I0816187

FIVE BULLETS

The Story of Bernie Goetz, New York's Explosive '80s, and the Subway Vigilante Trial That Divided the Nation

ELLIOT WILLIAMS

PENGUIN PRESS NEW YORK 2026

PENGUIN PRESS
An imprint of Penguin Random House LLC
1745 Broadway, New York, NY 10019
penguinrandomhouse.com

Illustration credits appear on page 341.

Book design by Daniel Lagin

LIBRARY OF CONGRESS CATALOGING-IN-PUBLICATION DATA

Names: Williams, Elliot (Writer on Goetz's trial) author
Title: Five bullets : the story of Bernie Goetz, New York's explosive '80s, and the subway vigilante trial that divided the nation / Elliot Williams.
Description: New York : Penguin Press, 2026. |
Includes bibliographical references and index.
Identifiers: LCCN 2025038082 (print) | LCCN 2025038083 (ebook) |
ISBN 9780593833704 hardcover | ISBN 9780593833711 ebook
Subjects: LCSH: Goetz, Bernhard Hugo, 1947– Trials, litigation, etc. |
Trials (Assault and battery)—New York (State)—New York |
Trials (Attempted murder)—New York (State)—New York |
Subways—New York (State)—New York | Self-defense (Law)—United States |
Assault and battery—Law and legislation—United States |
Vigilantism—United States | LCGFT: Trial and arbitral proceedings
Classification: LCC KF224.G63 W55 2026 (print) |
LCC KF224.G63 (ebook) | DDC 345.747/02555—dc23/eng/20250815
LC record available at https://lccn.loc.gov/2025038082
LC ebook record available at https://lccn.loc.gov/2025038083

Printed in Canada
1 3 5 7 9 10 8 6 4 2

The authorized representative in the EU for product safety and compliance is Penguin Random House Ireland, Morrison Chambers, 32 Nassau Street, Dublin D02 YH68, Ireland, https://eu-contact.penguin.ie.

For Mitzi

The worst man has the right to live the same as the best, and no one may attack another because his general reputation is bad.

—*PEOPLE V. RODAWALD*,
NEW YORK COURT OF APPEALS, 1904

PAUL KERSEY: Nothing to do but cut and run, huh? What else? What about the old American social custom of self-defense? If the police don't defend us, maybe we ought to do it ourselves.

JACK TOBY: We're not pioneers anymore, Dad.

PAUL KERSEY: What are we, Jack?

JACK TOBY: What do you mean?

PAUL KERSEY: I mean, if we're not pioneers, what have we become? What do you call people who, when they're faced with a condition or fear, do nothing about it. They just run and hide?

JACK TOBY: Civilized?

PAUL KERSEY: No.

—*DEATH WISH*, 1974

CONTENTS

Part II
GUN-TOTING HONKY

Part III
CODA

PREFACE

Anyone who rides the New York City subway will, at some point, encounter a roving performer or panhandler. There are the breakdancers, mariachi bands, beatboxers, doo-wop singers, Peruvian flautists, garbage can drummers, and classical string quartets, to name just a few, and even—as I saw on the No. 2 train once in 1999—an old, wizened woman in a ratty fur coat smoking a cigarette with two inches of ash dangling from it slowly walking the aisle and railing in a British accent against "Mayor Ghouliani. And yes, you heard me right. I called him *Ghooooul*-iani."

Nothing connects New York City—its geography, its businesses, its people—like its subway system. Its 248 miles of tracks make it one of the largest and most comprehensive in the world. Even after massive drop-offs during the Covid-19 pandemic, the system still sees upward of a billion riders a year. As America's densest city is also home to some of the country's worst traffic, paying the $2.90 for a speedy ride underground is almost always the most efficient way to go.

Its tight quarters and centrality to city life make it one of American society's few true levelers. Like an emergency room or department of motor vehicles, the New York City subway is a rare space in which human necessity blurs almost all social division. And so for twenty-four hours a day, the subway displays the city's vibrant diversity: wealthy white finance bro crammed in next to struggling Asian hip-hop brutha; immigrant from the Dominican Republic brushing knees with priest from the Dominican Order. Mere miles of track connect Queens, which produced Donald Trump and Archie Bunker, with Brooklyn, which produced Shirley Chisholm and Clair Huxtable. It is a beautiful urban mess, with no other environment on the planet like it.

Jordan Neely, a regular presence on the subway, was an autistic thirty-year-old whose mental state had been further impaired by the murder of his mother when he was about fourteen. At around age four, his father introduced him to the music of the Jackson 5, and as he got older he developed a killer Michael Jackson impersonation. He dropped out of high school and ended up on the streets, unable to find steady work. When scraping for money, he would work the subway dressed as the *Thriller*-era King of Pop—red vinyl jacket, Jheri curl, rhinestone-studded socks, and a single glove—moonwalking down the aisles to "Billie Jean." Still, whatever joy he brought the world through his craft, his behavior was erratic. According to his father, he would regularly stop taking the medications that had been prescribed for his suite of serious psychological concerns.

On May 1, 2023, in the midst of an apparent psychiatric episode, Neely boarded an uptown F train and immediately began screaming. He removed his jacket and threw it to the ground, shouting, "I don't have food, I don't have a drink, I'm fed up. I don't mind going to jail and getting life in prison. I'm ready to die." There is little dispute that multiple, if not most, passengers in the car were frightened by his behavior. Several got up to move away. One said that she was "scared shitless" and that Neely had "scared the living daylights out of everybody."

Daniel Penny, a college student and former Marine who was seated close by, got up and took Neely down from behind in a tight chokehold. A four-minute cellphone video from a fellow passenger shows

Neely's arms flailing and his legs kicking as he struggled to free himself, before two other passengers held down his hands while Penny maintained the chokehold. A few other passengers can be heard on the video, one saying that they should ensure that Neely not defecate on himself, and that "[y]ou don't want to catch a murder charge. You got a hell of a chokehold, man." The three men then rolled a motionless Neely onto his side. A passenger can be heard on the video saying, "He's all right. He ain't gonna die."

The passenger was wrong. Neely was pronounced dead shortly thereafter, with his death ruled a homicide from compression of the neck. Penny went on trial for the incident the following year and was acquitted of criminally negligent homicide.

The central legal question in the trial for the murder of Jordan Neely was the "reasonableness" of Penny's use of deadly force. That question came down to two factors: whether his fear of Neely was justifiable, and whether his actions aligned with how society would expect an ordinary person to act under the same circumstances. That formulation—a confusing jumble of both the subjective appropriateness of a man's thoughts and the objective social acceptability of his actions—was forever etched into law and American consciousness four decades earlier in the case of Bernhard Goetz.

On a sleepy Saturday afternoon just before Christmas in 1984, Bernhard Goetz boarded a dingy subway car in Manhattan's West Village and encountered four black teenagers from the Bronx. Barry Allen, Darrell Cabey, Troy Canty, and James Ramseur were rowdy: raising their voices, hanging on the bars, doing pull-ups, pounding on the seats, shadowboxing, and approaching other riders for matches. While their fellow passengers later reported being alarmed, if not frightened, by the behavior, none of the four teenagers attacked or harmed anyone. Canty then took an action that would prove to be a key moment in a decades-long saga about race, crime, vigilantism, self-defense, and a host of other very fraught, and very abstract, nouns: he asked Goetz for five dollars.

Goetz argues that the four saw him as easy bait and were planning to mug him violently. In contrast, the four teenagers say that Canty was simply panhandling. Either way, Goetz slowly rose and, in a fury, emptied his silver Smith & Wesson revolver into their bodies, leaving all four bloodied and strewn throughout the subway car within seconds. Goetz then jumped off the train and vanished, setting off a frenzied nine-day manhunt. By the time he turned himself in, much of the media had turned him into a sort of hero—an armed avenger who (finally) struck back against the forces of decay responsible for a historic crime wave. He eventually went to trial and, in a polarizing decision, was acquitted of all violent crime charges, and convicted of only a minor gun-possession offense.

In some respects, Goetz's and Neely's cases are strikingly similar: city on edge; black rider frightens other passengers; white rider perceives threat; homicide (or at least an attempted one); ensuing national debate about heroism in the face of threat. Both men became causes célèbres, particularly on the political right. Campaigns were quickly set up to fund the defendants' legal defenses, as politicians from across the country with no connection to New York tripped over themselves to heap praise on both men's actions. The racial dynamics of the cases were unmistakable; the public would never have embraced either Goetz or Penny with the same glee if either was a black man who, in plain view, left white carcasses lying in a subway car.

Freud would say that sometimes subway violence isn't just subway violence. The cases, playing out in the same underground forum, both tapped into the same vexing issues that extend far beyond the borders of 1980s New York: race, crime, fear, safety, self-defense, political polarization, and the media's ability to skew reality. By many metrics, America is healthier, happier, and safer than it was in 1984. Nevertheless, a close look at Goetz's case reminds us that we are still afraid, still haunted by America's racist past (and present and future), and still very quick to kill strangers.

The tour this book takes through Goetz's story is based on the rich public record of the case and extended interviews with many key figures: police in New York and New Hampshire who investigated and ultimately apprehended Goetz more than forty years ago; the judge and lawyers at the center of a decade of high-stakes legal drama; an eyewitness in the subway car who feared that he, too, could have been shot that day; one of the jurors who heard the case; reporters who covered the story; activists who protested aspects of the case; a former top official at the National Rifle Association; the courtroom sketch artists who spent years silently capturing the essences of every key figure in the case; and even one lawyer who had nothing to do with the shooting but who had to deal with the pain in the ass of having the Trial of the Century take place in the courthouse on a day when she was just trying to get to work.

Writing about a decades-old event—particularly one with death as a regular backdrop—provided constant reminders about the ruthlessness of time and the fragility of human existence. I am grateful to have interviewed Mark Baker, one of Goetz's attorneys, multiple times and relied on him as a resource over email throughout much of the reporting of this book. He died a few months before it was released.

Some well-known names were gracious with their time: Al Sharpton, the civil rights activist turned MSNBC host, and Curtis Sliwa, the founder of the patrol group the Guardian Angels, sat for lengthy interviews. Others did not. The media mogul and *New York Post* owner Rupert Murdoch declined a request for an interview; former New York City mayor Rudy Giuliani, through staff, did not respond to multiple requests.

I made dozens of attempts to interview the teenagers—now men approaching old age—whom Goetz shot. They, or their families, were either unreachable or declined to be interviewed. Much of the public record that still exists about them relates to their criminal history, and, sadly, that is much of the way we will get to know them in this book. Still, I tried to reconstruct as much of the rest of their lives as I could from other sources.

I did, however, speak with Bernhard Goetz.

"Those guys needed shooting, for starters, just for starters. That's not why I shot them, but they absolutely needed shooting."

I spoke with Mr. Goetz on March 1, 2024, and in perhaps the most striking moment in a telephone call full of them, he shared a ruthless moral judgment about where his five bullets ended up. No amount of prissy postmodern handwringing is going to tell him he didn't commit an act of community service. According to Goetz, it was his fortune, good or bad, to mete out the justice that four young men had brought upon their own damned selves.

He's also a bigot. Much has been made over the years regarding his use of vile racist slurs in public on at least one occasion. He, and those who support him, has worked overtime to explain away the comments. He may well possess a worldly tolerance "in his heart," as his supporters claim. That said, he had no hesitation in saying minutes after he got onto the phone with a black man he had never met, "I don't care if you like hearing this or not, but there was a bad problem in a lot of the blacks back then about fucking with people in general, fucking with rioting, fucking with themselves." His comments on race all seemed to be the quiet part out loud—the kinds of comments that many perhaps might say in private but which are too déclassé to share in mixed company. Perhaps it was his forthrightness, not the comments themselves, that was the most jarring. He seemed to think of himself as a modern-day Cassandra, blessed with the ability to state obvious truths to a woke public that just doesn't get it, or refuses to. He has had support. Scores of lawyers, witnesses, jurors, members of the public, newspaper columnists, and many others over decades have done all they could to deny any racial backdrop to every aspect of Goetz's case or crime in the city overall. But take it from Bernhard Goetz's own unambiguous words: it was, at least partly, about black people.

I was born to Jamaican parents in a section of Flatbush, Brooklyn, which was ethnically mixed in a way few places in America are today. Like so many immigrant families in 1970s New York, we eventually fled to the comfort and perceived safety of the New Jersey suburbs. My dad worked two jobs in New York for most of my childhood, and my grandparents and several of my uncles and aunts remained there. Given the city's museums, parks, zoos, shopping, and our beloved (ahem, twenty-seven-time world champion) New York Yankees, we were there for one thing or another at least once a week. Most relevant to the events in this book, though, we lived squarely in New York's media market.

It's fascinating what memories linger in the backs of our minds across decades. My oldest memory of Goetz was from—as I now have pieced together—early 1985, right around when I was turning nine. The memory is fleeting: probably only ten or fifteen seconds. But I recall that it was a segment on the local nightly news, covering not the specifics of the story, but how the "Subway Vigilante"—the nickname with which the media had knighted Goetz—had become the subject of rap songs. I realize now how that moment was a perfect window into the obsession the country had with the case. This "Subway Vigilante" became almost a cartoon character, an avatar for a public that felt unsafe and finally fought back. He was, to many, more than the central figure in a true crime story. He was a hero.

During those years, New York was fiscally mismanaged, facing allegations of rampant police brutality and corruption. Foremost, however: its people were terrified. Pop culture fueled the sentiment. The mid-to-late 1970s bred an entire genre of extremely successful dystopian films about the city: *Death Wish, Taxi Driver, The Warriors, Escape from New York,* and even *Saturday Night Fever* all depicted a hellscape that, though it might have had good pizza, would probably leave you dead. Goetz represented a solution to many New Yorkers (and to others as well, those watching from afar, either concerned about their own hometown or fantasizing about how bad someone else's was). Somehow, in the rush to turn Goetz into a national sensation, the public overlooked, or chose to disregard, that the case was rife with complexity. His victims may not have posed the threat to him that he believed them to, and his background turned out to be not as angelic as the public dreamed. He also was odd.

None of that ultimately mattered. Fear and anger sell newspapers (and today, generate clicks on social media). The media pounced to pump out daily articles that fed into the hysteria: their success at the newsstand led to more articles, and in turn led to more fear. (One can debate which came first: chicken or egg; ominous headline or paranoid public.) And finally, public voices on all sides of the case, figures no less prominent than Giuliani, Sharpton, and Murdoch, kept the story in the news as it became a critical part of their own origin stories. The story of a loner who shot up four forgotten members of society on a Saturday afternoon could easily have never made it past the police blotter. Something else gave it life.

Goetz himself, when speaking with police after turning himself in, touched on perhaps the biggest theme in his story, noting that "it's important to be afraid." Fear, one of the most basic human emotions, protects us from that which can do us harm. It stops us as children from climbing a jungle gym we are not ready for, or from touching a stove that has burned us before. It also can go too far, paralyzing us with terror about monsters that are not, in fact, hiding under the bed. While Goetz was afraid of something on the train, the question of what exactly he was afraid of is a complicated one. Was it the city's high crime rate? The possibility of being mugged? Was it that the four teenagers on the train with him were in a group? Was it black people? Was it the fact that even if he were a victim, the city wouldn't do anything about it? Was it the blow to his pride if he were to be smacked around like a plaything in public? It seems that, to some extent, each played a role in his split-second decision to pull the trigger—and then again, and again, and again, and again.

Goetz's fear was legitimate. The city *was* unsafe (or, at a minimum, was facing violent crime rates that are incomprehensible today). He had been victimized before, in a prior incident that had caused him great embarrassment and left him injured. I speak from experience in acknowledging that the subway then was scary, even if everyone relied on it. Goetz's opponents have, through the years, strained to defend his victims, overlooking plenty of evidence that even if the four did not mug Goetz, they clearly caused alarm to him and others.

This said, legitimate fears can lead people to do illegitimate things. Though the public has regarded him and his actions with increasing skepticism over the decades, his story invites us to think about entitlement and empowerment: What exactly can someone get away with when he is scared? When it comes to conferring such authority, the law and public opinion do not necessarily work together. Many people through history have gotten away with behavior that swaths of the public found disgusting. Many others have found themselves in jail for actions the public supported. What seems to matter most to how people's actions are judged is who has the biggest microphone at a given time, and whether society is willing to listen to them at that moment.

The nickname "Subway Vigilante" romanticizes Goetz. Notice that he was never called the "Subway Terror," the "Subway Assassin," or anything else less ambiguous. Segments of America love the idea of a vigilante, a noble (most likely white) warrior who acted out not because he wanted to, but because he felt he had to. In recent years, many such men have been rewarded handsomely. Mere days after being acquitted following Jordan Neely's death, Daniel Penny joined then President-elect Donald Trump as an invited guest in his suite at the annual Army-Navy football game. Less than two months later, he had a job offer from Andreessen Horowitz, the top venture capital firm in Silicon Valley, if not the world. Similarly, in 2020, Kyle Rittenhouse left his home in Illinois to help protect local businesses during Black Lives Matter protests in Kenosha, Wisconsin. Armed with an AR-15-style rifle, he fatally shot two men and wounded another. A segment of the public lionized Rittenhouse, and he was lauded with offers of congressional internships, legislation named in his honor, and a speaking tour through conservative media outlets. From a state a thousand miles away, Florida governor Ron DeSantis praised Rittenhouse's actions, saying that he did "what we should want citizens to do in such a situation: step forward to defend the community against mob violence." Rittenhouse was acquitted partly on the basis that he had acted in self-defense (the shots were fired during a violent altercation). But his self-defense argument launders the fact that he crossed state lines to a jurisdiction in which he did not live, to keep the peace at a riot he had no business in. How seriously can you take his complaint that society has broken down, after he himself decided to test its legal boundaries, if not violate them?

For many, Goetz, like Rittenhouse and Penny, was more idea than man. Each tapped into fantasies about how best to keep the public safe, and who the real threats were. But there is something perverse in America's rush, both then and now, to create heroes out of limited, or skewed, information. A *New York Times* column from a week after the 1984 shooting captured the point: "When people begin to feel so unsafe and so fed up on the subways that they will adopt as their vicarious champion a man with a gun who sets up his own criminal justice system and takes private vengeance, then a kind of madness has started creeping into the social system."

This book, beyond being the story of a man, four teenagers, and the struggling city around them, is about human nature. People are violent. Yes, people are loving, empathetic, creative, collaborative, nurturing, and a host of other beautiful things. We also kill each other a lot, often with firearms. Societies have long tried to impose order on themselves, in the form of governments and the social contract, all in an attempt to stem the state of lawlessness Thomas Hobbes once called "the war of all against all." Still, our noble nation has violence baked into its DNA. We are one of a handful of places to have won our independence by force and kept it—only to remain a nation after a vicious civil war. Our laws recognize an inherent right to bear arms yet provide ambiguous standards on when the use of deadly force is acceptable. As historian and president emerita of Harvard Drew Gilpin Faust has written, "The rule of law seems historically and inextricably enmeshed in the tolerance—even the encouragement—of violence." What if violence is just part of who we are as Americans? It might explain a lot.

Bernhard Goetz was in equal parts a reviled figure and a cultural icon. No other person in American history has had pop, hip-hop, and punk songs written about him; run for mayor of New York; given rise to the modern gun rights movement; partly been the inspiration for the lead character in an Academy Award–winning film (2019's *Joker*); sparked a generation of discussions about crime in cities; been the answer to a Trivial Pursuit question; and been a Rorschach test about race in the criminal justice system—all after nearly being convicted of a quadruple attempted homicide. There is much to be said about Bernhard Goetz. But perhaps we can learn more about what his two minutes on a dirty subway car in 1984 say about the rest of us.

PART I

LIVE FREE OR DIE

CHAPTER ONE

The Powder Keg

July 13, 1977

NEW YORK CITY

The city went dark.

Violent thunderstorms rolled across the region on a sweltering, humid evening. Lightning strikes clapped down on the earth below, with perhaps the most consequential one in New York history striking a substation about an hour north up the Hudson River in Westchester County at around 8:30 p.m.. The crash tripped two circuit breakers, sending a surge that cut off power from the massive Indian Point No. 3 plant, which served much of the region. Soon after, a second strike cut off power from another nearby plant. As surges knocked out substations one by one, demand increased on other parts of the region's power grid. As a result, a series of catastrophic power failures quickly crept southward, finally nestling in America's largest city.

By 9:30 p.m., New York City's five boroughs and most of Westchester County were literally, and figuratively, powerless. Tunnels leading into and out of the city had to be closed due to lack of ventilation. Thousands were evacuated from pitch-black subway cars that were becoming unbearably hot. Screaming riders got stranded in darkness atop Coney Island's Wonder Wheel, a rickety fifty-seven-year-old Ferris wheel. Reporters in the *New York Post's* newsroom had heard over police radio monitors that blackouts were cascading south from the Bronx through Manhattan. Mindful of the city's geography, they did not panic when, a moment later, their lights went out too. Frank Sinatra, cozy on the thirty-eighth floor of the posh Waldorf-Astoria Hotel, passed the time by consuming the "rapidly thawing contents of the refrigerator." A pilot landing a cargo plane of strawberries at JFK Airport watched in shock as its runways vanished into the miles of blackness around them. As the plane circled above, he asked the control tower in exasperation, "Where is Kennedy Airport?" and "What am I supposed to do with the berries?" The control tower, dealing with problems of its own, responded simply, "Eat them." Both JFK and LaGuardia Airports would soon stop all arrivals and departures for the next eight hours, gumming up air travel across the planet.

For a time, the only three lights that remained on New York's silhouetted skyline sat atop symbols of the city's greatest areas of pride—its financial dominance and historic embrace of diversity. Somehow, only the blinking airplane beacons on the World Trade Center and the Citibank Building, and the torch being lifted by the Statue of Liberty, punctuated the shadows. In retrospect, the metaphor was almost too on-the-nose to be real.

Perhaps the blackout of 1977 should not have been anything remarkable; every region with an electrical grid loses power at some point. Indeed, the region had confronted a massive fifteen-hour blackout just twelve years earlier. In 1965, even as 25 million lost power, the public reacted with romance and cheer. People got out of their cars at clogged intersections and directed traffic. Others handed out candles to passersby. Some weary travelers, knowing they could be stuck in Grand Central Terminal for a while, settled in for a night of sleep, unconcerned (or unaware) of any risk. Citywide, police made only ninety-six arrests, mostly for minor offenses. Within days, advertising executives published a book of cartoons titled *Where Were You When the Lights Went Out?* The experience, almost instantly, became a thing of amusement and nostalgia that unified a resilient city.

The 1977 darkness brought its own moments of magic also. Restaurants on the chic Upper West Side of Manhattan moved their tables outside for al fresco dining. A motorist who spotted an elderly woman struggling to feel her way home was seen spinning his car around so that his lights could help usher her inside. As the lights went out during a performance at the Metropolitan Opera, the orchestra's harpist broke into an impromptu solo of "Dancing in the Dark."

Oh, but 1965 this was not. For the next twenty-four hours, arson, looting, and violent crimes tore through the entire city. The predominantly black and Hispanic neighborhoods of the South Bronx, East Harlem in Manhattan, and Bedford-Stuyvesant and Bushwick in Brooklyn were among the most devastated. Some 1,037 fires, 50 of them serious, were the most seen in a single day in New York history.

Rioters smashed through the steel door and windows at a Pontiac showroom in the Bronx, speeding off with fifty new cars, valued at $250,000. On Broadway in Brooklyn, the night air was filled with the sounds of iron store gates being forced up and windows smashed open, exposing troves of electronics, furniture, and clothing to be looted. Near Columbia University in northern Manhattan, people were reported to have hooked cars up to the doors of electronics shops in order to tear them off, making way for others to clear the shelves. Even the Brooks Brothers on tony Madison Avenue in Manhattan saw its shelves emptied. A lucky bride-to-be made off with a lace gown from a shop in the Fordham section of the Bronx. All told, 473 shops in the Bronx and 700 in Brooklyn were attacked, and the rioting led to a billion dollars of damage. *Time*'s next cover story, echoing the words of Mayor Abraham Beame, dubbed the event a "night of terror."

Police, themselves dodging snipers and flying rocks and bottles, made 3,776 arrests—more in a single sweep than ever before in the city and some eight times more than were made during massive riots following Martin Luther King Jr.'s assassination in 1968. Before long, every cell in the city's seventy-three police precincts was full. Some in the NYPD turned instead to just cracking heads, in an egregious exercise of force from a department confronting years of allegations of widespread police brutality. Violence broke out in a jail in the Bronx, while several prisoners escaped in the darkness from Rikers Island, a 413-acre prison island and the city's largest jail. Across the city in lockups, the absence of working lights or air-conditioning was the least of the inmates' problems. Facilities were packed far beyond their capacity; one 29′ x 25′ holding pen was reported to have held thirty-six men. Sweaty bodies pocked with welts from nightsticks and open cuts from glass, all in need of immediate medical attention, were crammed together. Forget debating the wisdom of the city's criminal justice practices; the city had a brewing public health crisis.

Even before the first light bulb went out, though, the city was already on edge. A mysterious serial killer, who came to be known as the "Son of Sam," had been terrorizing the city throughout 1976 and 1977. In April 1977, Jimmy Breslin, a prominent columnist for the *New York Daily News*, received a handwritten note from the Son of Sam mocking the police and warning the public not to forget one of the shooter's early victims, continuing that "[s]he was a very sweet girl but Sam's a thirsty lad and he won't let me stop killing until he gets his fill of blood." Though David Berkowitz, the Son of Sam, killed or wounded only eight of New York's seven-million-plus people, his unpredictability and the police's inability to catch him bred fear that a menace could emerge anytime, anyplace, anywhere.

With a serial killer on the loose, the teenager running down the street with a looted television wasn't your biggest problem. The desperate mayor called NYPD leadership, pushing for them to do more. Ed Koch, then the congressman who represented the Village, was more direct and at one point called District Attorney Robert Morgenthau, screaming. "The city's verging on chaos," he railed. "If the cops can't do anything, can't you?"

While the blackout and threat posed by the Son of Sam would soon pass,* they remained vivid symbols of two unassailable facts: many New Yorkers did not feel safe, and New York in the late 1970s could not manage itself. Nothing captured the city's woes better than a line in a film review from *The New York Times* in 1974: "New York City is a mess. . . . It's run by fools. Its citizens are at the mercy of its criminals who, as often as not, are protected by an unholy alliance of civil libertarians and crooked cops. The air is foul. The traffic is impossible. Services are diminishing and the morale is such that ordering a cup of coffee in a diner can turn into a request for a fat lip."

A fiscal and political crisis in the mid-1970s had left the city broke and unable to borrow money from banks, credit markets, or Washington. Unable to make payroll and with the city almost bankrupt, Beame called for the first layoffs of city workers since the Great Depression, and at midnight on June 30, 1975, the city dismissed some nineteen thousand civil servants. More would follow, and in time the city would lay off approximately sixteen thousand teachers (four thousand from elementary schools), four thousand hospital staff, and thousands of others. All told, the city would slough off a quarter of its municipal workforce between 1975 and 1980. Those who managed to hold on to their jobs often threatened to strike, as wages stagnated under the weight of the crisis.

With a total collapse of the city's—and by extension the state's—economy a real possibility, the city sought a bailout from the federal government. On October 29, 1975, in a speech to the National Press Club, President Gerald R. Ford said he was "prepared to veto any bill that has as its purpose a federal bailout of New York City," leading to

* Two years later, an even more ominous threat would emerge, with the kidnapping of six-year-old Etan Patz on his way to school one morning in Lower Manhattan. His body was never found. Far more terrifying than any riot or serial killer was the specter that not even innocent children were safe. It became yet another gripping national public safety story inextricably tied to New York.

one of the most famous headlines in history: "FORD TO CITY: DROP DEAD." Ford eventually relented and committed $2.3 billion in federal assistance to the city, but not before sniping with New York state and city leadership.

As local and national politicians bickered, law enforcement agencies were hit by cutbacks, and this became a matter of triage for the city. The city's transit police force was cut by 25 percent between 1975 and 1980. The city focused its energy on major crimes, turning its focus away from policing the more common but less serious crimes that made daily life difficult: the snatches-and-grabs, the petty thefts, the burglaries. Said Robert J. McGuire, the city's police commissioner, "I think it's intolerable for the police to walk away from any crime, but the system is so overcrowded with other stuff, it's a matter of priorities."

Unfortunately, the city's management failures and extreme belt-tightening came just as it was confronting a historic spike in crime. Three hundred and ninety people were murdered in New York in 1960. That number ballooned to 1,117 in 1970, and 1,787 in 1980—a massive increase in a period in which the city's population had *declined* by close to one million. By 1979 the city led the nation in violent crimes and muggings. By 1984 a crime was reported in the city, on average, once every eighteen seconds. So many burglaries were reported in 1980—a year the NYPD reported to be the worst year for crime in city history to date—that police would simply shrug and direct callers to notify insurance and grease the windows of their apartments.

Many police officers didn't like the situation any more than the public did. Plainclothes members of the police union would greet new visitors arriving at LaGuardia Airport with flyers reading "WELCOME TO FEAR CITY," featuring an eerie silhouette of the Grim Reaper providing advice such as "Do not walk" and "You should never ride the subway for any reason whatsoever." It was quite a way to start a vacation in the Big Apple.

Even if authorities managed to make arrests, odds were that they were all but powerless to do anything with them. The Manhattan district attorney's office was horribly under-resourced in the late 1970s, with many of its prosecutors having no telephones. In 1978, at the Manhattan Criminal Court, an average of seventeen judges tackled 85,512 misdemeanor cases. That year, the court held only 164 trials. Adjusting for the fact that most criminal cases do not end up going to trial, the figure is astonishing. By 1980 criminal court judges handled up to 120 cases a day. Morgenthau was furious at the situation and complained that the city's criminal court "had ceased to function as a court."

Meanwhile, the city was hemorrhaging its white residents, thereby losing their incomes (and support to the city's tax base). Between 1950 and 1976, the city's white population plummeted from 90.2 percent to

76.6 percent. The Bronx, in particular, saw its complexion change. The white ethnic stronghold of the 1950s became far more diverse in the decades to come, with its white population dropping nearly 50 percent in the 1970s, from 1.08 million to 554,000.

While the city has long thought of itself as a progressive multiracial haven, rapid demographic change has an ugly conjoined twin—racial resentment. Nothing is more American than mom, apple pie, and suspicion of people from different backgrounds (particularly when they don't stay on their side of the street). As a result, the city that is guarded by the welcoming two-monument flotilla of the Statue of Liberty and Ellis Island incubated a stunning number of searing, high-profile racial incidents in the 1970s and 1980s. Their constant but invisible stress characterized the era more than perhaps any other aspect of city life.

For instance, in 1981, Willie Turks, a thirty-four-year-old transit worker, was dragged from an automobile and savagely beaten to death by a group of fifteen to twenty men shouting, "Nigger, get out of here," when his car stalled in the Gravesend section of Brooklyn.

In 1984, Eleanor Bumpurs, a sixty-seven-year-old mentally disturbed grandmother was shotgunned to death by New York City Police as she stood naked in the kitchen of her own home resisting an eviction.

In 1986, Michael Griffith, a Trinidadian immigrant, was traveling with friends from Brooklyn to Queens to pick up his paycheck when their car stalled. He and two others walked approximately three miles to the Howard Beach neighborhood where they were accosted by a group of white residents brandishing tire irons, baseball bats, and tree limbs, yelling racial slurs and screaming at the three to get out of the neighborhood. Griffith was severely beaten and, while trying to flee, was struck and killed by a vehicle as he tried to run across a highway.

In 1989 Yusuf Hawkins was shot to death by a baseball bat–wielding mob of ten to thirty white men in the Bensonhurst section of Brooklyn. The group had been lying in wait for black youths who were believed to be attending a party at the home of a teenage girl. Hawkins hadn't even known the girl in question; he had come to the neighborhood with friends to look at a used Pontiac.

In 1991 two children of Guyanese immigrants were hit by a car in a prominent Orthodox rabbi's motorcade, which had run a red light in the Crown Heights section of Brooklyn. One child, Gavin Cato, died, and the other was seriously injured, triggering widespread rioting and looting of stores and Jewish homes.

They never felt like isolated incidents. As the city calmed from one, another would hit the news. They would play out, Al Sharpton (still a local activist beginning his path to national stardom) would show up at a protest, the mayor would issue a statement calling for calm, and it would blow over, a city's rage pushed back under the surface until next time. And for each incident that became national news, there may well have been countless others that were narrowly avoided, did not end in violent tragedy, or did not get picked up by newspapers or activists. None happened in a vacuum, as New York, like America, has never been the melting pot it thinks it is. Rodney King, years later, would be terribly naive; we could not, in fact, just get along.

Today, in many New York neighborhoods, one is far more likely to trip over a purebred labradoodle than a crack pipe. Given that reality, it is almost impossible to comprehend the mythic level of unrest that characterized life in New York just a few decades ago. "It was not an easy place to be," said a woman who was in her twenties in the city at the time. "It wasn't an easy place to be female. It wasn't an easy place to be white. It wasn't an easy place to be black. It wasn't an easy place to be anybody."

Even with crime rates having ticked back upward in recent years, the same city is almost unrecognizable today. The same holds true across America. Fear may have crept back into American consciousness, but the city and country are safer places to live than they were four decades ago.

The *New York Daily News* ran a devastating opinion piece on July 22, 1980, titled "There's No Help on the Way," all but saying that New York was beyond control. It even quoted a senior Legal Aid attorney—hardly a role typically held by rugged police-loving authoritarians—as saying "[w]e have a social problem that transcends anything a cop with a stick or a judge with a gavel can do." The piece ended with an ominous line: "New Yorkers are going to have to do a lot to save themselves."

One prominent criminologist of the era wrote of the prevalence of the concept of "inevitable victimization": the notion that people had largely given up and accepted that, at some point, they, too, would be mugged—or worse. Still, most New Yorkers chose not to take crime fighting into their own hands. But the combination of a rough public safety climate, an impotent government, ongoing racial tension, and America's ready access to personal firearms provided just the right climate for the right person—who was most likely a white man—to be embraced for stepping outside the law.

Enter Bernhard Goetz, who moved to Manhattan in 1975, and four teenagers who had grown up in the Bronx: Barry Allen, Darrell Cabey, Troy Canty, and James Ramseur.

CHAPTER TWO

Claremont Village

1984

THE SOUTH BRONX

In 1978, Taito, a Japanese electronics company, debuted a creation that would forever change entertainment and commerce: *Space Invaders.*

The films *Star Wars* and *Close Encounters of the Third Kind* had captivated the universe a year before, and engineers at Taito, inspired by their successes, designed a coin-operated arcade game that would also transport people to outer space. Game play of *Space Invaders* is at best quaint by today's standards. The player blasts rows of aliens as they descend from the top of the screen. There is very little to it; the game uses only two colors—white and a fluorescent green—on a black background. The aliens look no more menacing than crude, pixelated shellfish.

However simple it was, *Space Invaders* was revolutionary. It was a pioneering "no limit" game: it had no time clock to cut off game play and no way to win. So the better someone got, the longer they could play. In addition, the game popularized the "high score" concept, in which a machine would track and display the highest scores achieved on it. A player now had several incentives to continue playing, thereby shoveling quarter after quarter into the machine's coin slot. An urban legend held that *Space Invaders* was so popular in Japan that the hysteria around the game led to a shortage of the 100-yen coins used to play it at the time.*

The game's success led to explosive growth in the industry, ushering in a period often called the "golden age" of arcade games. Pop culture–defining games like *PAC-MAN*, *Frogger*, *Centipede*, and *Donkey Kong*—each of which built on *Space Invaders'* innovations—soon followed. It all meant big business; the number of arcades in North America doubled between 1980 and 1982 to a peak of about ten thousand. Coin-operated arcade machines would soon be ubiquitous across New York City, in restaurants, liquor stores, bodegas, and other cash-based businesses.

There was a problem, though. The overnight video game boom presented a huge challenge for urban businesses: the new infusion of cash into video game machines turned each one into a giant piggy bank that could hold thousands of dollars at a time. Breaking into an early 1980s arcade game was almost too easy; a quick payday awaited anyone with a little ingenuity and a long screwdriver. Thefts became so common that arcades started hiring bouncers to hover by the machines.

A cold calculus went into someone's decision to steal from video games or engage in the sister petty crime of using their mouth to suck subway tokens out of turnstiles.† It was lucrative; it wasn't hard for a

*The 100-yen-coin myth has widely been debunked. See Charles Paradis, "Insert Coin to Play: Space Invaders and the 100-Yen Myth," *The Numismatist* 29 (March 2014): 46–48.

†Token theft might have been the ickiest form of petty theft in human history. To do it, one would jam a coin slot with cardboard or chewing gum so coins could not fully fall in. Not knowing the machine was obstructed, an unsuspecting rider would drop in a token that could not fall all the way in to activate the turnstile, realize they were stuck, and end up having to go elsewhere in frustration. The teen watching nearby would then approach, put his or her mouth over the coin slot, and powerfully suck the coin out. In 1984 each token had a face value of 90 cents and could easily be resold. One could make fifty to a hun-

thief, often a teenager, to make off with several hundred dollars a day doing it. Getting caught might mean at most thirty days in Rikers, rather than the far more severe sentence that might come from mugging someone or burglarizing a home, probably for the same payout. And more importantly, a youngster would need to be caught red-handed to even stand a chance of getting punished. Cops were probably not going to spend precious resources hunting down a kid who had run off with a bunch of quarters from a *PAC-MAN* machine. And getting caught wasn't all that likely in many parts of the city. As one Bronx teenager said at the time, "It's bad to bust machines around here or, say, up in Harlem, because the owners go after you. Downtown they just call the cops." In short, petty theft carried all of the reward and little of the risk.

Stealing from video machines was largely how Barry Allen, Darrell Cabey, Troy Canty, and James Ramseur, then four teenagers in the Bronx, made money. Canty and Allen had probably known each other the longest, but the four were all familiar with one another. (Though they had broken into machines together before, Canty and Ramseur first met because of a fistfight Ramseur had had with a friend of Canty's. As a result, the two weren't all that close.)

Odds were not good for most young people in the hood in the 1980s, a group once described by *The New York Times* as "average teenagers with less-than-average opportunities." Regardless of any conclusions that can be drawn from the four teenagers' personal backgrounds, each of their life stories says as much about society's failures as it does about their own. For many, the American Dream is a mirage that can't be brought to life through just pluck and gumption, and an unforgiving world can quickly extinguish glimmers of a better or even different life. Society is quick to let the four teens' copious rap sheets, which

dred dollars a day sucking and then reselling tokens. See, e.g., Ari Goldman, "Youths Stealing Subway Tokens by Sucking on Turnstile Slots," *New York Times*, February 7, 1983, B1; and Randy Kennedy, "TUNNEL VISION; The Kiss of Desperation: A Disgusting Practice Vanishes with the Token," *New York Times*, April 8, 2003, D3.

in places include some heinous crimes, drown out talk of whatever humanity might also be there.

Barry Allen, a slightly built nineteen-year-old Bronx native, was the eldest of the five children of Mary Allen, a switchboard operator. Allen never knew his father, who left when he was a little boy. He dropped out of school in ninth grade, and eventually enrolled in a graduate equivalency degree program in the Bronx. He was already a father of a son, Jason, who was likely born when Allen was seventeen. (Jason lived with his mother, Allen's former girlfriend. It is unclear what role, if any, Allen had in Jason's life.) Crack had not yet made it to the Bronx for much of Allen's early years, but cocaine was everywhere. Though a self-professed addict, he said that he wanted to enter rehab to "go right, to get a job, to step down from all this crime." Still, years later he described his younger self as a "go-getter" (which, in practice, probably meant being more brazen about committing petty crimes). "If it's a dollar involved, let's get it," he said of his approach. "Let's go." He had already gone to prison for assaulting a man with a BB rifle, and racked up time and probation for thefts. In 1984 Allen was facing jail time in state prison for prior probation violations. Allen's mother, who said she had seen Allen and his friends around the neighborhood but had no reason to believe they weren't decent, went on to say about her son—whether ominously or with resignation—"I can't say what he is capable of and not capable of." The statement was pregnant with meaning, recognizing that even if her son didn't have many choices, he owned the ones he made.

Troy Canty was a wiry five-seven nineteen-year-old. With a slow and methodical personal manner, he was described as a "thinker" by his friends. He lived at home with his mother and older brother and had had repeated psychiatric and behavioral issues in school, the most severe being a suspension in middle school for beating up a teacher. Like Allen, he had also dropped out of high school in ninth grade and quickly started running into trouble with the system. Canty was first arrested at sixteen for stealing toys and tape recorders for needy children. He was arrested three months later for stealing shirts from Bloomingdale's in Manhattan. Two weeks later, he was caught stealing $130 of merchandise from Macy's, and then a year later from a poker machine from a bar in the Bronx, and then six months later from a video game machine in Penn Station. He had picked up another larceny charge for breaking open a video game machine at a bowling alley just three weeks before the Goetz incident.

Drugs had also been a constant in Canty's life. He first smoked pot at about age thirteen or fourteen, and started snorting cocaine two years later. Like too many in the South Bronx in the 1980s, he eventually became a regular crack smoker, starting at around seventeen or eighteen, at times spending fifty dollars or more a day on the drug. According to his brother, he was high on the morning of December 22, 1984.

Little exists in the public record about eighteen-year-old James Ramseur. Though his parents, James and Bessie, moved at some point to New York City from North Carolina, it is unclear where James or his four brothers and sisters were born. Beyond that, Ramseur, like too many of his generation, can easily be reduced to being little more than a criminal record with a name. He had been arrested multiple times for burglary, larceny, and robbery, and had four pending warrants issued for not appearing in court.

The last in the group, nineteen-year-old Darrell Cabey, was born in Queens and had five siblings. His mother, Shirley Cabey, was a food service worker for the state. She was fiercely protective of her six children, encouraging them to entertain themselves at home, never allowing them to have friends come over to the apartment. She feared that her children's young playmates would use the time to case the joint and eventually come back to rob it. Though Darrell enjoyed dressing up and looking good, his mother avoided buying him or his siblings fancy jackets or bicycles, believing that having flashy things could make them targets for crime themselves. Perhaps more than anything, she wanted him to finish school. "I tried to talk to him," she said. "I told him, 'You have two strikes against you, you're black and you're poor, so you better get back to studying.' I told him there's more to life than hanging out in the streets. If only he had used a little common sense." At the end of 1984, he was awaiting trial for armed robbery charges.

Shirley was the only parent at home, as Darrell's father, a taxi driver, had been crushed to death in 1973 by his taxi in Queens while trying to fight off a carjacker. Shirley, a religious woman, prayed that Darrell would escape the neighborhood. Maybe one day he could make it north to the kind of leafy Hudson Valley town that was the final destination for the trains that they would watch zipping by their neighborhood without stopping.

Darrell's friends described him as "laid back" and a "follower," perhaps the kind of kid who would even be more prone than the others to go along with easy trouble as it presented itself. "He was staying outside a lot and I didn't know what he was doing," Cabey's mother told *The New York Times.* "Knowing the situation out there and the area around here, I just should've known."

The "area around here" Ms. Cabey spoke about was the South Bronx. The Bronx, which on its own would be America's eighth-largest city, is home to twelve colleges and universities, the largest urban zoo in America, the largest botanical garden in New York State, and thousands of acres of rolling hills. A quarter of the borough's land area is given over to parkland. Despite its green space, it was also home to incomprehensible blight, even when compared with struggling cities nationwide.

A number of plausible theories might explain what turned the South Bronx's condition from challenging to catastrophic. Perhaps it was the construction of the Cross Bronx Expressway, a pet project of urban planner Robert Moses that cut a gash across the borough, all but imprisoning its southern residents into an eternal Land of the Have-Nots. It might have been the flight of one in four manufacturing jobs from the borough. It could have been the redlining by banks that refused to grant mortgages to black people. Perhaps the borough was hit hardest by the city's refusing services deliberately in order to depopulate the area prior to rebuilding it (a concept known as "planned shrinkage"). Whatever the reason, parts of the South Bronx, by the 1980s, matched the *Hartford Courant*'s description of "the nation's most publicized urban wasteland."

More than any other factor in the decimation of the Bronx that sealed the borough's fate was the widespread arson that occurred over an extended period. Property values in the area had plummeted, and many owners could not pay to maintain their buildings. At one point in the 1970s, one in three walkups and one in five elevator buildings had defaulted on taxes. Many owners simply gave up and determined that it was far more cost-effective to set their buildings on fire and collect the insurance.

The result was an epidemic of urban destruction, from which it took decades for the South Bronx to recover. One hundred thousand housing units were lost to fires from the early 1960s to the early 1980s. At the height of the tragedy, there were an average of ten fires a day, with seven thousand in two years. In their wake was a vast terrain of unsalvageable building skeletons. Some two thousand square blocks of the South Bronx were leveled. Windows not blackened by fire were nailed shut or cemented over.

Welcoming bluish-green shutters and flowers in windows were often an illusion; the city had glued vinyl decals to some window frames to try to enhance the buildings' curb—rather, rubble—appeal, as funds weren't available to make actual repairs. After the state legislature passed a law that disincentivized setting one's own property on fire, landlords merely abandoned buildings and left the city holding the bag. By 1981 at least half of twenty-nine hundred vacant buildings still standing in the South Bronx were destroyed beyond repair and simply had to be demolished.

Even the most famous residents of the South Bronx were not immune.

As the New York Yankees played Game 2 of the 1977 World Series, an inferno swallowing an abandoned apartment building could be seen off in the distance from the stadium. Network television would cut back repeatedly to air images of the fire throughout the game. The Yankees went on to win that championship. However, in what should have been a moment of joy, New York's greatest shame was exposed on national television, narrated as a Howard Cosell play-by-play.

Public figures were quick to capitalize and use the blight as a backdrop to promote themselves. Nonetheless, a press conference outlining a bold vision for the future, no matter how well intentioned, will not fill today's potholes. For seventy-five minutes in 1977, President Jimmy Carter visited the ashes of a particularly leveled stretch of the Bronx's Charlotte Street. As he gave remarks promising to "turn it around," spectators screamed at him, "We want jobs!" and "Give us money!" His future opponent for the presidency, Ronald Reagan, used a separate vacant lot on Charlotte Street to blast Carter for failing to address the decay. He, too, was met with Bronx cheers, heckled with cries of "You ain't gonna do nothing! Go back to California!" He snapped back, "I can't do a damn thing for you if I don't get elected!"* Over the years, Senators Ted Kennedy and Daniel Patrick Moynihan, President Bill Clinton, and Pope John Paul II would participate in high-profile media events on and around Charlotte Street or elsewhere in the South Bronx. When running in the 1984 Democratic presidential primary, the Reverend Jesse Jackson theatrically spent a night in a South Bronx housing project to call attention to the plight of America's poor. Even Mother Teresa would eventually make a stop at America's own Calcutta.

To the extent that it was possible to find a refuge from the world around them, the Allen, Cabey, Canty, and Ramseur families found theirs in

*As president, Reagan would cut federal housing programs nationwide.

Claremont Village, a sprawling housing project in the Morrisania* section of the borough. Designed in the 1960s, Claremont Village was heralded by the New York City Housing Authority for lumping multiple smaller housing projects into a single behemoth—a concept that had not been seen in a generation. The result was a residential development the size of a university campus, spanning thirty-six acres across multiple city blocks. Though its four thousand units were originally designed to hold seventeen thousand residents, the total number of residents may have been closer to thirty thousand, given multigenerational families and the likely doubling up of friends. More than half of the residents were under the age of twenty-one.

Poverty and all it carries with it were common in Claremont Village. On cold, heatless days, old women would bundle up in lobbies, their eyes fixed out the window as they waited to snatch up their Social Security checks before someone else could run away with them. Still, from the late 1960s to the late 1980s, developments in the New York City Housing Authority (also known and pronounced as NYCHA) were safer than the city as a whole. As neighborhoods got rougher, the projects provided a safe space. In 1981 tenants in New York's housing projects were less likely to be victims of murder, assault, robbery, and rape than those who lived elsewhere.

The peace was not eternal. One new tenant would soon catapult an unmanageable wave of crime from the streets into the halls of the projects: crack cocaine. Crack hit New York around 1985, and soon the only thing it sent higher than people who smoked it was the crime rate in subsidized-housing facilities. In 1985 NYCHA's crime rate spiked 21 percent. Then, for the rest of the 1980s, the rate of violent crime within public housing projects grew much faster than it did elsewhere in the city (which itself was skyrocketing). Crack singlehandedly

*The neighborhood got its name from Gouverneur Morris, the author of the Preamble to the United States Constitution. At the time, he had sought to have the town be the capital of the United States—a decision that would have changed the Bronx's entire trajectory in immeasurable ways.

robbed the residents of the projects of the notion that their home could be protection from the harsh world around them.

It was overcast, foggy, and lightly drizzling on December 22, 1984, an unseasonably warm day that signaled there probably wouldn't be a white Christmas that year. Barry Allen and Troy Canty met up in Claremont Village with plans to go "get some money" by heading down toward Pace University in Lower Manhattan to break into video machines. The two bumped into James Ramseur; he had previously acted for them as a "blocker"—pretending to play the game as a diversion while others broke into it*—and it made sense for him to join. Darrell Cabey came along as well. Between them, they were carrying three screwdrivers for the job. Canty was careful not to have one on him. He knew that if caught, having a screwdriver on him brought an extra charge of possession of burglar's tools. So he quietly ensured that the screwdrivers were with the others.

At 169th Street and 3rd Avenue, they snuck through the back door of the bus without paying. They got off twenty blocks later, at 149th Street, the stop for the downtown No. 2 express Interborough Rapid Transit line (the IRT), and jumped the turnstiles. Within minutes, a train jangled its way to the platform, its seventh car pulling to a stop in front of them. Once its middle doors opened, the four walked through and started roughhousing. The other passengers would later remember that the four were loud, but they disagreed as to how much of a nuisance, or even threat, the young men were. For example, a woman noted that while she didn't see the youths threaten anyone, their behavior made her feel "concerned" and "afraid," to the point of her considering moving to another car. Another person said that the

*After a successful theft, the people who did the physical work of breaking open the machine would always keep a bigger payout than the others who "blocked" it, or acted as the lookout. See Trial transcript page 5329, Box 7, Folder 5, Bernhard Goetz Closed Case Files, New York City Municipal Archives, New York, New York.

young men were "talking loud" and "saying dirty words." One rider described their behavior as "harassing" but also referred to them as little more than "teenagers" and "average kids." Another woman testified that she kept her eyes on them at all times, concerned about what they might try. On the other hand, one male regular rider had said that he had seen groups of riders acting in a similar manner before and found nothing alarming about it. Most passengers reacted as just about anyone else would: by putting their antennae up, by moving seats, or by clutching their purse a little tighter. These were young men having a good time, however annoying (or scary) the scenario might have seemed.

As the train creaked along the tracks, the four settled in for their ride, excited about whatever payday might be awaiting them downtown.

CHAPTER THREE

Bu

1947

QUEENS

"Hey! Quit kicking that sand in our faces!"

Anyone who has opened a comic book published between the 1930s and the 1990s has probably seen an advertisement in the back pages for Charles Atlas's Dynamic Tension fitness program. In one of the most famous ads, "The Insult That Made a Man Out of 'Mac,'" a skinny guy is roughed up on a beach by a sand-kicking meanie, while his winsome date watches on. Even her attempts to make him feel better are backhanded at best: "Oh don't let it bother you, little boy!" He responds to Atlas's ad, and in the next frame he has morphed into a beefcake. He returns to the beach, gives the bully swift justice in the form of an uppercut to the jaw, and struts off with his date, who declares, "Oh, Mac. You ARE a real man after all!"

In the pantheon of American underdogs, there is a special place for the bullied who go on to win their pride by force. Sure, one can teach a tormentor a lesson with wit or guile. But the nerdy runt who learns how to punch back? Give that fellow a medal. Many of America's cultural icons are Davids who are fed up with being manhandled by Goliaths, and pop culture is loaded with examples of protagonists, or at least beloved antiheroes, who, after being pushed around, chose violence. Paul Kersey in *Death Wish* (much more on that later), Travis Bickle in *Taxi Driver*, Bill Foster in *Falling Down*, Arthur Fleck in *Joker*, and a host of others across movie history were bullied (white) guys who, for various reasons, had had enough.

As an early schoolteacher said about the young Bernhard Goetz, "He was picked on. He wouldn't say anything. He always kind of walked away." His brother-in-law would say, "Bernhard is basically a wimp." One member of his eventual defense team described him by saying, "Bernie—bless him—for lack of a technical term, is a schnook. He was a very nerdy pocket protector kind of guy." As an adult, Goetz echoed the sentiment. "Was I picked on?" he mused. "I accept that it's part of human nature for some people to attack the weakest." After the shooting, much of what the world would come to focus on about Bernhard Goetz was how much he had been pushed around.

Beyond his meekness—descriptions of which would follow him through his life—Goetz lived an existence of relative privilege and comfort. Still, his background shaped him into the human he would become and has bearing on what happened on that subway car. As Gregory Waples, the man who prosecuted him, would say years later, "To really understand what happened in this case, you have to take a long, hard look at the defendant in this case. You have to take a long, hard look at Bernhard Goetz."

Bernhard Hugo Goetz, nicknamed "Bu" as a child, was born in Kew Gardens, Queens, on November 7, 1947, the youngest of the four children of Bernhard Sr. and Gertrude Goetz. His mother was Jewish; his father, rigidly Lutheran and known for "authoritarian tendencies."

According to *The New York Times*, his father, who had emigrated from northwestern Germany, was trained as a scientist and engineer.

Upon moving to the United States, the elder Bernhard went to work in Queens with a bookbinding company, and within a few years owned it. In the 1940s, he bought a dairy farm in Clinton, New York, about two hours north of New York City, where Goetz's father split his time by working for the company during the week and at the farm on weekends. In 1949 the family moved to the farm and lived there full-time.

In 1960 the Goetzes bought Silver Lake Dairy, a distributorship the family would go on to own for decades. They eventually purchased property in nearby Rhinebeck, a bucolic rural town in the Hudson Valley with rolling hills and a historic downtown. The elder Bernhard moved his bookbinding company to Rhinebeck, where young Bernhard would spend the rest of his childhood. In school, he was studious, loved science, did not take much interest in sports, and never got into trouble.

One incident that year permanently shaped the Goetz family's relationship with the town: the senior Bernhard was arrested and charged with eighteen counts of "moral wrongdoing" for allegedly molesting two fifteen-year-old boys at the farm. The family maintained his innocence, arguing that the issue may have been pushed by political opponents of the powerful, wealthy, and connected Goetz. They questioned the teens' honesty, alleging that the two simply lied to incriminate and defraud him. The boys were regarded as troublemakers in the town, with one having been expelled from school while the other was a dropout. According to a book written during the younger Bernhard Goetz's legal proceedings, there had long been murmurs in the community about the elder Goetz's troubling conduct with other young boys. In his interview for this book, Goetz acknowledged some of the questions about his father's sexuality, saying as an aside, "My father was bisexual or whatever." He was convicted of eight of the eighteen counts and sentenced to six months in jail. After an appeals court tossed the conviction, the elder Goetz pled guilty to a single disorderly conduct charge. Wherever the truth lay about the conduct or case, young Bernhard was bullied and picked on because of it, and the event was a turning point in his journey toward disillusionment with the legal system. Themes he has echoed through the years overlap: the system is unfair, and some people who claim to be aggrieved are actually lying.

Perhaps to ease young Bernhard's anguish, in 1960 the family sent him to Institut auf dem Rosenberg in St. Gallen, Switzerland, in an idyllic lakefront medieval cathedral city where Germany, Austria, Switzerland, and Liechtenstein meet. Students studied Italian, German, and English, while having access to equestrian and ski trails. At the time, the school cost $12,000 a year; tuition in 2024 is over $100,000, plus another $63,000 in fees. It being the 1960s, he returned from boarding school with long hair, rankling his father.

In 1963 the Goetz family moved into a comfortable and tidy four-bedroom house at the end of a cul-de-sac overlooking a lake in Park Manor, a neighborhood in then-booming Orlando, Florida, where Goetz Sr. developed a semirural tract of homes. After another year of prep school in Poughkeepsie, New York, Goetz Jr. attended the now defunct Bronx campus of New York University. He graduated with a degree in nuclear engineering in 1970, before going back to Orlando to work with his father in the family business: development.

It was now the height of the United States' involvement in the Vietnam War, and Bernhard avoided being drafted by seeking psychiatric assistance on account of mental illness. He was later connected to the military as a navy contractor, working on safeguarding nuclear weapons.

The 1984 shooting wouldn't be the first major life moment to happen on a train for Goetz. He had met the lively and romantic Elizabeth Boylan on the train, and the two married in 1971. For the first six months of marriage they lived with Goetz's parents—a stressful environment for any young couple, let alone one in which the groom worked around the clock for his father's company. The two men fought bitterly, and eventually the younger Goetz moved out; the two wouldn't speak for the next decade. After a four-year rocky marriage, Bernhard demanded a divorce in 1975. According to a brother-in-law, "He kept talking about how much Elizabeth had hurt him. And when I asked what the trouble was, he never shared it. Bernhard kept his private life private."

After the divorce, he moved to New York City, where he incorporated and ran a business out of his apartment, testing, repairing, and maintaining electrical equipment for manufacturing companies. It was successful, and with business booming, he moved to an apartment in Courtney House, a white-brick twenty-one-story high-rise doorman building at 55 West 14th Street, a block away from the downtown No. 2 subway stop at 14th Street and 7th Avenue in the West Village. The neighborhood was gritty, with cut-rate electronics shops lining the street and discount-clothing racks obstructing the sidewalk. One would have to work to dodge the ever-present drug dealers and pickpockets trying to make their next buck. Litter and the occasional junkie dozing off on the stoop were everywhere.

For years, he lived in an apartment facing the chaos of 14th Street. Eventually, he moved to a much quieter one-bedroom apartment with a terrace on the ninth floor at the back of the building. His space was sparsely decorated, with a few pieces of impressive inherited furniture. He had covered his windows with stained glass, giving the space a curious religious feeling inside. Overall, it was ordered and impeccably tidy.

His neighbors regarded him as quirky, shy, eccentric, and even a little strange—a recurring theme in others' descriptions of him over the years. One described him as "intense and hyperkinetic," with an "obsessive nature." He walked very quickly, hands clenched as he moved through the building. Though not prone to raising his voice, he was known for tension in his speech and gestures. Another neighbor said that he was given to erratic moods; he might engage and be a pleasant conversationalist one day but ignore the person the next. Though some neighbors shared an "odd affection" for Goetz and noted that he would often brighten around children, adult neighbors found his eccentricities to be a lot to deal with. As one told the *New York Daily News*, "He is not the kind of guy you could joke with. He is the type who doesn't want to be harassed by anybody. You couldn't tell whether he was a sickie or not."

However impersonal and quirky his neighbors at the time found him to be, one subject consistently got a rise out of Goetz—public safety. He was frustrated by what he regarded as the city's failures to fight crime and mess. He believed, like the proponents of the controversial "broken windows" theory of policing would declare a few years later, that disorder inherently breeds more serious crime. As a neighbor who lived down the hall from him said, "He had a feeling of hopelessness of crime all around. He became discouraged that things weren't getting better." He was said to get particularly riled up whenever there were drunks outside the door of his building.

He pestered any neighbor who was willing to listen with his fusillade of new ideas about what to do with the community. A neighbor heading out of the building might get cornered for a conversation about mandating cleanups for all city buildings; she might return a few hours later and be immediately shown a document about street peddlers. Frustrated, he regularly marched petitions to City Hall and the police, blasting the level of protection provided to citizens, drug abuse in the neighborhood, and unlicensed merchants cluttering the block. He was particularly incensed when the building's doorman was assaulted. For months, he repeatedly complained to the city about an abandoned newsstand on the corner that had turned into a receptacle for trash and urine, and was a spot where people would frequently loiter. When it mysteriously went up in flames, some neighbors suspected, but never confirmed, that Goetz was the culprit. Either way, he was seen clearing away the debris.

He joined a community organization, For a Better 14th Street (or "FAB14"), and after it ran out of money, he donated three hundred dollars to pay an outside individual to empty his building's trash containers. He eventually quit the organization, frustrated that it wasn't working fast enough to rid the neighborhood of drug dealers. His frustration was reasonable but misguided. A host of factors led to the 1980s drug boom: wildly successful Latin American cartels' ability to get product into America; drugs that could be made cheaply and sold at a massive profit; brutal economic conditions in cities; underfunded police departments; not enough focus on social services. Goetz was correct that FAB14 wasn't getting rid of the drug dealers on the corner. Even still, the city's drug habit was far bigger than any co-op board could manage.

But for Bernie Goetz, the problem wasn't just crime; it also was black and brown people. At a tenants' association meeting in 1980, Goetz said "the only way we're going to clean up this street is to get rid of the spics and niggers." Neighbors were so incensed by the comment that they removed him from the group's board of directors. One longtime neighbor was shocked at Goetz's use of the terms, given Goetz's number of black and Latino friends, and a friend later said that he used the terms merely for their shock value, "just to get the liberals wild, because he's pissed at them."

That Goetz would continue to claim he wasn't racist, and that people would continue to defend him even in the face of the comments, is part of a far broader societal problem: the notion that racism is a binary. To think that "racist" is something someone definitely is or isn't ignores a basic truth: good people can sometimes do racist things. If using two of the most vile words in the English language, both of which have clear meanings and were used in perfect context and with full understanding of their hateful power, isn't "racist," nothing is.

While Goetz might not harbor a deep dislike of those of other ethnic groups, he is as capable as the rest of us of having nebulous and unquantifiable biases knocking around in his brain. And while we can't know the extent to which any of an individual's feelings, biases, and traumas factor into individual actions they take, one moment in Goetz's life probably led most directly to his eventual conduct on the subway.

On January 21, 1981, Bernhard Goetz, a skinny, bespectacled white nerd, was brutally mugged by three black teenagers. At that moment, the man who had spent all his thirty-three years getting sand kicked in his face by bullies had finally reached his breaking point. It was time to do something big to fight back.

CHAPTER FOUR

The .38 Smith & Wesson Airweight

January 21, 1981

CANAL STREET

Goetz's business was booming. There was one issue: testing, repairing, and maintaining electrical equipment meant that Goetz was often carrying around hundreds, if not thousands, of dollars of gear—and cash. On a cloudy, chilly January afternoon, Goetz found himself alone at around 2:30 p.m. at the subway stop at Canal Street with between $800 and $1,000 of equipment on him. Among the equipment was an oscilloscope that resembled a television set (a conspicuous object to carry openly in an environment widely believed—including by the carrier—to be unsafe). Three young men jumped him and threw him up against a plate glass window with a handle jutting out of it.

Charles Cozza, an off-duty cop, was sitting in a nearby restaurant when he heard the noise and saw a tangle of four bodies sprinting by.

He ran out of the restaurant and saw the three punching and kicking the stumbling, prone Goetz. As Cozza approached, two of them dropped Goetz's items and ran off, while the third, sixteen-year-old Fred Clarke, stayed behind and kept pounding him. In the scuffle, Goetz's sheepskin jacket (apparently what the boys were after in the first place) got torn. Cozza arrested Clarke on the spot.

The experience was frightening and humiliating for Goetz. Though he did not seek immediate medical care, the red welt now burned into his face was the least of his problems. When he hit the door and handle, he tore cartilage around his chest and ribcage. The injury would not heal for another six months. In addition, the fall seriously injured his knee, crushing his meniscus, the damage causing him pain that would last more than a year.

Cozza was the only eyewitness. From his vantage point, he only saw a group of individuals punching and kicking one another. He had no way of knowing for certain whether what he saw was a four-way brawl or three people jumping a blameless victim. As a result, Clarke was only charged with criminal mischief–intentionally or recklessly damaging another person's property* (here, the jacket, and perhaps any of the electrical items if they had gotten banged up). That legal outcome, however justified, does not jibe with basic common sense. Although the boys clearly tried to rob Goetz, without some evidence of theft, prosecutors would have had to rely on two competing narratives (Goetz's and the boys'). Even assuming Goetz was found credible, the case would have to beat the high reasonable doubt standard in court and likely wasn't worth taking the time to get there. Clarke pled guilty to a misdemeanor and was sentenced to six months in jail, serving only four.

Goetz derided the charge by complaining that all his aggressors were charged with was "mischievous mischief." But more than anything else, he was most troubled by how the police handled it and claimed

*See N.Y. Penal Law § 145.00.

that they gave Clarke better treatment than he got. He repeatedly pointed to his being detained for six hours and five minutes, while Clarke was released after two hours and thirty-five, all but citing the times to the precise minute. He was further incensed by Clarke's filing a cross-complaint against *him*, which argued that he, not Clarke, started it. Goetz, at least once, framed his frustration about the incident in terms of race. "I think it's kind of ridiculous," he said, "to consider that someone, let's say in my position, carrying things, would start up with three blacks alone, in the subway system."* He may have been frustrated, but what came out in a moment of vulnerability and candor was telling. Goetz, shaken up, returned to his apartment. The injury he seemed to complain about most was to his pride. According to his doorman, "All he could say was, 'Do you believe this? I spent all this time there and this guy walked out in two and a half hours.'"

Goetz pled with the police to take additional action, and on a call with them, he all but committed a crime, saying that "if you want me to lie, I'll lie. I'll say whatever it takes to, you know, to arrest these guys, or to get these guys." One of the officers immediately shut him down, telling Goetz, "Don't you ever say that." He appeared genuinely surprised that the police didn't bite. It wouldn't be unreasonable for him, as a victim of a crime, to assume that the police were, in effect, on his side; a basic function of law enforcement is protecting the needs of victims. Still, a brazen offer to lie to a law enforcement officer while assuming the officers' complicity spoke to an astonishing level of entitlement about law enforcement and public protection. Having grappled with a police corruption scandal in the 1970s, New York over the years had not been without its share of dirty cops. Goetz was inviting them to keep the tradition going.

---

*On another occasion, however, he made a similar point, but did not reference race, saying, "Is it conceivable that one person alone in the subway system, carrying packages, would start up with three people?" See Statement of Bernhard H. Goetz to Concord Police, December 31, 1984, Box 1, Folder 6, Bernhard Goetz Closed Case Files.

Goetz personalized the experience, regarding it as yet another of the city's many failings. Those who haven't been victims of violent crimes likely can't comprehend the sense of violation, vulnerability, fear, and fragility that must follow. But when discussing it, Goetz and those around him would speak in apocalyptic terms, ones that were breathtaking to the point of being comical. "As far as Bernie was concerned," one friend said at the time, "[the assault] was equivalent to a woman being raped."

Goetz had had enough. As he told police, "Once you have been beaten up, you'll never let it happen again." There was one way he felt he could ensure that that was the case.

It was time to start carrying a gun.

Goetz wasn't new to guns; he had bought at least ten since the 1970s. In 1970 Goetz purchased a .38 Smith & Wesson in Groton, Connecticut, and he claims to have bought at least one in the East Village in Manhattan. In Florida, on September 4, 1984—the day of his father's death—he purchased a 9mm semiautomatic handgun, producing a Florida driver's license and his father's Orlando address, in accordance with state law. (Goetz claims that he had dual residence in both Florida and New York.)

Any number of his guns may have been bought in Florida, a state that, as now, had far more permissive rules governing firearms than New York. While Florida dealers were not supposed to sell to out-of-state buyers, less scrupulous dealers, called "basement bandits," would sell from their homes or anywhere and would be far more likely to transact without making a record. They looked the other way as long as the checks cashed or the money was green.

Goetz claimed that he sold guns "at cost" to other people several times. Records of transactions were not a given, and it isn't clear what he did with all the guns he bought. In any event, those around Goetz knew that he had firearms. He is reported at one point to have shown a gun to four children who lived in his building.* Another neighbor, Theresa Winkler, told the *New York Daily News* at the time that she had previously seen a gun in a desk in his apartment and asked whether it was loaded and if he had a permit. She conveyed to Goetz that he ought to get one, given the trouble he risked if he did not. Goetz apparently did not respond.

Whatever he was thinking at the time of the exchange with Winkler, Goetz sought a concealed carry permit in 1982. Under New York law at the time, someone who wanted to carry a firearm outside of the home could get an unrestricted concealed pistol permit if they could prove that "proper cause" existed for doing so. If they couldn't prove proper cause, they could still apply for a restricted license, for activities like hunting, target shooting, or work. Because nothing is ever easy with the law, the state never really defined what proper cause meant, leaving generations of courts to interpret it. Over time, courts found it to mean that a person only showed proper cause if he could "demonstrate a special need for self-protection distinguishable from that of the general community." Merely living in a rough neighborhood would not be enough. Courts required evidence "of particular threats, attacks, or other extraordinary danger to personal safety." When denying an application, an officer would be required to give reasons "specifically and concisely in writing," but unless the denial had been done in an "arbitrary and capricious" manner—the legal standard for ruling without basis in fact or law—courts deferred to the decision.

In practice, outside of individuals whose work required them to carry large amounts of cash or jewelry on their person, not many people were approved for concealed carry permits in New York at the time. Affluent or high-profile individuals may have been among the

*Still, the children's father praised Goetz's character and said that "if Bernie got out of jail tomorrow, I would have no problem with having him play with my children." See United Press International (UPI), "Crime Frustrated Goetz, Neighbors Say," *Los Angeles Times*, January 7, 1985, 16, https://www.latimes.com/archives/la-xpm-1985-01-07-mn-11761-story.html.

rare ones to get permits. "Only folks like Donald Trump got licenses," said a former political director at the NRA, referring to the future president of the United States' past life as one of the most prominent Manhattanites in history. "Eleanor Roosevelt had one."* Still, Goetz relied on his regularly carrying cash as a basis for a permit. He noted to the hearing officer that given the cash-heavy nature of his business, he would at times travel with up to six thousand dollars on him. On his application, he also listed his military status as "4F," for having seen a psychologist or psychiatrist years before.

Goetz was turned down for failure to show sufficient need, with authorities ruling that he didn't carry large enough sums of money; his business was "not prone to robberies"; and he had not shown that he was in any "unusual danger." Goetz was furious. He claimed that he had shelled out two thousand dollars on filing the requisite paperwork and was, as he said, "trying to follow the rules." In reality, Goetz had little legal basis for complaining about the decision. Under New York law at the time, authorities had every basis for denying an individual a permit solely because he believes he needs one (the Supreme Court undid that law—and with it the country's entire basis for regulating guns—about forty years later in *New York State Rifle & Pistol Association, Inc. v. Bruen*†). While Goetz claims he was given no explanation for the denial beyond "we can't give everyone a license," there is nothing either arbitrary or capricious about denying a single firearm license in a city in which most people's applications were denied. Gun

*Donald Trump has acknowledged having a concealed carry permit in New York. See Emily Miller, "Donald Trump's Guns," *Washington Times*, November 14, 2012; Lorraine Woellert, "Missing from the Gun Debate: Trump's Own Experience with Concealed Carry," *Politico*, February 28, 2018. It is widely known that former first lady Eleanor Roosevelt regularly possessed firearms, going as far as carrying an unloaded firearm in the locked glove compartment of her car. See Ashley Thess, "Eleanor Roosevelt: First Lady of Concealed Carry," February 21, 2022, https://www.nrawomen.com/content/eleanor-roosevelt-first-lady-of-concealed-carry; John W. Barry, "Eleanor Roosevelt, Gun Owner," *Poughkeepsie Journal*, July 12, 2015.

†In *Bruen*, a 6–3 Supreme Court majority led by Justice Clarence Thomas broadly found that the right to carry personal firearms for self-defense in public is protected by the Constitution. See *New York State Rifle & Pistol Association, Inc. v. Bruen*, 597 U.S. 1 (2022).

rights advocates to this day argue that the very notion of a permitting scheme like New York's fundamentally violated people's rights (ultimately winning with that argument before the Supreme Court in *Bruen*). Still, the decision, even if not an outlier, stung Goetz and fueled his belief that authorities only care about "technicalities" and not about keeping the public safe. ("Technicalities" is a common term nonlawyers use about cases when they're not happy about having lost.)

Goetz's decision to arm himself could be rationalized: crime was up, the city was failing to manage it, and he had just been violently assaulted. For someone who feels victimized, few things probably level the playing field more than having an agent of lethal force tucked into his pants. He recognized that there may have been other ways for him to help ensure his safety; he just didn't feel like doing them. As he later told Nancy Grace, "I do not want to spend time taking karate classes and trying to put on weight and build up muscles and learn how to be a fighter." The frictionless ease of firearms was just too simple to pass up.

But using a gun isn't exactly simple, and Goetz had deluded himself into thinking he was proficient. In reality, there is no rational universe in which Bernhard Goetz could have been considered properly trained in firearms. At the time he applied for a permit, he said that he had taken a "very brief" gun safety course, which "basically consisted of 'don't point a gun at anybody.'" Beyond that, Goetz attributes much of the rest of his proficiency to his being a skilled "cowboys and Indians" player as a child—a claim he made in multiple interviews. Stone Phillips, in an interview in 1996 on *Dateline NBC*, (gently) pushed him on the claim:

GOETZ: But when I was a young boy, I used to play cowboys and Indians a lot with cap guns.

PHILLIPS: So cowboys and Indians was a—was a warmup for this?

GOETZ: Oh definitely. It's—it's a way of teaching a person how to shoot a gun. To shoot a gun proficiently, including speed shooting, is much less of a skill than typing.

PHILLIPS: Yeah, but we're talking about a real gun, real bullets, and real people.

GOETZ: Easier than typing.

Gun safety professionals will tell you to never point a gun at something you don't intend to shoot, if not kill. Whatever his goals were, Goetz had pointed loaded firearms at people at least twice prior to shooting four people in the subway.

Even the most experienced straphangers miss a stop from time to time. A rider who is daydreaming, lost in a book, or intoxicated by the steady hum of a train's engine at the end of a long workday can easily succumb to an ill-timed nap and be out of luck on a train that can't be turned around. One evening, for whatever reason, Goetz ended up at the wrong stop. A rational thing to have done, and one most riders would have chosen, might have been to walk across the subway platform to catch the next train heading in the opposite direction. Instead, Goetz inexplicably left the station and started walking. It was an approach that would have made total sense were he not on Central Park North. The street is bounded on one side by Harlem, a neighborhood that Goetz himself described as not "civilized," and on the other by Central Park, a place where in the 1970s, quite literally, the freaks came out at night.

An individual approached and, according to Goetz, said to him something along the lines of "OK, motherfucker, give it up." Goetz pulled out a gun. When he later recounted the story, Goetz, appearing amused with himself, said that upon seeing the gun the man instantly turned a shade of gray, paralyzed with terror. "I was so scared I was shaking. I thought I was going to shoot him. He thought I was going to shoot him . . . his knees buckled. He, he could hardly walk." Crisis averted.

On another occasion, on 6th Avenue downtown closer to Goetz's home, a white man walked up behind Goetz and started yelling. Goetz says he was "asking for money or something" but also berating Goetz, saying, in Goetz's retelling, things like "I hope I catch up with you, 'cause I'm gonna . . . and when I do . . ." Goetz then brandished a gun and the young man ran away. Goetz admits that in this instance, he bared the weapon out of annoyance, not fear. "I was pissed. But I didn't shoot him. He deserved to die."

Both scenarios, and particularly the 6th Avenue instance, are striking in that no matter how sincere Goetz's fear might have been, it was he who dramatically, and quickly, escalated things. He admitted that he didn't need to pull the gun on 6th Avenue. In a moment of self-reflection, he said that his doing so was "stupid," in that "I didn't have to pull out the gun and showing it was enough to make him run away. . . . I could have just as easily run in one of the stores."

By his own admission, Goetz was aware that he had other options besides carelessly brandishing weapons at people who were bothering him. At that point, it was still a question of if, not when, he would fire one.

December 22, 1984
THE WEST VILLAGE

Every year, Bernie and some old friends from school would get together for a pre-Christmas drink, and this time he was running late. He threw on a light blue windbreaker over a green plaid shirt and put on his gold wire-rimmed glasses. With haste, he made it to the subway stop at 14th Street and 7th Avenue, waiting for a downtown No. 2 express train. As one approached, he looked for a relatively empty car and saw that the seventh of the train's ten cars seemed to fit the bill.

He entered from the north, or rear end, and took a seat on a long bench on the far side of the car.

Of course, the last thing Goetz had packed before he left home was his .38 Smith & Wesson, which he had acquired a year and a half earlier. It was an Airweight, one of Smith & Wesson's variety of lightweight revolvers small enough to fit in one's pocket. (Picture the stubby revolver in the right hand of the potbellied tough known as Advanced Silhouette SP-83A, or "The Thug," on generations of police shooting range paper targets.) It weighed probably no more than a pound unloaded, with a shiny nickel-plated body. Its small size and reliability made it an attractive service weapon for police departments and security companies across the country.

Goetz took several steps to ensure that he could draw his gun quickly: He discreetly tucked it inside his pants, keeping it in a cheap leather "fast-draw" holster designed to enable the handler to immediately dislodge a gun to aim it at a target. He had his belt buckled to the side, rather than in the front of his pants, such that the buckle would not obstruct the holster or the gun. He had stopped wearing gloves, even in the winter, as gloves might make it harder for him to get his gun out if he ever felt he had to. Despite all the steps he regularly took to make it easy to draw his gun, Goetz later said that prior to that day, he hadn't fired one in five years.

After all, he'd said, "I'm not a gun nut."

CHAPTER FIVE

Car 7657

December 22, 1984

THE BRONX

Victor Flores rode the New York subway for one reason or another every day. Among those rides, twice a week he would make the almost two-hour-long trip from his home up in the Bronx to Brooklyn on the downtown No. 2 IRT express. There he would help out his brother, a building superintendent, at work.

Flores's regular ride, as it carved through three of New York's five boroughs, was a tour through an entire world crammed into a tiny geographic area that was evolving by the minute. The train started at the damp, dark, and dingy elevated platforms in the Bronx, the gleaming Manhattan skyline off in the distance. It entered Manhattan from its northeastern corner in Harlem, once the home of a great Renaissance and a place so rich with black history that Langston Hughes had romantically called it a "dusky sash across Manhattan." By 1984 it had transformed into a place crying desperately for help. The city owned almost 60 percent of the area's property due to foreclosures but did not auction off its coveted brownstones out of fear that doing so would lead to inevitable class and race conflict. So properties just sat, empty.

As the train headed south, and Harlem bled into the Upper West Side, rows of burned-out buildings morphed into renovated townhomes, bodegas became boutiques, and pedestrians and subway riders quickly turned younger, and whiter. A few stops away, the train would rattle under Midtown's most famous destination, Times Square, then a home to decadence, debauchery, and what Governor Mario Cuomo would call "the most crime-ridden block in the state." Onward to Chelsea, yet another Manhattan neighborhood where new housing units and converted brownstones couldn't stem an apartment shortage, and rents shot into the stratosphere.

On December 22, Flores arrived at the station and had just missed a train, so he jumped on the next one a few minutes later. After picking up two baguettes on a brief stop at Macy's along the way, he got back on and joined Goetz, the four teens from the Bronx, and maybe a dozen other travelers in the seventh car. It was an R22 subway car that had been built in 1957–58, and it looked and felt like it. An R22 was about forty-nine feet long and just shy of nine feet wide, with three sets of double doors evenly spaced along its sides. Its windows were held in place by 1950s-era rivets, slathered over with paint. It had a simple sign, with thin white capital letters on a black background, providing the train's origin and destination. Inside, a mix of shorter and longer benches ran along the sides between the doors. Riders could steady themselves on vertical poles or hold on to the spring-loaded handle grips that had replaced the synthetic leather straps found in the cars of the past. (The term "straphanger," even though technically no longer accurate, has a smoother ring to it than "spring-loaded metal handlehanger.")

Of course, this was how the car would have looked when it got off the assembly line. In reality, like the entire fleet in service in 1984, the car had fallen into disrepair. Across the city, subway car doors were frequently broken and lights flickered—if they were on at all. Riders were wise to know where they wanted to go *before* getting onto the platform, as maps frequently had been vandalized, graffitied over, or torn down. In 1984 a fire blazed somewhere on the subway system every day, and a derailment could happen every other week. Cars broke down an average of every seven thousand miles—an astonishing frequency for vehicles that traveled all day. The system's tracks were a minefield of hundreds of "red-tape areas," or places where it was unsafe for a train to travel more than fifteen miles an hour, far less than the cars' top speed of approximately fifty-five mph.

Posted signs advising:

Please NO
Littering
Smoking
Spitting
Radio Playing

were mere recommendations, and hardly ever followed. Strewn newspapers, spent cigarette butts, discarded fast-food containers, and untold other yucky detritus from thousands of daily riders permanently cluttered the floors.

Also, by the mid-1970s, spray paint's increasing availability in stores had changed the game for graffiti artists. What had started as a network of ornate names written in magic marker had evolved into a multicolor mosaic of bleeding figures that covered almost every inch of the city's six thousand subway cars. The act of tagging train cars—whether an art form or a symbol of social decline—became a citywide competition of sorts, and trains covered in graffiti were elevated to "masterpieces." By successfully "going all city" and tagging in all five boroughs, graffiti artists could become known to each other as "kings." As early as 1972, so many cars were tatted up that mayor John V. Lindsay declared an official "War on Graffiti."

Like other elements of the city's infrastructure, fixing the subway system came down to triage. In the 1980s, instead of trying to improve the condition of all cars, the MTA focused on keeping new or overhauled trains or buses in working order. The head of the MTA, like a sneakerhead who didn't want his new Jordans to get scuffed, even requested that the NYPD station two officers on just the newly overhauled cars *at all times* to keep them from being damaged.

And then there was the crime. If staying aboveground might have given some New Yorkers a sense of safety, heading underground eliminated it. The early 1980s saw roughly fourteen thousand felonies a year on the subway—some forty a day. It was a rate unrivaled among major public transportation systems across the planet.* Criminologists thought that the system's antique design, long corridors, blind corners, and poor lighting created a more hospitable environment for crime than in some of the newer, airier, and more physically open systems in other world cities. Crime on the subway was such a reality of life that in June 1985, at least one police officer rode on every train between 8 p.m. and 6 a.m. in a futile attempt to try to restore confidence in the system. Signs warned riders of ways to lessen their risks of being victimized during "chain-snatching season." The system was such a mess that the MTA's own chairman admitted that he wouldn't let his teenage son ride the subway at night.

In spite of the system's failings, riders still flocked to it—albeit out of necessity. Even in its leanest years, as riders were deterred by the litter, the persistent smell of urine, and the fears—however rational—of being mugged or worse, the system still hosted nearly a billion riders a year. As a column in *The New York Times* said, "The subway rider can't

*New York City's subway is one of the few in the world that is open twenty-four hours a day; more hours open in a vast system provide more opportunities for crimes to occur.

ignore [subway crime] as he might in someone else's neighborhood—because, for the moment, the subway *is* his neighborhood."

Over the course of the trip, one by one, an assortment of riders stepped onto the seventh subway car. Along with Flores, Goetz, and the four young men were, at least, Solitaire Macfoy, a West African–born computer engineer struggling with a package of two 41″ x 32″ panes of plexiglass he had just picked up; Mary Gant, an actress from Wisconsin heading down to the South Street Seaport at the southern tip of Manhattan; Josephine Holt, a chambermaid working in New Jersey on her way downtown; and Christopher Boucher and Loren Michals, two friends on their way to get some drinks and do some Christmas shopping in SoHo.

Garth Reid, an immigrant from Jamaica, often chose to sit in the seventh car precisely because it was next to the sixth, where the conductor sat. The public transit veteran knew that the uniformed conductor, providing an official set of eyes watching over the train car, might spook any troublemakers from trying anything stupid. Looking back in 2024, Reid said of the subway that "it wasn't as clean. But it was something, you know, that everybody just got used to." Like frogs unaware that water around them was slowly being brought to a boil, New Yorkers simply acclimated to the fact that their lifeline to the rest of the city was a regular place of fear and discomfort. Reid and his wife, Andrea, rolled their stroller onto the train and sat with their infant daughter on Garth's lap.

The train creaked its way up to its top speed for a short ride; the next stop, at Chambers Street, would only be about two minutes away.

It was now a little before 2 p.m., almost exactly a half hour from when the guys got on in the Bronx. As the doors sealed the car off from the world, Troy Canty, acting alone, rose from his seat and approached Bernhard Goetz.

CHAPTER SIX

Shiny Eyes

December 22, 1984

SOMEWHERE UNDERNEATH MANHATTAN

No matter what conclusions anyone might draw from the events of December 22, 1984, one thing is clear: from the moment Troy Canty approached Bernhard Goetz, whatever followed would permanently alter the lives of five men on the train, and with them, the entire city.

Canty, standing with his hand still clutching the hanging support, leaned close to Goetz and asked how he was doing. He later said he approached Goetz for no reason other than the fact that Goetz happened to be closest to him on the train. Accounts differ over how close Canty was to Goetz. Ramseur later said that Canty "was up in Bernhard Goetz's face," coming to within a foot of him. Other riders noticed the proximity; across the train, Andrea Reid leaned over to her husband and said, "Look at those four punks bothering that man."*

*There was some dispute about whether Andrea Reid had actually said "Look at those four punks *messing with that white man*" (emphasis added). The statement would ultimately be allowed at trial, but only after a contentious debate between the lawyers and judge over its

While seemingly innocuous, the approach would have been concerning enough for just about anybody in those circumstances to set off a red flag, or at least raise a yellow one. Even in a time and place far less intimidating than a dimly lit New York subway car in 1984, any reasonably vigilant person might have found it puzzling, if not frightening, to be approached in this way by a stranger.

Goetz did not make eye contact with Canty. He would later say, "You're not supposed to look at people a lot because it can be interpreted as impolite. So I just looked at him and I said 'fine.' And I looked down." He said he then kept the four in the corner of his eye. In his mind, though, even the mere greeting meant trouble. Goetz remembered that his doorman at Courtney House was brutally mugged in an encounter that started with an innocent "How are you doing?" This, Goetz thought, was probably going to be no different. As he said to Nancy Grace on CNN years later, "They were just typical street thugs. You get to know them. . . . They didn't even have to say anything. It was just by their positions."

As the train shot past the Franklin Street stop, the final local stop before its destination, Goetz's and the young teenagers' accounts differed as to whether Canty then either asked for, or demanded, five dollars from Goetz. It was an alarming amount to request from a stranger, about fifteen dollars today. Perhaps Canty was just "aggressively panhandling" Goetz, as the act was described by William Kunstler, Cabey's eventual attorney. Whether the words said to Goetz were a question, a demand, a violent threat, an order, or just a casual statement, we will never know. But as sure as there was a loaded revolver tucked into the front of his pants, Goetz was convinced that he was being threatened and was about to be viciously assaulted. As he told Nancy Grace, "I was very familiar with the streets of New York. I know a mugging when it's going down."

---

admissibility under rules prohibiting hearsay at trials. See Trial transcript page 6940, Box 8, Folder 4, Bernhard Goetz Closed Case Files.

But according to an NYPD detective from the time, as well as others, it would have been an odd time and place for anyone, let alone an experienced petty thief, to violently mug an individual. It was the middle of the day, with plenty of bystanders nearby and no real means of escape. Even if the four had successfully robbed Goetz, they would then have been stuck on an enclosed train car, surrounded by dozens of others, until the doors opened. Unless they'd planned to mug, kill, or violently silence everyone in the train car in the remaining ninety or so seconds until the train arrived at its next stop, trying anything rash would have been foolish. Even in their lack of academic or professional sophistication, the four were likely savvy enough to know that.

The situation was certainly tense, uncomfortable, intimidating, and scary. Most urban dwellers have been in similar situations before, where they were forced to ask themselves: Is something off here? Is this guy too close for comfort? Will he leave me alone if I look away? Though risk is a reality of life in a crowded urban environment, all humans at their core want to feel safe. Furthermore, it is not healthy (and is, in fact, a sign of civic failure) if people grow so accustomed to frightening encounters that they accept them as a way of life. Mary Gant, uncomfortable at how the four were looking at her, simply avoided eye contact and buried herself in her book. It seemed to have worked. Likewise, when the young men started acting up, Josephine Holt took a keen interest in her newspaper. Like Gant and Holt, most New Yorkers would likely have figured out a nonviolent way to defuse or avoid an unpleasant encounter.

Goetz pretended he hadn't heard Canty and asked him to repeat himself, buying time. He would later say he could not have walked away, claiming he was "surrounded" by Canty and Allen, if not all four. As Goetz would eventually tell law enforcement, "I had no intention of killing them at that time, but then I saw the smile on his face and the shine in his eyes, that he was enjoying this." Suddenly, the encounter was no longer about money. Bernhard Goetz believed that these four young men were treating him as a plaything. At that moment, this was not just about public safety, cleaning up the streets, or being mugged. This was about pride. A white-hot rage took over Goetz. He turned around and unzipped his jacket.

Goetz typically loaded his gun with two types of bullets. The first were standard hollow-points (called "dumdum" bullets on the street), which would expand on impact with a soft target like a human body. The second were higher-powered +P bullets, a type of ammunition designed to achieve a higher internal pressure than a standard bullet of the same caliber. Both were designed to maximize the damage they could do to someone.

Goetz swung back around, now holding his gun, and said or shouted something to the effect of "I'll give all of you five dollars!"* He quickly rose and and took a "combat stance," gripping his revolver with both hands and raising it. Goetz would later say that he fired the first shot without even aiming.

The first bullet struck Canty straight-on in the chest. Canty clutched where it hit him and fell limp to the floor, feeling his legs and arms starting to go numb. So consumed with fury, Goetz thought about using his keys to gouge out Canty's eyes but held back when he looked down and saw fear in them. One man down.

Pandemonium.

Passengers didn't even know if the loud bang had come from inside the train but immediately realized that something was horribly wrong. Multiple passengers referred to the gunshot as the loudest noise they had ever heard, or wondered if someone was firing off very loud fireworks in the train car. Barry Allen shouted, "Troy, are you all right?" Terrified riders lunged from their seats, dove to the ground, and began

---

*Goetz acknowledges that he may only have said, "I'll give you five dollars." Canty testified that Goetz's words were "You can all have it!," while Allen said that Goetz simply said, "I'll give it to you." According to the NYPD, Goetz said, "I have five dollars for each of you." See Nancy Grace, "Interview with 'Subway Vigilante' Bernhard Goetz," *Larry King Live*, CNN, December 17, 2004, https://transcripts.cnn.com/show/lkl/date/2004-12-17/segment/01; Margot Hornblower, "Wounded Youth Denies Intent to Rob New York City 'Subway Vigilante,'" *Washington Post*, January 10, 1985; Suzanne Daley, "Man Tells Police He Shot Youths in Subway," *New York Times*, January 1, 1985, Section 1, 1.

screaming and tripping over one another. Those who didn't panic played possum. Victor Flores and Mary Gant stayed frozen in their seats, worried that if they moved the shooter might come for them next. Garth Reid saw the white shooter and black victims and wondered if a hate crime or terrorist act was playing out, with Goetz planning on killing all the black people he could find. He and Andrea grabbed their baby and sprinted through the doors at the front of the car, hoping to find refuge in the next one. In the rush, they left their stroller behind.

Goetz appeared remarkably calm amid a swirling tornado, and multiple people, including Canty, would later comment on Goetz's equipoise. "He looked like he had the same expression he had for the whole ride" (as he fired the gun). Another eyewitness described his demeanor as "bland," "somewhat calculating," and "deliberate."

After shooting Canty, Goetz turned slightly to the right and shot Allen. Whether Allen was in the process of turning and running away or stumbling in a chaotic scene in a wobbly subway car was unclear. Either way, Allen was wounded in his back, a bullet lodged between his spine and left shoulder blade, and was now jumping around and shouting about how much it burned. He said years later that when he got hit, he thought he'd been shot with a "paralyzer gun." "My hand just went like this"—suddenly gesturing with a frozen limp hand, as if rigor mortis had set in—"I couldn't move it or nothing." Two down.

Multiple passengers later said that either Ramseur or Allen were desperately trying to flee from Goetz, even trying to run through the walls of the train as if being pursued by a slasher in a horror movie. Goetz then fired a third shot, striking Ramseur in the arm and chest. Three.

Cabey was in the rear of the car, either hiding or pretending to be wounded. One passenger said definitively that he saw Cabey seated and clutching a bench, with a look of terror on his face. After Goetz shot Ramseur, two bullets remained in the gun. Goetz fired them both. Though the sequence of how they were fired is unclear, within moments a panel on the train's interior would end up with a bullet hole, and Cabey with a serious gunshot wound.

According to the police report as well as a statement Goetz made later, he thought he missed Cabey the first time he shot at him. Goetz then stood over Cabey and said, "You don't look so bad. Here's another," then fired directly into his chest again. Goetz would go on to say, "I was so out of control, I would have put the barrel against his forehead and fired." It is not clear for how long or even whether Goetz paused at that moment; several people in the car perceived that Goetz fired all of the shots in rapid succession, emptying his gun in less than two seconds, never pausing long enough to give a final message to Cabey. As Victor Flores said, "He just kept shooting until he didn't have no more."

Either way, there was a brief silence after Goetz was done shooting. After the final shot rang out, Canty said he could hear Darrell Cabey cry, "Why did he shoot me? Why did he shoot me?"

Five shots fired. Four men down.*

Hysteria turned into shock. Piping-hot gun in hand, Goetz stood up and sat down a few times, and paced around for a bit. The police report said that Goetz checked on each of the men after shooting them. Goetz knelt down next to Canty, looked Canty closely in the face, and then shook his head and mumbled about how he needed to get out of there. All four were lying down, and according to Goetz they were "cold, no longer a threat." They were all in some state of consciousness—breathing but still, their eyes becoming glassy.

As four struggling bodies littered the moving train car, the rest of the passengers began to wonder what they had just witnessed. Mary Gant looked to her right and saw a young black man lying on his stom-

*In an interview in 2018, Barry Allen insisted that the four did not intend to rob Goetz. "If Troy's intention was to rob this man, bamboozle him, I would have been the first to know. Like, we all would have knew what was going down. Troy didn't give me a wink or nod his head; none of that shit. We were going to rob video machines."

ach with his head toward her, eyes open. They looked at each other in silence. A male voice, which could have been Goetz, or could have been a person who had shoved her in the scrum, called to her. "Miss, are you all right? Did I hurt you? Did I hit you?"

Someone pulled the train's emergency brake. It screeched to a halt before reaching the Chambers Street station, sparks flying from its wheels. After passengers yelled to Armando Soler, the train's conductor, that four people had been shot, he got on the public address system and called two urgent codes to the train's motorman: "12/7," to request police and ambulance assistance; and the dreaded "12/8," meaning that someone on the train had a handgun. He then ran into the seventh car and saw a calm Goetz seated there.

As Soler checked on the passengers, including the four young men bleeding out in his subway car, he asked Goetz if he was a police officer. That Goetz had the luxury of being politely asked the question is itself noteworthy; not every subway shooter would have been afforded that grace. Even the very question suggests a veneer of legitimacy for Goetz's actions. Put another way: Had Troy Canty—or, better yet, the other black men in the car, Garth Reid or Solitaire Macfoy—opened fire in a crowded train car, would they have ever been given the same courtesy?

Goetz responded, "I don't know why I did it. They tried to rip me off." Soler asked if Goetz had a permit for the gun. Goetz replied that he did not. Soler then urged Goetz to give him the gun; Goetz did not respond and turned and walked away. Given Goetz's "serene" demeanor, Soler assumed Goetz was waiting around and planning on turning himself in. Goetz saw two female passengers on the ground, paralyzed and cowering in fear. Thinking he had mistakenly hit them—another example of the extreme recklessness with which he behaved in opening fire in a crowded and enclosed space with at least one baby in it—Goetz asked them how they were doing and, with Soler, helped at least one of the two to her feet.

Goetz then had a moment of clarity. Law enforcement would be swarming the train at any moment. He knew that if he had a chance at getting away, now was his moment. It was a transit authority practice, in the event of a crime, to ground a train to prevent people, and the vital evidence they might be carrying, from getting off. Ironically, the practice enabled Goetz's escape. With the train stopped on the dark track, he could easily jump off without any difficulty. He walked through the service door at the south end of the train car and, in a fit of panic and brazenness, jumped down to the tracks below. Gun tucked into his pants, he sprinted southbound down the tunnel, splashing through puddles as rats scurried away.

Covered in filth, Goetz reached the Chambers Street stop, climbed up onto the platform, and ran upstairs. When he emerged on the street above, at Chambers and West Broadway, he slowed down to a walk, blending into the crowd with the sweet anonymity that only a New York street in the middle of the day can provide. Every few seconds, another caterwauling light-blue-and-white Plymouth Gran Fury police cruiser would shoot by, its riders unaware that the frail-looking white guy on the corner was responsible for the underground carnage to which they were speeding. He was right there in front of them, and they had no idea.

After walking a block east to Church Street, Goetz hailed a northbound cab about a mile and a half back home, where he changed his clothes and stuffed his blue windbreaker and gun into a duffel bag. He then walked several blocks from his apartment to Olin Rent-A-Car at 21 East 12th Street and got himself a blue AMC Eagle with New York plates. He drove out of the city and, before long, over the horizon.

Bernhard Hugo Goetz of Manhattan's West Village would become, and represent, many things in the days and weeks ahead. However, at that moment, in the middle of the afternoon of December 22, 1984, he bore a striking resemblance to a skinny, blond, middle-aged white male last seen jumping off a downtown No. 2 express train—an armed and dangerous fugitive.

CHAPTER SEVEN

The Man in the Blue Windbreaker

Arnetha Gilbert, deep into her newspaper in the sixth car on the train when the shots rang out, was startled by panicked screaming. Whatever unseen madness had just broken out in the next car immediately spilled into hers. One hysterical individual even landed right at her feet before jumping up and continuing to sprint toward the front of the train. After a few moments, she began to assume that people were hurt back in the seventh car and rushed to help.

She saw four young men lying amid the sticky filth on the floor, bleeding profusely, moving in and out of consciousness, eyes starting to roll back in their heads. Just to her right, James Ramseur, clearly in distress, leaned to her and mumbled, "Miss, I've been shot through the heart and I'm dying." Her response, whether delivered with medical precision or wry humor was "If you'd been shot through the heart, I don't think you'd be talking to me." She then quickly turned to Canty and checked his pulse. He said to her, "He shot me for nothing. I didn't do anything. I only asked for five dollars."

She next approached a still-conscious Darrell Cabey. He said to her, "I didn't do anything. He shot me for nothing." All the statements were made independently of each other and in a moment in which the speakers were not thinking clearly or in any position to collude. Each spoke to the young men's belief that they had done nothing wrong. Perhaps such was the case. Perhaps the statements were based on the men's morally suspect notion that there is nothing wrong with harassing people. They may truly have thought that getting in strangers' faces and hassling them is just what you do. Whatever the explanation, the statements were unambiguous and said largely the same thing. Cabey also later said to someone, "The guys I was with were hassling this guy, asking him for money. The guy threatened us and then he shot us." The statement simultaneously acknowledged that the young men were merely panhandling and did not intend to rob Goetz, but also that they were aware that the overture they had made to Goetz was not welcome. Regardless, these rare, real-time statements from shooting victims would be invaluable at any trial. That is, if they would be allowed in as evidence.

John Filangeri and his partner, both paramedics, had just finished with a patient at Bellevue Hospital. As they were getting back on the road, they heard over the radio that four people had been shot on the other side of Lower Manhattan. Though the job had been dispatched to another team, they knew that four gunshot victims would require multiple ambulances and rushed to the scene. After pushing through passengers, police, and a growing number of spectators, they got to the car and found Barry Allen on his hands and knees, crawling toward the motorman's cab at the front of the car. Cabey was still lucid enough to grab an officer's arm and ask that the officer not let him die. He and Canty, who was lying on the ground, were in severe shock. Given Canty's low blood pressure, racing heartbeat, and gunshot wound squarely in the chest, paramedics believed he was in the gravest condition. To stem his shock, they put him in pneumatic anti-shock trousers that forced blood to his chest and head.

The medics put Goetz's victims on IVs and oxygen, strapped them to stretchers, and rushed them out of the station. Allen and Ramseur were whisked across town to Bellevue. Allen, perhaps the least injured of the four, arrived in stable condition. He had been shot in the back an inch or two to the left of his spine, about four inches below his shoulder. Bullet fragments, which doctors left inside his body, had spread along his left shoulder. Doctors put a tube in his chest to drain fluid that had built up around his lungs.

A single bullet had hit Ramseur in his forearm above the elbow, passing completely through his arm and then piercing the left side of his chest. Doctors performed an exploratory laparotomy, which involved cutting open his abdomen to get to his injuries. They removed his spleen, which had been lacerated by the shot, and treated wounds to his diaphragm and stomach. Doctors never found the bullet that struck him, believing it to be lodged somewhere near his left adrenal gland. Over the next few days, they would treat him for a collapsed left lung and a small bowel obstruction. He left the hospital without being discharged on January 8, came back, and left again on his own on January 13, about three weeks after the shooting.

Canty and Cabey, meanwhile, were taken to St. Vincent's Hospital nearby in the West Village.* Ironically, despite having had a bullet tear through his lung and burrow into his back, Canty was in remarkably good condition. Doctors operated to drain his left lung of blood and fluid, and re-expand it. They removed the bullet a few days later. He was discharged within two weeks of the shooting, generally fine despite complaining that his wounds burned when it rained or when he took a shower.

Darrell Cabey, though, was in bad shape. A bullet had entered his

*Throughout history, St. Vincent's Hospital often seemed to show up in some of New York's highest-profile tragedies (and notorious cases). Founded in 1849, it was where survivors of the *Titanic* were received in 1912. As HIV rapidly spread in its earliest days, the hospital housed the first and largest AIDS ward on the East Coast. It also was the major site for the triage of survivors from the 9/11 World Trade Center attacks. After years of financial hardship, it filed for bankruptcy and closed in 2010. See Elizabeth Zheng and William H. Frishman, "The Closing of St. Vincent's Hospital in New York City: What Happened to the House Staff Orphans?," *American Journal of Medicine* 125, no. 5 (May 2012).

left side and ricocheted through his torso from left to right, its fragments puncturing both of his lungs. One severed his spinal cord, instantly paralyzing him from the abdomen down. Doctors inserted tubes to drain blood and fluid from his lungs (which by this point had partially collapsed). His condition spiraled as complications from his injuries compounded, each worsening the effects of the others. Given his paralysis, the muscles around his ribs couldn't expand and contract normally, preventing him from breathing deeply or coughing or spitting as fluid filled his lungs. As a result, within days, he had developed significant pneumonia in both.

Three weeks later, Cabey went into respiratory arrest. While doctors were able to respond quickly enough with CPR to maintain his heartbeat, he had stopped breathing for about eight minutes. He eventually fell into a deep coma, slipping into critical condition and being kept alive via a respirator. Cabey was in a persistent vegetative state, and his eyes, when open, would rove when he was prodded. His upper extremities were tight, rigid, and spastic, all signs that the cortical level of his brain—which is involved in reasoning, emotion, thought, memory, language, and consciousness—had been irreversibly damaged from the lack of oxygen. The surgeon who operated on him did not think that he would survive.

One of his last actions before slipping into the coma was holding his mother Shirley's hand, looking at her, and saying, "I'm sorry, Mom. I shouldn't have been there." The moment made devastatingly clear that any dreams of another life for her son were dashed. It would be another two months before he awakened, his mother still at his bedside. The Darrell Cabey who had existed before slipping into a coma was gone. Now, in addition to being a paraplegic, he had developed irreversible brain damage and had the mental capacity of a third-grader. He could propel a wheelchair but didn't have much coordination beyond that. His speech was slurred, and he was unable to follow two back-to-back commands, copy a square, or write his own name. He had little recollection of the incident that got him in that condition in the first place, let alone what day of the week, month, or year it was.

While the four were being treated, a frantic search was underway. The MTA shut off power to allow their search, thereby suspending subway service for two hours. Police, unaware that the unnamed assailant was long gone, rushed through the train. All they found were terrified passengers, still in shock from what they had just experienced; one officer found forty passengers huddled on the floor of the last car. Fifteen detectives canvassed the area aboveground, looking for any sign of people who might have seen the shooter fleeing. They also passed out twelve hundred flyers with an artist's sketch of the assailant to subway booths and other police departments. Underground, police searched the tunnel with flashlights for more than an hour, looking, in vain, for any sign of the man in the blue windbreaker.

A manhunt was on.

CHAPTER EIGHT

A Polite Note

It's safe to say that not much work gets done, anywhere, on the Saturday three days before Christmas. Most workplaces are closed on weekends to begin with, and even for ones that are open, workers have routinely checked out. To top it off, December 22, 1984, was the fifth day of Chanukah.

Though the NYPD was fully staffed for the day, its officers were starting to get into the holiday spirit. At the First Precinct in Lower Manhattan, both Sergeant Robert Thomkins, the chief detective, and his second-in-command, thirty-six-year-old detective supervisor Jim Levison, were already off. That evening, Levison was moments from walking out his door on the Upper West Side to go to a Chanukah event at his girlfriend's house when the phone rang. Had the call come a couple minutes later, he would have missed it entirely and been at the party. On the other end of the line was fellow detective Mike Clark. Levison knew as soon as he heard Clark's voice that whatever was coming wasn't going to be good.

Four kids shot on the subway. One of them (believed at the time to be Troy Canty, because of the location of his gunshot wound) might have been seriously injured. Levison knew that the guys who worked under him could handle most cases, but he also knew that he probably needed to be there if a major event had taken place. He asked Clark what he thought. "I think this is going to be a big one," Clark said.

Levison called his girlfriend to let her know that she was probably going to end up going solo to the party that evening, and got into his car. By the time he arrived downtown, swarms of media, law enforcement, and rubberneckers had made it almost impossible for him to get to his office.

The victims' bodies had barely made it to the hospital, but hysteria was starting to engulf the city and flood the world beyond it. The story hit television news later that day, and by the next morning, it had exploded. The public had barely any information beyond "subway," "man," "teenagers," "mugging," "gun," "white," and "black," but for many, that was more than enough to turbocharge a wave of support for the shooter. Callers lit up switchboards at radio stations across the country to talk about crime; at one San Diego station, calls supporting the gunman outnumbered others 4 to 1. Newspaper columnists from across America's racial and ideological spectrums found ripe new fodder for their essays. Politicians from far beyond New York's five boroughs now felt it was their duty to opine with authority about a subway system they had never ridden. The NYPD's tip line did not turn up any actionable leads, but instead brought hundreds of pats on the back for the gunman—"He did a great job," "He should run for mayor," "He did the right thing." Within days, the mayor was flooded with 240 letters; of them, 237 backed the shooter. Man-in-the-street interviews showed kinship with the shooter coming from both white and black people. A *New York Daily News* tip line was inundated with calls of sympathy and praise, with one caller offering the shooter the Bronze Star he earned for valor in combat in World War II. "It's scary on those trains," the caller said. "Did you ever have a punk ask you for money on a train?" Without more details, a public narrative wrote itself: in an unsafe city, someone finally had the guts to do what needed to be done. To many, this guy wasn't a violent criminal; he was Batman.

Officers still had almost nothing to go on. The shooter had been seen jumping off the train, but even that meant very little. Did he walk north or south in the tunnel? No one really knew. Did he reenter the train elsewhere and try to blend back in? Or get on another train somehow? If he managed to make it out of the tunnel, onto the platform, and into the streets, he'd have slipped into the most densely populated borough of the most densely populated city in the United States. Even though Manhattan is only twenty-three square miles in area and just over two miles at its widest point, he could have vanished into its 1.5 million people within minutes. And never mind if he got his hands on a car. States—and by extension, the reach of state and local law enforcement—are small in the northeast, and within a few hours, he could have been deep into rural Pennsylvania, Virginia, or New England, far beyond the jurisdiction of the NYPD. Add a few more hours and he could have made it to Canada and vanished without a trail, as biometric scanners and license plate cameras and tracking technology were still decades away in the future. It may have been 1984, but Big Brother wasn't watching.

Then, after days of coming up cold, a breakthrough: On December 26, an unidentified caller to NYPD's tip line said that someone named Bernhard Goetz matched the description of the shooter, carried a gun, and had vowed never to be mugged a second time. The caller might even have said that Goetz lived near the subway line. The tip was promising, but making an arrest would require police to have probable cause, or a reasonable belief that a person had committed a crime. What police actually had was much less than that.

Levison and his team ran checks to see what they could uncover.

Goetz had no criminal record. A record wouldn't necessarily mean that the person would be more likely to have committed a crime, but it would have been a place to start. Above all else, did the person's past suggest a pattern of committing crimes in a particular place or at a generalized time of day, or against a certain type of victim? Was there a type of weapon he always used?

Officers soon figured out that Goetz had once applied for a pistol permit. They knew that every permit application had to be submitted with a photograph. Bingo. Even if Goetz wasn't the subway shooter, the application would have enabled officers either to identify him or have witnesses exclude him as a possible suspect. They pulled the photo.

Levison says that they knew that at least one person not named Allen, Cabey, Canty, or Ramseur had gotten an extended look at the gunman: Armando Soler, the conductor. Soler had interacted with him at length. He had enough time to ask the shooter if he was a police officer. He had heard the gunman's claim that he fired the shots because he thought he was being robbed. The two had also had a long enough exchange for Soler to request, and be denied, the gun.

Unfortunately for the police, Soler did not identify Goetz as the shooter and claimed to not even recognize the man in the photo. Levison suspected that Soler simply didn't want to get involved. Police were at a dead end. Bernhard Goetz was one of perhaps hundreds of thousands of New Yorkers who might have fit the physical description; it would have been impossible to interview every middle-aged white guy in the city, in the hopes of finding one who wore glasses and always packed heat. In addition, the tip line had largely turned into therapy for callers who wanted to vent about crime.

Levison could not let go of his hunch that they were onto something. The tip felt just too specific to be false. Adding to the intrigue, Goetz lived mere blocks from where the incident had taken place. The 14th Street subway station where the shooter got on would almost certainly have been the preferred stop for someone who lived where Goetz did. A few detectives headed to his apartment to talk to him and, not finding him there, left notes at his residence and in his mailbox. At least one read "Mr. Goetz—Please contact the police A.S.A.P."

As detectives struggled, Mayor Koch faced a brewing political disaster. Even given the level of public support for the shooter, a long delay in nabbing him could make the police—and the mayor himself—look incompetent. With the ongoing criticism of the city's management and a fast-approaching election year, a public safety crisis was the last thing the mayor needed. More importantly, it was the height of the holiday season. Seventy-two hours before Christmas is probably the worst moment for an urban mayor's public to lose faith in their public transit system. The city anticipated a crush of some 3.5 million holiday riders. Empty subways could hurt the city's businesses, lead to more car traffic, and cause unease, all of which could come back to bite the mayor politically.

The city did what it and so many others have done through history when trying to project calm: throw more cops at the problem. At Koch's direction, the city drastically increased police presence on the subway system, sending out three thousand more city and transit cops to engage in "frequent and periodic" checks of riders.* The police department, still suffering from PTSD from the Son of Sam saga, was forthright that they had taken steps to calm the public. A return to that pervading sense of a mysterious threat at large could paralyze a city. In contrast, the mayor laughably claimed, in a break from his own police

*New York recently took a similar approach. See Maria Cramer and Ana Ley, "National Guard and State Police Will Patrol the Subways and Check Bags," *New York Times*, March 6, 2024, A11, describing an announcement from New York governor Kathy Hochul to deploy one thousand members of the State Police and National Guard to the transit system to conduct bag checks in the city's busiest stations (riders had the right to refuse a search, but officers could deny them access to the subway). They would serve alongside the one thousand additional police officers Mayor Eric Adams had ordered to the subways the month before.

Public reaction to the move was mixed. Civil libertarians, civil rights groups, mental health advocates, and transit advocacy groups uniformly blasted it; the transportation workers' union applauded it and said it did not go far enough.

Ironically, two hours after the governor made her announcement, a female subway conductor was hit with a glass bottle as the train pulled out of a station in the Bronx. The assailant got away without being arrested.

department, that the request had nothing to do with the shooting. According to the mayor, beefing up security was just intended to get people to avoid driving on the holidays. For the mayor, acknowledging the fear would have been an admission of defeat. The episode demonstrated the tightrope of managing the public's mixed reaction to the shooting. From the safety of their typewriters or telephones, people cheered the idea of a mysterious thug-busting gunslinger even if deep down, they were as terrified as they were excited. The mayor's initial response toed a line between panic and calm: nothing to see here, except thousands of more cops.

The city's transit union blasted the decision, with its president calling it a "hysterical overreaction" that would "put the public in further jeopardy" by removing full-time coverage from some platforms. They also thought it created an administrative mess by putting NYPD officers whose radios did not work underground alongside transit officers whose radios did (and operated on a different frequency). More officers would be visible, but what good would it do if officers couldn't actually communicate with one another? It would make New York's Finest look like Keystone Cops.

Whether the infusion of officers made subway riders safer (or at least feel so) is an open question. But days were beginning to pass, with little success at finding their man. Not the NYPD, the transit police, other subway riders, or just about anyone else in the city had any idea who—or, more importantly, where—the shooter was.

CHAPTER NINE

The Bug

Right after the shooting, a peculiar graphic began appearing on *New York Post* articles. Drawn in comic-book style, it featured an image of an ominous subway tunnel, its tracks receding off into a dark infinity. Its most prominent feature: a Caucasian (or at least unshaded) forearm and hand, in shirtsleeves, holding a revolver. A light appears at the end of the tunnel; it is impossible to tell whether it is on a train that is coming or going. Implicit is that the gunman just defused some trouble, or will be ready for it when it comes.

Breaking up the frame of the image were three bold words: "'DEATH WISH' VIGILANTE."

Ten years earlier, the movie *Death Wish* had made an impressive $22 million domestic box office haul, instantly etching itself into movie history by striking a nerve about crime in America's cities. The 1974 movie, which takes place in a violently dystopian New York, starts with architect Paul Kersey's wife and daughter being violently beaten and sexually assaulted in a home invasion. Kersey's wife succumbed to her injuries; his daughter was left catatonic and with an unexplained mental illness. Despite having been a conscientious objector during the Korean War, and having an aversion to guns following his father's death in a hunting accident, Kersey (played by Charles Bronson) turned to vigilantism. He walked the streets of New York gunning down criminals—both ones that he caught in the act and others that he lured into attacking him.

In many respects, *Death Wish* was a perfect analogue for the Goetz story. Both fact and fiction had at their centers an unassuming middle-aged white professional tired of living in fear. A few of Kersey's homicides even happened in a subway car, the same littered, graffiti-strewn 1950s-era mess that would be home to Goetz's shooting years later. Given the glaring similarities between the two, one can easily watch *Death Wish* and have trouble telling whether it was based on Goetz's case or vice versa.

But the reality of the comparison was more complicated. The film made violence sexy. Kersey is a complex lead character who engages in legally indefensible conduct (even if he had a moral explanation for it). At the end of the film (spoiler alert!), he is cast out of his community. Still, he is the film's protagonist. There is scarcely a moment in *Death Wish* in which you find yourself rooting for the detectives who pursue Kersey. *Death Wish* creates a cops-and-robbers universe in which perhaps the robbers are villains, but the cops aren't exactly the good guys. It's government's fault that Kersey is (and you, viewer, are) forced to live in such a crime-ridden hellhole in the first place. He's just cleaning it up for you. And if heroism requires shooting someone in the back who is already fleeing, so be it. Even Brian Garfield, the writer of the novel on which the film was based, was critical of the movie and its sequels. Years later, he said that their point was to show a character's descent into madness and, perhaps presciently, that vigilantism "was an attractive fantasy, but . . . only makes things worse in reality. By the end of the novel, the character is gunning down teenagers because he doesn't like their looks." He says he wrote *Death Sentence,* the sequel to the book, which features a protagonist who does not shoot to kill, as a "penance" for the violence in *Death Wish.* "Any idiot can kill people," Garfield said. "You can't teach someone a lesson by killing him."

The *New York Post* immediately began tying the movie to the shooting and the victims in its coverage. It used the movie's title on its cover two days after the shooting and included an article that walked through the similarities between the film and the events that had taken place on the subway. If life was not imitating art enough, Charles Bronson himself weighed in, saying in a *Post* article that "New York City today is almost like the Wild West, with violence and robbing making it open season on the law-abiding private citizen. If someone confronts you with a weapon, whether they're going to rob you or attack you in some way, you defend yourself." Though the piece appeared on a full page of articles about the shooting, Bronson claimed he was not speaking about Goetz.

Other tabloids instantly drew links between Goetz's shooting and the movie. The *New York Daily News* included the unironic language in an article that the shooter had become a "big-city folk hero, a living legend with a list of names that would insure him a permanent place in the city's Crime Hall of Fame: The Avenging Angel, the Death Wish Gunman, the Subway Vigilante." The morning after the shooting, as an aside in a quote from a transit cop at the scene who asked not to be identified: "It was a real Charles Bronson type of incident." (By 1984 Bronson's public recognition was inseparable from the character—think Mark Hamill and Luke Skywalker or Daniel Radcliffe and Harry Potter.) The graphic on *New York Post* articles, called a "bug" in newspaper lingo, soon followed. (In printed newspapers, bugs, or small standing logos appended to stories, were a common way of signifying a regularly appearing section, page, story, column, or feature.) A bug suggested that the story was sufficiently important to warrant enough articles, over time, that the paper's coverage would not be seen as a one-off. A reader could know that an article was important, and if they bought tomorrow's paper, they'd see another one like it. Even though there was no public knowledge of a suspect, investigative leads, or a motive, many in the *Post*'s readership were rooting for him.

Everything from watercooler chatter to police bulletins across the country were abuzz with curiosity, concern, and passion about the case. The attention made sense, as the circumstances of the shooting created a perfect environment for ongoing, frenzied coverage. It took place on a holiday weekend, as slow a news day as any. For the first few vital days as the story was taking off, it would not compete for column inches with the regular events of city life. In addition, a city on edge about crime was particularly touchy about the subway. Any old tragedy might dissolve into the racket of daily stories. But the story of a high-profile shooting or, even better, a high-profile shooting that sent a message to the kind of punks that terrorized the city every day? On the subway? Now *that's* news.

It took place in the West Village, an area that was still squarely urban but so much whiter than other parts of the city that many New Yorkers would have found the notion of a major shooting happening there unthinkable. People downtown might regularly have looked over their shoulder for purse snatchers, not mass shooters. "Something like [a vigilante shooting] probably happened a dozen times a year back then in New York City," Levison mused about the public's double standards about crime: disgust about violence in a place like the Village but nonchalance about the prospect of the same thing in a rougher neighborhood. "And it never even hit the papers."

Most importantly, it is hard to deny the racial realities of the story. One of the only hard details the public had about the incident was the race of the participants. A white shooter gunning down four black people was palatable in a way that perhaps no other configuration of races would have been. A black adult who shot and seriously wounded four misbehaving white teenagers would probably never have made it off the train, let alone captivated the public's imagination. Still, support for the shooter did not line up cleanly along racial lines. Two things could be true at once: black people may broadly have carried suspicions of law enforcement and feared being victimized by white bigots since America's founding, but were still capable of lining up behind a white vigilante.

The broad contours of the story were a gift to a press that thrived on sensation. Only three weeks before, the city's tabloids had had a field day with an unspeakable tragedy: the horrific assault and murder of Caroline Isenberg. On the evening of December 2, 1984, Isenberg, who had just attended a Broadway show, was attacked, dragged to the roof of her building, and repeatedly stabbed. She died at the hospital several hours later. To Detective Levison's point, while New York saw nearly two thousand homicides a year, most did not become national news. Isenberg, though, was as sympathetic a victim as one ever existed: she was a gorgeous white twenty-two-year-old from an affluent Boston suburb who had graduated from Harvard six months before and moved to New York to become an actress. The contrast to her assailant, Emmanuel Torres, a twenty-one-year-old Puerto Rican from the Bronx, was stark. Torres had a sad past: he had grown up in a destitute family on welfare, possibly suffering from severe and untreated brain trauma after being struck in a hit-and-run by a speeding car at age seven or eight as he was getting off a school bus. After the accident, his overall demeanor permanently changed, leaving him frequently agitated. Still, the narrative about him was painfully easy for the press to craft: Latino dropout who regularly got into fights; pot smoker and drunk; possible (though never confirmed, despite appearing in newspapers) street gang member. The *New York Post* devoted several full-page cover stories to the matter, with headlines such as "DEATH OF A DREAM," "SLAIN GIRL'S DYING WORDS," and "Grim Farewell to Slain Actress." The reporting was poignant and sensational. As in so much of the era's coverage of crime in the city, fear and outrage fed into each other in a never-ending loop: the public was scared, coverage made them more scared, the public stayed scared. Sinatra was only partly correct: if you can make it there, you can make it anywhere—as long as you're not stabbed to death soon after arriving. Stay afraid.

The very specific tenor of the city papers' coverage around crime can be traced to Rupert Murdoch's purchase of the *New York Post* in 1976.

Founded by Alexander Hamilton in 1801, the *Post* is the oldest continuously running daily newspaper in the United States. Ever a home to strong opinions, the paper had a conservative bent beginning in the early twentieth century. It began to shift leftward in the 1930s, particularly after its purchase in 1939 by banking heiress Dorothy Schiff. Over time, she led the paper's evolution into a powerful liberal tabloid, while keeping a close eye on its editorial policy. Its pages had a focus on human-interest stories, sex, and exposé reporting. It savaged previously untouchable figures such as J. Edgar Hoover, Senator Joseph McCarthy, and Robert Moses. Under Schiff's leadership, the paper wavered between making and losing money, leaving Schiff—who had a visceral fear of going broke—concerned that the paper may eventually lead to her financial ruin. Somehow, as its rivals folded one by one, it survived, becoming the city's only afternoon daily. Schiff endured being in the red a lot in the mid-1970s, so she decided to sell.

Rupert Murdoch, then a forty-nine-year-old Australian publisher, sat atop a kingdom of nearly a hundred publications in Australia and England. In the early 1970s, he went on a spree of buying up major American media properties, acquiring two papers in San Antonio. He had had his eye on moving into big northeastern media markets, when, at a meeting in 1976, Schiff mentioned to him that she was thinking about selling the *Post*. He pounced, and following three weeks of secret negotiations, the two closed on a $30 million deal. He also quickly acquired *New York* magazine and *The Village Voice* (he would not acquire *The Wall Street Journal* or found the Fox News network until decades later).

Though few knew at the time where Murdoch's leadership would take the *Post*, his holdings left some clues. His publications had a mass-market appeal, with their coverage focusing heavily on crime, sex, and other sensational stories that drew eyeballs. The content tapped into the adage popularized by William Randolph Hearst in the 1890s that "if it bleeds, it leads"; tragedies (and even sensational facts) sell papers. A classic story in the *San Antonio News*, a Murdoch paper, involved rape, starvation, torture of a divorced epileptic, and someone who claimed to have been buried alive in a bathtub of wet cement before being hanged naked upside down. It wasn't an outlier.

Because single-paper sales were a major part of tabloids' circulation, publications relied on "rack card" advertising—poster-sized displays with big headlines on vending machines and racks where papers were sold. Murdoch had figured out the concept of "clickbait" long before the internet, with his San Antonio rack cards featuring gems such as "ALIENS FOUGHT OVER URINE IN DESERT BATTLE," "MIDGET ROBS UNDERTAKER AT MIDNIGHT," "DISSOLVE OLD MAN IN ACID!" and "ANIMAL AUSCHWITZ." Around the same time, Murdoch had also founded *The National Star*, a tabloid to compete with the *National Enquirer*. Though not featuring fare as off-the-wall as his Texas papers, the *Star* trafficked in the scandalous and, most importantly, gave Murdoch a taste of participating in an arms race against a powerful competitor. Though the *Enquirer* was the industry's clear leader, the two consistently pushed each other to more salacious depths (or heights). After Murdoch's acquisition, *Time* wrote of the paper, "Murdoch provided a daily diet of rape and mayhem, tortured tots, and killer bees."

Regardless of where he would take the publication, *Post* staff were supportive of the deal for a large reason: Murdoch came with deep pockets and would surely pump money into the paper. Schiff framed the handoff as a continuation of the *Post*'s current path and success.

She said in a statement that "Rupert Murdoch is a man of strong commitment to the spirit of independent, progressive journalism. I am confident he will carry on vigorously in the tradition I value so deeply."

Murdoch was hands-on in the newsroom, often with a direct role in making the paper's headlines and text hit harder. Under his leadership, the paper created "Page Six," a gossip column featuring eyebrow-raising stories about the private lives of athletes, movie starlets, and politicians. Stories got shorter, photos and headlines larger. Whatever its overall nutritional value, the paper fed hungry readers steady helpings of fat and sugar.

The citywide blackout and the Son of Sam killings took place within a year of Murdoch's takeover of the *Post* and both provided ripe material for driving public outrage. The paper's coverage of the events viscerally tapped into fears, particularly among white residents in the outer boroughs (who by then were rapidly fleeing the city), around crime and public safety. "[The *Post*] handled the blackout stories by exaggeration and by scare headlines over their stories and on their front pages," said biographer Thomas Kiernan on a PBS *Frontline* TV documentary. "The impression was created that there was an impending threat of a kind of race war in New York." The paper immediately followed the blackout with a multipage special, with sections such as "A City Ravaged" and "City Under Siege."

Likewise, papers soared off the shelves as the *Post*'s coverage of the Son of Sam helped keep the public on edge (an August 1, 1977, headline, with the killer on the loose, read "NO ONE IS SAFE FROM SON OF SAM"). Sales of locks and guns skyrocketed. Still, Murdoch was livid that David Berkowitz, the Son of Sam himself, had chosen to send his missives to the *Daily News* and not the *Post*. The pressure was on for the paper to do anything—*anything*—to attract Berkowitz's attention and the readers that would follow. So Steve Dunleavy, the *Post*'s brash and charismatic metropolitan editor, cooked up one of the more bonkers stunts in news history: to use his staff to set a trap for a serial killer. Under the plan, two reporters, one wearing a blond wig, would wait in a car at night, pretending to have sex. (Dunleavy wanted to use only male reporters, to not risk getting any female ones hurt.) Joe DeMaria, a young photographer at the paper who had a gun permit, would hide in the back seat with a revolver and a camera. If Berkowitz showed up, DeMaria hoped to shoot him twice: once with a firearm to dispatch Berkowitz, and then, with any luck, a second time with a camera for a shot of his lifeless body. It would have been a photograph for the ages, or a disaster that ended with three dead reporters. It never happened, likely being scrubbed in light of the creepy similarity to the actual murder around the same time of Stacy Moskowitz, a blond woman shot and murdered by Berkowitz while in an automobile with a male partner.

The paper's coverage about crime and safety issues and politics was so intense that City Hall began to take notice. Following the blackout, deputy mayor Osborn Elliott sent Murdoch a letter that implied that the paper had aggravated the unrest in the city. Mayor Beame was less diplomatic, saying at a 1977 press conference:

> I am particularly saddened to see a fine old newspaper like the *New York Post* corrupted into a sensationalist rag by an Australian carpetbagger. He came here to line his pockets by peddling fiction in the guise of news. As a self-acclaimed kingmaker, the man from Down Under has openly used his publications to wage political war and engage wantonly in character assassination. No New Yorker should take Rupert Murdoch's *New York Post* seriously any longer. It makes *Hustler* magazine look like the *Harvard [Law] Review.*

The mayor's gripes about Murdoch and the *Post* may have been personal. Beame had first been elected in 1973, and his one term in office was known more for its troubles than for anything else: a near-bankrupt city, rising crime rates, and devastating fiscal cuts. In the 1977 primary, Beame faced brutal challenges from almost every corner of the Democratic coalition: moderate Manhattan congressman Ed Koch; liberal New York secretary of state Mario Cuomo; feminist activist and former congresswoman Bella Abzug; the city's highest-ranking black elected official Percy Sutton; and Bronx congressman Herman Badillo, the first Puerto Rican mayoral candidate in the country. Koch ran to the right of the others, pushing "law and order" as a core campaign message, highlighting the blackout and the city's public safety failures. The *Post* pounced. According to the *New Yorker* columnist Ken Auletta, the paper didn't just endorse Koch, it "anointed" him. In the month leading up to the primary, the paper's news pages ran nothing unfavorable about Koch, while regularly blasting his opponents. After the election, according to Auletta, "fifty of the sixty reporters on the paper signed a petition of protest to Murdoch." Murdoch challenged them to quit, and twelve reportedly did.

Unlike today, there were comparatively few ways to consume information. People got papers during the day and caught televised news broadcasts for an hour or two during the evening. CNN was born in 1980 but only available to those homes lucky enough to have cable, and its hold on ratings would not be challenged by Fox News or MSNBC until the 1990s. Critics were concerned that the *Post*'s shift in tone was destructive to the city—if the paper went to the gutter, it dragged the public with it. As put by Pete Hamill, the legendary *Daily News* columnist at the time, "Something vaguely sickening is happening to that newspaper, and it is spreading through the city's psychic life like a stain."

Though it never played in the muck as giddily as its competitor, the *Daily News* also turned up the sensation. In the months leading up to the Goetz shooting, the paper had gone through management changes of its own, with a new publisher taking the helm earlier in 1984 and a new editor joining that September. James Hoge, the new publisher, rejected any notion that the *Daily News* would engage in a daily war with another paper. Reality played out differently. In time, recognizing that a tabloid's front page was its greatest selling point, the *Daily News* would join the battle for readers with splashy front-page headlines such as "SCREAMS IGNORED, SHE'S SHOT DEAD" from early December 1984. Though the *Daily News* had been stylistically more conservative than the *Post* since the 1960s, loosening its necktie was good for its bottom line. A paper that had been on the verge of collapse as recently as 1982 was beginning to print money.

Coverage of the shooting tapped into daydreams of otherwise law-abiding citizens: What if we—whoever the "we" might be—fired back? Perhaps no sentences sum up the tabloids' line-blurring relationship with the shooter better than the *New York Post*'s urging, just days after the shooting, for the gunman to turn himself in, writing, "The editors and reporters of this newspaper understand your anger and frustration. . . . We endure the same fear and anger that exploded in you on Saturday."

The heroic saga starring the shooter was an alluring one for a public that had no concept of what precisely had gone down. Riders, quoted in the *Daily News* three days after the shooting, said that the four victims were "symbols of all thugs who have caused straphangers to look around and pray a cop appears," while the gunman was "an instant hero . . . a subway vigilante with his whole style of justice." The *New York Times* columnist Sydney H. Schanberg noted that the general public, with its limited knowledge, may have seen the world differently than those who actually experienced the shooting firsthand. "I wonder if the dozen or so passengers who, screaming and sobbing, dove for cover as the vigilante gunman fired at the four youths feel as sympathetic toward the shooter as do the people who telephoned the police hot line. Those scared passengers had no way of knowing who his next target might be." It is easy to want to see a man run for mayor when you have not stared into the barrel of his loaded .38 revolver.

Even before the days of social media and twenty-four-hour news cycles, inaccurate information quickly went viral about the shooter and the four victims. Some were innocuous, such as the *Daily News*' initial reporting from sources that had the shooter getting on the train at 96th Street rather than eighty blocks south in the West Village. While a relevant detail, it was one eyewitnesses may have initially gotten wrong in any investigation. On an express train, there are only a handful of stops between 96th and 14th Streets, and most people are not clocking every time a stranger walks into their subway car (this reality, coupled with human bias, is also why eyewitness testimony is regarded as one of the most unreliable forms of evidence in court).

The press made an even bigger error in its initial reporting: they ran with the inaccurate fact, apparently put out by police, that three of the men were carrying "sharpened" screwdrivers. The *Daily News* further suggested that the screwdrivers were brandished in an attempt to rob the gunman. Both points—that the screwdrivers were sharpened and that they were brandished to rob people—were untrue.* The falsehood was noted early on by *Daily News* columnist Jimmy Breslin, one of the few initial voices to push back on the rush to support the mysterious shooter (implicitly criticizing his own paper's reporting in the process). The information was not only false, but it served to taint public perception about both the shooter and his victims. By wrongly reporting that the men were armed, the public was left with little ambiguity about why Goetz shot them. No one would dispute that a crime was committed on the train on December 22. But who was the criminal?

Press coverage of the screwdrivers was particularly damaging in that even if the teens *had been* carrying sharpened screwdrivers (or even other weapons), they were never made visible to Goetz or any

---

*As recently as 2013, coverage of the incident in major outlets continued to erroneously note that the screwdrivers were sharpened. See, e.g., "NYC Subway Vigilante Goetz Charged in Drug Case," Associated Press (AP), November 2, 2013, https://www.usatoday.com/story/news/nation/2013/11/02/nyc-subway-vigilante-goetz-arrested-on-drug-charge/3381015/.

bystanders. Police reports never indicated that the teens showed the screwdrivers or weapons to Goetz. No witnesses had come forward at that point to suggest that they had seen any weapons. In short, the presence of screwdrivers had no bearing on the legal, or even moral, justification for the shooting. By way of example, if an individual pulls a knife or a gun on another individual, the second person can almost always, fearing a violent assault, use deadly force to defend himself. The same individual cannot kill a different stranger at random on the street and then justify it by publicly noting that the victim happened to have a rock—a potentially deadly weapon—hidden in his back pocket.

More recently, as the public was still learning of the facts of Michael Brown's shooting by a police officer in Ferguson, Missouri, in 2014, *The New York Times* ran a piece referring to Brown as "no angel." The article detailed Brown's recent history of having previously been caught on a security camera stealing cigars, getting into fights with a neighbor, and experimenting with drugs and alcohol. While there is no reason to believe that the information was untrue, its framing served to tar a shooting victim as federal and state law enforcement agencies were weighing whether to bring charges in the case. Most importantly, the officer would have had no way of knowing Brown's criminal history. Are we supposed to believe that even if the officer's reasons for pulling the trigger fell into a gray area, the fact that Brown had been caught with nicked cigars on a prior occasion somehow made his death justified? Facing a backlash over the article, the *Times*' public editor issued a column about the piece, noting her view that while overall it painted a nuanced portrait of Brown and the community's grief around his loss, broadly framing him as "no angel" (while referencing an anecdote earlier in the piece that referenced an "angelic vision") was "not a good choice of words" and a "regrettable mistake."

In Goetz's case, the fact that the press let a damaging fact quickly take hold is even more striking in an era that predated social media. Today it is more algorithmically rewarding to be quick than accurate. There is little reason as to why a 1984 news media that had the luxury of hours, as opposed to seconds, to put out their content could not have done a better job of checking a fundamental fact about a matter of profound public interest. Within days, though, the damage was done. Even if facts would eventually emerge that made the four victims appear more or less sympathetic, the narrative of them as a marauding gang of armed thugs was impossible for the press to pass up, and just about everyone was complicit in crafting the narrative about it all. Once the screwdriver was out of the bag, there was no putting it back in.

There is plenty that the world, led by the press, got wrong about the story. And to top it off, in all of the column inches written about him in New York's papers, no one had figured out the biggest fact of all: the most famous, or infamous, man in New York was actually nowhere near the city. While everyone was distracted by their hot takes about the shooter, he was very quietly making his way to a place hundreds of miles away.

CHAPTER TEN

Joseph Adams

December 22, 1984

A COUNTRY ROAD

Within hours of disappearing from the subway car, the mystery man was deep in the woods, alone with his thoughts. After leaving New York, he headed north into New England, intending to return home in a few days. The choice of location was deliberate; he would later say that he went that way because "heading north is the way to go if there's a problem." New England was a world away, despite its closest border being mere miles from the city. It provided a peaceful backdrop for an individual needing to cool his jets after having just tried to slaughter four people in a fit of fury. Regardless of the motivations he might have had for fleeing, he had to have been aware that law enforcement was looking for him. Whether motivated by cowardice or entitlement, he chose to run, frustrating authorities' efforts to get to the bottom of what had happened.

To this day, no one is clear on what route he took there, precisely how long it took, or wherever else he stopped along the way. Goetz's first documented stop was near Bennington, Vermont, a quiet, historic college town nestled in the rural corner of the state where New

York, Vermont, and Massachusetts come together. After checking in at a small motel on the outskirts of town, he drove farther out into the country, parking on a side road about forty miles north. In the frigid night (Goetz would later claim that he almost died out there, as he was wearing only a light jacket), he took a walk in the woods and disassembled the .38 Smith & Wesson, burying its parts in the snow. According to *The New York Times*, at that time he also burned the blue windbreaker he wore during the shooting. He then got back into the car, drove to town, and spent the night in the motel.

December 23, 1984
NORTH SUTTON, NEW HAMPSHIRE

The next day, he headed about two and half hours northeast, landing in North Sutton, New Hampshire, a tiny town in the middle of the state. He checked in to the Follansbee Inn, a 140-year-old lakefront bed and breakfast. Though the forced intimacy of a bed and breakfast could easily blow the cover of a fugitive trying to avoid attention, a sleepy town in the middle of nowhere was as good a place as any to hide. Little more than lakes, rustic valleys, and a small mountain in the distance dotted the horizon. Here, and elsewhere, Goetz did his best to keep his identity hidden; he paid in cash and checked in as "Joseph Adams of 959 Maret Street, Red Hook, New Jersey." He told the people there that he was only "traveling." It seemed believable enough and they left him alone.

Christmas Eve 1984
SUNAPEE, NEW HAMPSHIRE

'Twas the night before Christmas, and all through New England, Bernhard Goetz was still on the move. He drove from Sutton about fifteen miles southeast to Mount Sunapee, a quiet ski area nestled in a state park. He checked in at the Mount Sunapee Motel, a tiny brick-and-wood building nearby. Again, the meek-looking man traveling alone did not seem to set off any alarms for those he encountered. "He was a very nice guy," said the motel's owner. "He was just a regular customer who was very nice and polite and stayed two nights."

A Few Days Later
WARNER, NEW HAMPSHIRE

Warner, New Hampshire, is another tiny town about a half hour southeast from Sunapee. It is home to Mount Kearsarge, the small mountain that was visible in the distance from the Follansbee Inn in North Sutton. Visitors to Warner seeking to embrace the full country experience would often head to a remote area about four miles outside of town to Hillside Books, an antique bookstore. There they could sit by the fire and chat with its owner, Thomas Stotler.

On a snowy December 26 or 27, Goetz walked in and perused the aisles, looking for books on science and electronics. In what would prove to be Goetz's longest face-to-face encounter during his time on the lam, he told Stotler that he was nearly broke and could not afford the thirty dollars or so it would have cost to purchase the books. One of the first things Stotler noticed was that his visitor had New York license plates. The two struck up a conversation about the city and why Goetz was in New Hampshire in the first place. Goetz told Stotler he was from New York but wanted to get away for the holidays. "He said that he wanted some peace and quiet and that he liked the people up here," Stotler told the *New York Daily News* in 1985. "He said he had been here before. He left the impression he was dissatisfied with the atmosphere in New York." The conversation then quickly turned to crime in the city. Goetz told Stotler that he had been mugged five times and spoke at length about how unsafe the city was. "I think it's out of control," Goetz told the bookseller. "It's not safe in the streets. If the police arrest somebody they are out again in no time." Goetz also claimed that he was once jogging in Central Park when he successfully ran down muggers who had taken a woman's purse. He claimed that police showed no interest in catching them.

Stotler then asked Goetz whether he had heard about the fugitive "vigilante" who had shot four young men on the subway whom he believed had been threatening him. While Goetz initially pretended that he had not heard about the shooting, he took a keen interest in the matter and asked questions, trying to get to the bottom of how Stotler had heard. "He was interested in it," Stotler said. "But he didn't try to pin me down for details." Before leaving, Goetz asked Stotler and his son whether they had any New York newspapers.

Goetz didn't know it at the time, but he may have found as welcome an audience as a vigilante could have hoped for when he stumbled into Stotler's shop. According to the *Daily News*, Stotler was a member of a right-wing organization called Freedom Through Strength, which advocated that the United States arm itself as heavily as possible. After their encounter, Stotler would largely echo Goetz's underlying message, saying that "I sympathize with him, because when the police can't look after you, you have to do it for yourself."

December 29, 1984
55 WEST 14TH STREET

Little is known about where and how Goetz spent much of his time while in Vermont and New Hampshire. Police suspected that while he may have done some business with electronics firms in New England, he kept moving, likely using different names along the way. He also apparently made several phone calls, including to Myra Friedman, a woman who had lived in his apartment building for six years.

Myra was quirky. She wore heavy makeup and large eyeglasses, and was described by multiple sources as being a dead ringer, in style and demeanor, to Lily Tomlin's brash and zany telephone operator Ernestine from *Rowan & Martin's Laugh-In.* Her apartment was quiet; she lived at the back of the building, far removed from the bustle and distractions of 14th Street. It had also gotten quieter over time, as the tenant who had previously lived above her, a "boisterous" sex-show producer, had moved out. A quieter tenant had moved in afterward. Able to find a moment of calm among the city around her, she settled in for a Saturday nap.

The phone rang, jolting her up from her midafternoon bliss. On the other end of the line was a voice she didn't immediately recognize, one that seemed equal parts tense and frightened.

"Myra, this is Bernie," crackled the voice.

"Bernie who?" asked Myra.

"Bernie Goetz."

"Bernie, what in the world . . . ?" Myra said, stunned at receiving any call from Bernie Goetz, her quiet neighbor from the upstairs apartment. They had a relationship she described as "hundreds of brief encounters," often in the lobby, when the two would periodically run into each other on breaks when working from home. They were familiar with each other but, as she described it, "hardly the closest of friends."

"Listen, can you rent a car?" Bernie asked.

"Rent a car? What are you talking about?"

"Do you know where Route 95 is to Connecticut?"

"Connecticut! What are you talking about?"

"Please, just listen to me. You can get a map and figure it out. Route 95. Take Route 95 to Connecticut, go off at Exit 6, and meet me at the Howard Johnson's there with a couple of the Guardian Angels and a tape recorder."

It is no surprise that Goetz was trying to get some help from the Guardian Angels, the volunteer unarmed civilian patrol group founded by Curtis Sliwa in 1979 as New York crime rates were skyrocketing.

The first Guardian Angels were a few young men Sliwa managed on an evening shift at a McDonald's in a rough part of the Bronx. The predominantly black and brown young men and women can still often be seen on subways and street corners and at public events, purporting to patrol neighborhoods without consideration of race or background. The group has exploded into a network of several thousand people in fifty-one cities worldwide, wearing their trademark red berets and white T-shirts emblazoned with the words "Safety Patrol" under red satin baseball jackets. The Guardian Angels' existence had blurred the line between "us" and "them" in the ongoing struggle to make sense of safety in the city. As one shopkeeper at the time said, giving the Angels some backhanded praise, "The thing about these kids is, they may come from the worst parts of town, but they're on our side."

Whatever their goals, the Guardian Angels were the very embodiment of Goetz's worldview: the notion that leaders had failed to make the world safe and that it fell to individuals to step in. Still, what they saw as perhaps their greatest selling point was their biggest flaw: they were only accountable to themselves. As Joe Allen, the renowned restaurateur of West 46th Street's Restaurant Row, said about them in 1988, "They have a certain advantage over the police, in the sense that they don't have to read anyone his rights." The police largely took a different view. "We would prefer the Angels not step in," a NYPD spokesman said at the time. "The problem is, they are not trained and don't have authority." The organization had a chilly relationship with Koch, who referred to them as "paramilitaries" who ought to join the police force if they wanted to do good. Sliwa, however, today pins the blame almost directly on Koch. "People say, 'Oh, the Guardian Angels are vigilantes,'" he offers. "We're not. . . . You don't want Bernhard Goetz? You don't want Daniel Penny? There should be more cops. And if there were more cops in 1979, there would never have been the Guardian Angels."

Myra paused and took it all in. And then it hit her. Bernie was tall, lanky, and blond with a thin face, and wore wire-rimmed glasses. She also hadn't seen him for at least a week, the same week in which the world was looking for a tall, lanky blond man with a thin face who wore wire-rimmed glasses. Her stomach started churning.

"You? My God!" she exclaimed.

"Yes."

"Where in the world am I going to find Guardian Angels?" she asked, still apparently not grasping that an obvious fugitive was seeking her assistance in running from the cops.

Friedman was a writer and had worked as Janis Joplin's publicist. Her biggest work up until that point had been a biography of the rock legend. She quickly realized that she had stumbled right out of a Saturday nap into her next major story. She was now likely the only person who knew for certain the identity of the blond man on the train. Without thinking twice, she took out a tape recorder.

Now, simply knowing who Goetz was and agreeing to speak with him could get her in huge trouble. Given that risk, Friedman still somehow stayed on the phone with him for a remarkably long time. He began by mentioning more than once that he needed her to do him a "favor," and that she should tell no one that the two were speaking. Even as a young writer hungry for the next big break, she was now beginning to flirt with unimaginable personal risk. Honoring just about any request from an individual fleeing law enforcement—short of "Can you please feed my goldfish?"—could subject her to being an accessory after the fact to a crime.

After Friedman asked him to tell her what had happened, he gave what can best be described as a meandering series of monologues, with her cutting in only periodically as he rattled on about the farce of the legal system; showed disgust about his own viciousness; complained about the coverage the case was getting on television; doubled down on the reasonableness of the shooting; railed about the city's gun laws; claimed that the fact that the screwdrivers in the young men's pockets were never brandished was a "technicality"; stressed how much he knew about fighting; opined about the effects of adrenaline on the body; explained his understanding of the concept of premeditation;

and repeatedly pointed out to her how little she knew or understood the case, even saying at one point, "See, for you, it's easy to say, 'Go ahead and do this and let's get all the dirt out.' Myra, rather than go through this, I'd rather put a bullet in my head."*

After Goetz was through speaking to Friedman and they hung up, she went downstairs and learned from the doorman that police had come looking for Goetz. She debated calling a detective she had periodically seen around the building and with whom she was familiar, but instead took an additional step toward being complicit in Goetz's acts: she slipped up to the ninth floor and retrieved the note the police had left on his door. She also went down to his mailbox and took the note they had left there. She claimed to have wanted to give Goetz an opportunity to turn himself in on his own and feared that "notes from the police might prove to be too much of a shock for him," perhaps leading him to stay on the run. Though her actions were explainable—they were committed by someone who had empathy for a person she had a peculiar fondness for—she was nonetheless breaking the law. She behaved with the sense of invincibility that can be possessed only by someone who believed that the police were on their side, unafraid of what might happen if an encounter with law enforcement were to go south. It is hard to imagine someone in the South Bronx getting away with openly discarding a note from police, under the rationale of looking out for the fragile feelings of the suspect in an attempted quadruple homicide.

December 30, 1984

Around noon the next day, Friedman heard footsteps coming from the apartment upstairs. She furiously dialed Bernie's number. No answer.

*Extended excerpts of the conversation, as relayed by Myra Friedman, appeared in an issue of *New York* magazine. See Myra Friedman with Michael Daly, "My Neighbor Bernie Goetz," *New York*, February 18, 1985, 35.

She then rode the elevator downstairs to the doorman and learned that Bernie was home. She rushed back to the elevator. As the doors slid open, there he stood, on the way to do his laundry. Oddly, though, he was holding only a dirty blue sock.

"I can't talk right now. I've got a lot of things to do. I can't talk," he said. They went their separate ways.

About two hours later, she heard a faint knock on her door. It was Bernie, and she let him in. He immediately mentioned that he had found a note from police under his door. She suggested, as she had done at least once on their call the previous day, that he turn himself in. Worried about the "commotion" if he did so, Goetz said that he could not face the police in New York and had planned to hide out in New Hampshire "until this blows over." He paced around her apartment, repeatedly standing and sitting, unable to clearly articulate what had happened on the subway. He also mimicked a gesture that he claimed Ramseur had made to him that suggested that Ramseur had a weapon in his pocket.

"Bernie, what's with the guns, for God's sake?" she asked him, aware of his history of gun possession.

"Oh, Myra. I grew up on a farm. Guns are nothing on a farm. I knew about guns when I was a kid."

He then went back into his theory of the case—that the justice system is stacked and unfair, and that "hoodlums" could get away with just about anything short of killing someone. "They can fracture your skull. They can squash your brain. They can ruin your kidneys. They can break your legs. They can wreck your spine." After more conversation, he suddenly jumped to his feet and ran out of the apartment.

Within an hour, Friedman heard another faint knock at the door. It was Goetz with a neatly folded brown paper bag in a shape that was about two feet by a foot, and no more than a few inches tall. He walked in and said, "Can I leave this with you for a few days?"

"What is that?" she screamed.

"This is not the weapon that was used."

Clutching the package, he darted toward her bedroom, but she immediately stopped him, yelling, "No, not there!" Panicking, she then pointed to a hall closet, asking, "Will it explode?"

He answered, "There are no bullets in there." She asked if he had a license for whatever was in the package. He responded that its contents—without saying what they were—were purchased legally. She refused to touch the package, and he placed it in the closet and left.

The entire exchange was over within five minutes.

A little later, Friedman went upstairs to Goetz's apartment to ask him to take the package back. No response. She went back inside her apartment and stared at the package as it sat ominously on a shelf in her closet. She did not open it, knowing that whatever was in there could probably get her in enormous legal trouble. Still, she did not call the police. Later that night, she called an attorney.

New Year's Eve, 1984

Early the next morning, Friedman's phone rang. It was an anxious, stammering, heavily breathing, fatigued Bernie. He had fled New York once again and was thinking about turning himself in.

CHAPTER ELEVEN

Live Free or Die

New Year's Eve, 1984

CONCORD, NEW HAMPSHIRE

I am the person they are seeking in New York."

The few officers at the police headquarters in Concord, New Hampshire, didn't quite know what to do when a man in a leather bombardier's jacket, jeans, and white sport shirt walked in and calmly identified himself. He didn't need to say much more than ". . . the person they are seeking in New York." The search had been on for nine days, and the case was now one of the biggest news stories in the country. There he was, in Concord, in the flesh: just a skinny, shivering guy miles from home, standing there with his glasses fogging up.

The action the Concord police saw usually was standard for a small city: a shooting or homicide every now and again, but more than anything, just domestic calls and complaints from neighbors when local bars got rowdy. It was a small department, with only a few dozen officers and about seven or eight police cars covering an area of only sixty-four square miles. They worked out of an unspectacular two-floor 1970s redbrick building that would have seemed right at home in a boring middle-class suburb anywhere in America, not a state capital that predated the American Revolution. New Year's Eve was an even quieter day than usual at the office, as a number of detectives were on a stakeout at a local bank following rumors of a robbery that never materialized.

As a veteran of the force said in the understatement of the year, "Although you might say we are in the sticks, amazing things can happen anywhere."

Bob Libby was the watch commander for the day, stationed at the office as the point of contact for any sergeants who were out on patrol. He was sitting at his desk when a stunned Jim McGonigle, the department's energy resource officer, came in with the news that a man claiming to be the New York shooter—*the* New York shooter—had just walked in. Libby was familiar with the story. He had read about it in the local Sunday paper just the day before. But why Concord, and why now? Libby didn't even believe the man's claim as to who he was. Having worked as an officer for more than fifteen years, he knew to approach confessions with a little bit of skepticism. People have all sorts of reasons for claiming they committed an offense, and it wouldn't have been out of the question for someone to want to capitalize on the attention around the biggest story in the country.

They confirmed Goetz's name from his Florida driver's license and American Express card. They then notified Dave Walchak, Concord's police chief, saying that a man who was "a little strange" or "different" (Walchak later described Goetz as an "interesting fella") had just walked in, claiming he was the guy everyone had been looking for. Realizing that this one might take awhile, Walchak called his girlfriend and canceled his New Year's Eve dinner plans.

When officers realized that Goetz wanted to confess, they immediately read him his Miranda rights, advising him of his right to remain silent, that any statements he gave could be used against him in court, and that he had a right to have an attorney present. Doing so was probably not out of the officers' burning desire to protect his rights. There was also a practical reason: not reading him his rights could have meant that anything he said in response to questions could be kept out of court one day. Still, Goetz talked. Years later, he told Nancy Grace that he was as forthcoming as he was because he believed that if he told the police the whole story, it would simply go away. He was so convinced that law enforcement would regard the entire thing as an honest disagreement that he assumed they would let him drive himself back to New York that day. He had not even fed his parking meter.

Goetz first spoke to Warren Foote, a Concord detective, from about 12:40 p.m. to 2 p.m., in a cramped eight-by-eight room on the second floor of the station. Foote described Goetz as "nervous, very nervous at that time." Officers then asked Goetz to give an additional statement, which they could record. Goetz agreed, and spoke at length with Foote and a second officer for the next two hours. After a secretary typed up the notes from the conversation, Goetz read them over and signed them. He had now given more than three hours of detailed statements to police without an attorney present.

Later that night, a team from New York arrived. Clearly, the city was taking this case more seriously than most; they had sent an inspector, an NYPD detective, a New York transit detective, and a prosecutor from the Manhattan DA's office to handle the interrogation.

The camera started rolling.

Goetz sat in his white shirt, hair parted to the left, wire glasses perched on his nose. He was positioned at the head of a shiny wood-grain interrogation table, an orange wall behind him. Throughout his confession, he sat fidgeting, arms closely wrapped around his midsection, his upper body curled into an upright fetal position. His left leg was tightly crossed over his other. To his right was Transit Detective Dan Hattendorf. To Hattendorf's right sat Assistant District Attorney Susan Braver, who rushed down from a skiing vacation in Vermont to Concord. Across the table, to Goetz's left, sat New York City detective Michael Clark.

Goetz was explicit at the start of the interview, saying, "I don't want to talk to you." Whether he was simply annoyed by the people around him or seeking to revoke his earlier choice to speak, the interview should have ended right there. With that sentence, he had asserted his constitutional right to remain silent. Clark coaxed him back into compliance: "Just relax"; "Sit back." Goetz went along with it and got back to talking.

As the New York officials interviewed him, Goetz maintained the same posture—tense, tightly wound, and kinetic. The only exception was whenever Susan Braver was speaking. Something about her set him off, and he reacted almost viciously whenever she spoke. When she began at the start of the conversation, "So you indicated to the detectives here that you would speak . . ." he immediately grimaced, leaned forward with his arms gripping his midsection even more tightly, and let out a grunt of revulsion about her accent. "Just when I hear New Yorkers speak . . ." he spat out, trailing off (an odd criticism from an almost lifelong New Yorker).

It would not be the only time he was rude to Braver, with a reflexive change in his posture, tone, and demeanor whenever she opened her mouth. When she had introduced herself, "I'm an assistant district attorney from Manhattan," he blurted out a snide "Congratulations." At one point, he suggested that she was on a personal crusade to take him down, spitting at her, "Don't you love it? . . . It's going to be great for your career, isn't it, Miss?" When she asked Goetz what might have been in his head at the time he encountered the teens—a necessary question for determining whether authorities would have enough to charge him with a crime, he insulted her personally. "You are so far removed from reality, and yet they send you here as a professional . . . to investigate this. It's beyond belief." He echoed a similar point elsewhere in the interview, saying that the NYPD and DA's office "shouldn't have sent [Braver] up here," on account of her not being "familiar" with violence (another curious point to make to a city resident who prosecuted local crimes).

Goetz's several hours of confessions to two different sets of police were a chaotic tangle of feelings. He was equal parts cerebral and disordered, arrogant and crippled with self-doubt, acerbic and polite, defiant and meek, angry and ashamed. Each new moment seemed to bring another mood swing.

He made clear in his interview with the Concord police that the violence was something that only he, not yokel cops from New England or snobby ivory tower lawyers, could truly understand. "You have to think in a cold-blooded way in New York. . . . If you don't . . . think in what society's going to brand it, as being you know cold-blooded and murderous and savage and monstrous. . . . How can you understand that here in New Hampshire?" "The robbery has nothing to do with it," he said later after the New York team had arrived. "How can people like you be familiar with violence? Have you been beaten into the ground?" He pinned much on the legal system, decoupling police from prosecutors and courts. "The problem isn't the police," he sneered at Susan Braver. "The problem is you. It's your legal system. . . . Oh, if you knew how sick your legal system makes me. . . . Do you know how sick your legal system makes me, Miss?"

He blasted city management, with "[T]he government of New York City is a disgrace. The services are disgraceful. Now, forget about what happened on that subway to me. That's just one thing. This happens all the time. The subway system itself is a disaster. The school system is a disaster. The crime system is a disaster. And [the case] is getting all the attention."

Throughout, he spelled out his own legal code. Time would tell if it would align with society's. If he were to be charged for shooting another person in self-defense, his guilt would almost certainly hinge on his thoughts and feelings at the time he pulled the trigger (the critical legal concept of criminal intent or mental state, known by the Latin term *mens rea*). As such, prosecutors were keen on trying to figure out how afraid he was on the subway car. Did he fire his weapon out of fear that he, or others, were about to be victims of a violent crime? Did he fear a robbery (which, under New York law, would have allowed him to use deadly force)?

He didn't do himself any favors by suggesting that the shooting wasn't really in self-defense. Without hesitation, he admitted that he knowingly shot at least one individual who was trying to get away from him. As he volunteered, "They say I shot him in the back. It doesn't matter. I wasn't even aiming" (a statement that spoke to both his cruelty and the extreme risk to which he subjected all bystanders), and "It seems as if he was trying to get through the steel wall of the subway car. But he couldn't. And I let him have it."

He also was unclear about how much he feared a robbery. He noted that he did not regard it a threat when Canty approached him. However, coupled with his prior mugging, he claimed to have had a nebulous fear of what *might* eventually happen that led him to lash out. He was dismissive of the four, saying that "[t]hey know the rules of the game . . . in New York and they're very serious about the rules," a statement suggesting some sort of code of human interaction—how to act and how to react—whether it be out in the streets, in back alleys, or in the subway. Even being asked "How are you?" was part of the ritual. "It normally means nothing," he said. "But in a certain frame of reference, there's an implication." He said that his doorman at Courtney House had been brutally mugged in an encounter that began with "How you doing?," thus suggesting that it was unlikely that the four young men were simply offering a warm greeting to a wayward traveler. Moreover, Goetz was convinced that even if the young men hadn't said anything to him, he knew based on context that the situation was about to go south. "What they said wasn't even so much as important as the look, the look," Goetz said. "You see the body language . . . you have to, you know, it's, it's, uh, you know, that's what I call it, body language."

In his rambling statements, he admitted multiple times to wanting to kill, even using the legally significant term "murder." (To kill is just an act; to murder is a crime.) He said that he wanted to "[m]urder them, to hurt them, to make them suffer as much as possible," and that "[t]hey didn't die, well, . . . that's what God has wanted evidently, if there is a God. But I, in my heart, was a murderer." He admitted that his rage led him to want to maim the young men, saying, "[I]f I had more bullets, I would have shot 'em all again and again. My problem was I ran out of bullets. And I was gonna, I was gonna gouge one of the guys' eyes out with my keys afterwards." He claimed to have said to a bleeding Canty, "You better learn a lesson from all this," suggesting far more than a desire to protect himself.

In many respects, Goetz's confessions were a meditation on fear, often framing it in terms of its importance in the animal kingdom. He returned to a metaphor he had used on the phone with Myra Friedman, involving what might happen if a rat were attacked brutally. "If you corner a rat and you are about to butcher it, OK?" he mused, "the way I responded was viciously and savagely, just like a rat." He continued, noting that he would be fine accepting his fate if he were to be killed instantly, but that he had a real fear of being played with "like a cat plays with a mouse." He said that "what being afraid does for you is it makes you think and analyze, and it speeds up your mind. . . . It builds up your adrenaline a little, okay?" Regarding New York's streets as a war zone, he noted how critical fear is to combat, as it makes and motivates better warriors. "The lower levels of your brain are going to take care of everything for you. You have speed, you have your—your visual capabilities. . . . [I]t's all visual. Your perception changes, your field of view changes. You see everything. Your sense of hearing becomes unimportant. . . . You react not—not from second to second. You react from maybe a tenth of a second or a twentieth of a second."

Even in his frenzied brazenness, Goetz repeatedly showed revulsion at his actions. "I know violence now from both sides," he moaned. "It's the worst thing in your life when you're on the losing side, and when you're on the winning side it makes you sick." At another point, his voice trembling, he said, "If there's a God, God knows what was in my heart. And it was . . . sadistic and savage . . . that was me."

After the confessions, the authorities transported him to the Merrimack County Jail, about twenty minutes north in Boscawen, New Hampshire. During processing, Goetz was almost in tears, telling a corrections officer, "I'm sorry for what happened, but it had to be done." A version of the quote appeared the next day as the lead headline on what would become an iconic *New York Daily News* front page.

With Goetz safely in custody and not going to run any farther, law enforcement confronted the problem they had to deal with anytime

Flutie tosses 45-28 Cotton Bowl victory

Huskies beat Sooners in Orange Bowl, 28-17

Stories on pages 64 & 65

Manhattan ★★★★ Sports Final

DAILY NEWS

30¢ Wednesday, January 2, 1985 — NEW YORK'S PICTURE NEWSPAPER® — Cloudy High 54 Details page 2

'I'M SORRY, BUT IT HAD TO BE DONE'

Death Wish suspect talks; fights return to New York

Suspect's life a jigsaw puzzle

Stories begin on page 2

Bernhard Goetz at Concord N.H., police headquarters yesterday someone is arrested in one state for a crime he committed in another. Under the law, a state can't simply take custody of an individual from another state without legal proceedings first (or getting his consent to be moved across state lines). After a testy back-and-forth with Susan Braver, Goetz decided not to fight extradition but made clear that he did not want to go to New York immediately (though the choice was not his), saying, "I don't have the strength to go through this again."

An unshaven and weary Goetz was led, handcuffed, into a Concord courthouse. He was charged in New Hampshire as a fugitive, an approach that let authorities keep him in custody pending his transfer over to New York. At the hearing, Goetz simply said to Judge Michael Sullivan, "I'm willing to go back." His trip back home was set, with NYPD detectives to arrive to transport him in the morning. As police led the handcuffed Goetz away, a reporter asked him if he had anything to say.

"Vultures," Goetz said.

Asked to clarify if he was referring to the four men he had shot, Goetz gave a one-word reply to the crowd of reporters: "You."

January 3, 1985
NEW YORK CITY

The circus was about to come to town. Stephen Crane, a former Wall Street lawyer who at age forty-eight was a rising star on the New York bench, was waiting with his wife for a bus on Lexington Avenue in Manhattan. He glanced at a nearby newsstand and saw blaring headlines on all the city's papers that Goetz had surrendered in New Hampshire and was about to be extradited to New York. He turned to his wife and said, "Oh, do I pity the judge who gets that case." He jinxed himself.

A caravan of press cars followed an unmarked NYPD car that took Goetz slowly down to Manhattan for the entire five-hour drive. Upon arrival, Goetz was not brought to the First Precinct's station house, as would likely have happened in an ordinary case. Fearing a spectacle, police instead took him to the city's main police headquarters in Lower Manhattan. Mindful of Jack Ruby's killing of Lee Harvey Oswald (then still a vivid memory for many people), the NYPD took particular care to ensure that Goetz got in and out of where he needed to be without incident. Double barricades lined the streets near the station, and traffic officers diverted all traffic from the area in advance of Goetz's arrival. Emergency services officers with shotguns were perched atop nearby buildings, and more than sixty officers wearing flak jackets, several of them on horseback, patrolled the streets below. Goetz was taken directly to central booking and processed for arraignment on weapons possession and attempted murder charges. Outside the building, several of the forty or so spectators who had gathered to wait for the caravan chanted a chorus of "Let him go! Let him go!"

In retrospect, Jim Levison admits that leaving a note for Goetz at his apartment that asked him to come talk to the police "wasn't a great piece of detective work." Still, he credits it with letting Goetz know that police were on his scent and spooking him enough to turn himself in. "He knew the jig was up," Levison said, noting how close they came to never making an arrest. "Knowing how investigations unfold, it would have been almost next to impossible to identify this guy."

But once Goetz was safely in custody, one question continued to puzzle the detectives. Why New Hampshire? If Goetz had made the decision to turn himself in, it seemed silly to do so hundreds of miles away. The question so dogged Jim Levison that he instructed his guys to ask Goetz about it directly, and a clerk finally got ahold of Goetz as he was being booked.

It turned out that, after more than a week in the woods, Bernie Goetz had no idea of how big a celebrity he was. "He said he was afraid that the New York police would beat him up because he caused so much trouble," Levison said. He chuckled, then continued:

"*Beat him up?* Half of the city wanted to give him a medal."

PART II

GUN-TOTING HONKY

CHAPTER TWELVE

Power to the Vigilante

January 3, 1985

NEW YORK CITY

The drive from New England into Lower Manhattan often ends on the FDR Drive, a parkway running along the East River. By New Year's Day 1985, drivers would be greeted by the words "POWER TO THE VIGILANTE–N.Y. LOVES YA!" crudely spray-painted on a wall running along the highway. Within weeks, "Ride with Bernie–He Goetz 'Em!" and "Bernhard Goetz: American Hero" bumper stickers funded by pro-gun groups would be all over the city.

The mysterious shooter was now real. Though he had not uttered a word publicly, Bernhard Goetz now had a name, an identity, and a history people across the world could try to decipher. An absurd arms race was on between the tabloids to find out what they could about Goetz, or at least get the first photo of him. The *New York Post* sent a reporter, Richard Esposito, on a twelve-hour stakeout of Goetz's apartment. When that didn't pan out with anything usable, Esposito snuck past detectives in the Courtney House lobby and slunk up to Goetz's place. He cracked the front door's lock with a credit card, slipped into the unit, snatched Goetz's passport, crept out, and handed it off to a photographer for a photo, then stole back in to replace the passport. The police figured out what was going on and called up to him on the apartment's intercom, "You had enough fun. You need to get out of there now." Recognizing the trouble they could have gotten into for trespass or burglary, Esposito and the photographer were terrified. But they'd gotten their shot.

Millions saw Goetz as either a bigot with an itchy trigger finger or an unwitting everyman who did what needed to be done. The split was best summed up by a newspaper headline: "Trigger Happy or Caspar Milquetoast?" People across the city differed vastly, if narrowly, as to what it meant to feel safe, how to address crime, and exactly what message to take away from the shooting. With results that traversed age, income, education, race, gender, political affiliation, and geography, *New York Times* polling from soon after the shooting found that half of New York's residents believed that crime was the worst thing about living there. Even with violent crime up, people were divided as to whether they backed Goetz, with slightly more than half saying they generally supported what he had done.

Likewise, the racial divide in the city over the incident was perceptible but not stark, with 45 percent of black people, 48 percent of people of Hispanic origin, and 56 percent of white people in favor of Goetz. There was a small gender divide: 56 percent of men supported Goetz to 48 percent of women.

When asked "Do you think there are so many muggings and holdups in New York City that people have a right to take matters into their own hands, or not?," 43 percent said yes, and 47 said no. There are many ways to interpret that result. Clearly, the public was closely split over whether it was acceptable to take matters of law and order into your own hands. Another way to look at it could be that those who found it

OK to step outside the law were outnumbered by those who thought it wasn't. Or, perhaps more troubling, it meant that things were so bad that almost half of New York City supported vigilante behavior.

Jimmy Breslin at the *New York Daily News* continued his string of columns that were critical of Goetz and his actions, hammering the point that despite many in the public "cheering lustily" in support of Goetz's act, much about the case made Goetz's "valor seem . . . a bit questionable." Another major media voice who challenged the prevailing narrative around Goetz's heroism was Les Payne, an editor and columnist at *Newsday*. A 1974 Pulitzer Prize winner for Public Service Reporting and a founder of the National Association of Black Journalists, Payne was one of very few black columnists at the city's major papers. Payne wrote powerfully about race and the public's relationship with it. He was suspicious about aspects of the case that many seemed quick to gloss over: whether the four asked Goetz for money in concert; how others on the train reacted once Goetz began firing; and, most importantly, how two ended up with bullet holes in their backs. To Payne, the public's warm embrace of Goetz could almost exclusively be traced to Goetz's and his victims' races. "What if the gunmen had been black and his victims four white teenagers?" Payne mused in a column soon after Goetz arrived back in New York. "The media would have dragged its cameras to the scene and doggedly pursued the best attainable version of the truth. In the Goetz case, the media dispensed spoon-fed police details." He continued, using language that would be noteworthy in any major newspaper, even decades later: "In picking up the guns Goetz, the blond hero, struck a blow for white manhood."

In contrast, Mayor Koch complained that Breslin, Payne, and another prominent columnist, Earl Caldwell from the *Daily News*, were the ones responsible for inflaming racial tensions in the city, calling their columns about the Goetz case "racist." Koch, who frequently tangled with the press, noted the races of all three journalists (Breslin was white; Caldwell and Payne, black) and protested, "They seek to make everybody a racist who supported Goetz." Koch then further singled out Payne and Caldwell, and noted, without basis, that the two "are devoted to securing a black mayor, not a mayor that is good." Koch, like so many before and after him, wrongly regarded the mere discussion of race as an inherently political, if not partisan, issue. Fred W. Friendly, the former president of CBS News and a prominent observer of the media, took note. Koch "ought to be able to take the heat without mixing it up with racism," Friendly said. "In a city like this, with a big ethnic and religious schism, it rings alarms when the Mayor attacks black journalists. But we're all fair game. He's the Mayor. It's a free country."

In that free country, however, for every Breslin, Payne, or Caldwell, there were dozens of louder voices painting Goetz as a savior. In a high-profile example, a staff editorial in *The Wall Street Journal* all but accepted as fact that the climate justified Goetz's behavior, noting, "If the 'state of nature' has returned to some big cities, can people fairly be blamed for modern vigilantism? Is it more 'civilized' to suffer threats to individual liberty from criminals, or is it an overdose of sophistication to say individuals can never resort to self-protection?" Mike Royko at the *Daily News* wrote gushing columns about Goetz, including one titled "They Deserved It, Sure as Shooting," in which he posed the question that when harassed, "What are you supposed to do—draft a motion to the conductor to file it with the Supreme Court?" Also in the *Daily News*, conservative syndicated columnist William F. Buckley analogized the matter to the My Lai massacre. My Lai had been a war crime committed by U.S. Army personnel in 1968 that involved the mass killing, gang rape, and mutilation of hundreds of unarmed Vietnamese men, women, and children. Buckley suggested that both scenarios took place in wartime (one against the Viet Cong, the other against crime and city leadership), and essentially that, in the fog of war, shit happens.

Papers around the country similarly joined in the fascination, latching on to the narrative that the nation's cities were in crisis, with the shooting a mere reflection of the country's urban troubles. Pieces about the shooting would often include a perfunctory aside about the fact that violence is fundamentally wrong, before going on to offer a full-throated defense of the conduct. Newspapers were flooded with letters of support for Goetz. In Atlanta, *The Journal* and *The Constitution* did not receive a single critical letter. In one, a man who claimed to be black wrote to the wounded young men: "Take time to think that whitey didn't do you in. You sure get no sympathy from us peace-loving, law-abiding blacks. We will even contribute to the guy that taught you a lesson . . ."

Goetz quickly became a fascination in pop culture as well. It didn't take long for someone to come up with a Monopoly-style board game, the Subway Vigilante Game, in which two to four players—each represented by a pewter handgun (all of them different types of revolver or semiautomatic pistol)—would race to survive a ride between Brooklyn and the Bronx. They would start the game with six bullets to use on their journey. Along the way, players would draw cards such as "Cops help stop punks: ROLL AGAIN," "Wild chase leads to detour: GO TO PENN STATION," and "Punk shot, but still moving: USE TWO BULLETS."

Over the airwaves, Goetz became a muse for everything from the headbanging grit of hardcore 1980s punk to the percussive beats of hip-hop that were then the soundtrack of urban streets. Ronny & The Urban Watchdogs, a group that appears to not have existed prior to the Goetz shooting (or produced any material afterward), released a single called "Subway Vigilante," an ode to a beloved fighter who, with his gun, "*Drove the rats back into hidin'.*" Pallas, a synthesizer-heavy Scottish progressive rock band that sounded like a mix of Styx and early Peter Gabriel, came out with "The Executioner (Bernie Goetz a Gun)": "*I have the right to clear this garbage from the street / If someone touches me / They'll suffer for their ignorance.*" The hardcore punk band Agnostic Front released the cheekily titled ode to Goetz, "Shoot His

Load," with the almost grandiose: "*Tired of being preyed upon / By the scum of the earth / Tonight he'll be the predator.*"*

Howard Stern, then very much a drive-time shock jock still decades from evolving into the more sober presence he cuts today, once called for Goetz to get a Congressional Medal of Honor. While couching his material in vulgar boundary-testing satire, Stern commiserated with Goetz. He noted how frightening the subway could be, given that an ordinary encounter with a group of tough guys could lead to disaster. In one segment, he questioned whether Goetz's being unaware of the screwdrivers on the men was somehow relevant, saying, "You're supposed to wait to find out what they're going to do with these screwdrivers? You must wait to see if they have them? These guys are just menacing on their own?" (The comments, though made in 1987, still pushed the notion that the screwdrivers were sharpened.)

A memorable segment on Stern's show played a parody a musician had made of the pop culture vigilante, "Bernhard Hugo Goetz What He Shoots," sung to the Rolling Stones' "You Can't Always Get What You Want," which matched the original's meter perfectly: "*Four bad ass dudes asked for five dollars / But he gave them five bullets instead.*"

Decades before psychologists coined the term "implicit bias," many black politicians and civil rights activists spoke out forcefully about how

*For years after the shooting, references to Goetz continued to appear in popular music, particularly hip-hop. For instance, Lou Reed's critically acclaimed 1989 "Hold On" about 1980s strife in the city, after mentioning the smells of the subway and the weapons one might carry down there, reminds the listener that they're not Bernhard Goetz and that "*There's no Mafia lawyer / to fight in your corner / for that 15 minutes of fame.*" Also in 1989, the Beastie Boys' "B-Boy Bouillabaisse: Stop That Train" colorfully covered all the things one might see on the hours-long ride southbound on the D train to the beaches and amusement area at Coney Island in Brooklyn. The song carried an explicit reference to the shooting, with "*Pickpocket gangsters, payin' their debts / I caught a bullet in the lung from Bernie Goetz.*" Wu-Tang Clan's 1993 "Clan in da Front" included a punny aside to the case, "*God squad that's mad hard to serve / Come frontin' hard, then Bernhard Goetz what he deserves.*" In the most commercially successful song to reference Goetz, Billy Joel's 1989 number one Billboard Hot 100 hit "We Didn't Start the Fire" ended a verse with "*Foreign debts, homeless vets / AIDS, crack, Bernie Goetz.*"

the case reflected a perfect example of how society's subtle, unconscious prejudices can drive everyday encounters between people of all races. For example, Charlie Rangel, a Harlem congressman who would go on to be a fixture in New York politics for half a century, stated soon after the shooting, "I wish the roles were reversed, where the perpetrator was black and the kids were white, to see whether or not we would have found the same sense of support that we get (for Goetz)."

Many prominent Republican politicians were unequivocal in their support for Goetz. George Clark, the head of New York's Republican Party, said that Goetz was merely "defending New York society" with his actions. Using language that throughout history has commonly been used to subconsciously (or consciously) label black perpetrators as "animals," "monsters," and other spooky subhuman threats, he personally offered to donate five thousand dollars to Goetz, "because he was scared of some of the creatures" found on the city's subways. Alphonse D'Amato, New York's junior U.S. senator, had offered to testify at any trial and suggested that the four young men "who tried to harass [Goetz]" should be the ones hauled into court, and not Goetz. Like many, he framed the incident as representing a broader clash of cultures, stating that "we are living in fear. We are the oppressed," not needing to clarify who precisely the "we" were.

The case had so gripped the nation that even the most prominent Republican in the country was quickly asked for his opinion. President Ronald Reagan carved out a middle ground and gave both Goetz's supporters and detractors a few words to indicate that he spoke for them. "In general," the president said at a press conference in response to a question from ABC News' Sam Donaldson, "I think we all can understand the frustration of people who are constantly threatened by crime and feel that law and order is not particularly protecting them." On the other hand, he continued, "I think we all realize there is a breakdown of civilization if people start taking the law into their own hands. So while we may feel understanding or sympathy for someone who was tested beyond his control—his ability to control himself—at the same time we have to abide by the law and stand for law and order." Donaldson's next question embraced the central issue behind the support for Goetz: "Many Americans feel that there is no law and order, that the police either are unable or not sufficiently in force to do their job. What, then, is the alternative for Americans?" In response, Reagan expressed a view that continues to animate discussions about public safety decades later: as a society, we have just gone too soft on crime. "I don't blame the police so much for what we've seen over the years as a kind of an attitude in the whole structure of judicial and everyplace else in crime in which it seemed that we got overzealous in protecting the criminals' rights and forgot about the victim." Stricter enforcement, and stricter punishment, he said, would necessarily lead to a decline in crime.

As the case and what it represented gripped the nation, no two figures better embodied New York's fraught relationship with it than its mayor, Ed Koch, and its police chief, Benjamin Ward.

Born in 1924 in a still heavily Jewish South Bronx, Edward Irving Koch had had a steady rise through city politics, having served as a local Democratic Party district leader, city council member, and congressman before being elected mayor in 1977. Koch stood out for some of his contradictory quirks. His imposing height almost seemed offset by a high-pitched voice, wisps of graying hair curling around a bald dome, and a smile permanently bent into a mischievous rictus. In public, he was a garrulous backslapper who used colorful language (various critics were "moral lepers," "elitists," and "wacko"), but underneath the veneer he was deeply introverted and intensely private.

In 1977, with the mayoral primary just weeks after the arrest of the Son of Sam and the citywide blackout, Koch ran, as he put it, as a "liberal with sanity." He ran politically to the right of most of the field, promising to fight crime with tough policing and the death penalty.

He attacked unions and called for slashing city budgets, raising subway fares, and giving private developers more latitude to build. After a close seven-way primary, he comfortably beat New York secretary of state Mario Cuomo (who ran on the Liberal Party ticket) in the general election to become New York City's mayor.

His first term was widely seen as his most successful. Inheriting huge deficits and a city that had barely staved off bankruptcy, he kept spending down, scrapped with unions, and budgeted the city's credit into better shape. He focused on improving bridges and streets (the kind of work on which urban mayors' fortunes rise and fall), and worked to reduce friction between glittering, glassy Manhattan and the grittier outer boroughs. One of the ways in which he kept spending down was by canceling contracts with antipoverty organizations, infuriating black leaders. (His standing with the black community started off on a bad foot, after the city's closing of a Harlem hospital in his first term.) It all led to his getting easily reelected to a second term in 1981, when he became the first mayor in city history to wrap up both the Democratic and Republican nominations. A booming economy had led to a $500 million surplus and a growing tax base. Koch rehired city workers and brought back municipal services. He put in place housing programs, improvements in the city's educational system, and programs to get people off welfare. Love Koch or hate him, New York was coming back.

New York City holds its mayoral elections in odd-numbered years. By the time the popular mayor ran for his third term in 1985—the year immediately following the Goetz shooting—he was beginning to lose his sheen. In a stunning move, several of the city's prominent black leaders refused to endorse him for reelection. Behavior that voters had once seen as charming and outspoken they now began to regard as arrogant and bullying. In addition, the corruption scandals that would eventually put a cloud over much of his third term were already brewing. Within months of Koch's easy election victory in November 1985,

Donald Manes, the Queens borough president and a loyal Koch ally facing corruption charges, attempted suicide (succeeding in a second attempt two months later). Though Koch himself was never accused of wrongdoing, a series of indictments for bribery, extortion, perjury, and conspiracy would soon take down many of his closest allies in city government. The scandals provided a constant distraction for his remaining time in office, and Ed Koch, the pillar in New York politics, had lost his mojo. Fish and guests begin to stink after three days. For New York mayors, it seems to be three terms.

As 1985 turned into 1986 for the start of what would be his final term (he would lose four years later to David Dinkins, one of the black mandarins who had refused to endorse him), other frightening menaces had begun to haunt the city. Hundreds of New Yorkers were gravely ill and dying under gruesome circumstances of a disease—AIDS—that the public health community did not yet understand. As Koch was pilloried for his pace in responding to the crisis, his critics, particularly in the LGBT community, accused him of being a closeted gay man who was running scared of being outed if he were to be seen as taking the crisis on too aggressively. (Koch was defensive of both the criticism and his sexuality, vociferously claiming to be straight whenever asked. Koch was indeed gay, and years after his death, *The New York Times* ran a long, controversial feature on his painful struggle with his keeping his homosexuality a secret for his entire public life.)

As crack cocaine was beginning to tear through black communities, and with homelessness on the rise across the city, the mayor further saw his standing worsening with black New Yorkers. Comments he made over the years further rankled the community, particularly an instance in which he referred to black and Hispanic leaders as "poverty pimps" and "poverticians." As one black activist from the time said, "The problem was that the mayor . . . had a very politically toxic relationship with the black community at the time. This is what Ed Koch had run on, and built his mayoralty on."

In a city brushed all over with a patina of racial tension, relations between a mostly white police force and black and brown communities were particularly fragile. The city had faced years of allegations of police brutality, amid a constant drip of high-profile incidents: the 1978 beating to death of businessman Arthur Miller Jr.; the Thanksgiving 1976 shooting of fifteen-year-old Randolph "Randy" Evans (from a distance of two feet); the 1979 point-blank shooting of Manuel Martinez and his nephew Domingo Morales Jr.; the 1983 beating to death of graffiti artist Michael Stewart (while in police custody); the 1984 killing of Eleanor Bumpurs (a mentally ill grandmother being evicted from a Bronx apartment after missing four rent payments of less than one hundred dollars a month). Far more atrocities than anyone could comprehend would follow in the years to come.

Politicians can often smooth over bad blood with a constituency by being generous with political appointments. Still smarting from criticism for his having passed over a black deputy schools chancellor for the top post,* pressure was on Koch to appoint someone black to something senior. As Police Commissioner Robert J. McGuire signaled that he was leaning toward retiring, some of Koch's staff began nudging him about the role. "I thought we should make a real effort to find a black of quality and merit," said Deputy Mayor Kenneth Lipper (using language that would certainly elicit cringes today), "and the Mayor and I turned out to be on the same wavelength."

The city's corrections commissioner, Benjamin Ward, was already the highest-ranking black official in the administration and was a natural choice. A public servant for more than three decades, Ward had served as an Army police officer in Europe in the 1940s and then worked in New York with the sanitation department before joining the police force and being assigned to be a foot patrolman in Crown

*Ironically, Koch's top choice for schools chancellor, Gordon Davis, was black. Davis turned the role down after what he described as "very serious" entreaties by the mayor and his allies. See Sam Roberts, "Political Realities and Koch's Decision to Name Black Police Commissioner," *New York Times*, December 24, 1983.

Heights, Brooklyn, then the only black officer in an all-white neighborhood. Realizing that he would hit a ceiling without an advanced education, he went to Brooklyn College and got associate's, bachelor's and law degrees while working full-time. Ward shot through the department's ranks, eventually becoming deputy commissioner for community affairs. Future big roles followed before Koch appointed him the city's corrections commissioner. Though the image of the mayor standing with a newly appointed black police chief was clear, and Koch had taken criticism that he caved to public pressure in appointing a black man to the role, Koch denied that race was a factor. At an event announcing Ward's appointment, Koch placed his hand on Ward's shoulder and said with his characteristically wry candor, "He's black, there's no question about that. If that is a help, isn't that nice?"

Tall and confident, with a booming voice, Ward aspired to be a "cop's cop" and carried a 9mm semiautomatic Glock that had been banned by the NYPD. Still, like many black people in law enforcement, Ward had a complicated relationship with the badge. His unique position perhaps gave him latitude to be one of the nation's first prominent proponents of community policing, a model focused on preventing crime by increasing community involvement in law enforcement. Though community policing is common today, it was still seen as extremely progressive—if not radical—in the 1980s. He also was candid about the realities of race and policing in a way few officers were at the time. "As a young man, I tended to cross the street when I saw a policeman," he said in 1983. "I never went into a police station for any reason in my life until I became a police officer." At a news conference years later, he characterized the delicate line toed by many black people in law enforcement by saying, "Many people make the mistake of thinking that black people are liberal because they are black. I'm very, very liberal when it comes to race relations, but when it comes to law enforcement, I am very, very conservative. I certainly believe bad guys belong in jail."

From the moment the news of the subway shooting broke in late

1984, the city was hungry to hear from the tough-on-crime mayor up for reelection in a tense climate with soaring crime rates, and the erudite black police commissioner with complicated feelings about bias, crime, and the law. In the immediate aftermath of the shooting, Koch, still unencumbered by public opinion and a rabid news media, initially spoke about the incident in terms that were critical of Goetz, if legally unremarkable: he cautioned New Yorkers against "taking the law into their own hands" and reminded them that "vigilantism will not be tolerated in the city."

Ward was more pointed. Right after the shooting, the police commissioner challenged the self-defense narrative. At a news conference just days after Goetz's identity became public, Ward opined on vigilantism, saying, "I cannot imagine any circumstances under which a person would pull out a gun on a typical New York City subway and fire five rounds. I could not glorify that person and make him into a vigilante." He went further, suggesting that the case was just another incident in an unbroken tradition of racial violence in America: "I have a little different definition of a vigilante, too. I would equate—maybe it's my background—I think those fellows wearing those pointy white hats and white sheets call themselves vigilantes, too. When we asked them where the black people hang out around here, they would very frequently point to the highest tree and say, 'Right there.'"

Koch and Ward were not the only prominent New Yorkers from whom the public needed to hear. Prosecutors had to decide, soon, about what to do with whatever had gone down on December 22, 1984. That decision—which would likely reverberate across the country—fell to one man: Manhattan's venerated district attorney, Robert D. Morgenthau.

CHAPTER THIRTEEN

Three to One

Robert Morgenthau was well into the third of his ten historic terms as Manhattan's chief prosecutor. (Morgenthau's predecessor had served in the role for thirty-two years, meaning that the office was primarily held by two men from World War II until almost a decade into the twenty-first century.)

Morgenthau rode into the job with unimaginable wealth and privilege, blessed with a great-grandfather who had founded Lehman Brothers, a grandfather who was a former ambassador to the Ottoman Empire, and a father who had been secretary of the treasury. Coincidentally, Morgenthau's grandfather had grown the family fortune by buying up land that was skyrocketing in value along a new subway line on the west side of Manhattan—the same subway line that would one day thrust a mess into his grandson's lap.

Across decades, he had built a name aggressively prosecuting white-collar criminals and mobsters. He had already served two stints as U.S. attorney (the region's top federal prosecutor), first appointed by John F. Kennedy. The nation's thousands of district and state attorneys are "local" prosecutors, charged with enforcing state and local, as opposed to federal, law. But nothing is ever truly local in a city that is home to America's biggest media market by an order of magnitude. His charge was a sprawling office serving a sprawling city, with five hundred attorneys overseeing cases involving everything from pickpockets to Ponzi schemes; from minor domestic disputes to major criminal enterprises—as Morgenthau would put it, both "crime in the streets" and "crime in the suites."

As a result, Morgenthau's decades in office saw a constant stream of cases, many of which extended far beyond the five boroughs. Through the 1980s, the office prosecuted John Lennon's assassin, Mark David Chapman; Robert Chambers, the "Preppy Killer," notorious for strangling to death eighteen-year-old Jennifer Levin in Central Park; and the Gambino crime family. Over the years, Morgenthau took criticism for focusing too heavily on white-collar crime—perhaps encroaching on federal prosecutors' domain*—largely leaving the office's major work on violent crime to subordinates.

January 4, 1985
MANHATTAN CRIMINAL COURT

After being booked at police headquarters, Goetz was taken to court for his arraignment. It drew a larger courthouse crowd than anyone at the time could remember. Some 250 lawyers, judges, and other spectators filled the dingy wood-paneled courtroom, crammed into every one of its benches and lined up along its walls. The security inside the courthouse was especially tight. Officers set up three metal detectors for the occasion, requiring all spectators and lawyers to go through

*An obituary noted: "As D.A., he lacked the tools of a U.S. attorney, who could use grand juries and give immunity in ways that were off-limits to New York State prosecutors; but [Morgenthau], perhaps unwisely, ignored those obstacles and pressed ahead with cases that should have been left to the feds or not brought at all." (In "Robert Morgenthau, Longtime Manhattan District Attorney, Dies at 99," *New York Times,* July 21, 2019. See also Jeffrey Toobin, "The Morgenthau Family's Gilded Path to the Manhattan D.A.'s Office," *New York Times,* October 8, 2022.)

them. Normally a crew of four officers was assigned to a given courtroom; on this day twenty were on hand. Ten or fifteen more lined the hallways nearby.

Goetz was still wearing his burgundy bomber jacket with a shearling collar, a light plaid button-down, and jeans, but now his hands were cuffed in front of him. His face was scruffy as police did not let him shave prior to coming to court. He silently stood with his head down and, according to *The New York Times*, appeared distracted and occasionally mumbled to himself through the proceedings. He remained silent as Susan Braver read off the allegations, using the grave and terse tone only used in courtroom proceedings, "Detective Daniel Hattendorf is informed by defendant that with intent to kill Troy Canty, Barry Allen, James Ramseur and Darryl Cabey, defendant did shoot Troy Canty, Barry Allen, James Ramseur and Darryl Cabey with a pistol and attempted to kill them."

The proceeding was a critical step in the process, where a judge would set bail conditions such as whether to hold a defendant behind bars, set a money bail, release him, or set additional conditions (such as restricting his travel). The goal of the process is to ensure that the defendant will show up to future court proceedings (and not commit any crimes in the interim). Though Goetz had no criminal history and had lived in the community for years, this was a serious violent crime, and it was known that he had fled the city at least once already. A judge would have good reason to set a high dollar amount for bail or keep him locked up.

Goetz's appointed defense lawyer tried to make the case that he should be released. He argued that Goetz's choosing to turn himself in and give hours of testimony suggested that he had no desire to run away. This was silly. Goetz had accessible family in Michigan and Florida, where he might have a safe place to flee and hide easily if he so chose. Moreover, all parties were aware that Goetz had fled New York City twice after the shooting, only choosing to turn himself in hundreds of miles away and outside the reach of the law enforcement officials who were pursuing him. Legally, he was as true a flight risk as anyone.

Judge Leslie Crocker Snyder, a former prosecutor under Morgenthau who was handling the indictment,* was pointed in criticizing Goetz's alleged behavior. Despite agreeing to the prosecutors' $50,000 bail request, she said she thought it was too low, saying, "If Western civilization has taught us anything, it is that we cannot tolerate individuals' taking law and justice into their own hands." She also agreed not to put any travel restrictions on Goetz if he posted the cash bail. Goetz said nothing during the eighteen-minute-long hearing besides his name. Officers then escorted him from the courtroom.

The court was not prepared for the crush of spectators and it turned into a shoving mob that clogged up the hallway outside. Goetz then was taken to the Central Infirmary Unit at Rikers Island, a block that housed thirteen higher-profile defendants to lessen the risk that they got harmed. He shared the space with December 1984's other above-the-fold criminal defendant: Emmanuel Torres, the man who had just been charged with killing Caroline Isenberg.

As soon as news spread that Goetz was being held in jail and that $50,000 could get him out, offers of support started pouring in from around the country. One man, Jose M. Gonzalez, offered a $50,000 cashier's check that he claimed to be his life's savings. Gonzalez said that he had previously been robbed and assaulted, and that he "identified" with Goetz. Hundreds of callers reached out to the *New York Daily*

---

*In more than three decades on the bench, Morgenthau faced a serious challenge to his election only once, when some twenty years after the Goetz case, Snyder resigned from the bench to challenge her former boss. *The New York Times* endorsed her, arguing that despite Snyder's "worrisome fondness for publicity," she had a deep understanding of the role and would be an effective prosecutor for the city. Moreover, the editorial argued that after three decades, it was time for new leadership. Morgenthau still won the primary handily, 59–41, and coasted to reelection. Snyder entered private practice afterward and served as a legal analyst for MSNBC and the *Today* show, and made several guest appearances on *Law & Order* playing a role she knew well: a New York judge. ("When to End an Era," *New York Times,* August 30, 2005, https://www.nytimes.com/2005/08/30/opinion/when-to-end-an-era.html; Robert D. McFadden, "Robert Morgenthau, Longtime Manhattan District Attorney, Dies at 99," *New York Times,* July 21, 2019, https://www.nytimes.com/2019/07/21/nyregion/robert-morgenthau-dead.html.)

News with questions about the case and how they could support Goetz's defense. After the hearing, seven people who claimed to be friends of Goetz from the electronics business gathered in front of the courthouse to announce that they were starting the Bernhard Goetz Legal Defense Fund and were accepting donations. Small contributions streamed in from individuals. Curtis Sliwa, the head of the Guardian Angels, announced that the group would patrol the subway system at night, asking riders for one dollar to contribute to Goetz's bail and defense costs. They collected $225 within the first two hours of their drive, $110 of which they turned over to the defense fund. A retired Staten Island fire chief put a ten-dollar check into an envelope to the Manhattan district attorney's office, commenting, "This guy rendered a service. He is our John Wayne. I say enough is enough. Put away the kid gloves and show the punks we mean business. He's got my 10 bucks and I'll send more if he needs it." Other offers came in from sheriff's deputies in Georgia and from the comedian Foster Brooks (then nationally known as a regular on *The Tonight Show Starring Johnny Carson* and from his recurring roles on the 1970s celebrity roast circuit).

Despite the easy money flowing his way and additional offers from family members to pay the full amount, Goetz said that he did not want to accept any "publicly raised bail money," and posted his own. He did so in such haste that he surprised even his attorney. According to a spokesman for the corrections department, Goetz was whisked out of jail "in a private manner." Both to accommodate Goetz's wishes and to avoid a security problem, corrections employees processed his bail papers in a way that kept the release quiet.

The legal system in America is based on the concept that nothing is absolute. Take an easy hypothetical: we can look outside and all agree, as a matter of common sense (and atmospheric science), that the sky is blue. A court, however, could not simply rely on that accepted truth. Were the issue to come up as a factual question in court, the sky would not be considered "blue" unless either a judge found it to be so, the parties got together and agreed as such, or one side successfully made the case to judge or jury that it was, indeed, blue. A smart opposing attorney can easily question unquestionable facts: Are you certain the sky wasn't periwinkle or lavender, as opposed to blue? Weren't you wearing sunglasses at the time you looked up at the sky, which might have impaired your ability to determine its color? Weren't you drunk last night?

Consider the wording of the ultimate outcome in a criminal case. Juries and judges do not decide whether someone is guilty or innocent; they merely assess whether the defendant is guilty or not guilty. "Innocence" is absolute; the term "not guilty" says only that the decider—the jury or the judge—wasn't convinced of guilt. Though someone may have committed the act they are accused of, there may be a host of reasons that they might not get convicted. In Goetz's case, little was straightforward about the evidence. The events took place in a split second, in an environment in which most bystanders did not have a clear view of what had happened, and the whole thing centered on the issue of safety, an issue that every witness or potential juror would have strong personal feelings about.

For these reasons, legal cases are not reflections of reality. They represent competing narratives painstakingly crafted by lawyers around their client's (or the government's) version of the world. That work involves deciding what evidence to introduce and in which order; how to talk about individual bits of evidence for the strongest effect (do we refer to Goetz's video as a "confession" or a "statement"?); and, most importantly, which witnesses to bring forth.

In order for Goetz's legal case to proceed, the district attorney's office first needed to present a case to a grand jury, a group of sixteen to twenty-three members of the public whose job it is to hear evidence about the alleged crimes and to determine whether there is enough evidence to formally charge someone with felonies. As grand juries' work happens in secret with only witnesses, grand jurors, and prosecutors allowed in the room when the case is presented, most people never experience a grand jury firsthand. Typically defense attorneys aren't even allowed in. Given its secrecy and format, the grand jury is probably the aspect of the criminal justice process that the public understands the least.

Robert Morgenthau, though a consummate public servant, was a politician. And one does not get elected nine times across generations in a sprawling, evolving city without knowing which way the wind is blowing. He had a problem: the rare high-profile case in which many of his constituents saw the assailant, not the victims, as the sympathetic figure. He could not be seen as being too far on the side of the victims, even if the law might have demanded it. New York's grand jury laws presented Morgenthau a challenge that would linger over the case until its conclusion: as a default, witnesses—even unsavory ones with copious criminal records who might not have been blameless themselves and may admit to even more crimes on the stand—can't be prosecuted for most things they say to a grand jury.

The concept is called "transactional immunity." It is a legal protection that prevents a witness from being prosecuted for crimes he admits to or discusses in his testimony. New York is one of a handful of states that automatically confers it on grand jury witnesses. The rule is intended to give witnesses an incentive to testify; they are far more likely to tell the truth (or at least not hide facts that might get them in trouble down the road) if they have the security of knowing that they won't have handcuffs slapped on them the moment they step off the witness stand. Imagine a (partly) hypothetical example involving James Ramseur. In the summer of 1985—just a few months after the grand jury proceedings in the Goetz case—Ramseur participated in the gruesome rape, sodomy, and robbery of a young pregnant woman on the rooftop of a housing project. If he were a grand jury witness in a case in New York and, while on the stand, revealed to prosecutors for the first time that he had committed the sexual assault, they would be forbidden from prosecuting him for it. Knowing he could not be prosecuted would have given him an incentive to testify openly and honestly as a witness, but at what cost? To the public, it is irrelevant that prosecutors had no say in granting immunity to the witness. Prosecutors would be seen as responsible for the witness. It would have been a disaster for them once word got out that a witness they chose to put on the stand got away with (something perhaps as bad as) murder.* They would be seen as complicit in someone's horrible acts. In short, the idea of letting a criminal walk in order to go after someone else might make sense in law or philosophy seminars, but not on the pages of New York City tabloids. Or the campaign trail.

This said, prosecutors can still ask a witness to waive immunity and testify without it. There are any number of reasons why a witness might want to waive immunity. Among other reasons, he might feel he has nothing to hide, and that nothing incriminating will come up in his testimony. He may want to cooperate fully with an investigation. Or, most commonly, he may be self-interested. Waiving immunity and testifying openly could be a means of currying favor with prosecutors, in the hopes that they go easier on him if he is sentenced for something in the future. That is naive; prosecutors hold all the power in the relationship and are under no obligation to honor what was no more than a handshake promise they made to a witness. A common scenario arises when prosecutors go ahead and still prosecute a witness they feel has not been honest with them or—and this is subjective—that they simply feel has not adequately cooperated with them. (In general, it's best to avoid committing crimes in the first place, thus eliminating the need to pin one's hopes on the kindness of prosecutors.)

Given his injuries, prosecutors quickly determined that they couldn't call Cabey as a witness. Though they knew through counsel that Allen, Canty, and Ramseur were not going to waive immunity, prosecutors made the decision to call the three to appear anyway. The decision was unusual; it makes little practical sense for prosecutors to put wit-

*The issue never arose, and Ramseur was convicted of the sexual assault and robbery and sentenced to eight to twenty-five years for it.

nesses on the stand who they know are not going to agree to testify. Still, doing so was probably the best option Morgenthau had among a sea of bad ones. A first option, of ignoring the victims altogether, wasn't a great choice. They obviously were the central figures in the case, and failing to at least invite them to testify would have given the impression that Morgenthau was not serious about prosecuting Goetz. A second option, of having the victims testify, immunized, would surely have left the public with the impression, however inaccurate, that Morgenthau was coddling criminals by refusing to prosecute them for their own misdeeds. Instead, having the victims still come in as a pretense with the knowledge that they were not going to waive immunity might have been a savvy political move. It allowed prosecutors to shift the onus and the critical public eye away from his office and to the victims, saying, in effect, "Look, we tried, but the victims chose not to cooperate."

On January 8, 1985, Allen, Canty, and Ramseur were each individually led into the grand jury room. Braver asked each one the question: "Do you wish to waive immunity?" Each said that, on the advice of counsel, he did not. It was wise for the victims' counsels to advise them not to waive their immunity. Each of the three had little to gain and plenty to lose by turning down that gift of immunity conferred by the state. They took their lawyers' advice, and each answered his one question and was led out of the room. James Ramseur was moaning, holding his stomach, and said to still be in "excruciating pain" from his injuries the entire time he was there.

Goetz, ever on the hunt for angles to tell his side of the story, also weighed whether to testify. Goetz's lawyer wisely reminded him that once he got on the stand, prosecutors would only proceed if he waived his immunity as well. (Anyone is free to signify that they wish to testify, but the decision of whom to call—and how to conduct the questioning—is another that rests solely with prosecutors.) Testifying would have been a disaster for Goetz. He would be providing a sworn confession on top of two recorded ones that he had already given in New Hampshire. More testimony could have provided prosecutors three invaluable things: even more evidence; contradictory statements from Goetz that they could use to undermine him at trial; or evidence of new crimes prosecutors didn't yet know about. On the stand, he also would be face-to-face with a prosecutor who, rather than letting him blather on, would ask precise questions targeted at building legal support for criminal charges against him. He took his lawyer's advice, and did not testify.

January 25, 1985

Prosecutors asked the grand jury to consider four counts of attempted murder (one corresponding to each victim), four counts of assault, four counts of reckless endangerment, and a few counts related to Goetz's possessing guns illegally. Without testimony from victims or the shooter, the grand jury was left to make sense out of what they had: officer Warren Foote's police report from Concord, photographs, medical evidence, Goetz's statements, and live testimony from about a dozen witnesses, none of whom had overheard the interaction between Goetz and the four men.

After hearing evidence and deliberating in secret for seventy minutes, the grand jury returned an indictment with only one felony count of criminal possession of a weapon in the third degree, for carrying the gun used in the shooting; and two misdemeanor counts of criminal possession of a weapon in the fourth degree, for possessing two unlicensed weapons at home. It did not indict Goetz for any violent crime. The most serious charge—criminal possession of a weapon in the third degree—is a Class D felony, or the second-least-serious type of felony in New York, carrying at most a seven-year sentence. Unlike attempted murder and assault, though, the weapons possession charge did not carry a mandatory minimum sentence. Given that Goetz did not have a criminal history, if convicted he would serve very little, if any, jail time.

Although the grand jury did not disclose its reasoning, the prosecutor's office thought that the grand jurors believed that Goetz had acted in self-defense. One of Goetz's lawyers called it "practically an exoneration of our client." One of the victims' lawyers largely agreed that it was an exoneration—just not one anyone should be proud of. "He shot four kids with dum-dum bullets, two of them in the back," said Howard Meyer, Canty's attorney. "What kind of hero is that? He's white, and the four kids he shot were black. It is absurd to think he did not intend to murder them."

As with so many other aspects of the case, the public reaction to the grand jury indictment was swift, loud, and layered. For residents of Claremont Village, the decision hit close to home. Many who spoke out were disappointed in the decision. Shirley Cabey did not respond directly to reporters but indicated to *Newsday* through a friend that she was "very upset." A lawyer representing her described her as being "in shock," adding, "She said that what the government is now telling people is that it is all right to go out and shoot black people." One resident commented that "[t]his gives anybody the right to shoot anybody who asks you for $5. The way some of his statements have been coming out, he would have shot any minority children that day if they had asked him for a piece of bread." Another said, "Do I feel there might be more vigilantes? Yes, because Goetz made it possible. The kids didn't even touch him or pull out any arms. What this says to me is that if you're black and you get too close to a white person, that's your life."

Many civil rights activists viewed the situation similarly. One said that the indictment was "tantamount to a commendation. The grand wizard of the KKK would be proud of this grand jury. This really means that if you think a black kid looks menacing, shoot him."

Mario Cuomo, who had been elected governor in 1983, criticized New York's grand jury immunity law as "silly" and "unintelligent." In his view, automatically conferring immunity gave witnesses too much leverage, disincentivizing prosecutors from calling them in the first place. (Many other American entities, including the federal government, allow prosecutors to make the choice over whether to immunize witnesses.) As a result, he said, "the grand jury had to come to its conclusions on the skimpiest of conclusions and certainly not the best evidence." Still, given his long legal background, Cuomo also knew of the folly of commenting with any authority on a process that operates in secret. "You don't know what the grand jury was told," he said. "Why should we assume they acted irresponsibly? I'm going to believe they acted responsibly."

New York's mayor and police chief continued to exist like a planet and its moon: two distinct bodies reliant on each other for survival, tethered by gravity. In the days after the shooting, Koch conveyed sympathy for Cabey and noted how easily an innocent bystander could have been struck by one of Goetz's bullets, decrying the "instant justice" of a vigilante shooting. Koch's tone began to shift as public opinion became clearer, particularly from white voters in Brooklyn, Queens, and Staten Island on whom his fortunes depended. He first called the grand jury's decision to charge Goetz on gun possession but not any violent crimes "Solomonic," and said that it "pleased" him and that he believed Goetz was a victim. Days later, he went further and said that he thought the grand jury had been "right."

Moreover, his broader framing about the ills of vigilantism gently evolved into one of empathy toward a public that was fed up. "The frustration and anger are so obvious not only in New York City, but around the country," he said on WCBS-TV's *Newsmakers*. "The rights of society have been impinged upon, and what they're saying is they're fed up. I'm fed up, too." In calling for elected officials to address public safety, he (with the subtlety of an air horn) echoed Goetz's central animating point:

> I believe that most people believe that the criminal justice system is broken down, and that the rights of society are not adequately protected under the law, under court procedures, under the various things that go into it, and I think that this case

gives us the justification to get the legislature and the courts to do a better job.

The mayor had now picked a side. Whenever asked about the case (which happened just about every time he was in public), he would ask for a show of hands of who agreed with him. He previously had used a similar tactic with other issues that were emotional and polarizing for the city; he regularly did so on the 1977 campaign trail when asking audiences about the death penalty. At another point, when Koch was dedicating a shopping center in Brooklyn in 1981, a black member of the audience shouted out, "We want John Lindsay!," referring to the liberal former mayor from the tumultuous 1960s whom Koch blamed for a lot of the mess the city was in. Koch asked everyone in the audience to raise their hands if they wanted Lindsay back. A few in the audience—most of them black—did so. Koch paused, took in the scene, then bellowed, "Dummies!" The tactic well suited the mayor—he was a consummate retail politician. It allowed him to use the pretense of sincerely soliciting public opinion to serve a broader goal: outing and embarrassing those who disagreed with him.

Koch's evolution mirrored how he responded to the death of Eleanor Bumpurs, whom police killed with a shotgun during an eviction two months before the subway shooting. As the grand jury was considering manslaughter charges against Stephen Sullivan, the officer who shot Bumpurs, Koch commented, "Just as I said I would not comment on the Goetz case and the grand jury, I will also accept the outcome of the grand jury in the Stephen Sullivan case." Two days later, following protests by police officers and a demonstration by seven thousand cops in front of the Bronx courthouse, he said that a manslaughter indictment that had been returned against Sullivan was "wrong"—hardly an acceptance of the grand jury's outcome. When pressed, he said he did not need to explain his change in tone. "I am simply saying that over a period of time, there is greater discussion, greater understanding in the public's mind and in my mind of what took place," he said. "I don't believe if you look at my statements you will find them necessarily in conflict. And even if they were, it isn't a question that I am a computer." Koch's formula was straightforward: speak from the heart, check public opinion, speak from the head, then claim that both positions were consistent all along.

The two cases were quite different: one involved action by police; the other, action by a private individual. In spite of those differences, they uncovered an unspoken but overwhelming dynamic: raw emotions about race relations. Both, like countless others today, involved bullets fired at black people who were deemed to pose threats and in which the shooter claimed some entitlement to kill. Depending on whom you asked, both were either proof positive of open season on black people and a devaluing of their lives, or a tragic but explainable cost of business in a country under siege. In New York in 1985, getting elected mayor required embracing the latter.

In contrast, it is not uncommon for police officers to bristle at court decisions that don't go their way. They may have spent months, or even years, working toward an arrest, only to have seen a court or grand jury toss it out on an arcane legal issue. Bear in mind, to make an arrest police only need to have probable cause, a far lower standard than that needed to convict someone in court. What may feel like a moral truth to an officer who spent months or years working toward an arrest may end up going nowhere once the lawyers and judges have their way with it. Benjamin Ward shared some of that sentiment in his comments after the shooting. He directly took the grand jury on, saying, "The facts that make out a self-defense argument are not there, based on information known to me and the information that's in the press. You don't shoot two people running away from you and say it's self-defense." When confronted with the fact that the mayor had taken a different position on the shooting, Ward stayed mum: "I didn't discuss it with him." He then fired a subtle shot at the mayor, winking at the fact that he, like the mayor, was a lawyer: "I don't think, legally, any lawyer believes that what Goetz did was self-defense, not as to the two with holes in their back."

Ward went further. He was not merely the city's top cop; he was one of the highest-ranking black people in city history. He all but begged the public to recognize a racial subtext to the case. He used the language of slavery when describing what he saw as a troubling amount of public support for Goetz: "I'm not surprised that you can round up a lynch mob. We were always able to do that in this country." He softened his tone when asked directly if race played in to the grand jury's process, saying, "I don't know of many things that happen in this country that don't have racial overtones, but I can't point to any overt situation involved in that case that I can say has racial overtones." Goetz, in an interview with *The New York Times* three weeks later, directly challenged the police chief's comments, saying that Ward had a "right to his opinion, but he has not been exposed to all the facts. The Commissioner wasn't there."

Morgenthau's public statements were uncontroversial. He made his disappointment known, while, as elected officials often do, giving a nod to the integrity of the process. "It was the view of the grand jurors that Mr. Goetz was justified in taking the force that he did," he said, also making an incontrovertible point that every case ought to be decided on its merits. "I don't view this as license to shoot people because they look at you cross-eyed," he said. "Anybody who shoots another person on the subway or anywhere will have the case presented to the grand jury, and they will have to establish justification." He acknowledged that more graphic descriptions of Goetz's conduct "might have made a difference in terms of public perception, but not as far as the grand jury was concerned. We post-mortemed this thing to death. I don't think if we had leaned on that grand jury it would have made any difference." Publicly, he resisted calls to reopen the case. "[J]ust because a prosecutor is not happy over a grand jury action is not a basis for re-presenting," he said. "We're not interested in tilting at windmills. I've got to have a substantial basis for doing it."

Privately, however, the district attorney was stung by the heat directed at his office and, by extension, at him. He was Robert Morgenthau, a legend in Manhattan, the man with an unimpeachable patrician résumé who had practically been bred for high office. That Robert Morgenthau, who regarded receiving less than 70 percent in an election a "race," was for perhaps the first time tasting the bitter flavor of public opinion gone south. He couldn't win; aggressive criticism came from all sides. From one side, Assemblyman Frank J. Barbaro, a Democrat from Brooklyn, called for Morgenthau's impeachment for "failing to get a more serious indictment." From another side, Morgenthau's view: "Women—lots of women, furious with me—but most of all, spewing hate on those black kids." More than anything else, he had taken for granted that he would always have the support of the black community. According to an aide to Cuomo, "It shook him. He's always seen himself as this bastion of progressivism, and suddenly here were blacks kicking the shit out of him."

The public continued to flood his office with letters, with those praising Goetz outnumbering those expressing sympathy for the victims by a factor of three. At a certain point, Morgenthau and his team began to confront a reality: the legal system does not exist outside of public opinion. Prosecutors often speak in the lofty, moralistic language of only bringing cases "without fear or favor," in which they adhere only to the rule of law and their unimpeachable morals. Their sanctimony aside, prosecutors—like judges, grand jurors, and all other figures in the criminal justice system—are human. No matter how idealized prosecutors' sense of self may be, they exist in the real world—one in which the news media, public opinion, and a fickle electorate can be vicious mistresses. "We thought we had a case against this guy," Morgenthau said. "I guess we underestimated the currents running in his favor."

Prosecutors now had two choices: figure out how to resuscitate what was left of their case or prepare for trial on a few tiny gun possession charges that would make not a single person happy. Not Goetz, who felt he had committed a public service, yet still could end up in jail. Not his supporters, who saw charging him with even gun possession as a travesty. Not the victims, who felt they had done nothing wrong but were now pockmarked with bullet holes and branded nationwide as Public Enemies One, Two, Three, and Four. Not anyone in America, who would find a way to be disappointed with the outcome.

And as it all played out, Robert Morgenthau's conundrum on the gun charges was of keen interest to another group of Americans quietly at work in Washington: the National Rifle Association.

CHAPTER FOURTEEN

Gun Fight in Cincinnati

In general," President Reagan said at a press conference in early January, "I think we can all understand the frustration of people who are constantly threatened by crime and feel that law and order is not protecting them." Reagan was about to be sworn in for a second term after one of the biggest landslide victories in American political history, partly due to the support of centrist "law-and-order"-focused "Reagan Democrats." His comments caught the ear of Richard Feldman, then a rising star at the NRA. The notion that the NRA should take a strong political stand on self-defense had, until recently, been a minority position within the organization. But Reagan's answer laid out the basis for what would be the next generation of the NRA's work: the principle that guns aren't just for shooting clay pigeons with grandpa. Feldman, a political liaison responsible for looking for new places to push the organization's agenda, couldn't have scripted the moment better.

Founded in 1871 by National Guard and former Army officers, the NRA stood to "promote rifle practice" and improve marksmanship. For generations, the organization focused on promoting hunting, conservation, and shooting. One would have been more likely to find an

NRA member at a Boy Scout summer camp than a political rally. Following unrest in the 1960s, Congress passed the Gun Control Act of 1968, which set up a licensing scheme and banned the sale of guns to, among others, people with felony convictions, drug users, and the mentally ill. Just four years later in 1972, Congress also created a new federal agency, the Bureau of Alcohol, Tobacco, Firearms and Explosives, commonly known as the ATF, which would be responsible for enforcing gun laws. As governor of California, Reagan was a vocal proponent at the time of stricter gun laws. He got far more vocal about the issue after witnessing heavily armed Black Panthers march in a protest at the state capitol in Sacramento on May 2, 1967—one of a series of Black Panther protests in the late 1960s that led to frightened political leaders and a turbocharged modern gun control movement.

In response, a new breed of gun rights advocate was born. They saw laws and federal agencies that limited firearms as un-American and believed that anti-gun forces were on a single-minded mission to take all guns away. And so began a rift within the organization: an old guard, committed to keeping it focused on the great outdoors, versus

a more activist, insurgent group dedicated to protecting what they saw as a civil, if not God-given, right.

The new mood within the NRA was perfectly reflected both by the organization's decision to incorporate a new registered lobbying arm in 1975 and by its choice to lead the lobbying group, Harlon Carter. Carter's aggressiveness about firearms and their purpose embodied the new NRA. He loved guns, in a romance that stretched back to his being convicted as a teenager of the murder of fifteen-year-old Ramón Casiano in Laredo, Texas, a border town. Carter's mother believed that Casiano had information about the theft of the Carter's family car three weeks previously. Carter told his mother that he would see if he could get Casiano and other boys to come and talk to her (though not to the police) about it. So he did what a teenage firearms zealot in 1930s Texas would have done when going to have a conversation with another minor: he grabbed a shotgun. He pointed the gun at Casiano's chest and demanded that Casiano come to Carter's family home to submit to questioning. Though what happened next is in dispute, minutes later Casiano lay dead, with a two-inch shotgun blast to his chest. Carter's conviction was later overturned on appeal, due to an issue the appeals court found with how the judge instructed the jury about self-defense. No evidence tying Casiano to the car was ever found.

An aggressive grassroots wing of the NRA, led by Carter and Neal Knox, a lobbyist and fellow hard-liner, was increasingly disdainful of the elitist scolds running the organization. They were particularly offended by a decision made by the old guard that summed up everything they thought was wrong with the old NRA: leadership's decision to move the headquarters from Washington, DC, to Colorado Springs. To them, nothing represented the organization's caving on an existential issue more than moving from the country's power center to the sticks.

They knew that the NRA's bylaws gave members power to vote at their convention for changes in how the group was governed. So they staged a coup. As the organization held its 1977 convention in a sweltering hall in Cincinnati, it began with the snoozy work of approving meeting minutes and reviewing business old and new. Suddenly, a group of rabble-rousers with walkie-talkies burst in and started working the floor. Ironically, the group of agitators pushing for the organization to focus less on the outdoors all wore the most recognizably outdoorsy garment possible: orange blaze hunting caps.

They called it the "Revolt at Cincinnati." Knox read the group's fifteen demands, including giving the organization's membership the ability to pick its leadership rather than leaving the decision to the board. The saga stretched on for hours—so long that the building's vending machine ran out of sodas as sweaty attendees got increasingly parched. By 3:30 a.m. on May 22, 1977, your grandfather's NRA was gone. Stunned old-guard officers had been replaced by new leadership, with Harlon Carter named the new executive vice president. By the time of the Goetz shooting several years later, the NRA was well on its way to becoming a political juggernaut.

Despite the new world order at the NRA, its leadership was still squeamish about wading too far into advocacy. The organization's focus was relatively new, and its leadership's hold on their newfound power was tenuous. Going too far could be counterproductive, locking them into a position they weren't prepared to take. Feldman was convinced that the Goetz case provided a perfect opportunity to catapult the NRA to even greater national prominence. Goetz was a perfect poster boy for everything the NRA wanted to push with its new messaging: he was an engaged member of the community who voted, paid taxes, and was involved in local issues. He was sympathetic, having been mugged at least once before. A politically liberal anti-gun state had denied him the opportunity to acquire guns legally. They didn't say it, but Goetz was also white, and his story would probably resonate with many white Americans across the country. He would probably resonate even more with people who did not live in cities. Americans have an amazing ability to vilify and be terrified of cities they have never been to, and Goetz's image sent an implicit reminder around the country about how unsafe places like New York were for everymen and everywomen. Activists were already speaking out about the case, and the media was all over it; there was a hole that the NRA could clearly fill.

Goetz presented one huge challenge for the NRA, though: even people who supported him had to acknowledge that he came with baggage. Not even the most die-hard Goetz supporter could say for sure whether he acted in self-defense. It would have been risky for the NRA to issue an unequivocal message of support for him. To get around that problem, they could use the occasion to highlight New York's gun laws, with Goetz's case being nothing more than the hook for the conversation. A bill had recently passed in Albany that a concealed carry license issued elsewhere in the state was valid anywhere but in New York City. In their reading, the law was a double standard that afforded city residents fewer rights than their neighbors elsewhere in New York. It didn't matter to them how densely populated New York was or that the city had a tragically high gun violence rate. To them, the fact that city residents faced tougher laws than others was a civil rights issue.

The NRA could also use Goetz's case to solidify support among gun owners. According to a *Washington Post*/ABC News poll from January 1985, people in homes with any guns approved of Goetz's actions 54–37 percent. In homes with only handguns, the gap was even greater: 62–32 percent (the numbers were just about the inverse for homes without guns: 38–54 percent). Notably, according to the polls, support and opposition did not change all that much depending on political affiliation: people who considered themselves liberals approved of the action 48–40 percent; people who identified as conservatives went 47–44 percent. Moderates more clearly disapproved of Goetz, 41–49 percent. Feldman saw an opening here as well. "I saw . . . that this could be a very bipartisan issue," he said. "It should have been. I wanted both sides to be on our side. I wanted both sides to say that there were limits. We have done a poor job of defining those limits."

Feldman had an audacious idea: do a press conference *in* New York. The group's leadership hated it. As he put it, "The NRA—in New York—didn't do things like that." They had all but written off traditionally Democratic strongholds like the New York metropolitan area, and going onto hostile turf to hold a press conference could have brought a total media disaster. There was another problem: the NRA was overwhelmingly white. The image of a group of white gun activists swooping into New York to give a press conference about a white man shooting four unarmed black teenagers would have given the NRA a national story, but probably not the one they wanted. It was crass, but they needed a black face onstage. They called Roy Innis.

January 10, 1985
THE OMNI PARK CENTRAL HOTEL

Innis cut quite a presence. He was tall and handsome, with a big smile, and still carried the frame of the amateur boxer he was in his youth. Whenever he opened his mouth, his voice showed traces of the sonorous lilt of his native U.S. Virgin Islands. More importantly, Roy Innis wasn't just any black conservative; he had once been a Black Panther who railed against Martin Luther King's nonviolent civil disobedience. As a black nationalist, he believed that integration robbed black people of their heritage and dignity. At a convention for the Congress of Racial Equality, the organization he would lead for years, he once said, "In America today, there are two kinds of black people: the field-hand blacks and the house niggers. We of CORE—the nationalists—are the field-hand blacks. The integrationists of the National Association for the Advancement of Colored People are house niggers." Over time, his black nationalism evolved into unabashed conservatism, often using his perch as the leader of a civil rights organization to push a vision for a race-neutral America, calling affirmative action "morally corrupt." No matter his politics, it would be hard for black critics of the NRA to label as an "Uncle Tom" a black man who thought that Martin Luther King wasn't gangsta enough.

Innis also was an aggressive advocate for gun rights. He was a lifetime member of the NRA and sat on its board for nearly a quarter century. He had lost two sons to gun violence, fourteen years apart. While others may have responded to the tragedy by supporting gun control measures, the incidents hardened Innis's pro-gun views. In response to a question from Peter Jennings about what informed his views, he said, "[I]t is because I learned the hard way. I don't want any other parent to be victimized the way I was, and to learn this lesson the hard way. I am living, and my sons were murdered in the city with the toughest gun law in the country." He believed that disarming law-abiding citizens aided and abetted crime, and as he told black people, gun control "was not meant to protect your safety; it was meant to deprive you of your freedom." At one point, he called for twenty-five thousand gun permits for civilians in New York, an idea Mayor Koch blasted as an "outrageously bad idea." He became a vociferous advocate in a growing "victims' rights" movement, and latched on to Goetz's case early. He offered to raise defense money for Goetz, calling him "the avenger for all of us."

On more than one occasion, he directly spoke to racial aspects of the Goetz case, though in comments very different from other black public voices. "Some black man ought to have done what he did long before," he said before continuing, "I wish it had been me." At another point, when denying any racial element to Goetz's case, he said that the case had "nothing to do with race, but with criminality. And this constant confusing of racism with criminality is the most moral situation we have in the '80's. These criminals and their apologists are a disproportionate percentage of our people." Innis was no stranger to supporting vigilante (or at least extra-legal) behavior; CORE kept around a "flying squad" of tough guys who knew martial arts and carried guns and protected the neighborhood around CORE's headquarters. "We own this block," he explained. "There's no crime around here. . . . We'd never tolerate those hoodlums like those who attacked Bernhard Goetz."

The lineup for the event was set. Innis would be the featured speaker, addressing the civil right of all New Yorkers, regardless of race or class, to be issued gun permits. Two Republican leaders, Brooklyn state senator Chris Mega and Queens assemblyman Douglas Prescott, would talk about their plans to introduce legislation that would prohibit localities from passing gun laws that were tougher than those in state law. Feldman would represent the NRA. They could not find a Democrat who would agree to appear with them.

Also, to coincide with the press conference, the NRA, CORE, and a local shooting organization took out a quarter-page newspaper ad with the headline "Self-Protection Is Your Right," which said that self-protection is a "basic right held sacred by all law-abiding citizens" who, due to law enforcement's failures, were left with a "personal decision: whether or not to protect yourself." It continued:

"The National Rifle Association believes it is your right and your choice to own a firearm for self-protection.

"The National Rifle Association offers training in safe and responsible use of firearms.

"Don't let anyone take away your rights, your life, or your livelihood."

It was direct and brazen.

Still glowing from Reagan's comment, Feldman, Mega, and Prescott gathered in a conference room at the Omni Park Central Hotel in Midtown Manhattan. As of 10:55 a.m., five minutes before the scheduled start of the event, neither Innis nor any reporters had arrived. The room (which already might have been too large for the event) began to feel cavernous for the men who had put the event together. An image of four gun advocates speaking in an empty room in liberal

New York days after the Goetz shooting would turn them into a laughingstock.

Then, at 10:59 a.m., the Second Amendment heavens opened and liberal *Newsday* columnist Murray Kempton walked in, followed by Innis. A moment later, a throng of reporters, including some from PBS, the local Fox affiliate, three other New York outlets, the BBC, and a Spanish-language network, all shoved in. Reporters from radio outlets arrived and quickly started getting their recording levels set, as several print reporters came in and took out their steno pads and tape recorders.

Soon after 11 a.m., Innis took to the lectern and spoke first. "Never before have I seen white people and black people so together on one issue, and that issue is crime," he said. "We've got to find some way to bring some kind of fear into a criminal. We have to make the streets unsafe for criminals." He announced that CORE would file a suit against New York City and State for "discriminatory practices against minority people" for denying citizens gun permits. Mega and Prescott spoke about their legislation.

Feldman took to the microphone and delivered a brief statement, attacking the mayor with a silly argument still used frequently today to criticize the gun policies of public figures who are under police or Secret Service protection: "When will Mayor Ed Koch provide the people the same level of protection that he enjoys riding in his armored limousine guarded by a phalanx of armed New York City police officers?" It suggested that somehow a public official relinquishes the right to be critical of private gun possession merely because (as the law often requires) he travels with police. Feldman ended the event with a line he and NRA leadership had rehearsed: "A government that cannot or will not protect its citizens has no right to deny them the means to protect themselves." It was official: The National Rifle Association, for the first time ever, had given a press conference in enemy territory about their growing focus on self-defense. Their new chapter had begun. The event became a major story, with national outlets in all media picking it up. The NRA rode the success a little longer and bought additional ads after the event on local New York television outlets.

At the press conference, they had barely said Bernhard Goetz's name.

January 27, 1985
THE WEST VILLAGE

Black civil rights activists, like the NRA, sensed the shock and anger of some in their communities. They, too, saw (perhaps cynically) that there might be ways in which they could use the polarizing case to raise the profile of their work and leaders. Roy Innis and Curtis Sliwa had already seized a version of a public narrative about the case and successfully made a symbol out of Goetz. Someone needed to counter the message.

The case to them was yet another instance of a criminal justice system that systematically devalued black victims while operating under a veneer of equal justice under the law. Many black leaders stressed that every outcome in the case—from media coverage to the words spoken by politicians to the outcome of the grand jury process—would have been vastly different if the victims had been white or the shooter black. In their view, a black shooter would never have been allowed to jump off the train, let alone spend a leisurely nine days gathering his thoughts in the New England snows. Data have long supported that black defendants get harsher sentences for the same crimes, that police more frequently shoot unarmed black suspects than white ones, and that black motorists are more likely to get pulled over for the same traffic offense as white ones. Each of the three is systemic, though not necessarily deliberate. (Officers rarely shout ethnic slurs when shooting black suspects or commit to pulling over black motorists just because they hate them.) But as long as America has had both laws and black people, people's biases have been a stain on our legal system. An imperfect system that is the envy of much of the world is still an imperfect one.

Prosecutors' not succeeding at indicting Goetz on any violent crime charges, while unsatisfying for some, might not necessarily have meant the end of the case. In America, there are multiple avenues for an aggrieved party to get recourse. For instance, the Manhattan district attorney's office sought to prosecute Goetz for violating New York *state* laws—laws only applicable in New York. Perhaps federal prosecutors could separately bring charges for any violations of *federal* law—laws passed by Congress governing the entire country. Federal crimes are regarded as more serious and tend to carry bigger penalties. (Blame Alexander Hamilton, James Madison, and George Washington, who, in their zeal to avoid having power concentrated in a king, pushed for what would become the patchwork of overlapping state and local authorities that make up American government today.) The Goetz case involved the use of deadly force by a white person against black people, followed by a grand jury decision that activists could argue was tainted by racial bias. Such a scenario could potentially support a federal civil rights investigation. In addition, if the feds decided to proceed with a case, it would come with their big resources and penalties. Goetz, if convicted of an attempted homicide under federal civil rights law, could technically face the death penalty.*

The activists knew that in order to capitalize on the intense media coverage the case was getting, they needed to make an announcement soon after the indictment. It also needed to stand out. Media outlets lack the capacity, or desire, to cover every stunt or event that comes their

*Federal death charges are rare and typically brought only in the most extreme cases. Though the law would have allowed it, federal charges for Goetz that involved the death penalty would have been miles beyond unlikely, given both uncertainty about whether the shooting was justified in the first place and the fact that none of the victims died. Still, federal civil rights law is written broadly and allows for death or life sentences for even attempted homicides.

way. The indictment decision had come down on a Friday; the activists planned their event for Sunday (the slowest news day of the week, and one in which a splashy event would be most likely to get picked up). As their backdrop, they chose a place that would instantly raise eyebrows: Courtney House, 55 West 14th Street—Bernhard Goetz's apartment building.

On a frigid January 27, 1985, a young overweight man stepped up to the microphone, and in the rising voice and cadence of someone who had come of age speaking in black churches, made the group's next steps known: "We're going to the U.S. Attorney's office to demand a meeting with either him or one of his assistants, and we won't leave until we get it."

The speaker was a thirty-year-old Pentecostal minister named Alfred Charles Sharpton Jr., whom many called "Reverend Al." The man with whom he was demanding a meeting was Manhattan's top federal prosecutor, a former Democrat turned rising star in the Republican Party, Rudolph W. Giuliani.

CHAPTER FIFTEEN

When Rudy Met Al

Young Al Sharpton was a spectacle. At an average five-ten and a far-from-average 305 pounds, his signature two-toned track suits clung tight to his belly and chest, pants draping loose to his sneakers. His round face was framed by sideburns and a handlebar mustache. And he was perhaps most recognizable for two features he never seemed to leave home without: a corona of heavily processed hair and a large gold medallion hanging from his neck.

The last two features were homages to individuals he had come up with in his youth. The gold medallion had Martin Luther King Jr.'s image on it, matching the one his mentor Jesse Jackson and many of MLK's other lieutenants had worn over the years. The hair, which he got permed once every six weeks, was a nod to the singer James Brown, who took Sharpton under his wing after his son, a friend of Sharpton's, was killed in a car accident.

Sharpton had been a Zelig who always seemed to show up alongside black cultural icons in the 1970s and 1980s. He preached his first sermon at age four, was an ordained Pentecostal minister at ten, and toured the country as a "boy preacher" with Mahalia Jackson by eleven. While promoting a concert for Brown in what was then Zaire, he befriended the flamboyant boxing promoter Don King and ended up a ringside fixture at major prize fights. After Sharpton and King threatened to boycott Michael Jackson's 1984 *Victory Tour* because "black promoters ought to have a piece of it," Jackson agreed to hire Sharpton as his community relations director. For $500,000, Sharpton promoted the tour by distributing tickets to disadvantaged members of the black community.

Sharpton carried baggage as well. For years, he had worked as an informant for the U.S. Department of Justice, secretly recording and reporting on the activities of mafia figures and, according to reports that Sharpton denies, on black civil rights leaders. At one point, he owed his landlord $7,000 in unpaid rent. He failed to file tax returns for years and incorrectly registered the fundraising activities of a youth organization he ran. In the following years, there would be allegations of antisemitism,* following Sharpton's comments after the 1991 death of Gavin Cato, a black boy who was killed by a Hasidic rabbi's motorcade in 1991 (the incident that helped incite major rioting in Crown Heights, Brooklyn). In remarks to a Reform Jewish organization years later, Sharpton acknowledged that he could have "done more to heal rather than harm."

Still, Sharpton was immensely popular with the black community. Disaffected young black people who were skeptical of the city's leadership saw him as bold and compelling. Timothy Mitchell, a prominent pastor in Queens, said at the time that Sharpton "represents a defiance that many older blacks are not used to. He represents a new kind of politics that many so-called 'moderate' politicians resent be-

*During Gavin Cato's funeral, Sharpton made a number of antisemitic comments, such as disparaging the Brooklyn neighborhood's Orthodox Jewish population with "Talk about how Oppenheimer in South Africa sends diamonds straight to Tel Aviv and deals with the diamond merchants right here in Crown Heights. The issue is not anti-Semitism; the issue is apartheid. . . . All we want to say is what Jesus said: If you offend one of these little ones, you got to pay for it. No compromise, no meetings, no kaffe klatsch, no skinnin' and grinnin.' Pay for your deeds." See William Saletan and Avi Zenilman, "The Gaffes of Al Sharpton," *Slate*, October 7, 2003, https://slate.com/news-and-politics/2003/10/the-gaffes-of-al-sharpton.html.

cause it is not the usual clubhouse system. They admire his courage." Tactically, he was aggressive in ways many activists were not. "We had never gone to white people's houses or to their neighborhoods to picket and march," he wrote in his 1996 autobiography. "We created drama. That became my technique, to dramatize issues and events until something had to be done about it by the authorities. That's one of the things it means to be an activist in the media age."

His behavior had also won him detractors in the black community. Andrew Cooper, the publisher of *The City Sun*, the rare black-owned newspaper that would frequently skewer black politicians, was far less charitable. "Alfred is the perfect black leader for white people because he validates their racism," Cooper said. "He's fat, he has show business hair, a gold medal, a jump suit and Reeboks. He's a perfect stereotype of a pork chop preacher." Sharpton brushed off the criticism from Cooper, whom he had known for twenty years, saying that "Andy has been aligned with people politically that I've been opposed to."

Given Goetz's ever-growing platform, the families of his victims saw Sharpton as essential to bringing attention to their sides of the story. After the press conference at Goetz's house, Shirley Cabey called Sharpton directly, pleading for him to take the case on. Sharpton said that thereafter he became "attached" to the case. He had engaged in plenty of activism throughout New York City; now it was time to go national.* Moreover, to him, the case provided a mass media avenue to getting the country to talk about race as being more than just a black

*Sharpton went on to become a *Saturday Night Live* host in 2003, a presidential candidate in 2004, and since 2011 a polished, three-piece-suit-wearing, slimmed-down MSNBC commentator and host. However, through the 1980s, he was a sharp-elbowed street activist intent on building a national platform and had many detractors.

To this day, he is dogged by his role in the Tawana Brawley case. Brawley was a black fifteen-year-old who claimed she had been gang-raped by a group of white men (including a cop and a prosecutor) who had scrawled racial slurs on her body with feces. The case, which became a national media sensation, turned out to be a hoax. But Sharpton, as Brawley's spokesman, was merciless in pushing the case and still stands by his work on it. "[A] grand jury is not a trial," Sharpton said in 2023. "She deserved to have a day in court. Let us bring the case to court. And this prosecutor would not do that." See Michael Winerip, "Revisiting a Rape Scandal That Would Have Been Monstrous If True," *New York Times*, June 3, 2013; Caroline Downey, "Al Sharpton Stands by His Handling of Tawana Brawley and white issue. As he said in 2024, "Some media covered the case as being about race, some covered it as just vigilantism. So I could see that we had to fight to try to make race an issue. . . . And many in our community saw it as 'he wouldn't have done that to four white kids.'"

At the press conference and in comments around it, Sharpton was bombastic about the explicit racial overtones of the case. (Roy Innis picked up on this and blasted the very idea of activists holding a press conference, saying it was "poppycock, nonsense and foolish fraudulence," and that "the easiest thing in the world is for someone to scream out 'racism.'") Still, Sharpton was deliberate in explaining that two things could be true at the same time: Goetz's victims may not have been blameless, but nothing entitled Goetz to try to kill them and get away with it. "People feel we're for the boys," he said into the microphone. "We're not. If they did a crime, they should pay for it. They should go to jail, but so should [Goetz]." He was more blunt with the same sentiment when interviewed for this book. "The precedent to me was more important than the individuals involved," he said. "A kid might have been rowdy on a train and said something threatening. And therefore you got the right to blow their brains out?"

January 29, 1985
THE U.S. ATTORNEY'S OFFICE

Rudy Giuliani agreed to meet with Al Sharpton and the other activists. Giuliani was politically astute and couldn't plausibly say no; citizens wished to speak to him about one of the highest-profile criminal matters in the country, in which emotions around the city and country were raw.

Talent, ambition, and savvy had led Giuliani to his current job. He

---

Rape Hoax," *National Review*, January 13, 2023. He argues today that it was the Goetz case, not the Brawley case, that first made him a national figure.

had such a penchant for publicity that local law enforcement officials feared that when he was appointed his attention seeking might get in the way of his ability to serve the public. Just forty years old, he led the most prestigious prosecutor's office in the United States, the U.S. Attorney's Office for the Southern District of New York (serving Manhattan, the Bronx, and a few northern counties). He seemed almost too immature for the role, with a handsome, boyish face and a sibilance that slurred some of his "s" sounds. His seniority was only apparent in his conservative dress and aggressive left-to-right combover that, at least for the time being, concealed the creeping hair loss below. After years as a prosecutor in Manhattan, he had already held the number three job at the Justice Department headquarters in Washington, where he oversaw the federal government's policies for enforcing laws around narcotics and organized crime. It was a promising career at a relatively early age, and there were few places in government or the private sector that he couldn't have gone after.

Moving back to New York technically was a demotion; by becoming U.S. attorney, he was moving down the org chart to a role that reported to the one he had just left. But some demotions are promotions, and throughout history many former inhabitants of the office went on to much larger things: Secretaries of War Elihu Root and Henry Stimson, Governor (and presidential candidate) Thomas Dewey, and the most famous local prosecutor in America, Robert Morgenthau. A bright, ambitious young man with his eye on local or national politics could do well by building a long record taking down mobsters and crack dealers in America's craziest city.

He wasn't central casting for the role, in a break from the Upper East Side WASP patricians who had held it for much of recent history. He had been born in the Flatbush section of Brooklyn, where his father ran a small restaurant. Ascending the ranks of government and industry wasn't the birthright it might have been for some of his predecessors; he had planned on becoming a priest after graduating from high school. As a young prosecutor, his supervisors described him as "brilliant" and a master at cross-examining witnesses. He was also known as a compulsive workaholic, found at his desk every day at 7:30 a.m. What some saw as "toughness"—a trait that would follow him through the decades he would spend in public life—often manifested as a legendarily hot temper. He readily admitted to screaming at employees who made mistakes, and colleagues described him as having problems dealing with others on a personal basis.

Even upon agreeing to take the meeting with Sharpton, Charles McKinney (an aide to Harlem congressman Charlie Rangel), C. Vernon Mason (a prominent civil rights lawyer in the city), and several other civil rights and religious leaders, Giuliani suggested it was unlikely that his office would open a prosecution. "The federal civil rights laws in this area give the federal government a very limited role," he said. "I don't want to create public expectation one way or another. There are very significant legal problems." Under federal civil rights law, the government can bring charges if some of a defendant's behavior was done with a racial motivation or was taken to deprive someone of the right to participate in a federally funded activity, such as riding the subway. The possibility that Goetz might have felt his life was in danger could complicate an argument from prosecutors that he acted with racial animus. No evidence so far (at least any that someone could point to with certainty) established a racial motivation for the shooting that would hold up in court.

The meeting lasted about two hours. Most legal questions are not entirely straightforward and can require coming up with ways to fit a square argument into a round statute. The group knew this, as McKinney said in remarks soon after the meeting: "We tried to suggest imaginative, creative approaches to overcome possibly legal, technical obstacles to a Federal investigation." Giuliani and Sharpton did most of the talking, with Giuliani challenging the activists on some of the points they raised. Sharpton today describes the meeting as "mildly contentious, but not hostile."

Over the weeks following the meeting, the U.S. attorney's office investigated the case, reviewing files from Morgenthau's and Goetz's lawyers, Myra Friedman's conversations with Goetz, Goetz's confession in New Hampshire, and interviews of others. Giuliani's office also reviewed the racist remarks Goetz made at a community meeting about "spics and niggers." The public was increasingly becoming aware of the comments; Myra Friedman had referenced them—and her and her neighbors' shock at them—in an article in the February 18 issue of *New York* magazine.

Goetz himself was not interviewed by Giuliani or anyone from his office, a sign that Giuliani was not thinking about referring the case to a grand jury. (Prosecutors who are going to move ahead with charges often give subjects of investigations a final opportunity to plead their case.)

February 25, 1985

As predicted, Giuliani found that federal civil rights laws didn't provide a basis for opening an investigation. He said that his office had found that Goetz acted out of fear, not racial animus. "The facts . . . refute allegations that Goetz was acting out of racial motivation," the investigation found, "or an intent to deprive anyone of his right to use the subway."

The report, having made a legally sound point, should have stopped there. It did not, and went on to make a few statements that tiptoed close to sounding like advocacy for Goetz. The report noted that Goetz was on his way to meet people for drinks, not because he was "patrolling or marauding" on the subway. Such a statement was a value judgment of Goetz's conduct. While "patrolling" a subway in search of black men to shoot would certainly be a basis for civil rights charges, the law would not have required Goetz to have been doing that—it only required prosecutors to prove that his actions were motivated by race.

The office's handling of Goetz's "spics and niggers" comment was equally perplexing. Giuliani said that while the comment was "troubling," the facts indicated that Goetz had never shown any bias against black people. Responsible investigators would have scoured evidence for information related to such a comment, and inquired whether it was part of a pattern or corroborated by other evidence, and it appears that the U.S. attorney's office did so. An isolated statement is, in most cases, not going to be enough to warrant legal action and was not here. Still, whether anyone cared to admit it, Goetz had previously shown bias against black people. His own plain statement—which he does not deny making—was itself evidence of such. He may not have used the language often, but he had brazenly done so, and everyone who heard it at the time was troubled enough by it to take action. Racist words used about other races in a racist way are racist. When we deny that fact, we—whether a gun-toting everyman, the U.S. attorney for the Southern District of New York, or anyone else—are at best naive and at worst complicit.

It is not a prosecutor's job to scold a subject for his distasteful views. But there are many ways to characterize an individual's statements, and here, Rudy Giuliani and the U.S. attorney's office were simply wrong in how they explained Goetz's worst (known) one. Even if the statement didn't justify bringing federal charges on account of the shooting—it was an isolated statement, made years before—it hardly squares with the notion that Goetz had not shown racial bias. In its subtlety, Giuliani's report gave Goetz's behavior a free pass where it did not have to.

Nearly two months had passed since the shooting. Just as the initial excitement of a teenage crush fades, Goetz seemed less dreamy to the world the more it learned about him. News of Cabey's paralysis and brain damage were now public, and he resembled more a suffering young human than the black face of urban terror. It was a given that Cabey would come out of the ordeal brain damaged, but how badly? Would he ever again be able to walk, speak, or feed himself? Would he ever even wake up? The question would also likely have repercussions for Goetz; as a matter of public perception, killing someone is very different than maiming them.

New York's NBC affiliate had also broadcast recordings of Goetz's conversations with Myra Friedman. As statements such as "the way I responded was viciously and savagely, just like a rat" reverberated over the airwaves, the public heard Goetz's volatile mix of emotions for the first time. Fear and fury, anger and shame—Charles Bronson he was not.

The public had begun to realize that the story was a little more complicated than just Goetz's getting pummeled by four rowdy black thugs brandishing screwdrivers. There is a very fine line between a heroic "Death Wish Vigilante" and a bloodthirsty madman. It was starting to become less clear to the public which of the two the real Bernhard Goetz really was.

CHAPTER SIXTEEN

Reasonably Reasonable Reasonableness

The grand jury's decision stood. Any question about whether the shooting was justified was, at least for now, purely academic. As Morgenthau figured out what to do next, he handed the case over to a top acolyte, thirty-seven-year-old Gregory Waples. Waples had a reputation as a respected, if humorless and intense, presence in the office. Tall and handsome, with wavy brown hair and modest gold-rimmed eyeglasses, he was prone to the understated, rumpled dress of a career government servant: boxy off-the-rack suits, unflashy neckties, and oxford shirts with button-down collars. He had the lean build of a dedicated runner, having finished several marathons in under three hours (mostly staying away from the New York City Marathon, which he found too crowded and clogged with pesky tourists and unserious weekend warriors). He would regularly jog the five or so miles from his Upper West Side apartment to work in the courthouse, carrying files and other effects in a bright orange Jansport backpack, which he still has today.

Originally from Iowa, he had graduated at the top of his class at Columbia Law School. Classmates described him as the kind of student who would sit at the back of the law school's wood-paneled lecture halls rarely raising his hand. Though if called on, he would deliver concise, brilliant answers that demonstrated an enviable grasp of complex subject matter. After a federal clerkship, he went to Cravath, Swaine & Moore, one of the most prestigious law firms in the world. With a chuckle, he says that his time there was "miserable." He wanted out. He hoped to be a federal prosecutor, but a recession had led to hiring freezes at the city's two U.S. attorneys' offices. Waples had never considered being a local prosecutor but was so desperate to leave Cravath and frustrated with the feds' hiring process that on a Monday in late 1977, "on a lark," he wrote Morgenthau a letter. Morgenthau received it the next day, and seeing the young attorney's stellar credentials, immediately called him in for an interview. On Wednesday, Morgenthau offered him a job on the spot.

Colleagues described Waples as "serious," "unpretentious to a fault," and "not flamboyant, but workmanlike and quietly organized." He aggressively avoided publicity and made his annoyance known whenever colleagues spoke to reporters about him. His intensity paid off. Starting in 1982, he had been given the coveted title of senior trial counsel, joining an exclusive group of about twelve senior lawyers whom Morgenthau expected to be able to take on any type of case and "handle them extremely well." A longtime alum called it the highest honor in the office, and "not a title that's given away lightly." Even among such a rarefied crowd, Waples was arguably the best of the office's four hundred trial lawyers, with a gift for explaining complex issues of evidence. The ability to distill, explain, and argue evidentiary issues is invaluable in any case, let alone one that was most likely going to depend on evidence that might not be admissible. Any prosecution of Goetz—even just for gun possession—would hinge on hearsay statements made by victims and others, at least one missing weapon, and a defendant who had repeatedly spoken to the press and whose original confession may have violated his constitutional rights—all among a host of other tricky technical issues that would require skilled lawyering.

Waples was not the only master tactician now working on the case. After being initially defended by state-appointed attorneys, Goetz sought out the services of a firm led by a man who claimed to be the best criminal defense lawyer in America and "liberty's last champion," Barry Slotnick. Though both brilliant at their craft, no two individuals could have been more different in style and approach than Waples and Slotnick. Slotnick countered Waples's back-of-the-house intensity and studiousness with front-of-the-house polish and pizzazz. (The contrast carried over even to the little things: at trial, Waples drank from a court-issued paper cup; Slotnick drank from a tall glass.) Slotnick's tall, thin frame could often be seen in an elegantly tailored $2,500 three-piece bespoke William Fioravanti suit, with a $15,000 gold Piaget watch poking out from under a monogrammed cuff and an alligator-skin briefcase in each hand. He released his tightly wound energy through smoking cigarettes and a habit of unfolding and chewing paperclips, discarding them in a trail on the floor. As a former Republican candidate for state attorney general, he carried a politician's charm and slickness.

His law practice had treated him well, affording him the fancy suits, the home in Scarsdale, the chauffeured rides to work every morning in a black Cadillac Fleetwood. He had represented several very high-profile clients, including Meir Kahane, the leader of the militant Jewish Defense League, and Congressman Mario Biaggi, a Brooklyn Democrat who had faced bribery, fraud, and conspiracy charges. No matter the undeniable reality of who many of his clients were, he bristled at one description of his past work: "mob lawyer." In addition to his white-collar clients, he had represented some of the biggest names in organized crime, including an associate of John Gotti and Joseph Colombo. Gotti and Colombo were the bosses of the Gambino and Colombo crime families, two of the "Five Families" that have dominated New York organized crime since the 1930s. Slotnick was standing a yard from Colombo when Colombo was shot and paralyzed at a rally, and continued to visit Colombo twice a week until his death.

Slotnick's response to criticism of his work ranged from denying the existence of the Mafia (he believed the term to be "more of an ethnic slur than a reality") to expressing the philosophical basis of the important role defense attorneys play in the criminal justice system. As he told *The New York Times*, "I represent people who are accused of crimes, many of them unjustifiably," noting that other talented lawyers represent "so-called organized crime figures." His bookish law partner, Mark Baker, found what he saw as Slotnick's ethics as a reason to join the firm. "Considering some of the clients [Slotnick] has had, it's important to know where the line is drawn between professional involvement and personal involvement," Baker said at the time. "He very clearly charts where the line is and doesn't cross it." Like lyrics complementing music, the two fit together perfectly. "Barry was always the outer-directed one, and Mark was the inner-directed one," said Gillian Coulter, the firm's paralegal. "Mark has that incredibly incisive mind and that feel for writing and connecting. And Barry performs it."

Slotnick initially bristled at the thought of taking the case on. "I don't represent people who shoot black kids in subway cars," he said to a common acquaintance who first proposed that Slotnick agree to do it. Perhaps the Goetz case provided the small, but powerful, firm an opportunity to launder its reputation to avoid further association with the mob. Maybe it was another case that affirmed the reason Slotnick claimed to have chosen to practice as a defense lawyer: to defend the individual against overweening state power. Whatever it was, one thing probably sealed the deal: the hordes of paparazzi and television cameras he saw camped in front of Goetz's apartment building the first time he went there. Slotnick immediately knew that untold attention would come his way for representing Goetz. Whatever his motivations, Slotnick was spellbinding at what he did, relying on meticulous preparation, withering cross-examinations, and slick courtroom tactics to win acquittals in most of the cases that he had taken to trial.

March 1, 1985
THE MANHATTAN D.A.'S OFFICE

Judges rarely give permission to prosecutors to reopen a grand jury, but there are exceptions. A major change in a victim's condition could be an avenue for reopening. In Goetz's case, as none of his victims had died, prosecutors had sought only an attempted murder charge. As an illustration, had Cabey succumbed to his injuries, prosecutors would likely have gotten permission to reopen the grand jury to ask for a murder charge. But even that may still not have changed the grand jury's decision. If a grand jury wasn't persuaded that they had enough evidence to bring charges the first time around on an attempted murder, they probably also wouldn't bring charges on a completed one. The two crimes require almost the same evidence, which the grand jury had already once found lacking.

Prosecutors can also get permission to reopen a grand jury if new evidence comes to light that was not available to them originally. Immediately after the grand jury decision, Morgenthau, who typically did not get intimately involved in the day-to-day matters of the office's cases, began huddling quietly with Waples and others to brainstorm for ways to resuscitate the case. On March 1, they got new evidence that allowed them to do exactly that. Through his lawyer Howard Meyer, Troy Canty said he had changed his mind and was willing to testify against Goetz—even without immunity if it came to it. "I want his story out, and I think his testimony comes under the heading of new information," Meyer said. "Justice should be done in this case. The grand jury should hear someone from the other side." Separately, James Ramseur also agreed to testify.

This time, prosecutors changed course and pressed forward with calling Canty and Ramseur to testify, without insisting that the two waive their immunity. Even in the face of opposition from many in the public, prosecutors believed that an attempted homicide had taken place. The only way they were going to be able to have a prayer of prosecuting it was with the two young men's testimony. Even though Canty's lawyer had suggested that his client was willing to proceed without immunity, there is no indication that Ramseur would also have done so. Perhaps as a means of ensuring that they got the testimony they needed, prosecutors took the path of least resistance and did not put up a fight on immunity with respect to either of the two.*

March 12, 1985

On March 12, Morgenthau formally announced that on the basis of "significant new evidence," the office was opening a second grand jury probe. Given the secrecy of the grand jury process, Morgenthau did not publicly identify that the new evidence was, at least in part, the testimony of two of Goetz's victims.

Ramseur, who testified before the grand jury for about forty-five minutes, spoke about his fear of both Goetz and Goetz's supporters, who had begun sending him "many" threatening letters. In public, neither he nor Canty provided more substance about their testimony. In an interview with the *New York Daily News*, though, he made several noteworthy statements. First, when walking past a video arcade, he lowered his voice and said, "That's why we were carrying the screwdrivers," and then with a chuckle, said, "Yeah, they work." Ironically, he made the statement to one of the newspapers that was partly re-

*Grand jury materials and prosecutors' files are not public (and the events in question took place four decades ago). As such, it is nearly impossible today to reconstruct what transpired behind the scenes as prosecutors weighed how to proceed before the grand jury. For instance, Gregory Waples, one of the few living people with firsthand knowledge of the matter, does not recall today why the office did not also call Barry Allen as a witness. He speculates that perhaps the office believed at the time that they had enough to proceed in the case with just the testimony of Canty and Ramseur. That is an entirely plausible explanation, given the much lower bar prosecutors have at the grand jury stage than at trial. In an attempt not to overload grand juries with evidence, prosecutors often will put on only the evidence they need to convince a grand jury that a crime was committed and that they should issue an indictment.

sponsible for pushing the false narrative about the screwdrivers in the first place.

At another point, he touched on a broad concept: the power of fear and bias. "Just because we all have criminal records, everybody thinks we're bad people. That just ain't so." He may not have realized it, but he was making a plea about whether the system could fairly address a harm to an unsavory victim. Ramseur had a long rap sheet and may not have been blameless in the shooting. At a minimum, there was some dispute as to how concerning the four teens' behavior on the train was. But could a justice system, and society, that often tends to see things in black and white make fair sense of an encounter that was quite clearly gray?

One of his statements in the interview would surely come back to bite him: "I want to see Bernie Goetz fry." Even though he followed the statement by saying that he told the grand jury the truth and that he thought Goetz shot him "for no reason," the statement could be construed by a future trial jury as showing bias that called his credibility into question.

The grand jury heard evidence for eight days. After he finished presenting his case, Waples explained the law the grand jury would need to apply in the case. The assault and attempted murder charges Goetz faced hinged on a critical word that has an obvious meaning in everyday speech but did not have a settled definition in New York law at the time: "reasonable." The state's courts were all over the place on how to judge whether a defendant's use of violent force was reasonable. The law was not clear, and there are at least two ways the legislature, which had written it decades before, could have meant for it to be interpreted. The law might have intended to impose a *subjective* notion of reasonableness, in which a defendant could not be found guilty if he sincerely felt threatened at the time he used force. Under this approach, Goetz would have been justified in shooting if he had a sincere fear that Canty and the others were about to rob or hurt him. Conversely, the legislature might have intended a more prosecution-friendly *objective* idea of reasonableness, in which a defendant could not be found guilty if his behavior aligned with how society would expect a normal person to have behaved in the same situation. Under that reading, Goetz would have been justified in shooting if an ordinary, or "reasonable," person would also have.

Gregory Waples was in a bind about how to explain the concept of reasonableness to the grand jury. He and his colleagues felt strongly, as they had put into a legal brief at the time, that a purely subjective standard, in this case, would give "a license to kill to any subway rider like [Goetz] who is asked for money—or the time—by black youths, simply because he honestly, but totally . . . believes that every such encounter with young members of a racial minority is potentially life-threatening." Unfortunately, given the uncertainty in the law, he felt that if he attempted to argue a purely objective standard—that regardless of the sincerity of his fear, Goetz's behavior did not align with how others in society should behave—the court would reject it as not accounting for the reality of a threatened person's fear.

So Waples did a very human thing when confronted with a difficult issue: he avoided it. Demonstrating the intellectual ability to speak with nuance that he showed even as a young law student, Waples cleverly framed the concept of reasonableness in an open-ended way. He told the jurors it was their job to determine "whether the evidence creates reasonable cause to believe that any shot he fired was not a reasonably necessary response" to what he had perceived. It ducked the question of whether the grand jury should follow a subjective or an objective standard. In somewhat circular legalese, he essentially directed them that if after hearing the evidence, they had a gut feeling that Goetz's shooting was unjustified, they could indict.

A perceptive (or confused) grand juror asked Waples for clarification, wondering how to judge reasonableness in terms of what the juror called the defendant's "psychiatric" state—essentially asking how they should consider the real fear a shooter may have experienced.

Though the juror's wording was inartful, the grand juror had asked a question that invited a response from Waples that would go on to upend generations of New York law. Waples knew he was stuck and had to address the subjectiveness of human fear in some way. "I felt I had to take the bull by the horns," he said. "If I just continued with a kind of a namby-pamby instruction that obfuscated the issue, Judge [Stephen Crane, who had since been assigned the case] . . . would find the instruction confusing [or] misleading, and dismiss the indictment on that ground." So he tried again, continuing:

> *So there's both a subjective and objective element to this.* First of all, you have to determine whether the defendant, in his own mind, believed he was in the kind of peril that permitted him to use deadly physical force. You must also then determine whether his response was reasonable under the circumstances, [if] a reasonable man who found himself in the defendant's situation would have behaved the same way. (Emphasis added)

In short, he called for a hybrid test for determining whether one's use of self-defense was appropriate. It required a jury, when judging self-defense, to first consider the defendant's subjective perception of a situation (how he felt), and then separately the objective reasonableness of it when judged against the rest of society (how society would expect others to behave in the same circumstances). Waples had given an entirely new reading of New York law, and the defense would surely challenge any indictment based on it.

A day before the grand jury completed its work, Goetz emerged, again hoping to testify. He and Slotnick crafted a plan for a partial grant of immunity that would protect him from prosecution for any testimony he gave regarding three guns he purchased in Florida. Not wanting to let him steer their case, prosecutors rejected the offer, and Goetz did not testify.

March 27, 1985

Waples's explanation worked, and on March 27, the grand jury gave its answer: indictments on all thirteen charges the prosecutors had asked for. The grand jury once again brought the three charges in the first indictment: two counts of fourth degree criminal possession of a weapon and one count of third degree criminal possession of a weapon. In addition, the grand jury added four counts of first degree assault (for deliberately injuring a person or showing "depraved indifference to human life" and injuring someone); four counts of attempted murder; one count of first degree reckless endangerment (for showing "depraved indifference to human life" and recklessly acting in a way that causes a "grave risk of death" to someone else); and one felony count of second degree criminal possession of a weapon. Oddly, Goetz was most bothered not by the attempted murder or assault charges, but by the reckless endangerment accusations, complaining to his defense team in exasperation that "I trained and was so careful! I wasn't ever going to endanger anybody else."

If the jury found Goetz not guilty of assault or reckless endangerment, they could also consider second degree, or less serious, charges for the two. If convicted, Goetz would face up to twenty-five years in prison on the attempted murder counts, five years on the assault and gun counts, and seven years on the reckless endangerment count (each figure is merely set by law, and few defendants, particularly those without criminal histories, are ever sentenced to the maximum).

The defense predictably moved to dismiss the indictment. The decision of what to do next fell to Justice Crane. Judges come from all corners of the legal profession, and like just about everyone, they bring their past experience into how they approach their work. Crane was a scholar, having written numerous articles on many weedy areas of civil and criminal practice. Moreover, after leaving private practice, he had worked as a top lawyer in one of the state's appeals courts, a wonkish role that required pondering complex questions about how laws are applied. As a result, he relished the opportunity to take on a confounding and unsettled area of New York law.

He, too, struggled. Deep down he felt that a trial that judged only whether Goetz felt subjectively scared would have meant a "slam dunk" for acquittal. Personally, Crane did not see an outright acquittal as completely fair or rational, based on what he knew about the evidence in the case. As an experienced jurist, though, he knew that his personal views did not matter. After poring over nearly a century and a half of New York case law, he felt constrained by precedent and ruled in Goetz's favor. In a nine-page opinion throwing out all the case's murder and assault charges (the ones that hinged on the reasonableness of self-defense), he wrote that the language "he reasonably believes" that appears in the law makes clear that the reasonableness of an action depends on a defendant's viewpoint at the time at issue, not how others might have behaved under the same circumstances. In Goetz's case, the reasonableness of his actions against the four teenagers depended on how Goetz felt at that moment, not on how anyone else in his shoes would have acted. According to Crane's decision, an indictment that required otherwise did not comport with the law.

Only weapons possession and reckless endangerment remained in the indictment. Morgenthau immediately announced that his office would appeal, noting a real-world impact of the decision: "A subjective standard justifies any use of deadly physical force even under circumstances which almost everyone in the community would think inappropriate," he said. "We do not believe this code of the Old West is appropriate in New York City in 1986."

With the most serious charges now dismissed, Crane's decision was a win for the defense. Still, parties often ought to be careful what they wish for. Had defense not moved to dismiss the indictment, the case would have gone to trial on the subjective standard. Were that the case, as Justice Crane had noted, Goetz stood a remarkable chance of getting acquitted. Given that, under the law, prosecutors are not allowed to appeal acquittals, the case would have been closed, with Goetz a free man.

However, prosecutors are allowed to appeal a judge's decision to throw out an indictment, and once Justice Crane ruled for Goetz, prosecutors were now free to appeal the decision. An appeals court with an eye on correcting confusion in the law can, with the stroke of a pen, reshape an entire state's (or country's) laws.

July 8, 1986
ALBANY

The Court of Appeals, housed in downtown Albany in a domed white marble building framed with Ionic columns, is the highest court in New York. Like its prettier and more popular step-sibling, the U.S. Supreme Court, it only takes on a small number of the cases that come its way. Such courts of "last resort" typically only hear cases in which there is a major dispute among lower courts over how to interpret a consequential area of law. There is plenty of work for such courts. Laws are often written in an open-ended way, and even centuries into the American experiment, courts still grapple with a constant stream of novel questions. New York's highest court had one in front of it now.

On July 8, 1986, more than a year after Justice Crane's decision, the Court of Appeals ruled: In a 7–0 decision, the court blessed the view Waples had made to the grand jury. The opinion, written by the court's chief judge Sol Wachtler, found that the notion of a "reasonable belief" in New York law included both a subjective and an objective element, thereby aligning New York with a majority of states at the time. It was an important precedent that would reverberate far beyond Goetz's case for decades, clarifying, among other things, when people should go to jail for trying to kill each other. In the short term, however, it meant that Goetz's attempted murder and assault charges were back. The case would be sent back to Justice Crane to oversee the trial, this time with clearer instructions on how to understand the indictment.

Everyone connected to the issue knew of its immediate significance. Wachtler and Crane had been friends for years and crossed paths at a program in Manhattan soon after the decision. Wachtler approached Crane, saying, "Steve, I hope you weren't too upset about our reversal in the Goetz case." Crane, without missing a beat, quipped, "Sol, I'm not the defendant."*

It was the middle of the summer of 1986 in the city. After two years, the scaffolding had finally come off the Statue of Liberty, following a much-needed facelift in advance of the landmark's two-hundred-year anniversary. Mayor Koch was trying to manage a tight budget, and crime rates were still heading up. Protests around the city raged following subway rate hikes.

The outdoorsy Gregory Waples was away from it all on a long vacation. He had met his cousin in Colorado, and the two had driven up to Alaska for several days of hiking in the scenic Brooks Range, a place almost as far—literally and figuratively—from New York as one can be while still in the United States. At dinner in Fairbanks, Waples saw a banner headline on the local newspaper in three-inch bold letters: "GOETZ INDICTMENT REINSTATED."

He headed back to New York without buying the paper.

---

*Wachtler had been best known for first delivering a line regarding the unchecked power of grand juries that every law student and criminal lawyer today knows well: "By and large, prosecutors could get grand jurors to indict a ham sandwich." See Marcia Kramer and Frank Lombardi, "New Top State Judge: Abolish Grand Juries & Let Us Decide," *New York Daily News*, January 31, 1985, 3.

Ironically, Sol Wachtler soon became a ham sandwich himself. In 1992 he was arrested on charges of extortion, racketeering, and blackmail after demanding a $20,000 payment in exchange for compromising videos of a woman with whom he had had an affair and her boyfriend. After pleading guilty to harassing the woman and threatening to kidnap her daughter, he resigned from the court, lost his law license, and spent fourteen months in prison.

CHAPTER SEVENTEEN

Bingo

December 12, 1986

NEW YORK SUPREME CRIMINAL COURT

The right to a jury trial comes from the Sixth Amendment to the Constitution, which says "the accused shall enjoy the right to a . . . public trial, by an impartial jury of the State and district wherein the crime shall have been committed." The Framers had no concept of what the world would look like two centuries later: when a "public trial" might mean one that takes place in a city with a population of seven million, in small aging courthouses that hadn't been built to hold zoos. Finding an "impartial jury" would seem easy had the community not for two years been inundated with daily sensational information about the alleged crime or the participants in it. Just about any prospective juror had ridden in the same subway system where the crime had taken place, or knew someone who had, or had heard in graphic terms about someone who had been a victim of a crime. In one vivid example, in initial screens of groups of prospective jurors, Justice Crane began by asking for a show of hands as to who had ever been crime victims. So many hands would shoot up every time, he started asking how many people *hadn't* been the victim of a crime, and the court recorded that information instead.

As 360 randomly selected New Yorkers arrived on Friday, December 12, 1986, to have their jobs, education, hobbies, family history, personalities, joys, and fears picked apart for glimmers of how they might rule in a criminal trial, crime and safety issues provided a vivid backdrop across the country. Violent crime rates, particularly in cities, were up nationwide. More importantly, by 1986 crack had become a nationwide epidemic. The drug, and its users, was easy to demonize. It was cheap and potent, and one could draw a straight line from the trail of corpses in its path to gang violence in cities. Panicked horror stories of a generation of irredeemable "crack babies" born to trick-turning crackhead mothers became common (*Washington Post* columnist Charles Krauthammer called them a "bio-underclass . . . whose biological inferiority is stamped at birth").

The solution was not to declare a public health emergency, but to engage in combat. And thus the War on Drugs raged on. Its own Antietam came less than two months before jury selection in Goetz's trial, when, on October 27, 1986, President Reagan signed the Anti-Drug Abuse Act of 1986 into law. Among a host of other measures, the bill put into place a 100-to-1 sentencing disparity for crack versus powdered cocaine, a change that led to decades of packed federal prisons, public misconceptions about the dangers of crack versus powdered cocaine, and disproportionately severe sentences for black and Latino offenders. Concerns by members of Congress about the possible impact of the new law's approach did not drive the day; the bill passed the House 392–24, and the Senate 97–2. America was afraid of crime—particularly when it came from black people in cities—and willing to fight it by any means necessary.

To complicate things further, Goetz had spent the weeks after the shooting on a media tour to a welcoming press who ate him up. He gave a lengthy exclusive interview to the *New York Daily News*, in which he railed about how the city was "sick," and that people needed more guns and to be taught to use them. He joined Barbara Walters—then one of the most recognizable faces in America—for a meal after Walters, having heard that Goetz liked Chinese food, grabbed some on the way to his apartment hoping to land an interview with him. (Goetz apparently picked at the food without eating much and would not answer any questions on camera.) He also sat for an interview with Geraldo Rivera for ABC's *20/20*.

Before he had hired Slotnick and Baker, Goetz's initial legal team had tried to arrange for a television outlet to run his two-hour confession video in its entirety so the world could hear the story from his unchallenged point of view. Both *20/20* and CBS's *60 Minutes* balked, not wanting to cede editorial control (or a precious two hours of prime airtime). The *New York Post* secured perhaps the hottest byline in America, running a cover page on March 22, 1985, with the words "MY STORY BY BERNHARD GOETZ," with Goetz's signature beneath it. Inside was a three-page narrative about the story from Goetz's point of view. Editor Steve Dunleavy insisted that Goetz wrote every word of it, down to nitpicking about commas. At one point, Goetz stayed up until 5:30 a.m. giving newspaper interviews. His lawyers watched and cringed as it all played out. Anything a defendant says can either come in at trial in evidence or, more dangerously, be used to contradict, or "impeach," other conflicting statements he has made. His lawyers said that they repeatedly warned him of the dangers in speaking publicly. "We had those talks repeatedly," Mark Baker said in 2024. "'Bernie, what are you doing? This is all going to bite you in the ass.'"

Goetz wasn't alone in his appetite for the spotlight. Both suspect *and* victims readily took advantage of opportunities for ink and airtime. As media outlets on the hunt for the next juicy story zipped them around town in limousines and plied them with food and drink, the young men, for the first time in their lives, got a taste of the good life. Barry Allen gave *The Washington Post* a one-hour sit-down interview. Canty's brother Carl sold his story to the *New York Post* for $125 and allowed the paper to interview him while he was freebasing cocaine.

(Dunleavy said at the time that he had no knowledge that the paper had paid for the interview.) Canty said that he and Allen had sold their story to the *National Enquirer* for $300 and allowed the tabloid to take photos of their bullet holes. Immediately after, they realized they had been taken advantage of, as they could have sold the story for orders of magnitude more. It's no surprise that a slurry of all of it—the political climate, the crime in the city, the constant national and local headlines about crime, the parties' many press interviews—was knocking around potential jurors' minds as they came in to be screened.

The pool of jurors filed into the courtroom. In a quaint practice still used in New York courts today, a clerk spun a rotating drum (of the sort used to draw bingo numbers) that contained a card for each prospective juror. The clerk then called each juror back, one at a time, for five to ten minutes of private questioning. Jurors were asked questions such as where they lived, whether they rode the subway, whether they knew anyone who had ever been arrested, what they knew about the case, what they thought about gun control, whether they had served on a jury, and if they understood the difference between illegally possessing and illegally using a gun. One moment at the outset made it clear how difficult it would be to find twelve people who could set aside their feelings and judge the case fairly: when Goetz entered the courtroom for the first time, a few dozen prospective jurors broke out into applause.

Still, a juror's clear bias is not enough to get them excluded. Jurors who at first claim they can't be fair can often be salvaged by deft questioning by the judge or parties. One early prospective juror initially answered that he did not think that he could be fair in the case, as he had once been shot by a black mugger. Goetz himself chimed in and rehabilitated the juror, asking, "You sympathize with me because you once were a victim of a robbery. If the prosecutor could prove to you

Young and old looters empty the shelves at an A&P supermarket in the Bronx during the massive blackout that hit New York City on July 13, 1977.

Children play amid debris from abandoned and torn-down buildings in the South Bronx, June 27, 1977.

Former California governor Ronald Reagan campaigns for president in 1980 at a leveled stretch of the South Bronx, pointing to the neighborhood as a prominent example of urban decay.

The car holding Bernhard Goetz speeds away from court through a chaotic scrum of Guardian Angels, reporters, photographers, protesters, and onlookers moments after the verdict in Goetz's trial on June 16, 1987.

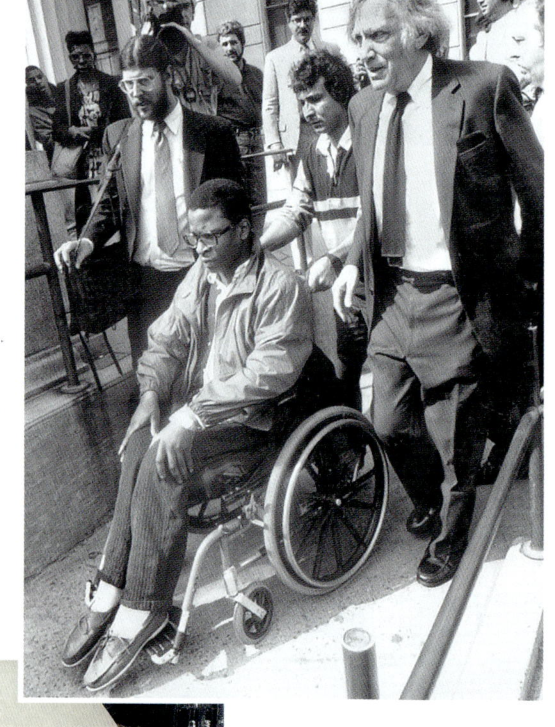

Darrell Cabey leaves the Bronx County Courthouse on September 26, 1990, flanked by his attorneys Ron Kuby, left, and William Kunstler, right, following a hearing in his civil suit against Goetz.

Goetz became a hero to many in the gun rights movement. In his first public appearance after his initial sentencing, Goetz received a plaque at an event celebrating the Federation of New York State Rifle and Pistol Clubs, for "wasting four vicious criminals and humiliating a gutless District Attorney." Here, at the event on April 24, 1988, he poses with three "Bernie's Girls."

that I was not the victim of a robbery and I shot four people without justification, would you lose your sympathy for me?" The juror immediately responded that he could. Despite having given an initial answer that was disqualifying, the juror ultimately gave the right answer and got added back to the jury pool. What matters is where a juror's answers end up, not necessarily where they began. Only those prospective jurors who, even after questioning, cannot commit to being fair are legally excluded (called being challenged "for cause"). Per standard practice, each side got to remove a set number of people for any reason. Waples felt that the defense framed questions to jurors in a manner that wrongly led them to believe that they couldn't be fair at trial. Many ended up getting excluded.

Jury selection often involves lawyers to try their hand at pop psychology (and even real psychology; Goetz's team, like many, brought in a professional psychologist to help them with the process). Just as George W. Bush claimed to have looked into Vladimir Putin's eyes and seen his soul, lawyers must look into a stranger's eyes and see someone who is going to vote their way. Engaged in the timeless human gamble of attempting to draw conclusions about people they hardly know, lawyers often look to other traits beyond a person's views in order to glean how they might perform as a juror. In any other case, prosecutors, not defense attorneys, might prefer having crime victims on a jury, under the assumption that crime victims typically are not sympathetic to defendants. Goetz's case upended that notion, as public support for Goetz was rooted in his being seen as standing up for victims. The defense also took an interest in whenever a prospective juror seemed curious about why one of the young men was shot in the back. It suggested a bias against Goetz.

Waples, on the other hand, knew there was a clear political dimension to how people saw the case, and was said to prefer what he saw as liberal "Greenwich Village types" who might be skeptical about someone who owned guns in the first place and concerned about the public safety threat posed by an armed individual to their neighborhood. This, too, may have been a miscalculation, as the Venn diagram of "liberals who do not like guns" probably overlaps with "liberals who are uneasy about sending people to jail."

Waples also used a hypothetical during questioning to nudge jurors toward understanding the hybrid standard for reasonableness that he and his colleagues had successfully gotten enshrined in New York law earlier that year:

> Let's assume, because of the very peculiar way my mind operates, that I believe that everyone who smiles at me is secretly plotting to kill me and that someday when I go back to my hometown in the Midwest I am walking down the street and the first man I encounter smiles at me and I kill him because I am in mortal fear of my personal safety.

He would then ask jurors whether they could appreciate that believing a smiling person was dangerous was not the same as reasonably believing it. If it seemed clear that a juror could not grasp the distinction, he would move to strike them for being biased.

Like bickering siblings testing the limits of what they can do to each other without getting into trouble, lawyers frequently slip improper points into questions to jurors. At least once, Waples made a reference to Goetz's mental instability in front of a prospective juror, a point that was plainly out of bounds, but which, once articulated, could not be unsaid. Goetz's lawyer, meanwhile, repeatedly referred to the four victims as "thugs and hoodlums." Crane admonished the lawyers whenever they tried to bend the rules. He got particularly frustrated when Slotnick suggested in questions that the jury was allowed to "nullify" the law or vote with their hearts and acquit in the face of evidence and explicit legal instructions that compelled them to convict.

When the state first filed charges against Goetz in 1985, it technically was still lawful for attorneys to strike jurors from serving on a trial on the basis of their race. By the time jury selection started in 1986, the U.S. Supreme Court had just forbidden the practice a few months before in *Batson v. Kentucky*. Even then, the rule applied only to prosecutors. Goetz's defense team could have attempted to strike all black prospective jurors from the pool and gotten away with it. It would be years before the Court applied the principle to strikes by defense attorneys. Goetz's lawyers did not make a concerted effort to keep black people off the jury. This was not a sign of their virtue; they kept black people in the jury pool because it would have been a bad tactical idea to try to get rid of them. First, as a practical matter, support for Goetz did not line up cleanly along racial lines, and many black and brown New Yorkers shared Goetz's frustration with crime in the city. One prospective juror originally from Puerto Rico was blunt when asked about the victims' criminal records: "I mean if they have records, they have been arrested. . . . [A] person doesn't get arrested for not doing anything. I have been in this country for 40 years and I have never been arrested." Moreover, there was a chance that being seen as having struck black people might backfire. Baker said that they welcomed having black people on the jury; given the level of "heat" in New York City on issues surrounding race, "the last thing we wanted to do was participate in it for either side." Keeping black people in the jury pool wasn't just morally upright; it simply looked better.

While the law now forbids striking jurors on the basis of race, gender, sexual orientation, and other legally protected characteristics, jury selection is largely a free-for-all in which attorneys have wide latitude to do what they can to get the jury they want. For example, one of the prospective jurors was an Episcopalian nun who came to court wearing her habit. The defense felt that her choice of vocation (or calling) might, among other things, confer a sense of moral authority that could get in the way of deliberations. They attempted to challenge her for cause. The judge denied the motion, given that she had a First Amendment right to wear her habit, not unlike that of an Orthodox Jew's right to wear a yarmulke in court (ironically, the prospective juror sitting next to the nun in court was an Orthodox Jewish man wearing a yarmulke). In the end, the defense struck both.

One by one, prospective jurors came up, representing both Manhattan's diversity and the challenge in picking a jury in such a high-pressure case: rabbi, psychic, martial arts expert, social worker, financial analyst, engineer, bus driver, retired civil engineer, World War II veteran, police department aide, computer operator. Like most humans, many were hard to slap labels onto, particularly prospective black jurors when it came to speaking about race. One prospective juror from Harlem referenced the Howard Beach case in which Michael Griffith was killed by a car while fleeing a white mob that was beating him. She noted that she thought all white people have some fear of black men in groups, saying, "Sometimes these fears are played out in very ugly ways." It was unclear whether she would be more useful to the defense or to the prosecution. Her recognition that white people often fear black people may have legitimized Goetz's fear, maybe leading to an acquittal. Or her solidarity with black victims may have benefited the prosecution. No one could tell for sure, and she ultimately was let go.

More than anything else, the city's safety and self-defense were constant backdrops to jury selection. One prospective juror who made it into the pool identified with Goetz, saying that Bernie "defended himself and he had the right to do it. If I have been in the same position and I had a weapon, I think I would have done the same." One woman questioned had worked for decades with veterans with PTSD; as the case was going to focus on Goetz's mental state, the defense saw her as too much of a liability and struck her. Another prospective juror who had said that while he believed in limits on self-defense, he sympathized with Goetz and that "I think the day of turning the other cheek is behind us." He made it through.

April 24, 1987

Winter turned into spring as the trial remained a constant presence in the background of New Yorkers' lives. Jury selection had to be delayed several times for Slotnick's representation of one of John Gotti's codefendants in a federal racketeering trial. All that time left plenty of room for more press about the case, and the public was hungry: a new profile of Goetz here, an article about where public opinion was on the anniversary of the shooting there.

After multiple rounds of questioning across four months, the final seated jury consisted of eight men and four women. Ten were white and two were black. Six of the jurors had been crime victims, with three of those crimes happening on the subway. Waples, upon seeing the full jury seated, felt that the trial was now almost a "fool's errand," given what he saw as a strong pro-Goetz bias among several of the twelve who were seated. He thought that though he might be able to get a conviction on the counts involving Cabey, getting a unanimous vote for conviction on anything else was unlikely. "Let's just say I didn't have warm and fuzzy feelings about the jury from the very beginning," he said.

Instantly, the group became the twelve most famous people who no one had ever heard of. The city's media outlets scrambled to be the first to learn whatever kernels of information they could. *Newsday*, treating the trial as theater, devoted two-thirds of a page to a graphic with detailed background information on the "Cast of Characters": Goetz, the judge, the lawyers, all four victims, and all twelve jurors. It even included an overhead sketch of twelve jurors in a jury box, with each person's body, hairstyle, and attire drawn slightly differently to reflect the order in which they would be seated once the trial started.

In addition, immediately after jury selection was completed, reporters from New York's ABC and Fox affiliates and CNN attempted to contact each of the seated jurors directly, seeking to schedule interviews immediately after the verdict. Justice Crane was furious. He called an emergency hearing with the attorneys to figure out if the contact was problematic enough to require him to declare a mistrial. While he did not, he threatened to sequester the jurors for the rest of the trial. (Judges try to avoid sequestering jurors at all costs, given the profound burden on people who are already being pulled out of their normal lives for weeks or months at a time.) The news organizations apologized and agreed not to contact the jurors again until after the trial.

After jury selection, the defense tried to get the trial postponed, arguing that they still needed to interview several fellow passengers on the train whom they thought could bolster Goetz's self-defense argument. Justice Crane declined, saying, "There comes a point where the need to keep this puzzle together outweighs my desire to accommodate." He noted that more big delays might warrant impaneling another jury (a tall undertaking, given that it took several months to pick the current one, partly due to the defense's own scheduling issues). As trial approached, reports also surfaced that Goetz offered to plead guilty to misdemeanor charges, in exchange for a one-year prison sentence. Prosecutors apparently resisted, not wanting to accept a plea for anything short of at least one attempted murder count. Even setting aside that prosecutors would not have brought a case they did not think they could win (under prosecutors' guidelines, it would have been unethical for them to have done so), turning down Goetz's plea offer made tactical sense. Prosecutors were already feeling public pressure over the two years of waffling and ham-fisted efforts to get Goetz indicted and brought to trial. Agreeing to let him walk with barely any prison time would have been a public relations disaster. Still, like all plea decisions, prosecutors' not taking the sure thing was a gamble. Going to trial and failing to convict Goetz on any of the more serious charges—murder, assault, or reckless endangerment—might still end up an embarrassment for them.

And that was it. In three days, on Monday, April 27, 1987, some twenty-eight months after shooting four men on the subway, Bernhard Goetz was going to trial.

CHAPTER EIGHTEEN

Room 572

The courthouse, an unimpressive but imposing cube of 1960s-era brutalist cement at 111 Centre Street, was now ground zero. Journalists, who swarmed the courthouse from long before it opened until well after it went dark, mobbed everyone with any connection to the case. "It was insane," Gillian Coulter said. "It was like paparazzi in Hollywood. It was like we were doing the Academy Awards red carpet every other day."

Spectators and protesters from all walks of life, representing a jumble of competing views, showed up to make their cases from a safe distance behind blue police barriers. Black and white, liberal and conservative, pro-gun and anti-gun, they were all in agreement about one thing: Bernhard Goetz was the perfect symbol of their movement. Police decked out in riot gear stood guard, ready to jump in if things went south between the bizarre multiracial coalitions that formed.

On a drizzling, overcast day, about twenty Guardian Angels paraded in front of the building with signs reading "Bernhard Goetz: Blame the Criminals, Not the Victim." (They were a constant presence at the trial, with a large one nicknamed "Mountain" providing daily security for Goetz and escorting him to and from home.) They were countered by about a dozen members of the Revolutionary Communist Party marching in a circle and chanting, "Goetz is a racist, not a hero!" and holding signs reading "Bernhard Goetz: KKK: Different Names, Same Game." Members of New York State's Conservative Party, which had been unequivocal in its support of Goetz, demonstrated in front of the courthouse, wearing buttons that read "Mug at Your Own Risk." William Kunstler, a leftist lawyer representing Darrell Cabey who had made a name for himself defending the Chicago Seven, a famed group of anti-Vietnam protesters, arrived and distributed copies of a poem he had written to the press about the "Vigilante of the IRT":

Who, stimulated by imagined threats,
Let bullets raise him from obscurity. . . .

(As any good lawyer would, he made sure to copyright his poem before handing it out.)

All of it got in the way of locals just trying to get on with their lives, annoyed at the latest loud urban drama that had gummed up their commutes. The courthouse was still a workplace for hundreds of people who had nothing to do with the trial. Clogged elevators, congested hallways, limited seating, and distracted security made life difficult for everyone. Fern Fisher-Brandveen, a legal services lawyer who was representing a client in an eviction proceeding on the same day, blasted the hassle and media frenzy caused by Goetz's trial. "Look at that. Bernie gets all the attention, and that means the rest of us will have to suffer," she said to reporters. "If you people would spend as much time on cases that affect people's lives every day, like housing, maybe you could do some good. The housing courts here are underfunded and overcrowded. But all you're interested in is a headline and all the hoopla that goes with it."

On nice mornings early in the trial, some members of the defense team would walk the few blocks to the courthouse from their offices.

They eventually stopped, given the hordes of people surrounding the courthouse that made getting there a pain. (Barry Slotnick avoided the drama; he was always chauffeured.)

The courthouse was old, cramped, and musty. Its hallways were crowded, filled with the chatter of desperate lawyers hawking their wares to those unlucky enough to need them. The constant sirens whizzing by on the streets below could often be heard inside the building. Every morning, when the building opened at 9 a.m., spectators at the front would rush to the elevators to the fifth floor, where they lined up in front of Room 572, its largest courtroom. At 9:30 sharp, spectators would go through magnetometers and take whatever seats were available. Among the daily hundred or so who attended every day were several dozen reporters from around the world sitting some four rows deep on both sides of the courtroom. Some days, everyone got a seat. Other days, the line would stay open, with lucky attendees getting their chance whenever one of the uncomfortable wood-paneled seats freed up.

Roy Innis was often there, giving interviews in support of Goetz to all who would listen. Lubavitchers sympathetic to Goetz, identifiable by their dark hats and curly locks, crammed into seats next to black activists and the actor Treat Williams. Educators at all levels saw the trial as an opportunity. Columbia Law School professor George Fletcher attended the entire trial, wanting a firsthand account for a book he intended to write about the legal minutiae around self-defense and reasonableness. Mary Ann Romano, a sociology professor at New York University, brought students from her class "Deviance and Social Control." She came in with her mind made up about Goetz's morality: "This isn't a case of self-defense," she told *The Washington Post.* "Society feels blacks and Hispanics are threatening. Goetz is a member of the white middle class. He had a built-in hostility." Some tweens got to see the case firsthand. Barbara Taylor, who ran a small school in Harlem, brought seven students to the courthouse for a living civics lesson. "They're concerned about racism. They're concerned about vigilantism," she said. "But I feel sorry for Goetz, too. He's a victim of our society, as well. I know one thing, though. Had Mr. Goetz been black and the youths white, it would have been a whole different story." Even Gregory Waples's father and stepmother had flown in from Palo Alto to watch the young star prosecutor's big moment.

Also seated in the courthouse were representatives from the NRA, perhaps to keep an eye on the return on their investment. The NRA Civil Rights Defense Fund, founded by the organization in 1978 to provide legal and financial help to people who used firearms for self-defense, had given Goetz $20,000. Given the dynamics of the case and his own admitted conduct, Goetz was not an ideal face for any organization. Still, no matter how much the NRA had tried to distance itself from Goetz's antics and racist comments, it ponied up for him when it counted. The case was heavy with social baggage that might have made some NRA supporters uncomfortable. Regardless, it had a clear self-defense angle, and to many, Goetz was a hero. With an expensive trial coming up, and with the NRA on its way to becoming a national political force, the organization probably needed Goetz as much as he needed it.

In criminal cases, the prosecution always argues first. After the judge kicked off the proceedings, Gregory Waples addressed the jury for the first time.

Unofficially, lawyers use their openings, like so much else in trial, to play mind games with jurors. Attorneys are deliberate about everything, from the words they use for the other side ("the defendant" is far less sympathetic than "Bernie"; "the state" sounds meaner than "the people") to the little ways they break the rules here and there that they hope will squeak by a judge who isn't paying close attention.

Waples's biggest mind game was so subtle that few may have noticed it: he sat alone. Parties are allowed to bring however many bodies they can fit into court and the judge allows—paralegals, legal secretaries, other attorneys, consultants—a veritable white-collar pit crew to help the race go smoothly. Waples, however, almost always sat by himself at the prosecutor's table, his staff seated anonymously elsewhere in the courtroom. This was by design: he wanted to make himself look small. As a means of making defendants seem more sympathetic, defense attorneys often argue (or suggest) that prosecutors come to work with the blessing and limitless resources of an oppressive government bent on taking down an individual citizen. (The implication about limitless resources is ironic, given that it was Goetz's attorneys, not Waples, who often showed up to court in chauffeured black cars.) He wanted to be seen as Greg Waples, a rumpled public servant here to do his level best, not Gregory L. Waples, agent of a five-hundred-attorney megalith with a $75 million budget.

He rose, placed a large stack of paper on a wooden shelf next to the jury box, and began to address the jury. He spoke for about an hour, his hands shaking with intensity. His words rose and fell for effect, doing their best to cut through the courtroom's awful acoustics. Some of the facts were mundane and indisputable: a ten-car IRT No. 2 downtown express train left White Plains Road in the Bronx at 12:36 p.m. and pulled into the 14th Street station at around 1:40 p.m. with about twenty people on it.

Quickly, though, the presentation turned from a recitation of agreed facts to a passionate argument. "Suddenly, however, that day that had begun so ordinarily, turned into a nightmare. Suddenly, every passenger on that train, every passenger in that car, was jolted by the electrifying and terrifying spectacle of Bernhard Goetz—this gentleman on trial here—standing on his feet, firing shots in every direction from a gun he was holding in his hand."

A fundamental question in any criminal proceeding is whether a defendant intended to commit the act for which he is on trial. In a murder trial, the question is often whether the defendant intended to kill, had a legal justification for killing, or simply did so by accident. The defense made clear that they were not going to raise an insanity defense, or a defense that Goetz could not be held accountable due to a psychiatric condition. But that did not stop both parties from delicately stepping up to the line of calling Goetz's mental capacity into question at trial. As a result, Waples walked a tightrope. Starting with his opening statement, he had to establish that Goetz, while paranoid, was still in control of his actions. He had to do so without crossing the line into making specific layman's accusations about Goetz's psychological health—dangerous territory that, if he probed too far, would be grounds for a mistrial. In his opening, Waples chose words that suggested that Goetz, while having his faculties, had succumbed to a rage and hatred that drove him to attempt to commit the unthinkable. He spoke of Goetz's "blind, self-righteous, volcanic fury," and attempt at carrying out a "cold-blooded execution." He leaned into attacking Goetz's character as much as the judge allowed, calling him a "tormented" and "troubled" man, an "emotional powder keg one spark away from a violent explosion," a "self-appointed vigilante," an individual with a "very twisted and self-righteous sense of right and wrong," a man with a "moralistic and self-righteous zeal" who possessed a "corrosive frustration that was eating away inside of him," and an individual with a "jaundiced mind" (the last one drawing an objection from the defense, which Justice Crane sustained).

Without explicitly making the case about gun rights, Waples called Goetz's attachment to firearms into question (an approach that, even in spite of New Yorkers' concerns about personal safety, would likely have landed well in the politically liberal city). He referenced the "small arsenal" in Goetz's apartment, noted Goetz's "attachment to this gun," and called Goetz's unwillingness to venture outside his home without a firearm "pathetic." He also called attention to Goetz's use of both a quick-draw holster and hollow-point bullets, two items that, even if legal, suggested that Goetz had every intention of drawing a gun quickly, to cause as much harm to others as possible.

Waples walked the jurors through several points that would be critical for them to understand. First, according to the prosecution, the case, at its core, would come down to jurors' notions of the appropriateness of self-defense. An extended back-and-forth in the weeds of the subjective and objective reasonableness of a suspect's behavior would be lost on most normal human beings. The jurors, who may well have confronted some of the same fears and threats as Goetz, and like so many before and after them, might botch their interpretation of the law. They needed self-defense explained to them in a way that they could understand, and in a way that made them suspicious of Goetz's behavior.

Waples made the point that from the moment he unholstered his gun, Goetz's self-defense justification made less and less sense as each moment passed. If Goetz intended to frighten the young men, Waples noted, merely brandishing the weapon should have been sufficient. According to Waples, even if brandishing the gun weren't enough, and Goetz truly felt he was justified in shooting Canty, he had no need to shoot either Allen or Ramseur, as both had turned and started fleeing once the first shot rang out. And even if Goetz felt justified in shooting the first three, he had no plausible reason for shooting Cabey, who was seated at the time. Finally, even if he felt he had had a reason to shoot Cabey once, his standing over Cabey and saying, "You don't look so bad; here's another," before firing was clear evidence of cold-blooded intent. Though not conceding that any of the shootings were justified, Waples gave the jury several off-ramps from which they could find that every action that followed broke the law.

The air was thick and stale in the creaky courtroom. Waples had to work to keep his audience. He used a poetic flourish to explain a core point the jury would need to understand in order to convict: "[P]rovidence alone prevented any of the many innocent men, women, and children from being killed or seriously injured by the defendant's wild shooting." He was, creatively, using human connection to explain the law of reckless endangerment (speaking of "providence" and "men, women, and children" lands very differently than the icy legalistic language "creating a substantial risk of serious injury to another person").

It was an important point to make, and one lost in so much of the frenzied coverage that for two years had focused so aggressively on black versus white, safe versus unsafe, noble vigilantes versus marauding bandits. There were other people, including at least one infant, on the train car. Any of them could have met Darrell Cabey's fate, or worse. At least one bullet fragment appeared to have struck one of the train car's side panels. Goetz is lucky he did not kill a baby that day. Even the notion of calling Goetz a "vigilante" in the mold of Paul Kersey from *Death Wish* misses a huge point: Even if Goetz was justified in trying to neutralize a threat, he still put almost two dozen innocent lives at risk. Was it all worth it? The next weeks of trial would try to sort that out.

More than anything else, Waples wasn't naive. He buried in his opening statement a wink to the reality of trying a case at the center of a public maelstrom: "For whatever reason, right or wrong, this case . . . has touched a raw nerve in the American anatomy. For whatever reason, this case has not become simply a media sensation, but something of a cultural phenomenon, and indeed, with a haste and stridency that says quite a bit about ourselves and the society in which we live today."

His work was cut out for him.

Gregory Waples was adept at crafting lofty intellectual arguments that appealed to his audience's highest sense of reason. Barry Slotnick was even better at kicking opponents in the teeth. Few lawyers in the country were as fun to watch flicking away each building block of a prosecution's case as Barry Slotnick. He rose.

"[Y]ou're going to see that those four were committing a robbery," he said, calling on the jury to question the very legitimacy of the case and suggesting that the four men, not Goetz, were the guilty ones. "They're not on trial here, by some strange reason, which is not explainable, Bernhard Goetz is." Gliding through the courtroom and alternately addressing jury, judge, and audience as if carrying out choreographed stage directions, he went on, noting that he would be "prosecuting" the four young men. "I'm going to try them for robbery, I promise you that. And you're going to convict them and acquit him."

He never used the term "victims," instead using a litany of loaded terms across his remarks to reinforce that they, not Goetz, were the true aggressors, calling them "vultures," a "gang of four," "predators of society," "low-lifespans," "hooligans," "punks," and "mean, vicious-looking men, without pity in their eyes." Knowing that at least some of the men would testify at trial, he was aggressive in suggesting that the jury had reasons to disbelieve anything they had said.

When he got to Ramseur, he was particularly brutal. By then, Ramseur was spending years in prison for his participation in the horrific sexual assault of a pregnant woman. "[Ramseur] will take this witness stand," Slotnick noted, "and he will be asked the following, 'James Ramseur, where do you live?'" And then, modulating his voice to separate questions from answers, he continued:

"And he'll tell you, 'state's prison.'

"How long have you lived in state's prison, Mr. Ramseur, or how long do you expect to live in state's prison?

"And he'll tell you, 'I recently got sentenced to eight and a third to twenty-five years.'"

Slotnick spread on the schmaltz. After each time he posed a question, Slotnick would cup his hand behind his ear, and lean in to the witness stand, as if riveted by the quiet words of the imaginary witness. With each response, he feigned being more and more stunned by what he was hearing.

"Mr. Ramseur, what were you convicted of? Was it rape, robbery, and sodomy of a pregnant woman . . . ?

"And the answer will be 'Yes.' And was it this same [woman], when you got done with her, who needed eighteen stitches in her anus, was taken off a rooftop and spent time in a hospital?

"And the answer will be 'Yes.'"

He made eye contact with the jury, particularly when talking about the stitches, shooting them exasperated looks, as if wondering if they were as disgusted by the words of the imaginary witness as he was.

Slotnick further suggested that in addition to not being trustworthy the men had incentives to be dishonest. Soon after the shooting, three of the men had filed multimillion-dollar civil suits against Goetz for their injuries (Canty for $5 million, Ramseur for $8.5 million, and Cabey for $50 million). While such civil suits from victims are not uncommon, defense attorneys can easily point to them as bearing on an individual's trustworthiness as a witness. A conviction for Goetz could come in as evidence in a future civil trial. Slotnick argued that the men had a big incentive to be dishonest to get Goetz convicted: buckets of money later.

Slotnick went further, though, and twisted the law by telling the jury that by getting immunity for their testimony, Canty and Ramseur, critical witnesses the prosecution had chosen to call, had been given a "license to lie." With the comment, he suggested that they had a blessing to lie on the witness stand (which would have been perjury—another crime). Though made in a brazen way, it was the kind of misstatement of a fine point in the law that most jurors would not have caught. As in any immunity arrangement, the men had been granted a protection from being prosecuted for *past* crimes. They could still be prosecuted for lying at trial. For some reason, Waples did not object to Slotnick's use of the phrase.

Though they would be given meticulous instructions, jurors would still be left to figure out the tricky question of what kinds of actions are reasonable on their own. To complicate things further, in order to convict, the jury would need to be convinced of Goetz's guilt beyond a reasonable doubt. Even though most people have heard the term countless times on police dramas, the definition is muddy at best. Instructions given to juries in New York are circular, framing a "reasonable doubt" in part as "an actual doubt, not an imaginary doubt," "a doubt that a reasonable person, acting in a matter of this importance, would be likely to entertain because of the evidence that was presented or because of the lack of convincing evidence." The most perplexing line sometimes given to juries in New York is that proof beyond a reasonable doubt "is proof that leaves you so firmly convinced of the defendant's guilt that you have no reasonable doubt of the existence of any element of the crime or of the defendant's identity as the person who committed the crime." Essentially, a reasonable doubt is a doubt . . . *which is reasonable.* How is a group of people, made of individuals burdened by their own notions of language, morality, society, and justice, to come up with a trustworthy outcome in any case? A cynical reading is that across time juries have tried to do their best but, in the end, just ended up doing what they were going to do.

The jury would also spend the next weeks figuring out how to follow the law as to the limits of when self-defense is appropriate. By the time the trial started, an international debate had broken out about self-defense in America. But how much of a hunch is enough for someone to be justified in pulling a trigger? In many circumstances, our society leaves it up to the fearful to make that call—and leaves it up to equally fearful people from the same community to hold them in judgment. Twelve imperfect people and one imperfect judge were about to make imperfect work out of an imperfect system.

A final challenge made the jobs of everyone connected to the case, particularly Justice Crane, difficult: how to manage the risk of prejudice presented at virtually every corner. "Prejudice" in the legal sense is only loosely connected to our common understanding of the term. In the law, "prejudicial evidence" is evidence that evokes emotion in either the judge or jury, but which does not add specific value to the case. It is yet another exceptionally vague standard in the law that, if botched, can have profound consequences.

The case involved a white defendant (who had previously been mugged and had used ethnic slurs in the past) who shot a group of black teenagers (who already had criminal records and had committed crimes since) with a firearm that had left them all with gory injuries. It was a minefield of potential prejudice. In addition, the Howard Beach attack and ensuing protests took place as the Goetz jury was being seated. In many ways, even if the word "race" was never spoken, New York's racial climate was as much on trial as Goetz's or Griffith's attackers were,* and (at a minimum) was part of the consciousness of everyone working on the case.

Of all the possible areas of prejudice in the case, Justice Crane particularly felt that allowing race to be addressed openly at trial could lead to problems on appeal. He barred the parties from open discussion of race at trial. His caution was not misplaced. There are areas in which the law explicitly allows consideration of race (recall activists' pleading with Giuliani to try to get him to open a civil rights investigation on the basis of race). This was not one of them. No matter how much the city's racial tension was a staple on the nightly news, the case was, at least on paper, about whether one man's fear was legitimate enough for him to open fire on people he felt were about to harm him. Gregory Waples largely stayed away from openly talking about race in court, only barely hinting at it once by suggesting that the defense was trying to make the case that some "persons are above the law's sanctions and worse, that some people are below the law's protection" (a line so open-ended it could have applied as much to class as it could to race).

*In all, nine people were convicted on a number of charges flowing from Griffith's death, with three convicted of manslaughter and assault and receiving sentences ranging from five to thirty years' imprisonment.

In contrast, the defense was smooth in nudging the jury on race. In perhaps the clearest example, for part of the trial, the defense kept up easels with blown-up photos of the four victims, each looking more menacing than the next. Waples suggested that the photos served no purpose other than to inflame the jury and were present to stoke jurors' racial fears. According to Mark Baker, who had thought up the idea for the defense, investigators were instructed to seek out the "meanest-looking photographs of each of these kids. . . . We put them on four easels and we [had] the jury staring at them. Four mean-looking pictures every morning." The intention was to frighten the jury. In response to Troy Canty first coming to court in a suit (something Baker referred to as "out of character"), Baker sought to remind the jury, however implicitly, that these were rough young men. The defense got away with toeing a fine line on race: plausibly denying that they had any racist intent while still benefiting from the parties' races. "The jury got the point," Baker said. "And look, they were black. I couldn't turn them into white kids. Would I have done that if I could? Probably not. But that's who they were and I wanted the jury to look at four guys in a circle like Bernie Goetz did."*

A few other aspects of the case, though not as incendiary as race, provided just as many tripwires. First, the court had to sort out what to do about the four victims' rich criminal histories, particularly evidence of several muggings Cabey, Allen, and Canty had participated in. Under the law, evidence of their past conduct could not be introduced simply to show that they were bad guys; it could only be brought in to establish that their behavior on the train matched a precise pattern of muggings in other incidents. Justice Crane did not allow the evidence in; the instances merely indicated that the four did, at times, do bad things with a buddy. That four individuals may have worked

*The photographs on easels turned into a standoff that played out over several days at trial. Baker would often arrive at court earlier in the morning than Waples and would set up the photos. Waples would arrive at court and take them down. Eventually the parties went back and forth until they, according to Baker, "came to a draw," and the defense withdrew the photos.

together in other very different circumstances would not pass muster for establishing that the four had a clear pattern of mugging people in a certain way.

Finally, the related issues of how to talk about guns, the damage they cause to bodies, and even the Second Amendment created more challenges around prejudice for the parties and court. A case about gun possession necessarily requires prosecutors to establish that the gun in question was, in fact, a gun. As the gun-ness of a gun is often not a real question anyone can dispute, parties will sometimes stipulate, or agree not to contest, that a gun is real and operable (as opposed to being a toy or model). Barry Slotnick argued aggressively for the parties to do so. He accused Waples, during the testimony of the firearms expert he had brought in to testify about the guns, of needlessly waving the guns around in front of the jury, in a way that was prejudicial to his client and not relevant to the trial. In a sidebar with the judge, Waples threw Slotnick's own behavior back at him. "Mr. Slotnick kept pictures of the four people Mr. Goetz shot on an easel for two days in front of the jury. . . . I think it's inappropriate to say now he's being prejudiced by the retention of a witness on the stand." Ever on the lookout for a Solomonic middle ground, Crane allowed Waples to continue questioning the witness about the operability of the guns but insisted that he keep them left on the evidence table. A court officer then showed them to the jury afterward.

Slotnick also objected during the testimony of one of the doctors who operated on Cabey immediately after the shooting. The witness walked through the mechanics of draining blood and fluid out of flattened lungs, the impact of respiratory arrest on a brain's oxygen levels, and a parade of grisly horribles that are the inescapable reality whenever speeding bullet fragments ricochet around someone's insides. Slotnick immediately called for another sidebar. He offered to stipulate to the idea that Cabey had suffered "life-threatening injuries," and claimed that Waples was "attempting to prejudice the jury with blood and gore." Crane allowed the prosecution to proceed (with both the surgeon and a neurologist who testified about Cabey's severely decreased intellectual capacity), stating that all was fair game in a homicide case: "the people have the burden of proof beyond a reasonable doubt, and they are entitled to call what witnesses they think are necessary to establish their burden, if they can do so."

As the trial carried on, the jury saw evidence from witnesses who served a range of purposes: highly credentialed experts, their testimony as boring as it was critical; straphangers who testified about what they saw on a day on which they, too, might have caught a bullet; and cops from states hundreds of miles apart who had been pulled into a mess they had never anticipated. And there were the sideshows. Kenneth Ditchfield, who sold Goetz one of his guns, arrived in court wearing a dark Stetson, enormous tinted eyeglasses, a three-piece Western-cut leisure suit, and a blood-red silk shirt unbuttoned down to his midchest. Accessorizing his outfit was a thick gold chain with a dangling bald eagle charm, a diamond-studded gold ring, and a bejeweled American flag lapel pin (the Orlando shop he owned sold both "self-defense weapons" and gold jewelry). Though there to provide ten minutes of straightforward testimony about the sale, he arrived in court with a 450-signature petition supporting Goetz. Immediately after testifying, he held an impromptu hallway press conference about the right to bear arms. After recounting an incident from years before in which someone on the New York subway tried to take his luggage, he told attendees that New York was "a great place to visit, but I'm glad to go back to Orlando."

Securing the testimony of defendants and victims is never a given; defendants have no obligation to testify, and victims may be uncomfortable testifying against someone who harmed them (if they are even alive or available at all). In many respects, the key figures in the case were caricatures; Goetz and his four victims were figures who, depending on whom you asked, wore either white or black hats.

Two of those caricatures—young men shot by Goetz whom much of the public had scarcely tried to understand—were now about to take the witness stand. Whether the jury believed them would be probably the single most important factor in whether Bernhard Goetz went to jail, or walked.

CHAPTER NINETEEN

Two Big Italian Guys

May 5, 1987

More than two years had passed since a grand jury first heard the case in 1985. After being embarrassed by the first grand jury's decision to indict Goetz only on minor gun possession charges, prosecutors had gone back a second time, armed with testimony from Canty and Ramseur. Finally, after more than two years, they both were going to have their moment at trial.

Gregory Waples had been deliberate about preparing the jury to accept that two things could be true at the same time: they may not trust (or even like) Goetz's victims, but victims they still were. He spoke about their drug abuse, poverty, criminal convictions, and unemployment, and put some of the onus on them, noting that "they had not labored particularly diligently to overcome the disadvantages" of their existence. He was blunt: "in all probability you folks will . . . find very little in common with any of these four young men. . . . Their lifestyle is, perhaps, totally alien." Waples was stuck with the young men as witnesses, and it was in his interest to control the narrative and frame the bad, the worse, and the ugliest of their backgrounds. (By preparing the jury for bad news, he could blunt the impact of Barry Slotnick's inevitable questions of "Sir, you've never had a job other than stealing from video arcades, have you?" or "What's it like living in prison?")

First, Waples walked Canty, who had been living in a drug rehabilitation center in Westchester County since early 1985, through the story of the shooting. There were a few big differences between Canty's and Goetz's accounts, starting with how their interaction went: He claims to have said, in a "normal" voice, "Mister, can I have $5?" followed by Goetz, a few seconds later, saying, "You can all have it!" and firing his weapon. (Goetz claimed that Canty leaned in close and with a menacing smile said, "Give me five dollars.") Likewise, Canty said that he wasn't sure where the others were standing when he first approached Goetz; Goetz had said that the four surrounded him. Canty also testified that he had thought that Goetz had paused for as long as ten seconds after firing the first shot before turning and firing the second. The testimony was in direct conflict with the central argument of Goetz's defense, which was that he didn't have time to think and blindly fired off all five shots in rapid succession.

The cross-examination brought the fireworks. The defense's entire trial strategy—undermining the four young men and implicitly putting them, and not Bernhard Goetz, on trial—was evident in Barry Slotnick's first question after he arose: "Mr. Canty, in December of 1984, when you were aboard the railroad train, you weren't wearing that nice suit and tie, and the shirt, were you?" Not far from Canty, on an easel, was the blown-up photograph of him, smirking, his arms crossed, very much not wearing a coat and tie. It was a two-dimensional reminder, in literal black-and-white, of the unspoken subtext of the case.

"And did you have many occasions in December 1984 to wear a nice suit and tie and shirt?"

"No."

What Canty was wearing was, as a legal matter, irrelevant. But with a casual question that could almost have felt like an aside, Slotnick had drawn blood. No matter how much Canty had been coached by prosecutors to sit up straight and wear fancy clothes, Slotnick wanted the jury to see him and his friends as nothing more than a street gang who had gotten what they deserved. As much as individual jurors would later profess to the contrary, they bought it.

Eliciting clipped, enunciated answers from Canty, Slotnick methodically walked him through a parade of facts that the jury could use to believe he wasn't credible or had an incentive to lie: his having beat up a schoolteacher, his time in rehab, the $300 he had received to tell his story to the *National Enquirer,* the $5 million lawsuit he had brought against Goetz.

Slotnick was skilled with slipping language past the judge, prosecution, and jury. At one point, he asked Canty if he made a living by "robbing and stealing." The law allowed him to probe questions about Canty's background to speak to his credibility, but Slotnick's use of the word "robbing" was significant. Canty had admitted on the stand that he and his buddies had regularly broken into video game machines. Robbery under the law is a very different act, committed against a person with the use of force, threat, or intimidation. By talking about the video games, Canty was only admitting to the far less exciting- (or menacing-) sounding *larceny.* Still, the question of whether the four had tried to rob Goetz was central to the trial. The very subtle elision of two different legal concepts furthered the defense's narrative that the group was a violent gang that made a living through intimidation and fear.

Back in 1985, prosecutors, who control the grand jury, had made the decision not to call Barry Allen as a witness. At trial, however, because Allen was not the defendant, nothing prevented the defense from calling him as their own. (While the Fifth Amendment forbids *prosecutors* from calling someone to testify against himself, nothing stops the defense from doing so.) Had the defense called him to the stand, they would have been able to guide his testimony and could have embarrassed him so much it would have gutted the prosecution's case. It therefore made sense for Waples to call Allen as a witness and be the first one to set the narrative about him.

Allen, like anyone else in an American court, still had the right to take the Fifth, or exercise his constitutional right not to testify so as not to incriminate himself for anything. Given Allen's criminal history, and the years of drama surrounding getting the three able-bodied victims to the witness stand, Justice Crane anticipated that Allen would do so. Crane called Allen to the witness stand outside of the presence of the jury, hoping to determine whether there were areas in which Allen could testify without getting himself into legal trouble. If there were not, the court would send him on his way. The defense, knowing that a prosecution witness repeatedly refusing to answer questions (and maybe even losing his temper) would play well for the defense in front of the jury, fought, in vain, to have the whole process play out in public view.

In a quiet courtroom, Waples called Barry Allen to the stand. Waples began with a basic question. "Mr. Allen, do you know a person by the name of Troy Canty?"

Allen instantly responded. "On advice of counsel I serve my constitutional rights against self-incrimination under the Fifth Amendment of the United States Constitution and decline to answer that question." Slotnick objected, claiming that there was no universe in which acknowledging a relationship could be incriminating. (In reality, as a defense lawyer, Slotnick certainly knew that such a question could open the door to far more incriminating ones, such as whether the two had ever committed crimes together. Still, ever the showman, Slotnick committed to the bit.) This went on for a few more questions.

Each time Allen pled the Fifth, Crane asked Waples if he would offer immunity for the question asked. Each time, Waples declined. After several questions, Waples sat down.

Slotnick came up for cross-examination and began, "Mr. Allen, my name is Barry Slotnick, and I represent Bernhard Goetz. How are you this morning?"

"Feeling fine," Allen responded.

"You got one in there, Mr. Slotnick," Crane joked. Slotnick next asked Allen where he lived. He gave his address. Slotnick then asked, "And did you recently leave prison?"

And that was about as far as it went. After each question Slotnick asked, Allen would invoke his right not to answer, Slotnick would ask Waples to grant immunity, Waples would deny it, Slotnick would ask the court to order Waples to grant immunity (something Crane rightly noted that he had no authority to do), and they would move on. The dance continued for about twenty minutes. After recognizing the futility of putting Allen in front of the jury, Crane decided to instruct the jury that Allen was a "missing witness," meaning that the prosecution had failed "adequately to explain" his absence. The law allowed the jury to infer from Allen's absence that his testimony would have hurt the prosecution.

In criminal trials, there are star witnesses and there are train wrecks. James Ramseur was not a star witness.

It was hot. A trial in which jury selection had started in the December cold and stretched through a delightful spring was now bogged down in a sticky New York summer. A miserable heat wave had taken over the city. Air-conditioning that worked well in the courthouse's hallways somehow did not make it into the courtroom itself, and the result was a courtroom that felt about ninety degrees. Virtually everyone in the court had trouble focusing by the afternoons, and Justice Crane frequently called breaks or closed early due to the heat, often referencing the parties' flaring tempers. "It's warm in the courtroom and I think we are all getting a little hot under the collar except Mr. Baker," he quipped during one particularly tense moment, noting Baker's generally cool demeanor.

Though Ramseur had by far the ugliest criminal history in the group and perhaps the most volatile temper of the four, Waples had no choice but to call him. "I knew he was not going to be a star or model witness," Waples said. "But I'd made my decision about immunizing him. I thought I had an obligation to put him on, for better or worse, and let the chips fall where they may."

As Waples predicted, moments prior to being called, Ramseur let Waples know that despite having been granted immunity, he was going to refuse to testify (doing so—refusing to testify while under a subpoena—is a crime). Waples warned Justice Crane that he was expecting Ramseur to be "contumacious" on the stand and tried desperately to come up with a solution that avoided putting him in front of the jury. Part of a jury's job is to judge witnesses' credibility, and a jury is far less likely to find someone credible whom they don't like personally. A combative Ramseur could end up a disaster for Waples, particularly given how central Ramseur's testimony was to the success of Waples's case.

It set off a heated debate over whether, as Slotnick wanted, the court ought to bring Ramseur in to take the stand and refuse to testify in front of the jury. Crane sided with Slotnick, making the point that if Waples disagreed with the decision, he could simply choose not to call Ramseur. Doing so would have been an equally bad outcome, as it would have either given the defense the opportunity to call him or led the judge to give another "missing witness" instruction that was already going to be given about Allen. Crane recognized the bind Waples was in but noted, either optimistically or naively, that "there is some persuasiveness to the observation that when he is in front of the jury, with all the people in the audience, he may very well cooperate by answering questions."

Ramseur did not, in fact, cooperate by answering questions. After Waples called him to the stand, the courtroom sat in awkward silence for fifteen unexplained minutes before he emerged, wearing dirty white jeans and a leather jacket. When a court officer attempted to swear in Ramseur, he pushed the Bible away and mumbled back, "I'm not taking the stand. I refuse to." Slotnick, never one to let a good theatrical moment go to waste, said to the judge, "Sorry, your honor, I can't hear the witness," to which Ramseur spat back, "I refuse to take the stand!" In a tense sidebar that followed, Waples went as far as offering to extend Ramseur's immunity to cover perjury (a risky step rarely taken by prosecutors). It was an act of desperation. Despite how Slotnick had mischaracterized immunity earlier in the trial, extending immunity to perjury would have given Ramseur a literal license to lie. For the rest of the trial, Slotnick would have eviscerated the prosecution for doing so. Waples was now running out of options. Reiterating that openly defying a lawful order to appear in court could get Ramseur charged with criminal contempt and get him even more jail time, Justice Crane again directed him to testify.

With his hands in his pockets, Ramseur made his response clear. "I refuse."

Ramseur would now be held in contempt of court. After he was led off the stand, Justice Crane directed the jury to disregard what they had just seen. He told them to "draw no inferences and make no speculations with respect to this matter. This conduct that has occurred in your presence has no bearing on your deliberations and this witness is excused," he said, directing them to somehow disregard something they had just seen clearly.

But the damage had been done. And the jury hadn't even seen the worst yet.

Later in the trial, the prosecution attempted to call him back to the stand. The second time around would have given Ramseur an opportunity to have his criminal contempt purged; if he came in and testified, he could avoid getting into legal trouble for not having testified the first time. Now wearing a jacket and tie, he took the stand. He sat slumped, mumbled his answers, and often spoke with his hand covering his mouth, repeatedly drawing reminders from Justice Crane to move closer or speak up. (At one point, he shot back, "Do you want me to put the microphone into my mouth?")

Ramseur contradicted other testimony in the prosecution's case in ways that, if unhelpful, were not fatal. His recollection of where he, Cabey, and Allen were positioned when Canty approached Goetz during the shooting did not match what Goetz, Canty, and other witnesses had said. He said he was largely minding his business and looking away when Goetz opened fire (a very different explanation from everyone else's). Likewise, he introduced that Barry Allen yelled, "Oh shit, Troy!" when Canty was shot, which no other witness had noticed. Juries tend to pounce on minor inconsistencies in witnesses' narratives to suggest that a whole story does not add up. Even so, none of the discrepancies between Ramseur's account and other witnesses' were insurmountable. They weren't hard to explain away: it was a moving train with flickering lights; the whole encounter happened in under a minute; chaos broke out once the first shot was fired. Even if the witnesses differed on which facts they remembered, no one could dispute that four men have bullet holes in them and that one of them will never walk or think clearly again.

But it wasn't the factual inconsistencies that made the afternoon so disastrous. On the morning of the shooting, Ramseur was already on the hook for ninety days in prison for failing to appear in court for four separate cases. Even worse, at the time of the trial, he was serving eighteen to twenty-five years for his part in the brutal sexual assault and robbery of a young woman that Slotnick had skewered Ramseur over in his opening statement. It was all fair game for Slotnick to bring up again.

Also, three months after the shooting, in a bizarre twist, Ramseur had faked his own kidnapping. On March 25, 1985 (within days of providing his testimony to the second grand jury), Ramseur called

911, claiming that his name was Darryl Thompson. The so-called Mr. Thompson claimed to have seen two "big Italian guys" grab James Ramseur, who "is involved in the Goetz Case," off the street, force him into a blue Lincoln, and speed away. Detectives rushed to Ramseur's apartment in Claremont Village and canvassed the neighborhood for witnesses. Ramseur showed up a few hours later, telling the police that the two armed men had driven him about five miles north to a playground, where they said they planned to kill him. He said that he ran away as they fired at him, then walked back home. He also went to the site with detectives and further explained what had happened.

The city threw tremendous resources at trying to avert the public relations disaster that would come from a hit being carried out on one of its victims and key witnesses. The police brought in several officers and a sketch artist, and brought the case to the attention of Benjamin Ward, Robert Morgenthau, and the city's chief of detectives. Quickly the cops figured out that the story did not line up, and a few days later, Ramseur admitted to faking it. He said that he had done so out of a fear that, if baseless, was not irrational: he thought that given the climate around the case, Goetz's friends would soon come after him. He wanted to test the police response to a scenario in which a black man was a victim. James Ramseur, like so many other Americans, including, ironically, Bernhard Goetz, did not trust that the legal system was looking out for him. He simply had a different explanation as to why.

In the end, Ramseur was arrested and given a minor charge: filing a false police report. It is not a stretch to conclude that part of the reason prosecutors let him off so easily was that they knew they would need him to testify against Goetz. Another big conviction would have only made that tougher.

The defense, having been given a witness list from the prosecution prior to trial, had plenty of time to brush up on Ramseur's background and criminal record. In addition, they had already observed him once in court and knew he would not be hard to set off. On cross-examination, Slotnick barely questioned Ramseur on some of the inconsistencies and discrepancies in his testimony, and went right to attacking his credibility. It did not take much to get under Ramseur's skin. For example, when confronted with a statement that he had made about the screwdriver in his pocket, Ramseur said that he did not recall saying it. When Slotnick asked to approach him to show the transcript to refresh his recollection, Ramseur refused, suggesting that Slotnick had made the transcript up.

Crane jumped in and attempted to redirect Ramseur. He made the point that Waples would have another opportunity to question Ramseur again after Slotnick, if it made sense for him to further clarify anything that came up during the cross. Crane reminded Ramseur that it was not his role to ask questions back to the attorneys questioning him and that if he did not understand a question, he should just say so. He even went as far as coaching Ramseur a little: "If you can't answer yes or no, tell him you can't answer yes or no. Don't volunteer anything."

Slotnick continued, moving to question Ramseur about a police report connected to the case. Ramseur again refused to look at the report, saying that the police and Slotnick were likely both lying and twisting information on it to trip him up. (Slotnick even tried some reverse psychology, suggesting to Ramseur that if he felt police were lying, he should point to which statements on the report were lies. Ramseur didn't bite.) The exchange continued:

SLOTNICK: If I may ask the Court officer to show Mr. Ramseur these two reports and read the yellow portion, perhaps it can refresh his recollection.

RAMSEUR: I don't want to read no reports.

CRANE: I need you to do that so you can answer the next question. All you have to do is take a look.

RAMSEUR: I don't need to read the reports.

SLOTNICK: Your Honor, I ask you direct the witness to read the reports.

CRANE: I'm directing. Mr. Ramseur, all you have to do is look at the report.

RAMSEUR: I know what happened. I don't—

CRANE: That's not the point of the question. Now, the point of the question is what you told other people and whether you remember what you told other people. One of the things that Mr. Slotnick is entitled to do is refresh your recollection. So please look at the reports and answer his questions. If you have any difficulty reading, Mr. Ramseur, we will have it read to you silently.

RAMSEUR: No, I'm reading it to myself.

CRANE: All right. Mr. Slotnick, we're ready for your question.

SLOTNICK: Does that refresh your recollection?

RAMSEUR: Nope.

Whenever Ramseur's sexual assault conviction came back up, he denied any participation and suggested a grand conspiracy to frame him:

SLOTNICK: Weren't you convicted of robbing from Gladys Richardson on the day that she was raped and sodomized, yes or no?

RAMSEUR: Yes, I was. I never committed the crime.

SLOTNICK: I guess the jury believed that when you were on trial, didn't they, yes or no?

RAMSEUR: I guess they did. They was paid to, one setup.

SLOTNICK: How many jurors were paid?

RAMSEUR: All of them. You probably paying the jurors now.

SLOTNICK [*flashing a wry smile at the jurors*]**:** I pay the jurors?

RAMSEUR: This could be a setup. I don't know. Fuckin know.

SLOTNICK: Mr. Ramseur, have we ever met?

RAMSEUR: No, we have never ever met, but I heard about you.

SLOTNICK: I hope it was nothing unpleasant.

RAMSEUR: It was unpleasant. I know all about you, baby.

Through his testimony, Ramseur rocked and swayed in his seat, appearing to get more and more impatient and frustrated as it went on. The tension between Slotnick and Ramseur became most intense as Slotnick began asking about whether Ramseur had any recollection of where he was and what he was doing on the days leading up to December 22, 1984 (presumably to undermine Ramseur's suggestion that he did not have much recollection of the time leading up to the shooting). At some point, Slotnick elicited that Ramseur was with a girlfriend on December 21. Crane attempted to get Ramseur to clarify his answer:

CRANE: Do you remember, Mr. Ramseur, what you did on December 20th?

RAMSEUR: No.

CRANE: You don't remember?

[*Ramseur nods.*]

CRANE: Your answer then is you don't remember.

SLOTNICK: Didn't you just tell this jury two minutes ago that you remembered what you did the day before?

RAMSEUR: I remember but I'm not going to tell you. It's none of your business.

SLOTNICK: Your Honor?

RAMSEUR: If I did, I'm not going to have to tell you.

SLOTNICK: Your Honor, I don't have to take this abuse, and I ask the Court to intercede.

CRANE: Mr. Ramseur, when a question is asked if there is no objection and it's not sustained, then you must answer, that's your obligation.

RAMSEUR: No.

CRANE: It's something that you promised that you would do when you took the oath.

RAMSEUR: All right.

CRANE: Would you please answer the question, please, to the best of your recollection.

RAMSEUR: What I'm doing with my girlfriend doesn't have nothing to do with this case.

CRANE: He asked only if you remember what you did the day before. He didn't ask what you did the day before.

RAMSEUR: That's none of his business.

CRANE: But do you remember it. That's all he asked.

RAMSEUR: I don't remember the whole day, but I remember some of the day.

CRANE: You remember some of the day?

RAMSEUR: And I refuse to tell him.

James Ramseur had had enough. He repeatedly asked to be taken out of the courtroom, saying at one point, "He's playing games with me. This is a serious case. He playing games. He going to ask about some old bullshit. Take me out of here." He repeatedly conveyed cynicism about fairness in the system not all that different from Goetz's: "I think this all bullshit, they all fuckin together." He went as far as to invite more jail time: "If you are going to get me for contempt, go ahead. I'm in jail for something I didn't do. Time isn't going to hurt me."

It went on for a while. Slotnick gave increasingly preachy pleas to the court ("I would respectfully ask the court to deal with this witness accordingly. How dare he use the language he has used in this courtroom, and I'm sure the District Attorney joins with me, how dare he use and abuse the majesty of this court"). People in the courtroom observed that Crane was desperately "pleading" or "coaxing" Ramseur back into cooperating, if even briefly. Crane noted: "I am not a partisan here; I am a neutral and I'd like to see what is required in this case be done. You are almost finished. You are so close to the end and you are walking at the very finish line. . . . Don't you understand you are almost there?" There was a practical reason for his repeated attempts to breathe life into the questioning. Defendants, under the Sixth Amendment, have a right to confront any witnesses against them. If Crane did not allow the defense an adequate opportunity to question a witness who had been called, he would have to exclude the entire testimony or risk jeopardizing the entire case.

It didn't work. With a smirk on his face, Ramseur eventually went silent, refusing to even nod or shake his head in response to yes or no questions. Crane began holding him in contempt every time he refused to answer. It went on:

SLOTNICK: When was the last time prior to December 22, 1984, that you, together with Darryl Cabey, Troy Canty, and Barry Allen, committed a crime against another human being?

RAMSEUR: When was the last time you got a drug dealer off?

Waples had tried everything to persuade his witness to cooperate, at one point snapping, "James, why don't you shut up?" Eventually, Waples knew that he would have gained nothing from trying to salvage Ramseur's testimony and waived the opportunity to question him again. Crane excused Ramseur, and several armed court officers escorted him back to cellblock 74 on Rikers Island, where he was being housed.

Ramseur left an impression on everyone in the room. After the trial, a juror said that he appeared to be full of "pent-up rage" and that he reminded her of "a caged animal." The *New York Post* ran a large headline about his "ravings." In contrast, Waples describes Ramseur on the stand as "sullen," but not much more than that. "I mean, it was dramatic," he says. "[But] it would be a bit of an overstatement to characterize this confrontation as really high drama."

Justice Crane sentenced Ramseur a few days later to the maximum sentence for contempt: a $1,500 fine and an additional six months in jail. In striking all of Ramseur's testimony, he admonished the jury to disregard everything they had just seen. He further instructed: "You're not to speculate as to why the testimony has been stricken." Still, he knew that even in his best efforts to get the jurors to put a mental block around Ramseur's two times on the stand, the encounters had been devastating to the prosecution. It came through at sentencing, though: In a tone that wavered between pity and anger, Crane told Ramseur that his behavior "had conveyed viciousness and selfishness more effectively than words could. . . . Your conduct has played right into the hands of Mr. Goetz's lawyer. He owes you a vote of thanks. . . . You only have yourself to blame. The jurors saw your contemptuous conduct. That can never be erased from their minds."

Throughout the sentencing, Ramseur, in black leather pants and a black sweater with leather patches, stood silently with his hands clasped in front of him. He still refused to speak or to answer the judge's questions.

It is never good for a jury to see a witness misbehaving on the stand. Jurors take in everything and pass judgment on it all. Still, however recalcitrant he had been in the portions of his testimony that led to his being held in contempt, it was an action that James Ramseur *didn't* actually end up taking that probably did the most to leave jurors with a negative impression of him.

Throughout his testimony, more officers than usual were in the courtroom. As he testified, four armed officers—two on either side—stood behind the witness stand and inched closer and closer to him as the testimony went further and further south. At one point, Ramseur crossed his right leg over his left and bent over and removed his shoe. Slotnick deliberately cowered, giving the impression that Ramseur was about to attack him. Tension in the courtroom immediately tightened as three or four guards quickly moved in and hovered over Ramseur. Both the *Post* and the *Daily News* picked up the incident, leaving open the question of what Ramseur had actually done, or had intended to do, with the shoe. Slotnick, in his daily post-court press conferences some reporters had mockingly dubbed the "five o'clock follies" or the "five o'clock funnies," laid it on thick: "If he had a gun he would have shot me."

In reality, Ramseur likely had no intention of harming anyone. Earlier that day, Ramseur had told a court officer in the elevator on the way to the courtroom that he had a boil on his foot that had been bothering him. This officer was standing next to Ramseur at the time of the incident and later repeatedly stressed that he believed the simplest and least sinister explanation: the man had an itch. At least one juror confirmed this account. It didn't matter. The notion that Ramseur was an unhinged, violent witness was an easy one for jurors to embrace. The mix of Ramseur's own history, a media that was desperate to paint the four as violent predators, and Ramseur's behavior in the courtroom both times he appeared led observers to believe the worst. The jury watched it all, diminishing any chance that they might find anything he said to be trustworthy. The presence of a phalanx of armed officers surrounding him didn't help how he came across either. The jury and public had little incentive to like or trust him, and by his own combative behavior, they were never going to give him the benefit of the doubt.

Slotnick milked the moment as much as he was capable. The next morning, outside of the jury's presence, Slotnick started the day with a florid, minutes-long ode to the courtroom guards who came to his rescue against a witness's viciousness: "[T]o all of the court officers in this building and elsewhere, if I've ever taken you for granted, I deeply apologize for that. . . . [T]he record should indicate the gratitude that I have and I'm sure the court has, and I include my learned adversary. . . ." Waples, appearing bemused by his opponent's slathering of performative melodrama, stifled a smirk.

Three of the four people to have been face-to-face with Bernhard Goetz as he was shooting had testified at trial. In different ways, they all hurt the prosecution far more than they helped it. Without the jury believing or trusting them, the case was probably lost.

However, two years previously in a chilly New Hampshire police station, Goetz had poured his heart out to officers in a meandering hours-long recorded series of confessions. Playing them to the jury was about to be the prosecution's last best hope of salvaging the case.

CHAPTER TWENTY

Ante Up

Goetz was a mystery to the jurors. Though they had heard vivid narratives from the attorneys and witnesses of who he was and wasn't, they had never heard his voice at the trial. Every day, he sat in silence, already there when the jury filed in, remaining after they had gone. He made a flat impression throughout, wearing the same outfit every day—jeans, a plain long-sleeved shirt, sleeves down but unbuttoned—occasionally sipping from a blue thermos cup. Every now and again, there could be some insight into his mind: when he squirmed during the most graphic parts of medical testimony about his victims' injuries or when he burst into a grin when Waples savaged his character during the prosecution's opening. That was about it.

The defense initially considered calling Goetz as a witness. To practice, they called in Benjamin Brafman, one of the city's top defense lawyers and a good friend of Baker's, to review the videotaped confession and then do a mock cross-examination of Goetz.

It didn't go well. Baker joked that Brafman "proceeded to vivisect Goetz in about twenty seconds." Putting defendants on the stand is almost always fraught with peril, and it was clear that Gregory Waples, one of the best lawyers in the city, would have eaten Goetz for lunch.

With his serious demeanor and years of experience questioning witnesses, he would have patiently walked Goetz into traps and confronted him with his past behavior and incriminating statements. Within minutes, Baker knew that "there was no way in God's green earth we were gonna put him on the witness stand."

Allowing Goetz's videotaped confessions was another risky option. Goetz had given several detailed statements after walking into the police station in New Hampshire back on New Year's Eve in 1984. There was one potential issue: Justice Crane could easily find that the statements had been taken improperly and exclude them from court.

If someone is in police custody—not free to leave and in law enforcement's control—and either requests a lawyer or says he doesn't want to speak, any statements he gives in response to police questions are inadmissible. It is a judgment call as to whether someone is in custody at the time he was questioned. When Goetz started speaking to police, he technically had walked in off the street a free man and had not been placed under arrest. However, when he gave the statements, he was inside a police station to confess a crime. As a matter of common sense, Goetz, like most people, would not have felt that he was free to go and could argue that he was in custody. Likewise, it is not always clear whether a statement was voluntary or in response to police questioning. If police were questioning Goetz and he blurted something out unrelated to the questioning, prosecutors could argue that the blurted statement was admissible, even if everything else wasn't.

Statements are not automatically excluded, however. If Goetz's attorneys wanted a statement kept out at trial, they had to specifically object to it. On at least two occasions when questioned in New Hampshire, Goetz said, with full clarity, "I just don't want to speak to you" and "I have nothing to say." Had they tried, Goetz's lawyers could almost certainly have had everything said after that kept out of court. A judge would never have allowed such statements in court in their entirety, at least by the textbook.

Few things in Goetz's trial followed the textbooks.

Behind the scenes, Goetz's lawyers disagreed over how to approach the statements. The cerebral Mark Baker, whom Justice Crane once referred to as "the brains of the outfit," was responsible for the kind of pedantic attention to detail often required of appellate lawyers. His main job was to ensure that the team built an airtight record in the event that Goetz lost at trial and they ended up having to appeal the conviction. That meant making certain that the team did not commit any big legal mistakes, and, more importantly, that they raised a good-faith objection every time something came up in court that might come back to haunt them later. If they didn't object to the statements at trial, the law would forbid them from raising any problems with them for the first time on appeal. The thought of negligently failing to object to something consequential—or, worse, *intentionally* letting something consequential slip by—would probably give most appellate attorneys recurring anxiety dreams.

Still, Baker and the team decided not to object to Goetz's confession video being played in court. Yes, it was a confession, but they felt that Goetz's fury and combativeness would actually help their case. Everything was largely going to come down to one issue: the sincerity of Goetz's fear—a fear many of the jurors could likely relate to. In effect, the defense would follow the same rationale behind some sports' allowing an aggrieved team to decline a penalty; the fact that the rules allow one to benefit from something doesn't mean it's always in their strategic interest to go along with it.

Waples spaced the two confession recordings apart at trial. The audiotape came very early on, after a few police officers took the stand to testify about the basic facts of the crime scene. The courtroom was not designed for a world that was getting more and more technologically sophisticated: it had a constant echo, and witnesses were repeatedly reminded to speak clearly into the microphone on the witness stand. The acoustics were lousy with a spotty sound system. Early in the trial, technicians came in to try to improve it, eventually adding more microphones and speakers.

The quality of the audio recording was poor to begin with. To help the audience make sense of it, jurors got a forty-seven-page handout of the transcript and lightweight headphones attached to a handheld receiver. Jurors had to be sure to keep the antennae on their devices pointed at an amplifier at the front of the courtroom to avoid static. As Waples pressed play, one observer felt a pall cast over the room. "The mood of the courtroom shifted from excited observation to the meditative silence of parishioners absorbing an awesome moment," they said. And in that quiet church, through the crackling and hum characteristic of 1980s analogue recordings, Goetz's voice bellowed for the jurors for the first time. The two-hour recording spanned four thirty-minute cassettes; exactly every half hour a sudden silence would snap into the courtroom, broken only by the recognizable click of a cassette being replaced.

Jurors who were having trouble hearing didn't have much better luck seeing; a thick wood rail built across the front of the jury box obstructed their view. In the twenty-seven years since the court had been built, a generation of jurors had complained about the obstruction, to no avail. Justice Crane directed the court clerk to take care of the issue, and in a day, a team of carpenters came in and lopped off the top eight inches of the railing. One nudge from the judge overseeing New York's biggest case was all it took to slice through years of red tape (and a wood panel).

Waples saved Goetz's confession video until much later in the trial. While words on a page, audio recordings, and tangible items technically have the same evidentiary weight as live testimony, there is no substitute for the ability to watch a human being. Mannerisms, tone, and behavior say far more than words on paper can.

A court clerk wheeled in a large metal cart with a boxy twenty-seven-inch Sony Trinitron monitor perched atop it. The jury also got another transcript, along with the same wireless headphones as previously. With four other monitors set up around the courtroom for the judge, audience, and lawyers, the court dimmed the lights and the show began. ABC News had aired only brief portions of the audio in March 1985, three months after the shooting. Beyond that, the public had never seen the video of an equally tortured and brazen Goetz confessing to the shootings. Over the course of two hours, the courtroom watched Goetz rail about New York City and its legal system as he explained the actions he took on December 22, 1984. As the video played, the jury saw Goetz's exculpatory statement that he felt he "was about to be beaten into a pulp," offset by a growing mountain of incriminating ones: his wanting to gouge Canty's eyes out, his stated desire to commit a "cold-blooded murder," his plain statement that "if I had more bullets, I would have shot them over and over again." As the video played, Goetz remained calm and kept his eyes fixed on the defense table, avoiding looking at the screen.

The lights came back on. There was dead silence in the courtroom.

Despite the "terrible things" that Goetz had said, Baker was still convinced that the confession could work to their advantage. What if they disputed some of the very things their own client had said on tape? They could use Goetz's own confession against the prosecution, by highlighting every instance in which things he said did not match the forensic evidence, and making a broader point that Goetz, after nine days on the run, was out of his mind when he gave the statements.

After the tape played, Slotnick, privately showing a resignation that betrayed the bombast the courtroom saw from him, turned to Baker and said, "We're done." Baker took a different view. "You're crazy," Baker told him. "This is a very sympathetic take. He's showing what he's going through. And he's showing raw emotion."

Slotnick was still so unconvinced that he was willing to make a sizable wager. He said to Baker, “If we get this acquittal, you get a car.”

“A car?” Baker responded.

“A car.”

“You’re on, my friend.”

CHAPTER TWENTY-ONE

Exhibit Y

Judges, like anyone else, are captives of their own backgrounds, experiences, and biases. Also like the rest of us, most judges go to work every day and try to do their best. Spot decisions they make can have generational consequences. By writing a sentence, or by uttering just a few words, they can deprive someone's liberty for their remaining days (or give them a second chance when all seemed impossible). Through no fault of their own, many—particularly at the state and local levels, including New York's criminal courts to this day—are understaffed and overworked, and face daunting backlogs that often lead to justice delayed, if not denied.

Justice Stephen G. Crane was incredibly gracious when interviewed for this book. As we connected the first time, I learned that he was recovering from having Covid-19. He was trying to power through a conversation and apologized as we talked, his eighty-six-year-old voice getting increasingly faint and raspy about twenty minutes in. "I'm losing my voice," he said when it became too much. "I'm enjoying this lovely conversation and am going to have to go," immediately offering to pick up the conversation another time later in the week and expressing regret once again. We got on another Zoom call a few days later, and he was in better spirits, wearing a cozy New York Rangers hoodie, still as warm and candid as he had been when we spoke when he was not feeling well.

From two short conversations, it quickly became evident why those who appeared before him in his courtroom consistently trusted him and praised his manner. Mark Baker called him "the ultimate mensch." One of the jurors wrote after the trial that he found Crane to be "the essence of fairness" and later spoke of the jury's "tremendous respect" for him. Whenever Crane felt that he, too, had crossed the line into getting too personal or disrespectful to the parties, he did something not enough judges (or, for that matter, most people) do: he apologized. He managed to keep the court running smoothly even as tempers flared; one dispute over evidence got so heated that, as Gregory Waples said, "I lost it more than I probably have in a courtroom for perhaps my lifetime." Crane consistently cooled down a simmering courtroom. Ruth Pollack, a sketch artist who covered the case, was so impressed with Crane's demeanor and kindness that she asked him to officiate her wedding years later.

Judges are charged with mediating ongoing disputes between two parties that, at least in theory, are equals. (We can leave for another day the reality that judges often do play favorites.) Judges in criminal cases confront an added reality: most of the rights built into the system exist for the protection of one party, the defendant. Being found to have stepped on a defendant's rights is one of the few ironclad ways to get a righteous prosecution thrown out forever, or an innocent person sent to prison. Gregory Waples, even in praising Crane's smarts and professionalism, had one caveat: Crane would let himself get "worn down" occasionally by Slotnick and Baker, leading him to "cut the baby in half." Waples felt that Crane would sometimes try to give both sides victories where the law did not require him to do so.

Most of the time, unwarranted baby-splitting by judges ends up being meaningless to the outcome of a trial. Whether Crane was too cautious about the need to protect Goetz's legal rights, too worried about being seen as pro-prosecution in a politically thorny case, or simply unaware of his own biases, there were two moments specifically when he allowed the case to spiral out of control. Judges are human. But not all judgment calls are created equal, and these two brought the nonsense surrounding the case squarely inside Crane's courtroom. They could likely have been avoided.

May 29, 1987
AN ABANDONED BROOKLYN-MANHATTAN TRANSIT LINE PLATFORM

Late in the trial, the defense asked Justice Crane to allow a visit to a subway train that had the same look and dimensions of the one in which the shootings had taken place. Slotnick argued in court that the rendering of the car the prosecution had supplied was not sufficient to give jurors a sense of the scene of the crime. The visit to the car was Mark Baker's idea; he wanted the jury to experience the case not just as a generic subway rider (as all the jurors, like most Manhattanites, were), but as the accused, riding alone, surrounded by four frightening individuals in a relatively small space. The defense wanted the jurors to feel afraid. Slotnick said as much, acknowledging that he wanted the jury to understand firsthand what it felt like to be "trapped like a rat."

Waples responded with a practical argument: the trip was unnecessary. He made the point that diagrams and the testimony of dozens of witnesses, coupled with the common sense of twelve people who likely had intimate knowledge of the insides of subway cars, would have been more than sufficient. Slotnick responded that above all else, nothing prohibited the trip. Justice Crane allowed it, under the condition that the attendees remain silent. Attorneys would not be allowed to speak to the jury during the visit, and attendees would only be allowed to communicate wordlessly. Unlike inside the courthouse, the press would be allowed to photograph jurors.

Juries in New York had taken trips to visit subway cars before, however not in more than a decade, and not in any case that had drawn the kind of attention of Goetz's. Because of the rarity, setting up the trip was, according to a spokesman for the New York City Transit Authority, "somewhat involved." With that, the judge, jury, attorneys, and several court personnel went on, as Mark Baker called it, a "class field trip." Goetz would not attend, as according to Slotnick, "he didn't really want to go back into the subway car under these circumstances." He instead left the courthouse that morning through a back door and was met with gleeful chants of "Bernie! Bernie! Bernie!" from nearby construction workers.

In true class trip fashion, everyone loaded into minibuses. They rode a few blocks to the Chambers Street stop of the Brooklyn-Manhattan Transit line (the BMT, which had been merged into the NYC subway system decades before). Beyond the fact that this experience involved walking down several flights of stairs onto a dim platform, the tightly controlled conditions of the excursion differed from the real-life experience of Goetz. Most importantly, the car the transit authority provided for everyone to board was not the same one from the shooting. That car had been stripped down and taken out of commuter service and was now part of a train used to perform maintenance work. IRT cars, like the one from the shooting, were a little narrower than BMT cars, so everyone had to hop over a six-inch gap to get from the platform to the train. The car was oriented in the opposite direction as the one from the shooting. The car was also more congested than the actual one Goetz had ridden in. At the time of the shooting, only about twenty people were in the train car. At the field trip, the combination of jurors, alternates, lawyers, and court staff totaled about thirty. And perhaps the most striking difference between the train in the shooting and the one the jury saw on the field trip was that this train was clean. A transit worker had wiped down the seats and windows with a rag for the special occasion. The experience wasn't all luxury, though; graffiti still covered the car.

The carnival atmosphere surrounding the trip drowned out whatever shreds of seriousness remained of the moment. National media were obsessed with the trial, and the field trip provided a tantalizing opportunity for stories and images far more exciting and evocative than daily courthouse sketches. Several dozen reporters pressed against the windows, watching and popping photos of the group inside. (The encounter was made even more bizarre by the fact that the people inside the human aquarium exhibit were communicating using only hand signals and head gestures.) Somehow, members of the public began to figure out that something big was happening in an abandoned underground train station, and rubberneckers started gathering. One young sleuth yelled from the crowd, "Is this the Goetz car? Is this the Goetz car?"

By about a half hour in, the train experiment was fully off the rails. Onlookers and photographers had begun to make a scene. Crane ordered the train to edge a little bit out of the platform, beyond the public's reach. The excursion eventually finished, and everyone dodged the onlookers and headed out.

Because nothing in the law forbade Crane from allowing jurors to go on a trip to view evidence or a crime scene, Waples did not have much of a basis for objecting to it, and did not. Still, by letting the trip play out as it did, Crane invited yet another spectacle. If there was a chance that media access would jeopardize the integrity of the trial or hurt Goetz's chances of getting a fair one, Crane was free to limit or prohibit it. Such was the case here. A transit authority lieutenant spoke about the "zoo atmosphere" that transpired underground. Afterward, a juror called the moment "circuslike," and commented on the "extremely distracting . . . commotion" outside the train car as Crane was attempting to give them instructions and said that they felt like "fish in an aquarium." As a result of the field trip, several of the jurors were shown on television and in news photos at the scene, leading to their being contacted by friends, family, and colleagues about the case. Justice Crane therefore had to pause the action the next day to call them in, one at a time, to ask each about who contacted them and how, and whether they felt they could still be fair in the case. (All said they could. One merely had gotten a call from his mother to tell him that she thought he looked fat on television.)

The field trip was not even the most bizarre event to take place in the trial, let alone that week.

A fight over ballistic evidence, playing out via the competing testimonies of medical professionals and ballistics experts, was inevitable. The shooting took place on a lurching train car, with a spitfire series of actions across a span of seconds. Widespread panic broke out the moment the first shot was fired, with almost two dozen people screaming and diving through an enclosed space. Plausible theories could have supported that Barry Allen was shot in the back as he was running away or that he exposed his back to Goetz while ducking. But bullet wounds are messy and inconclusive; human flesh often splatters upon contact with an object traveling with the destructive force of a bullet, leaving more questions than answers. Competing theories of the case left open the question of whether Cabey, at the time he was shot, was seated and cowering in fear or standing up. There was even an open question as to whether Goetz's fourth bullet ended up in Cabey's body at all or was just an errant shot that had the good fortune of striking a wall, not a bystander's spine or aorta.

As the public began lining up outside the courtroom that morning, few could have anticipated what was going on inside: Slotnick and his investigator had spent an hour taping a full-scale outline of a subway car on the courtroom's floor. When all entered, they saw a reorganized courtroom, with the jury on one end and the prosecution and defense tables adjusted so the taped silhouette of an R22 train was in full view for all. Crane had the scene introduced into evidence, meaning it would remain in place for the rest of the trial. It was named "Exhibit Y."

Slotnick called Joseph Quirk, a former police officer, to testify as an expert on crime scene re-creation. Slotnick proposed using several props in court to aid in the presentation. He then directed the audience's attention to his props: four large, muscular, tough-looking black teenagers, dressed in jeans and T-shirts. The four, never named in court, were reduced to numbers: Visual 1, Visual 2, Visual 3, and Visual 4. They were all members of the Guardian Angels.

Waples objected. There was no practical reason to have live models stage a reenactment, and even if so, there was no reason court officers could not have played the roles. Assuming that the point of Quirk's testimony was to help the jury see how the parties were positioned on the train, court personnel could have stood in and played anyone they needed to. Slotnick argued that the individuals were properly prepared for what to do in court and that using them would save the court time. Justice Crane, somehow, agreed.

The truth of the matter is that they were not there for their understanding of exit wounds or ability to explain the mechanics of handgun operability. They were there to look scary. Baker, who also takes "full credit" for the episode and calls it a "brilliant idea on [his] part," does not recall whether he or Slotnick specifically asked for the men to be black. He says that it "doesn't seem to be compatible with [his] sense of propriety" to have "stoked the racial issue." He claims he merely told Curtis Sliwa, "Give me the meanest-looking guys you got."*

Sliwa, however, did not hesitate in saying that the casting choice of four black men was deliberate. He also urged them to act their most

*The closest anyone interviewed for the book got to providing insight on the dynamic between Slotnick and Baker on this question was Gillian Coulter, who noted that Baker was "a little more scrupulous" than Slotnick. Slotnick, she said, was more prone to being behind the "stagey stuff" put on at trial. Still, when asked about Sliwa and his role, she paused and landed on, simply, "That's where I felt more racial overtones that I didn't like." (Gillian Coulter, interview by the author, January 29, 2025, by Zoom.)

blatantly thuggish in the courtroom by "mad-dogging" and "eye-fornicating" the jury. When asked in an interview for this book why a ballistics demonstration being put on for the sole purpose of demonstrating bullet trajectories required black models, he was blunt: "Because they were black." He said that the defense wanted the jury to see the "reality" of what Goetz saw. Even when pushed about the highly technical purpose of the testimony, Sliwa did not waver: "This is what people experienced all the time. You know, let's be real. What was the likelihood of four white guys surrounding you and mugging you on the subway?"—a point that, even if true, has no bearing on how fast bullets were going or where they landed.

Slotnick, who had merely claimed in court that there was a resemblance and that the men were "proper heights," initially asked that the four men be allowed to sit in the front row of the court, immediately adjacent to the jury box. Crane refused and directed the men to sit at the back of the courtroom. Slotnick called them down, one at a time, by number, to be placed in the taped-out train car. In a courtroom that had now fallen silent, with jurors standing on their seats to get a clearer view, Slotnick positioned the four men around Frank King, a white investigator playing Goetz in the reenactment.

The four muscular black men in messy street clothes jostled and shoved the white Frank King. It quickly became clear that the defense had succeeded in turning the demonstration into more than expert testimony about how bullets whizzed through the air. The whole episode, while cloaked in a veneer of legitimacy, was put on to stoke the jury members' biases. Waples knew it immediately and echoes the point today. "They were looming, menacing, young black people," he said. "There was no accident about that casting by the defense." The problem for Waples: there was no real way to call it out. Waples, whom the *New York Post* described as "infuriated," did not have many

options for pointing out its racial undertones. Nothing precluded the defense from using black models, however deliberate (or sinister) the choice to do so may have been. In addition, both Justice Crane's caution about race and inevitable performative outrage from the defense made raising it pointless. Without question, the defense would have kicked and screamed, making it sound as if the accusation of racism was a far greater sin than racism itself.

In a bind, Waples resorted to trying to gum up the whole thing. He lodged "dozens" of objections as the odd demonstration played out, repeatedly noting the absurdity of it all. He made clear to the court that there was no scientific legitimacy to the display. He sat on the opposite side of the subway car, such that the Guardian Angels playing Canty and Allen blocked his view of the others. He requested that the Canty and Allen models sit down. This led to a standoff between Waples and Slotnick over whether Waples could just move his seat; Waples refused. Crane ordered the two Guardian Angels to sit down, and Slotnick proceeded with his demonstration, his momentum (and perfectly crafted scene) disrupted.

Crane does not recall what precisely led him to cut off the demonstration. After the court returned from a break, he ordered that court officers would serve as props for the remainder of the demonstration.

Multiple people over the decades have strained to try to explain away the episode's impact. Columbia Law professor George Fletcher, in a comprehensive book about the shooting, noted that there was "no legal warrant" for making the actors black. Even showing some discomfort with the deliberateness of the casting (calling it a "covert message of racial fear"), he, too, took for granted that the specific casting was a deliberate choice that didn't have to be that way. He noted that others, when casting the scene, had been conscious of race. He particularly noted that the television show *20/20* had used four black actors for its reenactment of the shooting. As Fletcher wrote, "If one were recreating the incident on the stage, there is no doubt that one would want to cast young blacks in the roles of Canty, Allen, Ramseur, and Cabey. Authenticity demands no less."

Does it, though? The men's race was but one factor about them, and one irrelevant to the purpose of Quirk's testimony. (Though the musical *Hamilton* and its diverse racial casting would not come for another three decades following the release of Fletcher's book, the notion that theatrical casting need always be race-conscious was not a remarkable one in 1987.) It is impossible to explain why the race of these "props" (or, for that matter, much else about them) was relevant to helping establish the purely technical nature of Quirk's testimony. In a city with seven million people, many of them starving actors who would be thrilled for even a small gig, none of this looks like a mere accident or coincidence.

Moreover, the defense did not work very hard to replicate many other aspects of the shooting besides the races of the four men. Above all else, the demonstration played out in a static, two-dimensional environment. No other outside actors were brought in to replicate the other riders on the train. Frank King looked nothing like Goetz. He had an enormous pot belly and was described in a biography of Slotnick as having "the ruddy face of a drinker, and the seen-it-all eyes of a disgraced big-city detective." All he physically had in common with the bespectacled, runty blond Goetz was his whiteness. Why, then, was such apparent care given to ensuring that the four bodies that appeared in court were black? Regardless of whether many care to admit it, race silently trumps almost everything else, particularly in questions of fear and public safety. According to Sliwa, "Here's a white guy, surrounded. He didn't know their backgrounds. He didn't know that they were thugs, that they had records. He just saw what he saw."

The term "props" was a dehumanizing description to begin with. Framing their casting as being solely based on their "scariness" is only part of the story. At least Curtis Sliwa was honest about the kind of dirty-but-still-within-the-rules game he was playing. In contrast, everyone else around him succumbed to two failings: they either saw the men's scariness as inseparable from their race or, perhaps even worse, were not conscious of what they were doing. Ironically, of all the city's papers, the unabashedly pro-Goetz *New York Post* picked up on the wink-nod racial subtext of the display, noting the races of the participants in its reporting.

It would have been hard not to have picked up on the racial dynamics roiling the city in the spring of 1987. Even five months after Michael Griffith's death in Howard Beach, the aftermath of the incident continued to dominate the news. Sharpton continued to lead protests in the neighborhood, calling out for accountability from police. In an obvious rebuke to the Guardian Angels, he had also formed the Disciples of Justice, yellow-clad patrols of black youths seeking to counteract "the threat of light vigilantism" in the city. Koch, now well into his bumpy third term, continued to be dogged by the city's climate around race—and antagonized by Sharpton and other activists. After Koch and twenty-three black leaders held a summit at City Hall to address "pervasive and systemic" racism in the city, Sharpton—whose influence as a public voice was growing greater and more polarizing by the day—blasted the meeting as a "coon show." Mainstream media coverage often focused on the concerns of white New Yorkers, framing articles around their anxieties about safety, while downplaying similar concerns from the black community.

Justice Crane, while not recalling the precise basis for allowing the demonstration, acknowledges that perhaps the defense was trying to "gild the lily" by using black Guardian Angels instead of white ones. He did make clear, however, that there is always a risk that a defendant can argue that he was prejudiced by not getting something consequential that he asked for. Judges must strike a balance, as Justice Crane did throughout the case. He took heat from all sides of the public for various rulings and even saw his chances of being put on a higher court evaporate (based on anger from his own Democrats) after he dismissed the first Goetz indictment.

Still, allowing the courtroom demonstration to play out at all was a mistake. Judges are gatekeepers, and in this instance, Justice Crane allowed the defense to blow right through the gate in the worst way possible.

CHAPTER TWENTY-TWO

The Champion

Some Time Before the Goetz Trial

THE LAW OFFICES OF SLOTNICK & BAKER

The law firm was several floors up in a gorgeous building at 225 Broadway in Lower Manhattan. From the firm's corner suite, light beamed in from tall windows that on one side faced City Hall and its surrounding park, and on the other overlooked the mud-colored bricks of St. Paul's Chapel, the oldest surviving church building in Manhattan. On a quiet afternoon before the trial had begun, Baker sat at his desk, thumbing through a favorite magazine of his, *The Champion*, a trade publication put out by the National Association of Criminal Defense Lawyers. Its usual fare is articles on arcane legal developments of little interest to anyone beyond the world of geeky criminal defense lawyers.

Baker came across an article about something he had never thought about before: the autonomic nervous system, a network of nerves that handle unconscious functions like a person's heartbeat, breathing, or fight-or-flight response. It focused on a police officer who claimed to have drawn his weapon but had no recollection of emptying it or of even stopping to reload. According to the theory the officer's lawyers had put forward, the officer, experiencing a few-times-in-a-lifetime adrenaline surge, had had somewhat of an out-of-body experience. His body had taken catastrophic actions of which his mind was not aware. Baker closed the magazine.

"Holy smokes, this is Goetz," he recalls saying to himself, realizing he had just come up with a clever theory for how to explain their side of the case to the jury. "If we can prove that the first shot was warranted—even if he shot three more times—this all goes back to the first shot."

June 10, 1987
THE COURTHOUSE

Barry Slotnick was not in top form. His five meandering hours of closing argument left the jurors and his co-counsel so bored that Justice Crane repeatedly called rest breaks. Hoarse with a case of the laryngitis that was going around (and for which Slotnick had worked with a voice coach in order to make it through the closing), he planted seeds of doubt in many aspects of the prosecution's case. Noting that every witness but one had recalled that Goetz had fired a blitz of shots in rapid succession, he undermined a core aspect of the prosecution's case: that Goetz had time to stop, decide where to shoot, and make the statement to Cabey that "you don't look so bad; here's another."

He was merciless in attacking the victims' credibility, identifying Canty as someone "freebasing drugs, who was a thief, who was a criminal, and who was the leader of a group." Perhaps recognizing that Ramseur's testimony was such a disaster that it didn't warrant much more discussion, he simply noted, "You saw the fear and hate and anger that radiated out of him when surrounded by court officers. Can you imagine what he looked like when he surrounded Bernhard Goetz with three of his other friends?" Going after the victims so directly served a few purposes. First, it suggested that they were a four-person street gang, which made them seem more frightening as a group and tapped into pervasive fears about gang violence. It also spoke directly to the central question in the case: Was the scene so terrifying, or a mugging so imminent, that any reasonable person would have opened fire in a moment of horrified desperation?

Slotnick noted discrepancies over how many people had approached Goetz and from what distance. More than anything else, he suggested that the jurors were better served by not thinking of themselves as fact-checkers, but as amateur psychologists. The defense stood the best chance of winning if the jury found themselves trying to divine what was in Bernhard Goetz's mind, not the chamber of his gun.

He wanted the jury to focus on the fact that Goetz was essentially in a trance when he fired the five shots. Taking the microphone from the lectern and pacing around the courtroom, he used Baker's lightbulb moment from *The Champion* to describe the actions of a man with deep psychological wounds: "The mind went off, and the body went into automatic pilot," continuing that the entire episode was far more the result of trauma than any malicious action. Beyond that, though, he suggested that Goetz's confession tape—perhaps Waples's single most valuable piece of evidence—was worthless. According to Slotnick, Goetz was not a fugitive from justice who deliberately evaded authorities for nine days in an attempt to justify a vigilantist philosophy. Instead, he was a man so shaken up after an intense experience that he was "the most unreliable source in the world." As a result, nothing Goetz had said—not even incriminating points that were supported by other witnesses' statements—could be trusted.

June 11, 1987

The next morning at 8:30 a.m., it was Waples's turn. He approached the lectern with a confidence jurors felt they hadn't sensed during his opening. His big job as a prosecutor was to steer the jury away from sideshows and toward cold application of the law to the facts. But he had a problem to overcome: the victims whose injuries he was avenging were unsavory people. On an intellectual level, the members of the jury, regardless of race, class, or gender, probably could connect with Goetz far more than they could with the victims. He addressed the point head-on. With some of the first words in his remarks, he implored:

> The law protects everyone from unlawful violence, regardless of his character. This case, I submit, presents a monumental challenge to this most precious tenet of a free and democratic society.

To rebut Slotnick's argument that Goetz had lost control of his ability to think clearly after a "moment of fear," Waples countered with seventeen points* on which the confession was corroborated by other testimony. Goetz, Waples's argument went, didn't get to have it both ways. Goetz could not plausibly have admitted on the video that he shot someone in the back—a fact supported by ballistic evidence and the testimony of other witnesses—while simultaneously suggesting that he was so confused during his police interview that nothing he said could be trusted. Waples reminded the jury that questions ranging from whether Goetz was standing when he shot to how he escaped from the shooting were all supported by testimony elsewhere.

Waples, like his opponent, was also guilty of trying to have it both ways. He conceded that Goetz may have uttered the "here's another" expression under his breath, or even said it in his own head, before

---

*See George Fletcher, *A Crime of Self-Defense: Bernhard Goetz and the Law on Trial* (University of Chicago Press, 1988), 175, fn. 9, which enumerates the seventeen points in which Goetz's account was corroborated by other testimony, such as who was sitting where when Goetz entered the train; that Troy Canty "asked" Goetz for five dollars; that Barry Allen was running away when shot; that Goetz fired the third shot at someone trying to "climb through the wall," which necessarily would have been Ramseur; and that Goetz fired twice at Cabey.

pulling the trigger the final time. Much of Waples's case hinged on establishing an unbridled viciousness that started with Goetz's being set off by Canty's facial expression and ended in his pausing, looking at Cabey, and articulating that his goal was to kill. Conceding that the "here's another" line may not even have been vocalized was a significant, if not devastating, concession.

Waples, like Slotnick, tried to appeal to the jury's common sense, albeit by inviting them to think like petty criminals. He argued that a key point to Goetz's defense—that he felt he was being robbed—was impractical, as committing a robbery would have been foolish. He argued that Canty, who had made the initial overture to Goetz, knew of the penalties for robbery. He could have stayed on the train for just a few more stops and made it to a video arcade, stumbling into a safer payout. The guys knew that robbery was a felony, carrying with it jail time and hassle that just wasn't worth it. In his closing, Slotnick had pointed out that two of the men had on reversible jackets, suggesting an intent to rip someone off, then try to disguise themselves by appearing to have switched outfits. Waples argued that if they attempted to commit a robbery in a sealed train car, they'd be stuck and surrounded by eyewitnesses. It was a challenging argument to ask a jury to believe; anyone with any knowledge of the New York subway system at the time was aware of the staggering numbers of crimes, including robberies, that still managed to happen there.

Waples referenced a point made by a ballistics expert that Cabey's jacket had two exit holes on one side and two on the other, but with blood surrounding only one hole. Somehow, Cabey's medical examinations had shown only one gunshot wound. (Cue mysterious music.) He introduced a novel argument: while Cabey was standing, the fourth bullet had hit only his jacket and passed through it. Cabey then slumped into the seat, at which point Goetz shot him again with the fifth bullet, wounding him.

Then, as he had rarely done, Gregory Waples got theatrical. He pulled up a chair in front of the jury box and, in a stunning moment, removed his jacket, took out Cabey's filthy, bloodied jacket, and put it on. It was as visceral a moment as the jury had experienced in the trial. Cabey, who had not testified, was now a specter in the courtroom, the stiffened blood from his paralyzed body brought back to life by the man standing before them. Waples demonstrated how Cabey could have first been standing, shot at, fallen into a seat, and then shot a final time and wounded—countering a defense witness's testimony that such an order of events was physically impossible.

In a sidebar, Slotnick went (both literally and figuratively) ballistic. Slotnick fumed that Waples had used the closing to improperly introduce new evidence to which the defense could not respond. (Waples countered that he was merely suggesting an alternate way in which the jury could think about the existing evidence, not trying to sneak new evidence in.) Slotnick repeatedly demanded either the opportunity to call another ballistics expert to rebut Waples's argument or the right to address the jury at least once more about the issue. Crane denied Slotnick's requests for a mistrial and the trial continued.

Despite showing tremendous discipline throughout the trial, Waples committed a grave unforced error at one point in his closing. He began by making a reasonable concession about the teens' behavior, saying that a reasonable person would have been "undoubtedly annoyed" and "intimidated," and also called the behavior "stupid" and "inexcusable." Even if he didn't believe it, the jury almost certainly was thinking it. He said that Goetz "deliberately" chose to sit among a group of "rambunctious young teens." He should have stopped there. But went on:

> If this defendant, simply because he's been mugged by a group of young teens in the past is now so anxious about his own safety, that he's going to perceive every unpleasant encounter such an ominous threat that it must be answered by gunfire and possibly death then I suggest a solution is not for the defen-

> dant to pull out his gun at the mere indication of approaching danger. I suggest a solution for the defendant [is] to pack his bags and go somewhere else where his fragile sensibilities will be least easily assaulted.

Waples had a point; Goetz had stepped onto the train with the brazenness that only an armed person could have. He knew that if trouble came his way, he could neutralize it with a pull of the trigger. Moreover, like any subway rider, he knew that one is always free to get up and move away from something that doesn't smell right. (Indeed, two of the passengers on the car, Loren Michals and Christopher Boucher, testified that they had done exactly that, once they saw how rowdy the young men were being.) This said, Waples's comment was condescending to a group of people who lived in a city with soaring crime rates, several of whom had been victims themselves. Was he suggesting that to avoid the risk of future violent crime, they should all consider moving, too? It smacked of an argument made against political protesters across the country today: *If you don't like it here, just leave*—a cheap shot that thrusts an onus onto a party to remove themselves from a situation beyond their control. One juror muttered, "this guy is insulting my intelligence"; another thought that the implication that New Yorkers ought to either cede their home to criminals or toughen up "alienated everyone" and was "the kind of comment that reinforced the image of the uncaring municipal justice system that Goetz had complained about in the tapes."

Waples noticed at that moment that for the only time in his career, he had jurors laughing at him. He was reminded of when he first saw the jury, thinking that the case might have been a lost cause. Though he acknowledges today that he "could have filtered the thought to the jury a bit more delicately," he does not regret saying it. "If I gave ground by conceding that Goetz was justified or was legitimately afraid . . . I was going to lose the whole case, including the shooting at Darrell Cabey." Pointing to Goetz's choice to seek out frightening situations was all part of Waples's strategy. "Maybe I was right, maybe I was wrong," Waples says. "Maybe it really didn't matter at all in the outcome."

Finally, Waples wove through this closing the notion that with each successive moment, Goetz had less and less of a justification for firing. As the argument went, Goetz's first decision to shoot Canty was itself unreasonable and not based on an actual perceived threat. His subsequent decisions to shoot Allen, Ramseur, then Cabey—twice, including after possibly making a comment to him—became less and less justified. By the time he got to Cabey, he was shooting with a calculated rage, with the full knowledge of the consequences of his actions. According to the prosecution, it was not Goetz's role to act as an executioner meting out justice where he thought the state had failed. "The public at large can believe whatever it wants about this case, whatever conforms to its preconceived attitudes, often forged in ignorance and prejudice, about these shootings," Waples said near the end of his closing. "But you are the jury, folks. You are different."

Over two and a half hours the next morning, Justice Crane read the jury the law it was obligated to follow. And then, at 1:20 p.m. on June 12, 1987, after seven weeks and forty-one witnesses, Bernhard Goetz's fate was in the hands of twelve New Yorkers.

CHAPTER TWENTY-THREE

Sympathy for the Vigilante

June 11, 1987

THE COURTROOM

Although Justice Crane sequestered the jury once closing arguments began, he was aware that a major event might keep them up late that first night and make for a rough morning: Game 5 of the NBA Finals, featuring one of the fiercest rivalries in sports history, the Los Angeles Lakers versus the Boston Celtics. "I need to start you at 9:00 a.m. tomorrow, so get a good night's sleep," he said, in giving them permission to watch. "Don't stay up too late in case that game goes into overtime." (It did not, with the Celtics winning, 123–108.) A rowdy night of watching a big game might have been a distraction, but it was never going to be an escape from the weight of the trial. For the entire time they watched the game, an on-duty officer hovered, ready to pounce and change the channel the moment any news flashed on the screen.

For however many hours, days, or weeks their job would take, the jury would live in a bubble of supervision that kept them from a fascinated public and prying reporters. Every day after they left court, they would be shuttled to a different hotel, usually somewhere out in Queens near one of the airports. They ate dinner at hotel dining rooms with court officers sitting nearby; if they needed to go to the bathroom, an officer would walk with them. Unable to watch most television, several in the group played cards until their 10 p.m. nightly curfew.

Over the months of the trial, the twelve strangers had spent plenty of time in the jury room, having been sent there during the countless side arguments between Slotnick and Waples they were not allowed to hear or see. They spent so much time in the room that they gradually gave it touches of home. Artwork made it onto the walls: a Jamaican tourism poster with a bikini-clad woman on a beach, a Mets poster, and a six- or seven-foot-long dot matrix printout of the judge's admonition not to speak about the case. An alternate juror took charge of the group's coffee and brought a pot from home, collecting cash for supplies. They rigged a trash can basketball hoop at one end of the room and had brought in cards and poker chips as two camps of card players emerged—the poker and fan-tan players. Some of the jurors brought in materials that gave one another small windows into each of their personalities and interests: crossword puzzles, trivia games, issues of *New York* magazine, paperback novels. Two struck up a romance during the trial.

After closing arguments, things were different. The jury room was now the office, not the break room. Cramped and windowless, it had a long seminar table in the middle, its lacquer peeling off. No two of the sixteen chairs around the table matched. There were two tiny bathrooms at the far end of the room. They set up smoking and nonsmoking sections (it was the 1980s, after all). Smokers stayed toward one end of the table, with a large ventilator overhead providing enough circulation to convince the nonsmokers that the smoke in the room wasn't an issue.

The twelve-person mini-civilization had some basic rules. Some were set by the judge: they weren't allowed to discuss the case outside of the jury room and could not consume any news or watch television (beyond preapproved fare such as the NBA Finals or Mets games).

Per New York law, they were not allowed to deliberate on Sundays. A juror would have to raise a hand to be recognized if they wanted to speak, and no one would speak out of turn. There would be no speaking when someone was out of the room. After some debate, they decided to have all of their votes be voice votes, rather than by secret ballot, so they could try to persuade holdouts in one direction or another if need arose.

June 12, 1987
THE JURY ROOM

The easiest charge for the jury to consider was the count for third degree criminal possession of a weapon.* The law defined the crime as being committed by anyone who possesses a loaded gun outside of their home. None of the jurors were swayed by the notion that Goetz's having tried to get a license legitimized his possession. Few reasonable juries could have voted to acquit Goetz on the charge; he had carried the gun, people saw him use it, and he admitted to having done so. With little debate, they found him guilty in about fifteen minutes and moved on.

Next came criminal possession in the fourth degree, based on Goetz's alleged possession of the two guns found in Myra Friedman's apartment on December 30, 1984. It is possible for Goetz to have possessed an object not on his person. The concept is known as constructive possession, or being in control of an item without having it in one's physical custody (the gun you have stashed under the seat of your car is still your gun, even if I borrow the car). A conviction on the count would have been painfully straightforward if the jury had believed the testimony of the dealers who sold Goetz the weapons, Myra Friedman's

*At the time, the crime was defined in N.Y. Penal Law § 265.02 (4), a Class D felony carrying up to seven years in prison. In 2006 the law was repealed and replaced by § 265.03, which made the same offense a Class C felony, carrying up to fifteen years in prison.

account of Goetz coming to her apartment with a package, and the officers who opened the package of guns at Friedman's apartment. One juror said that at the time they started deliberating, she was convinced that the prosecution's case on the charge was "open and shut."

There was a huge wrinkle for the prosecution, though: the jury did not find Myra Friedman credible. They thought that as a writer starving for a break, she had an incentive to craft an elaborate and exciting story, one from which she could make a buck. That she saw a financial incentive to keep talking to Goetz provided a rational explanation for allowing multiple conversations to go on for as long as they did. Her cause was not helped by the fact that after surreptitiously recording her neighbor, she sold her story, through an agent, to *New York* magazine for $4,000. (The magazine ran it as a major cover story on February 18, 1985.)

Jurors also recalled evidence that Goetz had sold guns to others for a profit in the past. Couldn't it have been plausible, they thought, that he had sold two guns to Friedman as well? They weighed considering Friedman an accomplice to the crime but could not find any evidence in the record that corroborated her testimony. (To avoid the risk of accomplices lying to try to convict each other, New York requires that testimony from accomplices be corroborated by other evidence.) Still, buried in the record was an unambiguous statement from Goetz to Friedman that "I have other guns . . . but I can't—I'm not willing to tell you about the other guns because it would jeopardize people who I know are good people." The statement implied that he was likely providing her with guns and that both knew the legal risks associated with his doing so. Add in the fact that her only action after the exchange with Goetz was to contact a lawyer (suggesting that she, too, knew that something was fishy), and the jury could easily have convicted Goetz on the charge. But after a few votes, they decided to acquit.

During his closing argument, Barry Slotnick had given a plain-language explanation of the mystifying reasonable doubt standard:

"People don't get convicted on possibilities." Even with a clear path to convicting Goetz on the charge, both the law's natural pull toward acquitting defendants and the jury's misunderstanding of constructive possession led to Goetz's escaping that conviction.

The next charges the jury considered were the violent crimes at the heart of the case.

Goetz would be guilty of attempted murder in the second degree if he "engaged in conduct which tended to effect" the act of causing the death of a person, without succeeding in finishing the job. New York law at the time would have allowed Goetz to have used deadly force with no duty to retreat if he believed that deadly force was about to have been used against him or that he was about to be the victim of a robbery.* In judging the reasonableness of the actions, a jury could consider the circumstances in the subway car, any relevant knowledge he had about the four teenagers, and any prior experiences—his mugging, perhaps—that could provide a reasonable basis for his believing that deadly force was necessary. As the law now required, the jury had the unenviable job of weighing both the subjective and objective reasonableness of Goetz's behavior.

The jurors quickly agreed that some threat had presented itself to Goetz in the train car. They had little doubt that he was reasonable in believing that whatever Canty had said to him was more than just a polite request for money. They felt that Goetz was reasonable in being on edge, given that crime rates were high. The law didn't require a finding that he *would necessarily* have been mugged, only that *it was a reasonable assumption* that it might have happened. Gillian Coulter, the defense's paralegal, believed that Ramseur's demeanor in court eliminated any ambiguity as to whether Goetz had felt threatened. "[It

*The crimes enumerated at the time that would allow the use of deadly force were kidnapping, forcible rape, and sodomy. See New York Penal Law 35.15 (2)(b).

was] very tough [after that] not to be able to imagine and understand, '[W]ow, this guy's scary,'" she said. "Not hard to imagine that with the four of them around him in the subway car, even without the screwdrivers, even without the words . . . that he could very easily and legitimately feel threatened by that."

Members of the jury were reflexive after the trial in saying that race played no factor in their approach to deliberating. They appear to have never even considered the question of whether Goetz felt he was more likely to be mugged on account of the fact that the four men were black. The defense was not shy about blowing into dog whistles about the four victims' race. In a way, given the broad latitude the law gave the jury to consider factors such as the defendant's and assailants' "physical attributes," "relevant knowledge" the defendant had about the youths, and the "prior experiences" of the defendant, a suggestion by Slotnick that Goetz was afraid of black people might have actually *helped* him under the law. The law requires that a defendant's fear be reasonable, not socially acceptable. Either way, we can never know how the jury might have approached the most damaging bit of evidence available on Goetz's thoughts about black and brown people: his own comment on getting "spics and niggers" out of the neighborhood. Perhaps they would have found a way to explain it away.

Goetz's ethnic slurs were kept out as not relevant to the specific questions at issue at trial. They were hardly the only evidence the jury was not allowed to see for one reason or another. For instance, Cabey had given a number of statements to paramedics and law enforcement soon after the shooting: one that "I don't know why I hung out with the others. They always get into trouble," and another that "Barry Allen went over with Troy Canty and Troy asked for the money," and a third that Cabey was going downtown with Ramseur "for a job." He had also told *New York Daily News* columnist Jimmy Breslin that, as summarized by Justice Crane, "Cabey said he sat down a couple of seats away and wasn't with [the other three], and that they thought he looked like easy bait, he looked like he had money. They asked him for five dollars. They didn't use any screwdrivers and . . . they were going to rob the defendant by just scaring him." All of the statements were considered hearsay, and Justice Crane kept them out.

Another group of statements the judge kept out was a closer call. Arnetha Gilbert, who had been seated in the train's sixth car, was prepared to testify to the men's statements "Miss, I've been shot through the heart and I'm dying" and "He shot me for nothing. I didn't do anything. I only asked for five dollars." Both could have been seen as either "excited utterances"—or statements made by someone in response to a startling event when they are still under the stress of the event—or "dying declarations," defined as statements about the cause or circumstances of one's own death, made by someone who believes he is dying. After debate between the parties, Crane ruled against allowing the statements in. He found that enough time had elapsed between the shooting and the statements that they didn't carry the excitement or shock that would sweep the statements into court as exceptions to the hearsay rule.

The rules of evidence that guide courts are ambiguous. Trial judges must make hundreds of consequential decisions on the spot in tense circumstances, and trials rarely rise or fall over the admission of one statement. Still, "I'm dying" sounds very much like the declaration of a gunshot victim who plausibly believes he is, in fact, dying, even if after a few minutes. All are a reminder that criminal trials are designed to create a limited version of reality, in which facts and statements all must be filtered through narrowly crafted rules designed to protect defendants. A critical statement from a key witness can still end up being worthless in the eyes of the law.

As in any attempt to make sense of the memories of dozens of people, the trial's witnesses left as many questions as they answered: Was Goetz approached by one or several men? Was he surrounded, or did he actually have room to try to flee? Did Ramseur suggest, even casually, that he had a weapon in his pocket? Did Goetz deliberately shoot Allen and Ramseur in the back, or were they just flinching and turning to the side when they saw the gun come out? Was Cabey standing or sitting? Did Goetz actually say the "here's another" line? Were five shots fired in succession, or did Goetz pause before shooting Cabey a second time?

All were fair questions, the sort that a jury ought to sift through in deciding whether a story adds up. In the end, none of them truly mattered. In practice, the case came down to a simple query: Did the jury believe Goetz's confession video? If they did, it would have been hard to justify acquitting him. Questions such as whether Allen was flinching and exposing his back or trying to run away from Goetz are largely irrelevant, given that the defendant was on video saying he intended to murder all four (while making them suffer in the process).

Many jurors, having already agreed that Goetz was justified in shooting at least Canty, if not Canty and Allen, made the case to the others that Goetz's confession could not be trusted, as it had been made in what they called an "adrenal haze." They latched on to a line from the confession video in which Goetz said that the moment extreme violence confronts someone is "like a picture" in their mind. They extrapolated that in his days on the run he had snapshots of the incident frozen in his mind. In an extended reverie, he filled in gaps of what he didn't remember with a vivid and deeply traumatized imagination. One juror suggested that they should extend him grace, given that he was exhausted and under stress after nine days on the run, and was increasingly frustrated after going through his story multiple times to the police. (No juror appears to have commented publicly that they had considered the alternative: that fleeing the police is a crime, that being frustrated at the indignity of speaking to police is no excuse for not being truthful, and that nine days is plenty of time for someone to take a deep breath and get his story straight.) Another commented that she thought they couldn't take Goetz seriously in the video as he was "near hysteria." Another suggested that Goetz's statements about wanting to fire a bullet directly into Cabey's head or gouge out his eyes were just expressions of rage and "emotional turmoil" from his life having been turned upside down. The juror thought that the statements should be discredited partly because they were "[t]he statements of a man who felt that his life was ruined, or at least that his life was irrevocably changed." After debate, they disregarded the testimony of Christopher Boucher, the only witness to have perceived Goetz pausing between the fourth and fifth shots long enough to deliver the "here's another" line. Some thought Boucher testified "in order to get a free trip to New York"; another cooked up a bizarre explanation (which not all others bought) that "he's a gay and gays are a persecuted minority in this country, just like blacks," leading Boucher to have a soft spot for Goetz's victims. Much of the deliberations seemed like expressions of empathy for someone they felt a greater connection to than the people he tried to kill. They didn't say it, but the jury saw themselves in Goetz.

The defense's strategy of using the confession video to their advantage had paid off. Goetz had made multiple extended voluntary statements in which he confessed to several attempted homicides. He had made the statements after being on the run for more than a week from law enforcement officials he knew were pursuing him. In the recordings, he made clear that he wanted to behave in a manner more brutal than a simple handgun would have allowed him to. After all that, members of the jury still somehow felt *sorry* for him. They recognized his eccentricities, using terms like "disturbed" and "quirky" to describe him, but still, in a way, they felt compassion for him. Whether blinded by their own fears from constantly having to look over their shoulder when walking at night or wowed by clever lawyering, the jury's sense of empathy for Goetz won out.

Finally, the jury made a natural mistake in thinking, as nonlawyers, about homicide: they confused, as many people do, the difference between motive and intent. One can intend to kill someone without having a prior (bad) motive for doing so. While Goetz may not have gotten on the train with a motive for killing the men, he made clear that he intended to do it. While a motive can help *explain* why someone pulled a trigger, the only point prosecutors need to prove is that the defendant intended to do it (the fancy legal language is that the defendant had the "conscious aim or objective" to carry out the act). "We needed a motive," one juror said after the trial. "The only motive that Waples presented us was this revenge. And we didn't buy it." Another posed the question, "Where have they proved the intent to murder?" In effect, they made their work more complicated than they needed to. Even without a motive, Goetz quite clearly said that he had intended to kill. The jury could have stopped right there.

They voted to acquit Goetz on all remaining charges. The same reasoning that led them to acquit on all the attempted murder charges also applied to all the assault charges: he was reasonably in fear of his fate, and his confession could not be trusted. To convict for criminal possession of a weapon in the second degree, the jury would have needed to find that Goetz possessed a weapon intending to use it unlawfully against someone else. Waples had argued at trial that Goetz had gotten on the train looking for trouble, and the jury voted to acquit.

Likewise, they acquitted Goetz of reckless endangerment, the charge for his allegedly putting all the others on the train at risk with his shooting. Given that they had already found that Goetz's actions were not unjustified, they couldn't find that they were committed with a disregard of "substantial and unjustifiable risk," as the law would have required. Perhaps the jury could have latched on to Goetz's statement that he opened fire without looking. Such conduct necessarily puts others in an enclosed, crowded space at risk. The jury felt otherwise.

Their work was done. After more than thirty hours of deliberation, they had a verdict. They applauded, shook hands, and embraced one another. Several burst into tears. Their only remaining job was to tell the courtroom, and the rest of America, what they had decided.

June 16, 1987

THE COURTHOUSE

The courthouse was buzzing. Spectators started murmuring about the rumor that the trial was about to come to a close. Any savvy court watcher would have known that any jury that spends a week deliberating probably isn't coming back with convictions and might even be helplessly deadlocked. Still, something unexpected could always happen. Within minutes of the rumor that the jury had reached a verdict, every seat in the courtroom was full.

The jury, putting on a straight face after their small celebration moments before, walked single file into the silent courtroom, neither smiling nor looking at the parties. Despite there never having been a major outburst during the trial, the whole thing had become an exercise in packing more and more officers into the courtroom. Today there were more than a dozen officers stationed around the room, expecting the worst.

The court clerk, Bob Hamkalo, asked if they had reached a verdict. James Hurley, the jury's foreman, said that they had and raised the verdict form. He read off the verdict for criminal possession of a weapon in the third degree: "Guilty." Goetz, wearing a nervous smile, dropped his head, appeared to sigh, and said something to himself. With that verdict, he was probably going to jail. The question was whether it would be for months or decades.

Hamkalo asked whether the jury had reached a verdict on the next charge, for criminal possession of a weapon in the fourth degree (for the Myra Friedman guns). Hurley responded that it had and read off the verdict: "Not guilty." Though it was the least serious charge Goetz faced, Mark Baker immediately knew that he could relax about the rest. While the defense team had not conceded Goetz's guilt on the third degree possession charge, they knew that it was a painfully simple one. By convicting Goetz on a straightforward gun possession charge, but not convicting him on a more legally challenging if less serious one, it was clear that the jury had considered each charge individually rather than convicting him of everything in a broad sweep. It boded well for Goetz's chances of being acquitted of the remaining, far more serious, charges.

Next came a rhythmic dance between Hamkalo and Hurley, a dry call-and-response during which Hamkalo would ask for the jury's decision and Hurley would answer: "Not guilty." The courtroom remained silent until they got to count 7. Hamkalo asked, "With intent to cause the death of Troy Canty, attempted to cause the death of Troy Canty by shooting him with a pistol . . . how do you find the defendant, guilty or not guilty?" Hurley repeated the words: "Not guilty." Loud gasps shot through the courtroom. They faded down to murmurs and came back after count 11, for the attempted assault of Cabey. After two more not guilty verdicts, it was all done. Goetz slumped forward, in apparent relief, onto the defense table. Applause broke out in the courtroom as journalists rushed to begin working the phones and tapping out their first filings on one of the biggest stories of the year.

Mark Baker and Gillian Coulter openly wept. Several court officers did as well. Coulter says that for her, it was a mix of feelings, but primarily relief at knowing that Goetz, someone she had grown to care about, would not see significant jail time. ("*Bernie Goetz* in prison?" she mused with a grimace. "That's not gonna go well.") She described the intensity of the experience on everyone—not just the defense, but Crane, Waples, and particularly the jury—and how it forged a unique bond between them. In the years to come, members of the defense team, court staff, and jurors—but not Gregory Waples—got together a few times to socialize.

I cynically posed the question to Gillian Coulter that if an informal social community eventually formed between jurors, the defense team, and court staff, why wouldn't it be fair to conclude that they all had been rooting for him all along? She had two answers. First, she thought that others didn't find Waples particularly affable, and his conducting the trial in near-total solitude gave off an air of "isolation." Moreover, she felt that at least Ramseur's testimony left an unspoken sense throughout the rest of the trial that virtually everyone in the courtroom was, in a way, united in their empathy for Goetz's fear. After witnessing Ramseur, "[d]oesn't it become immeasurably easier to imagine that Bernie sitting by himself in the subway car surrounded by the four of them . . . probably felt threatened?" she mused. "Do you think that that contributed to everybody being on that side? Yeah, I'm sure it did."

In discharging the jury, Crane told them about all they had missed in the world while avoiding newspapers and TV for months. They had missed President Reagan going to the G-7 Economic Summit in Europe (a trip in which he uttered one of the most famous lines of his presidency, "Mister Gorbachev, tear down this wall!") and a tragic episode in the Persian Gulf in which thirty-seven Navy personnel had been killed. After it all ended, Goetz shook hands with Slotnick and the team's investigator. Goetz, who had not made a public statement since the start of the trial months before, leaned to Baker and asked, "Can I go home now?"

A crowd of about two hundred people, many of them reporters, shouted and shoved outside the courtroom. Protesters held up signs, from "CONGRATULATIONS" to "CRIMINALS WATCH OUT, WE'LL GET YOU" to "GOETZ IS A NAZI." Upon leaving court, Goetz wanted to give a statement "to thank the people of New York for their support" but was concerned about his safety. One woman was injured after being slammed into a parked car by a camera crew; Mark Baker later said that all the jostling in the crowd aggravated a herniated disk in his neck. Goetz and the defense team jumped into Slotnick's limo and they pulled away, with Guardian Angels, court officers, and camera operators trying to sprint alongside it.

Goetz arrived home to, depending on whom you ask, a jubilant street party or robust counterprotest. Those celebrating shared space with protesters holding signs like "GOETZ RACIST MURDERER: We know what time it is!" He had to ask a handyman to remove a giant "WELCOME HOME BERNIE" banner that was hanging on the building and a collection box for his defense fund that his fellow tenants had been keeping in the lobby. Someone had also sent him celebratory helium balloons and a basket of food.

Meanwhile, the jurors, like the Beatles being chased by rabid fans through the streets of London at the beginning of *A Hard Day's Night*, rushed to get away. A mob of reporters sprinted after them as they rode off in a bus. *The New York Times* reported that several of the jurors flashed victory signs with their fingers through the bus's windows as it pulled away.

Like all jurors, they had been selected partly because they were uncontroversial and wouldn't draw any undue attention to the trial. Now, however, they were minor celebrities. A local dry cleaner offered to clean one juror's suit for him, while others approached him on the street just wanting to shake his hand. Freed from the strict prohibitions on speaking to the media, they were allowed, if not eager, to speak out publicly (if not cash in on the hundreds, or thousands, they were being offered for their stories). At least one juror had reporters waiting on the stoop of his apartment when he got home. Justice Crane could not blow up at reporters as he had on the day early in the trial when the jurors' identities became public.

Several did television and print interviews. They largely sought to justify their decisions, with periodic asides about how odd they found Goetz and what they thought of the lawyers' presentations (in general, they thought that Slotnick was mesmerizing and that Waples simply had a harder case to prove). No juror publicly suggested any curiosity about why the lawyers and judge so studiously avoided any talk of race during the trial, or even acknowledged the glaring racial realities of life in 1980s New York City. Instead, they jumped to immediate defensiveness about the issue. One commented that "race or racism was in no way a factor in our deliberations or in our decision" and separately said to a passerby as he was being interviewed, "This isn't a color issue. We all live in the city. There's a law and we have to follow it." Another, when asked about race, said that "we were doing nothing more than what we were charged by the judge to do. We weren't trying to send a message to the public."

A verdict usually isn't just a verdict. In the Goetz case, like in more recent ones involving world-famous defendants like O. J. Simpson and Donald Trump, the public's reaction often went far beyond simply agreeing or disagreeing with how the jury applied fact to law. Since time immemorial, our legal system has been a window into the zeitgeist. Was O.J., even with his Bruno Magli shoes, mansion in Brentwood, and clear evidence of guilt, still the face of a criminal justice system that didn't treat black people fairly? By being prosecuted and convicted was Trump a victim of political persecution, or a lifelong bully and fraud who, for once, didn't get away with it? Few can point to a single evidentiary ruling made by the judge or name a witness who testified in either case, but just about everyone has deeply held opinions about what the cases meant.

Every public leader in America had something to say about the Goetz verdict, and few kept their comments to a simple "I respect the jury's decision." Robert Morgenthau gave the standard prosecutorial line of "I think it was a fair trial. It was fair to the people and it was fair to Mr. Goetz." Still, he acknowledged being thrown off by the fact that some defendants are popular with much of the public. "I underestimated the anger," he said. He clearly understood that the legal system must sometimes bend the knee to politics and public opinion. The Goetz case represented more than a simple application of New York's definition of the term "reasonableness"; it was a Rorschach test about what safety meant in America and who has a right to feel safe in the first place. To much of a public not expert in the particulars of whether Ramseur's statement was an admissible dying declaration or whether Slotnick's statement that witnesses had a "license to lie" twisted the legal definition of transactional immunity, the verdict was clear: the city is unsafe, and perhaps vigilantism could fix it.

Despite having made political arguments about self-defense at trial, Barry Slotnick said in an interview later that the case stood for a "right" to defend oneself against threats. Curtis Sliwa made a similar unequivocal statement after the verdict, "This has sent a message to all decent people that it's OK to fight back." Such statements misstated the meaning of the law and fed into a vigilantism narrative. The case was about an individual's actions, not his rights or entitlement. The law in Goetz's case was clear; it provided for certain circumstances in which deadly force would be justified. It said nothing about a "right" to do anything.

Mayor Koch broadly made the uncontroversial statement that the case was unique and that the verdict did not endorse vigilantism. He called for strengthened gun laws but was noncommittal about whether he would write a letter to Justice Crane advocating for a harsher sentence for Goetz. His comments gave reasonable "trust the system" idealism, stating "there will always be those who say that racism played a role in the decision of the jury. I don't think this is an illustration of racism."

In spite of his optimism, he stepped into a mess a day later by speaking at a gathering of two hundred black ministers at the historic Mother A.M.E. Zion Church in Harlem, home of the oldest black church in New York State. It is not clear whether he had previously had the event scheduled or did so to try to quell possible unrest after the decision. Black leaders from across the city made it clear to Koch that the verdict could lead to more racial tension, if not violence, across New York. Koch's broad messaging fell flat, given the crowd. The event got so tense that Koch had to be rushed out of one of the church's rear entrances rather than pass through the crowd on his way out.

Immediately after the shooting, many black and civil rights leaders' statements coalesced around two broad concepts: that the world would have had a completely different reaction if a black man had shot four white kids, and that the verdict invited open season on black people. Congressman Floyd Flake said immediately after the verdict, "I think that if a black had shot four whites, the cry for the death penalty would have been almost automatic. You won't get that in this situation." Benjamin Hooks, then head of the NAACP, predicted that the acquittal "could well encourage others to take the law into their own hands, acting as both judge and jury." Major Owens, a congressman representing Manhattan, suggested that the reaction from white people who identified with Goetz would be "Yeah, we were right, let's go get 'em."

The civil rights leaders' rhetoric about what might follow was provocative. Even so, the city saw a host of incidents in the years immediately after that reflected some of their worst fears. Two years after the Goetz verdict, Yusuf Hawkins was shot and beaten to death by a baseball bat–wielding white mob for committing the crime of wandering into the wrong neighborhood. The Central Park Five matter came soon after, in which five black and Latino teenagers were accused of brutally assaulting a white jogger in Central Park. The ensuing media and public reaction focused heavily on the races of the victim and alleged perpetrators in calls for severe punishments for the incident (Donald Trump took out full-page newspaper ads calling for the death penalty for the convicted teens). The case proved to be the worst of the system on display as the five served years in prison before being exonerated by DNA and the confession of a convicted rapist and murderer who actually committed the assault. As the aftermath of a racially divisive incident in the city began to die off, the next one would always seem to crop up.

Still, as much as the case crystallized white anxiety, it exposed the conflicted relationship many black people have toward other black people around crime. A *New York Times*/WCBS-TV poll from soon after the shooting found that both black and white people were more afraid of rowdy black teenagers than of white ones. For many black people in New York, multiple things could be true at the same time. One might feel that the young men may have been a genuine nuisance, while still believing that they did not deserve to end up paralyzed or killed. Or that the city may have been historically unsafe but wasn't a modern Wild West, in which whites were free to fire away whenever a black person made them uncomfortable. A black resident may support a particular white vigilante's acquittal, while knowing deep down that, as a black person, the system might treat them differently for having done the same thing. Being black in America is complicated.

People in Claremont Village felt a mix of comfort, fear, sadness, resignation, anger, and confusion around the case. As the verdict came down, a basketball tournament was playing at one of Claremont Village's courts between the Claremont All-Stars and younger residents. Anger was immediately palpable on the sidelines when the news broke. In response, Johnny Hall, the public youth housing director, said to *The New York Times*, "These kids feel hopeless, and already they are carrying weapons to protect themselves. I'm worried about the future."

Joyce Robinson, who had lived there for eighteen years, saw it differently. "Robbery is a big problem up here, where crack is everywhere. When I walk the streets at night, I carry a weapon. If it were me in the same situation as Goetz, I would have shot them too. This is self-preservation, sweetheart."

CHAPTER TWENTY-FOUR

Inmate No. 78900316

October 19, 1987

THE COURTHOUSE

Sentencing day was a stark reminder that the world had far bigger things to worry about than Bernhard Goetz. By the time New York's sun had risen, Asia's financial markets had fallen. Just a few blocks away from the courthouse, panicked Wall Street traders were rushing to sell off whatever they could to whoever would buy it. They knew a cataclysm was coming. They were right. Moments after the New York Stock Exchange's opening bell rang, the Dow Jones Industrial Average was in free fall. It was Black Monday, and by the end of the day, the Dow had lost 508 points in the largest one-day stock market drop in history. The question of whether Bernie Goetz would get prison or probation felt like nothing next to the nearly two trillion dollars the world lost that day. Even though the country was already starting to move on from the shooting, the news of Bernie Goetz's sentencing might have been show-stopping news even the day before. That day, however, it was an afterthought.

Ironically, all the wrangling about witness immunity and the years-long fight over the word "reasonable" that ended up in New York's highest court were largely in vain; Goetz was acquitted on all the charges on which any of that would have mattered. He was being sentenced for only one gun possession charge, which carried a maximum seven-year sentence. Waples argued that in order to both punish Goetz and deter future bad actors, Goetz deserved a "substantial sentence." He said there was a huge disconnect between the "myth" that Goetz was an innocent victim of life in New York and "the sad reality . . . that this defendant is a sick man. . . . Far from being totally harmless, this defendant, in my estimation, is dangerous." Slotnick countered by begging Crane not to "break the heart of the People of the City of New York" by putting Goetz in jail. Slotnick also noted that due to the publicity, Goetz planned on soon moving out of New York.

Any member of the public was allowed to weigh in between the time of the handing down of the verdict and the sentencing with their views about how to punish Goetz. Of the thirty-six letters and legal briefs that came in, only eleven favored putting Goetz behind bars. Crane decided to sentence Goetz to six months in prison, along with a $5,000 fine, four and a half years' probation, two hundred hours of community service with a medical rehabilitation center, and psychiatric counseling with a therapist of his choice. Sentencing has a lower legal bar than trial, and judges often can consider conduct that a defendant was not convicted of so long as it is relevant to the offense for which the defendant is being sentenced. In announcing Goetz's sentence for gun possession, Crane noted Goetz's purchase of guns for others; purchase of a gun while his own criminal case was pending; having pulled guns on people at least twice prior to the subway incident; putting his guns in Myra Friedman's care; and use of a quick-draw holster and ammunition designed to cause maximum physical harm, all as reasons that supported why jail, and not just probation, were appropriate. In effect, all those factors made Goetz's illegal possession of the gun—the crime he was convicted of—seem worse. During Crane's reading of the sentence, a young black man in the courtroom stood up and said, "Excuse me your honor, can he get a mandatory year like I got a mandatory year?" Justice Crane politely told him to sit down. Goetz stared silently at the floor through the hearing.

Under a quirk in the law, Goetz would likely have faced less time under a one-year sentence than under the six-month sentence he received. He would have been required to serve ninety days under a six-month sentence; with a sentence of one year, he would have been required to serve only sixty days. So Goetz's defense team appealed, ironically seeking to get their client the *higher* sentence. Of course, if the public learned one thing through Goetz's legal process, it's that the appeals process takes time. It would not be until late 1988 that New York's appeals courts would issue their final decision overturning the sentence, finding that Crane should have followed the state's gun control law and given Goetz at least a one-year sentence. On January 13, 1989, some five years after the shooting, Goetz came back to court to be sentenced for good.

January 13, 1989

The courtroom was packed for Goetz's second sentencing; twice as many court officers as usual lined the walls, and the court's wooden benches were filled with Guardian Angels. Waples gave a brief, dry argument, asking for a two- to three-year sentence for Goetz. Slotnick, in contrast, laid it on thick. "How much more flesh can this one-sided system beat out of this man's body and soul?" he asked. "Judge, I appeal to your sense of equity, fairness and to all the powers that you possess to unbreak the hearts of the people of New York." Crane then asked Goetz if he had anything to say. Goetz rose.

"This case is really more about the deterioration in society than it is about me," he said, waving his arms, his voice filling the courtroom. He rambled about how Cabey had not shown up in court after shooting someone and how Waples's priorities were misaligned in going after Goetz. He continued: "I believe society needs to be protected from criminals," he said, now lowering his voice in a way that, to those in the courtroom, seemed to mask resentment at the fact that he was being sent away while others were "back on the street." He then started to say something else.

Barry Slotnick cut him off by tugging on his arm. "That's good; that's enough," Slotnick said to Goetz in a stage whisper. Goetz then repeated audibly for the court reporter, "Society needs to be protected from criminals." Slotnick stood up and said, "My client is ready to go to jail."

After considering the same factors as at Goetz's first sentencing and following the appeals court's order, Crane gave Goetz one year in prison. Goetz went off to Rikers Island, where he spent his days in an eighteen-cell protective unit for celebrity inmates. He shared the space with others whose even more heinous crimes had splashed across newsstands far beyond New York. There was Joel Steinberg, who was serving eight and a third to twenty-five years for manslaughter in the rape and killing of six-year-old Lisa Steinberg, whom he and his partner had illegally adopted; Steven Smith, the homeless man who had raped and murdered Kathryn Hinnant, a pathologist who was five months pregnant; and Adrian Lopez, who had savagely beaten and assaulted five-year-old Jessica Cortez.

Goetz spent his days in a windowless nine-by-seven cell (with a toilet, bed, sink, and table), or in an area with tables and chairs just outside the cells. Not many talented engineers spent a lot of time behind bars at Rikers, and the prison took advantage of Inmate 78900316's expertise, making him the first ever to work in the radio shop there. Every morning a corrections captain would escort him to the bus garage, where he would repair broken walkie-talkies and radios. Donald

Cranston, the president of the Correction Officers' Benevolent Association, noted what a bargain Goetz's services were, telling the *New York Daily News*, "He has an expertise in this area, and, frankly, it's good to see the city taking advantage of this bargain—where else could you get a deal like this for 50 cents an hour?" In all, Goetz took home forty-nine dollars for the work.

When Rikers closed for renovations, Goetz was moved to the Brooklyn House of Detention for Men. He was there at the same time as two men who were notorious for high-profile, racially motivated killings in the city: Joseph Fama, the triggerman in the angry mob that had beaten and killed Yusuf Hawkins for wandering into the wrong neighborhood in Bensonhurst, Brooklyn; and Robert Riley, one of the participants in the racial attack in Howard Beach that left Michael Griffith dead.

New York's "good-time" law allowed inmates to get a third of their sentences knocked off if they behaved behind bars. Goetz did, with one exception: he got two extra weeks for refusing to return a disposable razor, claiming that prison officials were giving him used razors that might cause him to get AIDS. His lawyers blamed the extra time as "retribution" for a lawsuit he had filed about the razors. According to Mark Baker, "He got screwed by the court, he got screwed by the parole board, and now he's being screwed by the Correction Department."

As Goetz sat in prison, a pivotal election season was playing out beyond its walls, and 1989 brought the political end of a figure whose fortunes had been tied to the drama of the era more than anyone else's: Mayor Ed Koch. A week before Goetz's release, Koch lost in the city's Democratic primary to David Dinkins, the Manhattan borough president. Dinkins, seeking to be the city's first black mayor, pounced on Koch's declining popularity over his handling of, among other things, crime, safety, and racial tension. Dinkins trounced Koch in black and Latino sections of the city, and cut into the mayor's majorities with white voters. Dinkins went on to win a close race in November over his Republican opponent, U.S. attorney Rudy Giuliani, who had recently left the office to run for mayor.

Eventually, Goetz served his time, and after a little more than eight months, at 12:01 a.m. on September 20, 1989, he quietly left prison through one of its back doors (to avoid reporters). He turned down the city's standard offer of a ride to the nearest subway station and hopped into an idling car. When he got home, he was greeted by a large banner his neighbors had hung over 14th Street: "Criminals Beware: We Are Watching You." He dashed from the car into a door at the back of the building.

And with that, nearly five years after his fateful subway ride, Bernhard Goetz was home. Even with reporters continually staked out at his building, he remained inside.

The isolation would not last for long. In a week, he had to head back to a courtroom, this time in the Bronx, to sit for a deposition. Things were finally moving along in Darrell Cabey's $50 million civil lawsuit against him.

CHAPTER TWENTY-FIVE

Peckerwood

1985

CLAREMONT VILLAGE, THE SOUTH BRONX

Back in 1985, within days of her son's shooting, Shirley Cabey started getting hate mail and death threats. "He won't be breakdancing anymore." "Drop dead." "I hope he rots in hell." "I hope his wheelchair has a flat tire." "Nigger." Fearing the worst, she approached famed civil rights lawyers William Kunstler and Ron Kuby.

Around that time, Darrell Cabey had filed a civil suit against Goetz for shooting Cabey "deliberately, willfully, and with malice." Even though Goetz was acquitted in his criminal trial, it would not be out of the question for a victim to win a civil case based on the same incident. While the central legal question was the same—whether Goetz's actions were appropriate—civil suits do not require that a plaintiff prove his case beyond a reasonable doubt. Rather, civil suits carry the far lower "preponderance of the evidence" standard—essentially, allowing victory if evidence suggests the plaintiff's allegations are more likely true than not. In addition, in a civil case, Goetz would have few of the legal protections that the law requires in criminal trials, starting with the big one: a civil defendant can be called to testify against himself.

At their tiny firm, Kunstler and Kuby pledged to take up "the fight for the poor, the oppressed and the downtrodden" in their representation. The two had worked on many high-profile cases, but perhaps their biggest was representing Yusef Salaam, one of the Central Park Five. Kunstler, however, died in 1995. "There are a lot of things that Bill did not see happen that he was confident would happen before he died," Kuby said. "The most noteworthy of which, as far as I'm concerned, is not the Goetz verdict but the exoneration of the Central Park Five." After his partner's death, Kuby took over the firm's cases. Whether at a courtroom or rally, Kuby struck a presence: huge personality filtered through traces of a midwestern accent, bespectacled and bearded, and a long, graying ponytail he still has not cut since 1989. For years, he sparred daily on talk radio as the liberal foil to his cohost, one Curtis Sliwa.

1996
THE BRONX COUNTY COURTHOUSE

Civil cases often wind their way through the legal system at a pace that appears, to the outside world, frustratingly slow. Cabey's was no exception. It was first put on hold until Goetz finished his criminal trial and all appeals in 1989. Goetz then managed to slow the case further by filing his own $100 million suit against his victims. For years, Goetz represented himself, his sloppy legal filings tapped out on plain white stock with his name and address typed off-center. Representing himself allowed what Kuby describes as "a series of delaying tactics, filing frivolous motions and the like," such as asking for the case to be moved from the Bronx to Manhattan in light of his refusal to ride the subway and inability to afford a cab to court every day.

Noticeably absent was the gold-plated legal representation Goetz had enjoyed through the 1980s. Slotnick and Baker specialized in criminal, not civil, litigation, but more importantly, they saw little good in continuing to represent Goetz. "We took a beating financially on that case," Baker said. Goetz's legal defense fund had only collected $60,000, a fraction of the cost of the decade of litigation Goetz's case consumed. By the time Cabey's case finally made it to trial in 1996,* Goetz had hired new representation: Darnay Hoffman, an attorney who had passed the bar only a year previously. Goetz's case was Hoffman's second trial ever.

It had by then been almost twelve years since the shooting, and the city was almost unrecognizable from the one that had made Goetz a celebrity. By the mid-1990s, the city's crime rate had plummeted to its lowest rate in thirty years. The city had spent much of the 1980s in a spiraling drug-fueled crime wave that left many feeling like a terrifying disaster was waiting for them. While this was no longer the case, the path out of that time had been bumpy. Each of the next series of mayors was a direct repudiation of the man who preceded him, in both style and substance. The city eventually tired of Koch's conservatism and abrasiveness. It turned in 1990 to Dinkins and his softer tone, focus on community policing, and calls for racial unity and inclusivity. That didn't work either, so after only one term, the city turned to the man Dinkins had narrowly beaten four years earlier, Rudy Giuliani. The brash Giuliani rode into office in 1994 with a "tough on crime" platform that resonated with voters concerned with crime and decay. (Giuliani, unlike his predecessors, warmly embraced the Guardian Angels.) It all came at a cost. The era's aggressive policing tactics disproportionately targeted communities of color, leading to

*In 1995 a judge dismissed suits that Canty and Ramseur had filed a decade earlier, for "failure to prosecute," or letting the cases go idle without pursuing them. According to Canty's lawyer Scott Greenfield, it was a deliberate choice to let the case wither. "Troy wanted to get away," Greenfield said. "He realized after the initial idea of, gee whiz, let's [sue Goetz], that this was just not where he wanted to spend the rest of his life." Either way, given the nature of his injuries relative to the others', Cabey's suit was the most likely in the group to be successful. (Scott Greenfield, interview by the author, November 11, 2024, by Zoom.)

allegations of racial profiling. Relationships between law enforcement and many communities around the city were strained throughout much of Giuliani's time in office.

Much looked different in the courtroom as well. In a huge departure from Goetz's criminal case, only a handful of the prospective jurors in Goetz's civil trial had been victims of violent crime. Also, the Bronx's far blacker and browner population yielded Goetz a jury with four black and two Hispanic people on it.

Kuby, from his opening statement, went right after Goetz's use of the terms "spics and niggers." Later in the trial, after calling Goetz to the stand, Kuby stayed on it for thirty minutes. Goetz repeated the terms, apologized, and called their usage "stupid." Still, he went on, attempting to justify the statement, saying, "I didn't want 14th Street to be a dumping ground for the Times Square element."

Over the years, Goetz showed far less ambivalence about the shooting. In a deposition, he had already contradicted the main defense in his criminal trial—that the whole thing took place in a dreamlike state in which he was not aware of what he was doing or saying. His acquittal having emboldened him, Goetz was now unrepentant about having known precisely what he was doing at the time: "I walked directly in front of [Cabey], put the gun in his ribs, and pulled the trigger again with the words, 'You don't look too bad, here's another.'" He admitted to wanting to slaughter the young men, saying, "I was trying to get as many as I could." He admitted to not checking to see whether he was in danger before shooting. He admitted to wanting to see the young men suffer as much as possible. He acknowledged being set off by Canty's facial expression. He spoke favorably about hollow-point bullets. He spoke about his use of marijuana and PCP, and compared the shooting to a drug trip, saying, "I've never experienced anything like it."

Much of what he said was already in the public record from his criminal trial, in his statements in New Hampshire, and in his news interviews afterward. But they had never all been collected in one place and never had come directly out of his mouth in a trial. This time he went even further, using graphic terms to suggest that the men he shot, including the brain-damaged paraplegic slumped in the courtroom with him, were little more than varmints that needed to be exterminated. He had already groused in public that Cabey was not the "mental vegetable" he claimed to be, suggesting that it was all a big hoax to generate sympathy.* Kuby confronted Goetz about a statement that he had made publicly before, arguing that the world would have been better off if their mothers had had abortions rather than giving birth: "I think that would have been a better solution, just like one practices population control with animals."

Kuby asked Goetz if he stood by it. Under oath, with Cabey's mother and grandmother just feet away, Goetz said in a low voice, "It would have been better off than the situation we have now."

Hoffman's closing statement, if anything, attacked Goetz as much as it defended him. He suggested that his client lived in his own world—"Bernie World"—when he shot the four men. In arguing that the four men singled Goetz out because he did not look threatening, he directed the jury to "look at that guy over there. He's a lot of things. He's a nerd, a geek, a peckerwood, a cracker." He suggested that his client had significant credibility issues, admitting, "Bernie has always been his own worst enemy in respect to the truth," "a lot of Bernie's words are damning," and "clearly Mr. Goetz has been having problems with his mouth since the case started." And in addressing Goetz's racial slurs, he made a concession that, while true, it was a

*In 1990, to support his claim, Goetz provided the media with a video of Cabey in a wheelchair at a rehab center, able to name Dinkins, who was to be inaugurated three days later. To get the video, Goetz's paralegal posed as the brother of a man seeking access to the facility and told workers that he wanted to introduce his brother to them. See "Judge Blocks Goetz's Access to Subway Victim," United Press International, May 25, 1990.

disastrous admission to make during a trial, saying that Goetz is "not the first white guy who talked like that."

After only five hours of deliberations, the jury unanimously voted in Cabey's favor, finding the shooting unjustified. They awarded him $18 million for pain and suffering, and $25 million in punitive damages. Kuby wept as the verdict was read.

Almost three decades later, Cabey still has not seen any money. Goetz filed for bankruptcy soon afterward, claiming that years of legal bills and not working had left him broke. In bankruptcy filings, he claimed a $1 million liability for an unfulfilled book contract, $16 million in unpaid lawyers' fees, and the judgment from the Cabey suit. He claimed about $17,000 in assets, made up of some electronics equipment, a $320 wardrobe, $500 in cash, and a pet chinchilla and guinea pig valued together at about $130 in cash.

In many respects, little was different between Goetz's civil and criminal trials. Both cases, stripped of the atmosphere around them, came down to how reasonably Goetz behaved. The NRA was also back, giving Goetz another $20,000 for his legal defense. By now, however, the organization was explicit that their support was predicated on what the case said about the right to self-defense and kept its distance from Bernie's bigotry and antics. "To us, this is a case about his ability as a law-abiding American to defend himself from criminal attack," a representative said. "But it's not a support of Bernie Goetz from A to Z."

Moreover, by the mid-1990s, the public had a fuller picture of Goetz's history on race, with the civil trial focusing heavily on his own statements. Both because of the strict rules that limit the kinds of arguments and evidence that can be brought up in a criminal trial and because of Justice Crane's extreme caution about race coming into the courtroom, race as an issue was noticeably absent from Goetz's first trial. Goetz's second trial was different and became a meditation on racism and its impact on fear. During their initial screening, jurors in the civil case were asked about their attitudes on crime and race, which might have been unthinkable in 1987 (compounded by the fact that Justice Crane had made clear that he would not have allowed it). Several prospective jurors had described their own experiences with casual racism—the taxi drivers who didn't stop, the looks from shopkeepers, the disrespect from court officers even as the jurors showed up for duty. At the trial, Hoffman attempted to explain away Goetz's behavior, suggesting that it was impossible to be racist and live in New York. "New York's a tough place to be a racist," he said, noting that the subway, which Goetz regularly rode, forced people of all races to have to coexist. In Hoffman's framing, for a racist, it would mean that "you're going to be rubbing shoulders every day with a lot of people you don't like." It was a statement that disregarded the reality that American history is replete with instances of racial violence that followed *directly* from people of different backgrounds being forced to rub shoulders. The city faced such incidents regularly. Kuby took a different view, echoing a sentiment that many Americans still struggle to appreciate: racism need not be overt. "Even [former Klansman turned presidential candidate] David Duke denies he's a racist. Come on! We all live in New York."

Bernhard Goetz was, by then, a relic. By the time a brand-new Waterford Crystal ball dropped in Times Square to ring in a new millennium, crime rates were nearing their lowest rates since the 1960s. Twenty-first-century New York, with its gleaming new skyscrapers, housing boom, and ubiquitous Whole Foods supermarkets might have been many things. But *Death Wish* it was not. If anything, the biggest threat New Yorkers felt that they faced were the police themselves. In the early 2000s, New York continued its role as the main character in a national drama about urban safety with the introduction of its aggressive stop-and-frisk program, which involved temporarily detaining, questioning, and at times searching civilians and suspects on the street for weapons and drugs. Between 2003 and 2013, hundreds of thousands of stops were made across the city per year, with the high point being a staggering 685,724 people stopped under the program in 2011. Once again, race was more than a coincidental backdrop to the employment of the aggressive tactic. Some 90 percent of the individuals stopped in 2017 were black or Latino, mostly between the ages of fourteen and twenty-four. The vast majority were found not to have committed any crimes. The cost of being tough on crime in the city, or even making it safer, often amounted to an extended period of shaking down black and brown teenagers.

Even if Bernhard Goetz had not evolved, the world had. And so began the next chapter in his life.

CHAPTER TWENTY-SIX

Saving the Squirrels

By 2000, Goetz had served a prison sentence, had a $43 million judgment hanging over his head, and was moving on in a world that each day viewed him with more skepticism. It became easier to see him for what he was: a not-that-sociable grown man in a cluttered apartment with only the company of a pet chinchilla (an animal he admired partly for its refusal, unlike a needy cat or dog, to give him any affection). "All he wants right now is to fade into the woodwork," Slotnick said right after the criminal trial. "This has been a terrible chapter in his life—he would like to go back to being an anonymous stranger in the streets of New York."

Goetz did not, in fact, attempt to be an anonymous stranger in the streets of New York. The man who had once bemoaned that publicity robbed him of the ability to be "just an innocuous gun-toting honky on the street" repeatedly managed to keep himself in the public eye. "He was no longer the story," Scott Greenfield, Canty's lawyer said. "He thought he was a star. And I don't think he could handle the transition of going from newsworthy to irrelevant." Greenfield said that Goetz would sometimes come to the firm's offices, long after the trial. "Bernie used to come sit in our waiting room," Greenfield said. "We'd go, 'Bernie, we're not going to talk to you.' And he'd just sit there and say, 'I'll wait.' And he would sit there for hours."

Any self-imposed exile ended in spectacular fashion in 2001, when Goetz ran for mayor of New York on the Fusion Party ticket, campaigning for vegetarian food in public schools, jails, and hospitals. He was perplexed that many of his thirteen hundred supporters did not vote for him on the basis of his platform, instead supporting him for the issue for which he will eternally be a poster boy: gun rights. He ran for public advocate (the city's ombudsman) in 2005 on a pro-vegetarian, anti-circumcision platform. "I think eating meat is primitive and barbaric, just like circumcision," he said. "Add that to shallow television, new chemical drugs, and national leadership that can't be trusted, and you have a lot of people who are confused and lost."

His advocacy on behalf of animal rights was not limited to his runs for public office. He has been spotted at animal rights parades and occasionally volunteered with an organization called the VivaVegie Society, dressed up as a sexy female legume (named "Penelo Pea Pod") wearing a sign around his neck that read "Give Peas a Chance," and saying in a high-pitched voice, "I was born in this costume!" and "Don't eat the animals!"

Over time, Goetz also grew committed to the cause of rescuing squirrels from New York's Union Square Park. Sliwa said that when he first went to Goetz's apartment in 1985, he was struck by the squirrels. "I said, oh man, is this guy a nut job? You know, he's got squirrels from the park," Sliwa said. "But I could see the squirrels had been damaged. He's helping to nurture them back." Goetz said at one point that he liked squirrels better than he liked people. A problem: however good a substitute for human companionship wild rodents are, they run afoul of New York building codes, and Goetz eventually faced eviction proceedings from his squalid apartment over them. Goetz's fondness for the animals was widely known to his neighbors, who referred to him as "Squirrel Man." According to court papers, neighbors observed him "washing a wild squirrel in the building's laundry room," with Goetz allegedly explaining that "the squirrel had fleas." A worker commented that Goetz would frequently be seen in the building trying to hide a squirrel, "holding it close to him, tucking it under his arm or shirt. But you can't miss that." Goetz's attorney argued that it was a "comfort animal," protected under the law.

Goetz's most recent known brush with the law came in 2013. On November 1, 2013, a female undercover cop approached him in Union Square and asked if he was selling marijuana. He told her that he was, and he went to his apartment and came back a few minutes later, and she arrested him. Goetz claimed that he wanted to give her the thirty dollars of marijuana for free, but she kept insisting on paying. He railed against what he saw as injustice, saying, "Undercover people are out there looking to make trouble and get arrests." America has evolved on the acceptability of cannabis use, and in an irony layered on top of irony, there are now at least five legal cannabis shops within a few blocks of where Goetz was arrested. Still, Goetz committed a brazen street crime he knew was unlawful at the time and got caught. It was far less an act of vigilantism than one of arrogant, entitled sloppiness.

Irony, however, cuts both ways. Goetz never saw any punishment for the crime on account of something he has complained about for years: bureaucratic incompetence. The case got dismissed as prosecutors had waited too long to bring charges. On the day the charges were dropped, he appeared in court wearing a white T-shirt with the word "VEGETARIAN" in big green letters, under an image of a large nine-leafed marijuana plant.

March 1, 2005

A RADIO STUDIO INSIDE THE STEINWAY BUILDING, 111 WEST 57TH STREET

Some twenty years after the shooting and nearly a decade after Goetz had been slapped with a massive civil judgment that few expect he will

ever pay, Goetz was seated in a cramped XM Satellite Radio studio. He was the guest on *The Opie and Anthony Show*, a shock-jock program that had recently been canceled from terrestrial radio for racking up hundreds of thousands of dollars in FCC fines for segments like "Teen Guess What's in My Pants?," a game in which the hosts asked a seventeen-year-old caller to remove her panties and instructed her to rub the phone against her pubic hair as they broadcast the sounds; one featuring the song "Teen Week," about father-daughter fellatio; and as the final straw, a live broadcast of a blow-by-blow account of a couple allegedly having sex in a vestibule at St. Patrick's Cathedral during mass.

For Goetz's spot, the hosts would prompt him with a question that allowed him to launch into a monologue on any of a range of pet issues: how vegetarianism will save humanity; squirrels; human nature; the Iraq war. As Goetz stayed in character, so did the hosts, regularly interrupting with gunshot sound effects and jokes that ranged from spicy to overtly racist. For example, after one of the hosts was unclear about whether it was four or five people whom Goetz had shot:

> **GOETZ:** It's a group. It doesn't matter how many there are. What you do is, if there's a group, you get as many as you can, as quickly as you can.
>
> **HOST 1:** So Bernie, it was one entity walking up to him . . .
>
> **HOST 2:** . . . because they weren't human to him, in his eyes. Just a mass of black heading toward him. A *big*, black cloud.
>
> **GOETZ** [*undeterred from making his point that humans are the planet's most dangerous animals*]**:** You know what? The most dangerous animal on the planet walks on two legs.
>
> **HOST 1:** Right. And lives above a certain street!
>
> **HOST 2:** And lives above 100th Street, Bernie? [*Hosts cackle.*]

Goetz didn't take the bait and just kept rambling about sociology in the animal kingdom. It was as if, for an hour, two conversations were happening at once: a group of fratboyish pucks giggling as they tried to out-fart joke each other while an affable older man prattled on, neither in on the joke nor reading the room.

Until the mood in that room changed.

Early in the interview, Goetz produced a home-burned CD of wordless ethereal-sounding New Age music for the guys to play. (While it played, Jim Norton, the show's sidekick, described it as "nice music to lay on a table and be jerked off by another man to.") Later in the show, with mics still live, Goetz got up out of his seat to look around for his CD, appearing to get increasingly agitated that he couldn't find it. In response, host Gregg "Opie" Hughes held up a CD that he claimed was Goetz's and began violently smashing it on the table, destroying it. (Hughes had switched out Goetz's actual CD as a prank, one that even if mean-spirited and odd was innocuous.)

Goetz, thinking it was his, lost it. "Well, you motherfucker!" he shouted, jumping up out of his seat and approaching Hughes as the rest of the men in the room howled with laughter. "You're asking for trouble!" All were now out of their seats, with producer Erik Nagel jumping between an agitated Goetz and Hughes to avoid a possible physical confrontation. A cameraman, sensing that something was off, rushed into the studio. Over hysterical hooting, a host shouted, "He's really mad! You pissed off Bernie Goetz! It's getting hot in here!" The goofy chaos cooled down after a few minutes, and everyone got back into their seats. After a pause, Goetz blurted out, "Fuck you! Keep the CD. I won't be here again," and stomped out, over tittering pleas from hosts and producers that he come back. They sent a producer to intercept Goetz as they broadcast the attempts to coax him back to the studio live. In a few minutes he was seated once again, and all were back to the lightness of the interview, almost as if nothing had happened.

The hosts' on-air reactions for a full twenty minutes after Goetz later left the studio were telling. While still in character and never breaking the show's carefree tone, all suggested that something felt off in the moment and that it wasn't all one big schtick. One host joked about how he could barely remember anything that had happened on the show before Goetz "snapped." One macabrely quipped that his mind raced when Goetz immediately reached for his duffel bag, continuing that if Goetz had shot Hughes, the show would "get the best publicity we've ever had." They patched in the building's security guard, who mused that the fifteen-second delay of the broadcast into his office would not have given him enough time to rush to the studio to defuse a serious problem. That led one guest to joke that "Bernie can do a lot of damage [in fifteen seconds]!" They gamed out whether they were all in a position to pounce on the fifty-seven-year-old Goetz if they needed to. They called him an "irate white man," likening him to Michael Douglas's character in *Falling Down*. "That's every thug's worst nightmare," Norton said. "Some bespectacled man with a pistol who gets mad that fucking quickly." Another said, "That guy would use a gun at the drop of a hat."

Though one does not go on a show like *Opie and Anthony* without at some point ending up the butt of the joke, Goetz had done the program four or five times before, and it should have been a layup. It was a friendly enough room and one that didn't challenge him on substance. Still, even if treated with affection and humor, he was not invited on the program as Bernhard H. Goetz, trained engineer, longtime West Village resident, and animal rights activist. He was there to be the beloved (?) cartoon character "Bernie Goetz." In a way, it is hard to know which was the worse way for him to come off: as a loose cannon or as a laughingstock. More importantly, even if they would not admit it, the hosts suggested through their (half-) jokes that on account of Goetz's history, they were taken aback, if not afraid.

The blessing and curse of notoriety is that one can never really shake what made him relevant. Comedian Bill Burr, who was also a guest that day, best summed up a truth: Goetz will never be separable from the man who shot up four teenagers decades ago. "That was great that we really got to see him do his thing," Burr said, almost sounding relieved. "No one gives a shit about him running for office. We want to see [him] snap and go into a murderous rage."

Goetz has had the good fortune of being able to attempt four homicides (though not convicted of attempted murder, he is unapologetic about having tried to kill the four men) only to persevere and go on to become a popular object of quirky bemusement. Coverage of him today focuses heavily on his eccentricities. He should be grateful for that. In contrast, the four men he shot largely went on to outcomes as tragic as they were predictable. Their getting shot only sped up the inevitable.

Troy Canty is the only one of the four to appear to have successfully moved on in a meaningful way. Four months after the shooting, he entered Phoenix Academy, a drug rehabilitation facility in Westchester County, and eventually took vocational training as an automobile mechanic. He got a GED in 1986, and for a time had plans to start cooking school at the Culinary Institute of America. Over the years, he racked up a string of petty offenses, the most recent appearing to be a 1990 conviction for stealing a home pregnancy test from a department store. For that he got a year of probation. He eventually left the city and, drawing on the training he received in vocational school, started a new chapter of his life as a mechanic. In a podcast in 2023, Canty's brother Carl said that the bullet "saved" Troy, giving him a second chance in life, a new purpose. According to Carl, Troy no longer returns to the Bronx or even speaks with the people he grew up with.

Darrell Cabey, forever scarred by the shooting, similarly left the city long ago. For years he spent his weekdays in a Bronx rehabilitation center, his weekends at home watching horror movies. Like Canty, he does not like the idea of spending much time in the city. Still, because of his brain damage, his recollection of the shooting is spotty. When deposed by Goetz in Goetz's civil suit, Cabey said he did not recognize Goetz and did not even know why he was there. Cabey's family declined to be interviewed or make him available for this book.

Barry Allen was in and out of trouble in the years after the case. As Goetz's case was pending, Allen had already been sentenced to prison for one to four years for grand larceny, for which he got out in 1988. In 1989 he was charged with mugging a fifty-eight-year-old diabetic man and making off with fifty-four dollars from him. He spent four years in prison.

He was back again years later. In an interview from prison in 2018—one of the rare instances in which any of the four have spoken out publicly—Allen continued to insist, more than three decades later, that the four had no intention of harming Goetz. "I didn't do nothing to that man," he said, his voice starting to tremble with anger. "I didn't say nothing to this fucking cracker. Or none of them other two, Darrell Cabey . . . James Ramseur didn't say nothing to that man. We was out to rob something. Not *somebody*. Something." According to the New York Department of Corrections, he died in custody in 2021.

James Ramseur also spent many years after Goetz's trial in prison. He was released in 2002 for the gruesome rape, sodomy, and robbery that Barry Slotnick had pushed him about during his short-lived testimony at Goetz's trial. He returned to prison in 2005 on a parole violation, finally getting out for good in 2010.

Soon later he was found dead, fully clothed and in bed in a dingy low-rent highway hotel room in the Bronx. A pill bottle was floating in the toilet, its label scratched off.

The day was December 22, 2011, the twenty-seventh anniversary of the shooting.

PART III

CODA

CHAPTER TWENTY-SEVEN

Plus Ça Change . . .

Within a minute of our getting on the phone on March 1, 2024, Bernhard Goetz set the tone for the rest of our conversation, volunteering: "I think we live a lot in a B.S. society." It was the first of twenty-four times he said "bullshit" or "B.S." in our forty-six minutes together: the bullshit about his case, current New York governor Kathy Hochul's bullshit housing units, bullshit books people have written about the case, the bullshit I've stepped into by writing a book about the case, the bullshit his case exposed—bullshit, bullshit, bullshit, it's all bullshit. With his actions and words, Bernhard Goetz, both then and now, still seems to see himself as the voice of a segment of the public that is mad as hell and not going to take it anymore. It's not "get off my lawn." It's "get out of my way."

When allowed to speak at length, Bernhard Goetz sounds, for lack of a better word, Trumpy. Bouncing around from idea to idea, he saw a kinship between himself and his fellow perpetually aggrieved New Yorker Donald Trump, even if he did not expressly say he supported the president politically. "I had the media turned against me just like the media has turned against Trump," he said. Like the president, Goetz seems sustained by a decades-long sense of grievance. Goetz's is based on a hodgepodge of personal views—that he never got the love he feels he deserved from the media, that leaders have failed to keep the public safe, and that the only thing we have to fear is the black male teenage superpredator itself.

He had the most gripes about the media. He complained that anyone who had a problem with media coverage in the 1980s was stuck, given how few outlets there were. "It's the thing that's comparable today. It was actually worse back then because we didn't . . . have the internet. But today you see ridiculous biased reporting in the media." He felt that in the old days, if a publication was misreporting facts—as he felt was the case with his story—one's only recourse was to go directly to the paper and try to get them to make a correction.

He is broadly onto something but drawing the wrong conclusion. It is true that there were comparatively few media outlets in the 1970s and 1980s, that news consumers had few choices of where and how to consume information, and that a world with more trusted media sources is a good thing. This said, the idea that he was on the wrong side of biased reporting is laughable. The very notion that Goetz was a hero in the mold of Charles Bronson came from, and was turbocharged by, the mainstream media. The public might have been hungry for the narrative, but someone had to keep feeding it to them. Even *The New York Times*, which he criticized as being the least fair to him of New York's papers, ran with the incorrect notion that the teens carried sharpened screwdrivers. That idea was instrumental in shaping the early narrative around what, and who, posed threats on December 22, 1984. There are few undeniable truths to Bernhard Goetz's story. Two are that the media have tremendous power to create heroes and villains, and that they, more than anyone or anything else, created Bernhard Goetz.

Beyond that, he was making the case for one of the most destructive aspects of our culture today: how fragmented we are. He argued that the internet now provides people the ability to tune out the outlets and reporting they find undesirable and seek out many others.

"The most important thing you can do in your life, probably, is to choose who you choose to be associated with, what people," he said. "And you have to be selective. The same applies to the media. I mean, I listen to NPR a lot, just . . . so I understand how people lie." Missing here is that the ability to tune out all critical voices leads to a population that is dug into echo chambers and radicalized, not better informed. Given how on edge the public was in 1985 as it was, we can only imagine how Goetz's story would have played in an age of deepfakes, AI, and misinformation.

When I first emailed Goetz to let him know that I was writing a book about the shooting and was interested in speaking with him, he wrote back barely an hour later (using "B.S." in the first sentence, natch). After agreeing to speak, he ended the email by cryptically attaching an image

of the cover of the October 31, 1982, issue of *The New York Times Magazine.* It featured a portrait of a youthful Mario Cuomo and his Republican opponent for the governor's mansion that year, Lewis Lehrman. In the bottom right corner of the image appeared to be a sticker with the words, scrawled in irregular, crooked, and almost eerie capital letters, "THE MEDIA DEFINES REALITY."

Two days later, after we had agreed to speak, he sent me (unsolicited) the magazine cover again, writing:

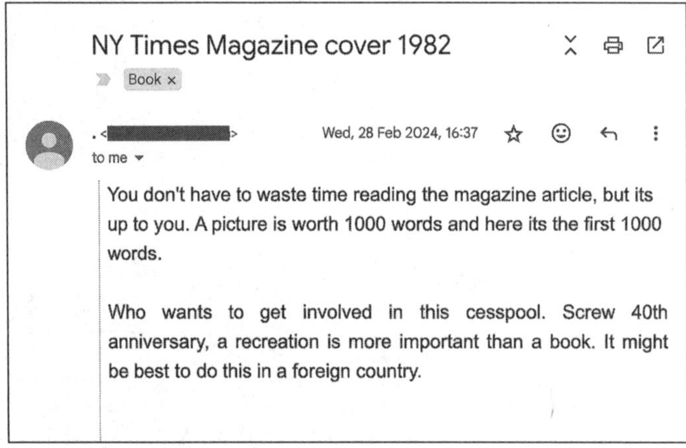

NY Times Magazine cover 1982

Book ×

. <> Wed, 28 Feb 2024, 16:37

to me

You don't have to waste time reading the magazine article, but its up to you. A picture is worth 1000 words and here its the first 1000 words.

Who wants to get involved in this cesspool. Screw 40th anniversary, a recreation is more important than a book. It might be best to do this in a foreign country.

"Recreation" is a reference to a physical re-creation of the shooting (an event he referred to on the phone only as his "incident"), which he was urging me to do. He felt that the media have consistently mischaracterized the story and that no one has ever given an accurate rendering of what happened. Truth, or the absence of it, was a recurring theme in our conversation. At one point on our call, he said that his criminal trial was not a demonstration of reality, laying some of the blame on the single person to whom he probably most owes his freedom: Barry Slotnick.

> You've got two psychos running the criminal trial. You have an attorney who wants to get anybody, his client off in any way he can, and you have a prosecutor who wants to convict someone

> any way they can. . . . Waples has more of an image of integrity, but Waples is even more dishonest than Slotnick. . . . [J]ust like an attorney tries to get their client off basically by misleading, taking out information—you know, whatever, misrepresenting things—you have Waples doing the same thing. A real fucking zoo. [*With that he chuckled.*]

Goetz's email would not be the last time he would bring up Cuomo to me. Like someone transported back to a special place every time he hears an old song—that deep, visceral feeling when a single guitar lick sends someone back to prom or a youthful road trip—something about Mario Cuomo seemed to touch something in Goetz. Cuomo was an enduring figure on the city, state, and national stage across more than two decades, from the 1970s through the 1990s. Goetz seems to see the liberal Cuomo, whose career spanned Goetz's formative years as an adult, as the face of the softness on crime and civic failure that troubled New York through those decades.

Goetz suggested that because of his case, he ended up being a bigger national figure than the governor:

> When Cuomo gave his talk in mid '85 in California, he gave a couple talks about—basically it was part of his presidential campaign—he was laughed at. They didn't boo him, but he was laughed at—my name recognition in California, in America actually, was twice—was above fifty percent and Cuomo was about twenty-five. My name recognition was double Cuomo's,*

*Goetz may have been referring to a Gallup poll from June 1985 about the name recognition of national Democrats, which placed Cuomo at 44 percent. (By comparison, Ted Kennedy and Jesse Jackson were at 91 percent; Joe Biden was at 6.) See Gallup Organization, Gallup Poll #1254G, Question 22, USGALLUP.071185.R1, Gallup Organization (Cornell University, Ithaca, NY: Roper Center for Public Opinion Research, 1985), Survey question, DOI: 10.25940/ROPER-31088107. In contrast, an ABC News/*Washington Post* poll from soon after Goetz was arrested in January 1985 found that 86 percent of respondents had "read or heard anything about the shooting in New York of four young men on the subway by a man (Bernhard Goetz) who said the four were trying to take his money." See

> so when people thought of New York, they didn't think about progressive policies to lift people out of poverty, they thought of Bernie Goetz and urban decay.

All the talk about Cuomo opened the door to an animating point of Goetz's that is also having its moment in American politics today: suspicion of liberal politicians and the media, key groups within a nebulous community now vaguely known as "elites." "[I]t was total bullshit because New York back then, I'm sure you heard the expression, the government and the media worked hand in hand." To many, an unfair press is just the symptom; the disease is collusion among the ruling class. As he described it, the country is run by fat cats in Washington and New York who scratch one another's backs, go to the same parties, and look the other way from each other's corruption. He isn't the only one who feels that way either; the sentiment helps explain why the country has been captivated by the connections between prominent Americans and disgraced financier turned sex offender Jeffrey Epstein. Compounding the public's disgust about Epstein's horrific and predatory acts against minors was the appearance that he existed in a rarefied world of rich and powerful people committed to covering for one another.

To Goetz, Cuomo was the face of a ruling class obsessed with social issues but either oblivious to or uncaring about society's real problems. The speech Goetz referenced on the phone—Cuomo's "A Tale of Two Cities" speech from the 1984 Democratic National Convention in San Francisco—was one of the most famous in modern political history and cemented Cuomo's status as the perpetual Next President of the United States. It focused on lifting up all Americans, regardless of race, creed, or class. However mellifluous and poetic a defense of post–New Deal American liberalism the speech was, Goetz found it, like so

---

ABC News/*Washington Post* National Poll, January 1985, Question 93, USABCWP.181.R47, Chilton Research Services (Cornell University, Ithaca, NY: Roper Center for Public Opinion Research, 1985), Survey question, DOI: 10.25940/ROPER-31086639.

much political rhetoric, to be hollow. (Or bullshit, really.) He saw Cuomo's lofty rhetoric about American values as gaslighting from elites that failed to do the one thing the public wanted (or needed): acknowledge that people felt unsafe. Goetz's decades-long declaration of war is as much directed at four teenagers as it is at fuddy-duddy elites who fail to recognize the public's fears.

If Goetz's reasons for mistrusting those in power sound familiar, they should: the notion has been a thread undergirding American politics for at least a generation, reaching its high point with Donald Trump's second election to the White House in 2024. One of the most devastating campaign ads in recent memory featured a parade of grainy images of transgender inmates over the voice of Vice President Kamala Harris speaking about trans issues. The tagline "Kamala is for 'they/them'; President Trump is for *you*" cleanly captured Goetz's animating principle decades after he became vocal about it. Half a century later, transgender inmates or MS-13 members pouring across the border in caravans can be swapped in for "black crime" and represent largely the same thing: a menace driving public fear that politically correct elites refused to even name. (Bernie was anti-woke before being anti-woke was cool.) This basic perception led, in part, to the remarkable ease with which a billionaire Ivy League nepo baby who resides in a gilded 5th Avenue high-rise could convince millions of working-class Americans for the second time that he was, in fact, one of them.

Goetz also said that his case, along with Sharpton's advocacy, took away Cuomo's "bread-and-butter political issue," which he seemed to regard as playing the "race card" in debates about public safety. Here we go. He explained:

> [T]he city actually was heading in a direction of [the 1981 dystopian film] *Escape from New York*. At the time of my incident, the kind of urban malaise that was spreading in New York and

> it was coming down from Harlem—still, it was still going on in the eighties, the urban decay was expanding at the time of my incident. . . .

I cut him off there, asking what specifically he meant with his view that New York's decay was "coming down from Harlem." His answer was one of many wide-open windows into his views on race, its role in society, and how it affected his case. Multiple times, Goetz, without hesitation, made sweeping claims about the direct nexus between black people and crime. On Harlem:

> [I]n the north part of Central Park, you have the black groups and everything even hanging out in the park at night. By the early eighties, you started having Central Park at night, the upper part of the park would have a significant number of, you know, unemployed blacks and stuff, basically people looking for trouble. By the time the mid-eighties came around, you even had these kids, it was incredible, you would have kids from Harlem in the summertime at 2:00 in the morning, 3 a.m. in the morning, running through the park in groups of thirty, forty. And they would go even to the south side of the park. No one knew how to handle crime back then.

It was the kind of statement cloaked in a vagueness that has given his many apologists over the years—friends, lawyers, jurors who have spoken out publicly—cover to say that he does not harbor racial biases. On its face, he was making points that were harmless enough: groups of youngsters hanging out in a rough Central Park at night were black, and given that Harlem, a predominantly black neighborhood, abuts the park to the north, it is not a stretch to conclude that some of the young people might have been from Harlem. Even so, a pattern emerged in statement after statement: his brand of what his defenders explain away as righteous straight shooting often just seems to be grousing about black people. Or at least his pointing to race but not poverty, class, or any of a host of ills that contribute to what plagues society.

His finger wagging about the dangers black people pose is more concerning when considered along his apparent view that the solution to trouble is more violence rather than social service. He noted in an interview years ago that the teens he shot were "functionally illiterate, even though they were 19½. I saw some of the forms that they had filled out in their handwriting. It was pathetic. They represented the failures of society." It was the closest he came to suggesting that even if the four were responsible for their bad acts, broader social forces helped get them there. That glimmer of grace did not last long, as he continued by saying that the shooting was an overall good in that it forced the city to address crime. It is a striking sentiment, given that a host of factors, starting with city budgets and nationwide attitudes toward crime, affected how cities across the country did so.

Moreover, a teenager ended up brain damaged and paralyzed as a result of the incident. Is Goetz suggesting that he made Darrell Cabey a martyr for the cause of public safety in New York? Whether Goetz was *legally* justified in using lethal force against the four is a discrete question, which a jury resolved. But who is Bernhard Goetz to decide, far beyond the four corners of the decision, that his violent act served some greater good? Surely few who thought the shooting sent an important message stopped to consider its rationality. For the public, Goetz fulfilled an enticing fantasy. And what makes fantasies so delightful is that one need not consider their consequences. It is doubtful that anyone with a "Ride with Bernie: He Goetz 'Em!" bumper sticker thought through what it truly meant to try to kill someone. For the shooting to make sense, we must accept a simple principle: sometimes violent acts will far exceed the threat that precipitated them, and that's OK.

But even if that concept is a basic fact about humanity (or at least American law), it's a terrifying way to live. Even in its barbarism, the

Code of Hammurabi's eye-for-an-eye concept, which says we ought to punish others in a manner commensurate to the harm they caused, makes rational sense. But it gets trickier with our modern conception of self-defense: an eye based on my fear that you might take my eye, even if you weren't planning on doing so. On balance, that looser standard may indeed prevent crimes and make the public safer. It also may lead to a lot of unarmed, harmless people wearing eye patches. We have made our peace with that.

Add it all to Goetz's comment from his civil trial that society would have been better off if Cabey's mother had had an abortion, and a comment he made on NBC that "Society is better off without certain people. . . . Whether one believes that they should be killed or—locked up, or used in forced labor, is just a matter of one's political point of view," and it is clear that Goetz isn't just all in on self-defense. He sounds like an evangelist for eugenics.

None of us were on the train on December 22, 1984, and we should extend Bernhard Goetz at least some grace. Grace, though, can go only so far. I asked him to explain his most obviously racist public statement: "spics and niggers." His response:

> I was smoking pot with angel dust in it that night, and I used a bad choice of words. I should have said "scum" . . . and it was a stupid choice of words. Anyway, what happens is the media grabs on anything, and then they try to say, "Hey, you're a racist," or, "These guys—race—they got shot because of race."

It echoed defenses for the comments he has used before. "I was a bit of a wild guy," "that was about 14th Street. It was a zoo," and "I used a bad choice of words." The explanation was telling for a few reasons. "Scum" has many synonyms. "Spic" and "nigger" are not among them. Still, he pushed back on the notion that the words have vastly different meanings, framing the disagreement as being the result of of my limitation, not his:

> You got to understand. Back then, the building was run by Hispanics and we called them "spics." You know, that was kind of . . . [A]ctually, one of my best friends back then was black, and I don't know if he was murdered or if he died of a heart attack, what the fuck. But anyway, you, you're just not going to get it.

If the issue truly was frustration with undesirable sleazy characters hanging out on the stoop, why the choice of two very specific terms, if he did not see a nexus between black and brown people and crime? Perhaps the weed and angel dust make the comments less, not more, defensible. One could argue that it was through the lowered inhibitions and looser lips of a drug-induced haze that we really learned what was "in his heart."

Moreover, when asked about the statement, he quickly made it the media's fault. Even in acknowledging the "bad choice of words," he pivoted to framing the issue as being whipped up by a "fucking bullshit left-wing media" that fixated on the wrong thing. How, though, is it unreasonable to conclude that someone holds racist views or chose to open fire on people at least partly because of their race, when that person has a history of making racist statements in public? Goetz, like so many others before and after him, seems to confuse whether his own words are his fault or someone else's.

Goetz has done a fair amount of media over the years, often in friendly outlets. He appeared on an episode of *Larry King Live* guest hosted by a comically uncritical Nancy Grace in 2004 and a more critical (but hardly hostile) Stone Phillips on *Dateline: NBC* in 1996. In more recent years, he has shown up here and there, with a nose for finding stories that have a self-defense angle: showing up at the funeral of a slain cabbie, giving his thoughts over the years to Fox News about Kyle Rittenhouse (one of the good guys) and Trayvon Martin (one of the bad ones). He rarely, if ever, seems to have agreed to confront much critical questioning. I noticed that while our conversation was cordial and was even humorous in parts, he only seemed anxious to get off the phone once I asked a few questions about the specifics of his case. No question I asked was all that pointed. When he brought up why the train car in which the shooting happened was empty:

> **GOETZ:** Yeah, so why? Why? If the other cars in the train were full, why was that—I thought maybe there might have been a homeless, stinky person in there or something when I walked in the door. I didn't know. Why do you think that car was empty?
>
> **WILLIAMS:** Well, I think I know your theory for it.
>
> **GOETZ:** Tell me, tell me what you think. Your theory, my theory. Why do you think it was empty? You think it was statistical?
>
> **WILLIAMS:** Well, [*chuckle*] let me characterize what I read in trial testimony and your own statements: it's that the four men were in that car and a number of witnesses testified that they were alarmed by some of the behavior of those men. That is my understanding. . . .
>
> **GOETZ:** Yes, yes. OK. Now, are people stupid? Are people—do you think it's not important for people in that subway train for them to have a seat? Why do you think that car was mostly empty? You think that people in New York are stupid? That they—why were people avoiding the car, plain and simple?
>
> **WILLIAMS:** Again, I can't, I mean . . .
>
> **GOETZ:** Okay. [*chuckle*]
>
> **WILLIAMS:** No, no, no, no. I understand. I understand all of this, but I just . . .
>
> **GOETZ:** No, no, I don't think you do. I don't think you do.

Immediately after that, he told me he had a busy day and needed to get going.

I can't know how he would have responded if I'd given the answer he seems to have wanted: that the car was empty (though, as multiple witnesses testified, it wasn't), because of the four people that, come on, weren't "teenagers" but scary grown men who were menacing the entire train car. As the conversation went on, I was struck that several times afterward, he repeatedly pointed out how little he thought I understood about him and the case, even once saying, "You don't get the picture. You're living in a different world." It echoed a main point he made to Susan Braver, and Myra Friedman, and others along the way who even hinted at having some skepticism about him: you just can't possibly understand. He seemed to see the world as divided into different parts, and he decided within about fifteen minutes of softball questioning that I wasn't part of his.

As the call wound down, I was curious about one big thing: after going to jail for gun possession, did he still carry?

> **GOETZ** [*laughs*]**:** What kind of a question is that?
>
> **WILLIAMS:** Well, it's . . .
>
> **GOETZ:** What kind of a question is that?
>
> **WILLIAMS:** Well, it's a fair one. It's a . . .
>
> **GOETZ** [*chuckling*]**:** Do you still jerk off? Do you still cheat on your taxes?

After some back-and-forth, he continued:

> [P]ut it this way, New York's problems are not going to be solved by legal carry. New York has bigger—[*chuckle*] the legal carry might help an individual . . . problem on the spot. You might eliminate some undesirables, but New York City's problems

> are a lot bigger now than . . . put it this way, for New York City, I don't care anymore what New York City does. The rest of the nation, I'm—New York City is not America. I do not consider New York City part of America.

Hostility toward New York was an odd sentiment to hear from someone who has resided there for half a century. A comment he made to *The New Yorker* after he ran for mayor did something similar: "*Despite the fact that I do not have a love affair with New York City*, I think that New York City does influence the whole world" (emphasis added). He seemed to recognize New York's prominence on the world stage while still resenting it. Decades ago, the jury was alienated by Gregory Waples's comment that if Goetz was so overwhelmed by fear in New York, then he ought "to pack his bags and go somewhere else where his fragile sensibilities will be least easily assaulted."

Waples, however unartful, still might have been onto something. Goetz railed not just about safety, but about any number of aspects of life in the city: the press, the management, the accents, the people. He said that initially people moved down to the West Village "to get the fuck away from the rest of society." Be that as it may, it's been fifty years. The West Village, like the rest of the city, is a vastly different place today and very much a part of the rest of society. Why, then, after life-altering notoriety, and his view that the place is truly so miserable—why not just go?

> Do I think New York City is blowing it right now? Yes. They are making it unlivable, unaffordable for good people here. But New York City still—people want to live here. You don't need—you can do more in New York City not owning a car—and owning a car is a big hassle; you leave New York City, you need a car to function—you can do more in New York City without a car than you can outside of the city with a car. Even though life

> might be more enjoyable and pleasant outside the city now. But anyway, I think New York City is lost.

In short, his hometown might be lost, mismanaged, and unsafe, but at least you don't have to drive. It was an odd leap, but much about Bernhard Goetz is odd.

Still, he does not seem particularly concerned about what others think about him, his eccentricities, or, most importantly, the fact that he nearly killed four people on December 22, 1984. As he told me, "My attitude is, I don't care if people like it or not. People in New York, [and] basically anyone who doesn't like it, can go fuck themselves."

Conclusion

This book ends where it began: in the middle of a once-in-a-generation power outage. Over time, the city has evolved into a place that has little use for a quirky lone wolf patrolling its streets with an unlicensed Smith & Wesson. Nowhere was that more evident than in the city's reaction to its lights going out in 2003.

At around 4 p.m. on August 14, a surge of electricity to western New York and Canada led to widespread power outages across the Northeast and Midwest, triggering the most catastrophic power failure in American history, upending fifty million lives. As lights and refrigerators clicked off, the city sweltered in humid air that felt far more miserable than the day's ninety-one degrees. Natural challenges arose when the power went away: people stuck in skyscraper elevators and subway cars; milk spoiling at bodegas; and at hospitals, long lines of vulnerable people who fought, sometimes in vain, to remain resilient.

The city was still reeling and barely done cleaning up the rubble from the September 11 attacks. But for some reason, this latest frightening disruption triggered far more bemusement than terror. Mayor

Michael Bloomberg hardly called for panic when telling the city that it should treat the day "like a snow day," continuing that "it wouldn't be the worst thing to take the day off." Restaurants rolled their grills outside and held cookouts. Tourists not allowed to go up to the Empire State Building's Observation Deck just took out their cameras and snapped pictures of the building from the ground below. Moments after the Metropolitan Museum of Art went dark, visitors pulled flashlights out of their backpacks and purses to get their final glances at art before heading home.

There were pockets of looting that evening, but nothing close to what transpired in 1977. Soon after the lights went out in 2003, a police officer sat in the 83rd Precinct in Bushwick, the neighborhood probably hit hardest in 1977, watching a scanner with very little activity flickering across it. "So far, so good," the officer said. "Nothing out of the ordinary. It's actually quieter than normal."

The sense of isolation and despair that precipitated the chaos in 1977 was no longer there. Many of the same communities that had been written off as they burned and got looted decades before were back, after years of investment. New housing, some of it affordable, had replaced stretches of burned-out facades. Crime rates that undid Mayors Beame, Koch, and Dinkins were long gone. For all its warts and ongoing challenges around allowing people of all races and income levels to feel safe, the city had figured out how to manage itself. If a rough city thought it needed Bernhard Goetz in 1984, it didn't particularly want him years later.

Mark Baker once said that Bernie was good for just about everyone who had a mission: self-defense advocates, the NRA, Al Sharpton, Rudy Giuliani, New York's newspapers, the Guardian Angels. (The case also worked out well for Baker, who ended up winning a two-tone blue and gray 1987 Isuzu Trooper out of it from Barry Slotnick, following their bet over the wisdom of playing Goetz's confession at trial.*) There is something in that. The case provided something for everybody. "He was a bumper sticker," Gillian Coulter said, looking back. "Some people were like, 'Yay! Woohoo! You're making the subway safe for nerds again!' Other people were like, 'Maniac! It's open season on black youth!' That all was us [more broadly in society]. That wasn't Bernie."

Read a certain way, Goetz's narrative is a compelling hero's saga. He was frail and bullied, a crime victim on whom the government had turned its back. Everyone loves an aggrieved everyman who lashes out and (finally) stands up for himself. Such is the entire appeal of *Death Wish* and so many films like it: they provide a safe outlet for bloodthirsty visions people may have but would never act on. There is something satisfying about watching a wimp who is down on his luck clap back and become the alpha male the good Lord intended him to be.

But it isn't that straightforward. Endorsing Goetz's behavior implicitly means buying that the social order has fallen apart. Put another way, supporting vigilantes means buying that cops need someone to do their job for them. As such, fully getting behind Goetz requires making a few mental leaps. No one saw a mugging happen on the train on December 22, 1984; Goetz may have been right that one was

---

*Mark Baker's good fortune was short-lived. The vehicle was soon stolen off the street and turned up in the South Bronx with its doors missing.

In addition, a month after Goetz's trial, Slotnick had his wrist broken in an attack across from City Hall. While Slotnick asserted that it was just a mugging, according to the *New York Post*, the beating came on orders from a Colombo crime family boss, angry about perceived failures in Slotnick's representation of the organization. The assailants made off with Slotnick's $15,000 Piaget watch.

Decades later, after a long career, Gregory Waples particularly does not enjoy talking about the Goetz case. "I mean, to get ten thousand pieces of hate mail—I got hate mail from New Zealand, from Austria," he says. "My office and the switchboard would be flooded with derisive calls. . . . . I had a listed phone number. It just wasn't a particularly fun case." Despite having worked on countless fraught and high-profile cases, this one took a special toll on him. "And it kind of consumed me for three years, and it just dragged on and on and on. I was extremely happy that it was in the rearview mirror at some point."

Darnay Hoffman had the most tragic outcome of any of the lawyers on the case. After years of struggling with diabetes and his finances, he broke into the home of his ex-wife (Sydney Biddle Barrows, the socialite and escort agency owner dubbed the "Mayflower Madam") and committed suicide by stabbing himself in the heart.

imminent, but by his own admission, none materialized. Without actual evidence of a violent crime, the public's rush to embrace him as a hero was based on either incomplete information or the *hope* that something bad had happened to him. No measure of the city's roughness or the specter of crime coming down from the projects means that these four threatened Goetz that afternoon. Yet somehow, regardless of what they might have done, they became a stand-in for every punk and thug across time who had ever hassled anybody. Many who celebrated Goetz were applauding the fact that he stood up on behalf of all who felt aggrieved, not necessarily for the idea that he was neutralizing a very specific threat. That is not a good thing.

Moreover, no one ever seems to have unqualified praise for Goetz. There is always a "but" or a "however." The National Rifle Association funneled $40,000 to his defense over the years and saw him as central to their political mission. Still, even as its leadership has gotten more radicalized over the decades, it has been measured in how it speaks about him. As Richard Feldman said at the NRA's press conference soon after the shooting, "We're not doing this to support what Bernhard Goetz did. That's for a court to decide. . . . Nevertheless, citizens should be able to defend themselves." One of his attorneys kept distance from his conduct, with the coldly legalistic "I don't make judgments about morality. That's personal. But legality . . . can be objective." Another who devoted much of a closing argument to bashing his own client made clear what a challenge Goetz was to represent: "Sometimes Bernie gives me lemons to work with. I'm in the lemonade business." "Bernie is a nut," said the jury consultant who worked on his criminal trial. "He just jabbered and wouldn't shut up." Even when praising him as a neighbor, others who lived in the building always seemed to have something to say about his oddities. Still, they all projected their feelings and visions about the world onto him. Years after the shooting, a *Newsday* column said it best: "All these years later people still look into Bernie's pasty face—and see whichever Bernie they want to see."

You wouldn't know it, but the country is objectively much safer today than it was in 1984. Most people do not go through their days with aggregated crime statistics in their pockets, and governors and mayors can't calm people by telling them, "Well, when your parents were toddlers, the murder rate was *way* higher." Ron Kuby said that it is all a matter of perception. "There are six subway crimes per day in a system which has 500 stations and carries 3.5 million people and has thousands of trains. Six crimes a day! That's struck-by-lightning kinds of odds." Without ignoring the suffering of any individual crime victims, the general message of the city's and country's overall trend toward being safer isn't sinking in.

In May 2022, New York's Mayor Eric Adams (on a remarkable decades-long journey from Al Sharpton's bodyguard to state senator to Brooklyn borough president to mayor before facing federal bribery and wire fraud charges that were suspiciously dropped by the Trump administration) said he had "never witnessed crime at this level," despite having been an NYPD and New York transit officer in the 1980s and '90s when the city's homicide rate was four times higher. Even the increase in violent crime around the Covid-19 pandemic followed more than two decades of dramatically decreasing crime rates. According to FBI statistics, almost every category of crime decreased from 2023 to 2024.

No matter how safe the streets might be, fear, like sex, sells. The *New York Post* mastered the art of engineering, and then handsomely profiting off of, outrage. It is no surprise that the paper today has the same ownership as the Fox News Channel. One is more likely to turn on their television to see images of pharmacies being looted in Philadelphia and San Francisco than images of children playing in parks that were patrolled by drug lords a decade ago. B-roll of menacing hordes of migrants swarming across the southwest border fails to mention that people who come to the United States to live are more likely to be religious, more likely to get or be married, and, most importantly, less likely to commit crime than native-born Americans. Panic defines an entire medium. A twenty-four-hour news cycle feeds Americans a steady diet of rare, but frightening, incidents that could be around the corner. Even if people are safer now, they may not know it or feel it, and it is in political leaders' interest to embrace that fact rather than fight or deny it.

Still, the more frightened people are, the fuzzier the line between vigilance and vigilantism can get. The crime rates of the 1980s led many in the public to form community organizations and neighborhood patrols. One estimate had that around the time Goetz turned himself in in 1985, ten million Americans were members of twenty thousand neighborhood anti-crime organizations. Local citizen pushes to fight crime were not limited to white suburbs. In Boston that year, callers flooded lines with names, addresses, and even license plate numbers when black clergy urged congregants to report information on drug dealers in the city. "There's no better way of curbing crime than to have citizens looking out for each other," said a Denver police lieutenant at the time. "We can't have a cop on every block." At its core, it is a good thing. The very concept of community policing, which made Benjamin Ward seem so progressive in the 1980s, is based on the unremarkable notions that communities should trust the cops, and that an alert and engaged population is a safer one. It just gets more complicated when people feel empowered to take a next step and stand in for the police.

Perhaps the information age has ripened the conditions for more vigilantism in America today. It is worth asking whether Kyle Rittenhouse, without a social media algorithm that fed him images of Kenosha burning, would have crossed state lines to go keep the peace there. It is undeniable that the Goetz case would have played out very differently in 2026 than in 1984. Above all else, a cellphone video of the encounter would have been inescapable. The only thing Americans enjoy more than feeling safe is putting videos on the internet of other people acting the fool. Any video of the encounter and its aftermath might have resolved for all whether it was an imminent mugging, a menacing threat, or simply just a kid asking politely for five bucks to play video games. Similarly, according to Al Sharpton, "[Jordan Neely] would have been like the Bernhard Goetz case if someone wasn't filming it, and you can see from the video what did and didn't happen. So we'll never know, because there were no iPhones in 1984." George Floyd's death in 2020 is the clearest modern example of the power of in-the-moment videos. Without video taken at the scene, the incident might forever have been relegated to a dusty file cabinet in the Minneapolis police headquarters under the misleading title of its original press release: "Man Dies After Medical Incident During Police Interaction." Likewise, the video of Neely's killing provided valuable context to the jury and public as they tried to make sense of what happened at the scene. Without more, Goetz's entire public was left to speculate, perchance to dream.

Goetz's public got there without the internet. Today the online public square would have emboldened the least defensible aspects of Goetz's vigilantism in a way that no 1980s tabloid ever could. In a fascinating coincidence, on the same day Daniel Penny's verdict came down, a ferocious manhunt was underway uptown for Luigi Mangione, the killer of Brian Thompson, the CEO of UnitedHealthcare. Thompson, who had been in Manhattan for an annual investors' meeting, had recently been gunned down as he stepped out of a hotel. Mangione, a University of Pennsylvania–educated computer engineer who had grown up in an affluent Baltimore suburb and had no criminal record, was found with, among other things, a handwritten manifesto that railed about the American health-care system. The incident unearthed a sickening amount of hatred online: not for the shooter, mind you, but for Thompson. "Thoughts and deductibles to the family" read one of the tamer comments online. "Unfortunately my condolences are out-of-network." It both can be true that an industry is notorious for treating its consumers like chattel and that extrajudicial killing is wrong. But that kind of basic nuance is impossible in a universal forum that, by design, rewards immoderation and fury with more attention. Even accepting that the failures of the health-care system can bring deadly consequences, no moral response involves cheering a delusional, self-appointed executioner who left a father of two bleeding to death on a sidewalk from bullet holes in his back. It is hard to imagine anyone—even those furious with their family's health coverage—making the same comments to Thompson's family. In our world, it is the acts of street justice, not compassion, that go viral. The bloodthirst is too delicious to not celebrate (from behind the comfort of a laptop, at least). Somehow, even as we have evolved, the internet has made us more a vigilante nation than we were in 1984.

Meanwhile, a number of factors in the world today might have made it tougher to pick a jury prone to acquitting Goetz. Even if the "racial reckoning" of 2020 following Floyd's death was short-lived (and sparked a backlash), society today has a different relationship to race in the criminal justice system than it did in the 1980s. In 1984 Benjamin Ward might have been seen as almost radical in supporting community policing or being candid about the complexities around being a black man in law enforcement. Today he would be in the mainstream among police chiefs in most liberal, if not politically split, cities. Juries reflect the environment from which they come. Although America still has far to go in its relationship with race, racial awareness is in the water in ways it wasn't decades ago. Moreover, society overall is more willing today to try to understand people, their backgrounds, their motivations, and their behaviors. Today Goetz's victims would not have been reduced to caricatures; Goetz's oddities would have been regarded with concern, not eye rolls.

Also, the improved public safety climate would likely work to Goetz's disadvantage. A central question in Goetz's case, as now enshrined in New York law, is whether someone's actions were objectively reasonable. New York's trains today would look like spaceships from another dimension to someone from the past: well lit, shiny, open, not covered in filth, the voice of a transgender woman announcing arrivals over the loudspeaker. Crimes happen but not nearly at the same rate as a half century ago. Someone opening fire in one, even if justified, would feel and look out of place—less "reasonable," rather—in a way he might not have in 1984. It would almost be gauche to bust caps off in the New York subway today. You might accidentally damage an LED real-time tracking map.

It is possible that Goetz's acquittal on violent crime charges was legally defensible but not just; supported by law but not morality. Even if we agree that Goetz's fear was sincere, what was the proper outcome? Barry Slotnick's suggestion that the shooting was an overall good for society misses the point; it suggests that Goetz's victims got what they deserved, and that one teenager's brain damage is worth society's contentment. In a way, the manner in which society is quick to conflate legal and moral judgments can be cruel. We allow people to kill or maim each other in the face of fuzzy threats. Even stipulating that Goetz's four victims said or did something menacing to him, what ought the punishment have been? The NYPD's Jim Levison thought that "[t]hey weren't muggers. They . . . might have been little jerkoffs and shakedown artists, but they weren't muggers." Even if they *were* muggers, it defies logic to match the punishment to the action. If the argument supporting or minimizing Cabey's paralysis was that it sent a message to others who might do the same, it is arbitrary and cruel. If it is that violent force is fine because—full stop—the law allowed it, it is reductive. Even considering the most damaging evidence in the case's record—that Canty demanded money from Goetz—it is hard to square that the aftermath was worth it. Perhaps part of life in America, with its ready access to guns and vague standards as to when self-defense is appropriate, is accepting that in order to make an omelet, sometimes you have to end up leaving a teenager wearing a colostomy bag for the rest of his life.

The law supported Goetz's acquittal. The jury appeared to do the best they could and handled the case professionally. Even in their biases, their hands were tied; they were interpreting laws that reflected policy choices made by lawmakers and interpreted by courts. Still, juries' decisions are reflections into the values of victims' and perpetrators' lives. While the trial of Derek Chauvin for murdering George Floyd revolved around the arcana of Minnesota's homicide statutes, the case, for the public, came down to bigger questions: How does society weigh the value of black victims? Can police be held accountable for stepping outside the law? Are there biases we all hold, of which we might not immediately be aware?

We can embrace Goetz's acquittal as an example of the system working but need not stop there. The fact that a legal outcome is supportable and sound isn't everything. Society's notion of what kinds of behavior it finds repugnant evolves over time. For instance, deep into the twentieth century it was still often against the law for women to wear pants in public, and America has been going to outer space longer than its courts have universally allowed interracial marriage. The legal system may have spoken in a case, but that may not necessarily be the final word. It falls to all of us as engaged members of the public to ensure that our laws and systems best serve an evolving society.

Also, conviction or acquittal at trial is but one metric, relevant only to whether a person ought to go to jail. It does not speak to anything else about a person or how society should regard them. America affords accused defendants the presumption of innocence and their absolute freedom if they are acquitted. That does not mean that society can't still judge someone's behavior. (Presumption of innocence aside, most people would not allow someone who had been charged with, but not convicted of, a sexual offense to babysit their children.) Legal decisions are not the same as moral ones, and some acts, and maybe even some people, are repugnant. Everyone is free to make their own moral judgments about others, as Bernhard Goetz certainly did. Perhaps history will do the same of him.

ACKNOWLEDGMENTS

In addition to the 95,720 words that make up this book, a few more: of thanks, for several people who made this all possible.

None of this would have happened without the years of support of my agents at WME, Bradley Singer and Howard Yoon. Howard gets a special prize for asking me at lunch on July 24, 2023, "Have you ever considered writing about history?" I hadn't, and the question kick-started my realization that the Goetz story has been bouncing around in my head for forty years. And now here we are.

I am grateful to Anne Godoff and Scott Moyers and the team at Penguin Press for seeing promise both in this story and in me as a writer. However, a special word about the editor of this book, Casey Denis. Casey was the sculptor who found the book that was hiding inside whatever mess I sent her. She also was masterful at emancipating me from my beloved parentheticals (though, come on, they come in handy sometimes!), helping me bridge the gap between writing a book report and telling a story, and most importantly insisting that I cut a two-page-long explanation of criminal intent that involved a detailed unpacking of the lyrics to Bob Marley's "I Shot the Sheriff." (It seemed brilliant when I wrote it one night at 1 a.m., but in retrospect, it would have put any reader to sleep long before they got to this acknowledgements section. And see: without Casey's edits, another parenthetical!)

No single person is more responsible for the completion of this book than my researcher, Will DiGravio. I remain mystified at the geeky joy Will finds in tracking down things like half-century-old newspaper ads. I also don't know many late-millennial-early-Gen-Z people who proudly possess working VCRs, so perhaps this all checks out. Finally, while *Five Bullets* is the final product we produced, the truest work of art is one no one will ever see: Will's meticulous multipage, tabbed spreadsheet that included hyperlinks, by decade, to perfectly cited and cleanly scanned versions of every one of the hundreds of sources that were the basis of this book. He brought order to the chaos of a challenging work of research while being a never-ending delight to be around.

Because of the far-from-normal world I am somehow blessed enough to inhabit, I am surrounded by a community of extremely successful writers, many of whom provided me with insights small and large about their own processes for getting books out. Particular thanks to Preet Bharara, Jonathan Capehart, Laura Coates, Garrett Graff, Maggie Haberman, Elie Honig, Scott Jennings, Alencia Johnson, Kate Marsh, Andy McCabe, Elie Mystal, Evan Osnos, Jim Sciutto, Bakari Sellers, Jake Tapper, Brad Todd, and Juanita Tolliver for their bits of wisdom along the way.

However, Devlin Barrett provided the most useful nugget of all: the best insights will come from friends who know nothing about your book and are kind enough to read early drafts. Thank you to Jason Cooper, Kristen Soltis Anderson, Jeremy Paris, Dan Swanson, and Alessia Viscusi (following her stellar work as an intern on the book) for providing unvarnished thoughts as nothing more than a favor to me. They made everything I did better, and without Devlin's remarkable advice, I would never have sought their help.

Danny Grooms never read a complete draft of the book—he wouldn't have been able to resist line editing it, which would have made me want to throttle him—but for nearly a quarter century he has been an amazing friend and sounding board for me on everything else. I couldn't have made it without his insight and suggestions on countless portions of this book.

Thank you to Robert Raben, Joanne Irby, Donald Walker, and my former colleagues at The Raben Group for their support in the early days of this project.

Joyce Carol Oates has said that disruptions and interruptions are the great enemy of writing. She is right, and I owe the world to two institutions that exist for a simple purpose: providing comfortable, distraction-free space to writers. I made tremendous writing progress at the Barn at Boyd's Mills in the Poconos. It is simply a magical place, and I would urge anyone who writes (or just needs some time to think while being fed spectacularly) to spend time there. Thank you to George Brown and the Highlights Foundation for founding and curating it. Thank you also to Donna Hemans who created and manages the DC Writers Room, a perfect coworking space close to home.

The staff at the New York Municipal Archives was a joy to work with and made it painfully easy to access and handle decades-old materials.

Also, a word of thanks to the staff at the Chevy Chase MedStar Health urgent care clinic for putting me back together after I fractured my right index finger (!) by slamming it in a car door (!!) about thirty-six hours before I needed to finalize and submit the completed manuscript of the book (!!!). Somehow, I, and my nine working fingers, got it in on time.

And finally, some extra-special words for a few extra-special people.

Mom and Dad, somehow, after coming to this country from an actual jungle in 1967 with almost nothing, you are now reading your child's thanks in the acknowledgments in a book. While America produced the despair and acrimony detailed in these pages, America, and only America, is capable of producing a story like ours. I cannot thank you both enough for all you have made possible for me.

Tracy, as the surviving sibling from said anything-is-possible-in-America household, thank you for remaining the only actual constant in my life since the beginning. And for being old enough (ha!) to fact-check information about our 1970s Brooklyn and Manhattan that I was too young to remember clearly.

Eileen, you have the questionable distinction of being the only person to have read every word I've written since we met. And only a person as savvy and empathetic as you could so quickly learn that 90 percent of being a writer's spouse is providing constant reminders that every word on the page is not, in fact, trash. Somehow you do everything I can do, but backwards, in sensible pumps. (Never heels, of course, after decades-old knee drama.) Thank you for simply being your wonderful self, every day.*

And finally, if there is anything I have learned from this process, it's that the only thing on earth harder than writing a book is having a parent who is writing a book. And so, Doodle and Vera Bear, while you did not choose to have your dad spend an entire year being distracted, you somehow responded with your typical tolerance, curiosity, and good cheer. Beyond that, you are the two most amazing human beings I know, and you make Mommy and me the luckiest people on the planet. Nothing else but your well-being truly matters to me. I love you more than you can comprehend.

However, now that this massive project is behind us, the three of us need to redouble our efforts toward our more important goal: convincing Mommy that it's finally time for us to get a dog. We've played nice for long enough. That stops today.

*The writer of this work can attest to the benefits of marrying very wisely.

NOTES

Citations from the trial transcripts provide page, box, and folder numbers and, unless otherwise noted, are found in the Bernhard Goetz Closed Case Files, New York City Municipal Archives, New York, New York. Citations from Goetz's two confession recordings are found in Box 1, Folder 6 in the Bernhard Goetz Closed Case Files, New York City Municipal Archives, New York, New York.

Author interviews are cited by the subject of the interview, medium of communication, and date.

PREFACE

xi **system still sees:** "Subway and Bus Ridership for 2023," Metropolitan Transit Authority, accessed February 28, 2025, https://new.mta.info/agency/new-york-city-transit/subway-bus-ridership-2023.

xi **country's worst traffic:** Celia Fernandez, "U.S. Drivers Lost 42 Hours—a Full Work Week—to Traffic in 2023: Congestion 'Hinders Economic Growth,' Expert Says," CNBC, June 26, 2024, https://www.cnbc.com/2024/06/26/most-congested-united-states-cities-inrix-2023-report.html.

xii **a regular presence:** Emma Seiwell and Larry McShane, "Shocked Father of Chokehold Victim Jordan Neely Recounts Son's Hard Life, Love of Michael Jackson," *New York Daily News*, May 3, 2023.

xii **on the streets:** Seiwell and McShane, "Shocked Father of Chokehold Victim Jordan Neely Recounts Son's Hard Life, Love of Michael Jackson."

xii **apparent psychiatric episode:** Maria Cramer, Hurubie Meko, and Amelia Nierenberg, "What We Know About Jordan Neely's Killing on the NYC Subway," *New York Times*, May 13, 2023.

xii **removed his jacket:** Cramer et al., "What We Know About Jordan Neely's Killing on the NYC Subway."

xii **"don't have food":** Chelsia Rose Marcius, "They Watched Jordan Neely Die. Did They Have a Duty to Intervene?," *New York Times*, May 17, 2023.

xii **"scared shitless":** Ben Kochman, Priscilla DeGregory and Kyle Schnitzer, "Daniel Penny Trial Live Updates from Nov. 12.," *New York Post*, November 12, 2024, https://nypost.com/2024/11/12/us-news/daniel-penny-nyc-trial-live-updates-analysis-reactions.

xii **four-minute cellphone video:** Cramer et al., "What We Know About Jordan Neely's Killing on the NYC Subway."
xiv **Goetz argues that:** Trial Transcript page 4886, Box 7, Folder 2.
xx **"we should want":** Pia Beumer, "Bernhard Goetz and the Roots of Kyle Rittenhouse's Celebrity on the Right," *Washington Post*, June 15, 2022.
xx **"feel so unsafe":** Sydney H. Schanberg, "A New Morality Play," *New York Times*, December 29, 1984.
xxi **"rule of law":** Drew Gilpin Faust, "The Men Who Started the War," *Atlantic*, November 13, 2023.

CHAPTER ONE: THE POWDER KEG

3 **crash tripped two:** Martin Gottlieb and James Glanz, "The Blackout of 2003: The Past; The Blackouts of '65 and '77 Became Defining Moments in the City's History," *New York Times*, August 15, 2003, A22.
4 **riders got stranded:** Associated Press, "Vignettes from a Night in the Dark," *Morning News*, July 15, 1977, 8.
4 **police radio monitors:** Susan Mulcahy and Frank DiGiacomo, *Paper of Wreckage* (Simon & Schuster, 2024), 65.
4 **"rapidly thawing contents":** Mulcahy and DiGiacomo, *Paper of Wreckage*, 69.
4 **dealing with problems:** Associated Press, "Vignettes from a Night in the Dark."
4 **police made only:** Selwyn Raab, "Ravage Continues Far into Day; Gunfire and Bottles Beset Police," *New York Times*, July 15, 1977, A1.
5 **book of cartoons:** Gottlieb and Glanz, "The Blackout of 2003: The Past."
5 **motorist who spotted:** Associated Press, "Vignettes from a Night in the Dark."
5 **lights went out:** Jonathan Mahler, "The Darkest Night," *New York Times Magazine*, October 5, 2003, 76.
5 **among the most:** Andrew Meier, *Morgenthau: Power, Privilege, and the Rise of an American Dynasty* (Random House, 2022), 683.
5 **Some 1,037 fires:** Gottlieb and Glanz, "The Blackout of 2003: The Past."
5 **the most seen:** Meier, *Morgenthau*, 683.
5 **speeding off with:** Raab, "Ravage Continues Far into Day; Gunfire and Bottles Beset Police."
5 **Broadway in Brooklyn:** Gottlieb and Glanz, "The Blackout of 2003: The Past."
5 **people were reported:** Jen Rubin, "Weekend History: How One Store Fought to Survive the Blackout and Looting of '77," *West Side Bag*, March 1, 2015, https://www.westsiderag.com/2014/04/05/uws-history-how-one-store-fought-to-survive-the-blackout-and-looting-of-77.
5 **the Brooks Brothers:** Gottlieb and Glanz, "The Blackout of 2003: The Past."
5 **lace gown from:** Associated Press, "Vignettes from a Night in the Dark."
5 **Brooklyn were attacked:** "The Blackout: Night of Terror," *Time*, July 25, 1977, https://time.com/archive/6853056/the-blackout-night-of-terror.
5 **a billion dollars':** Gottlieb and Glanz, "The Blackout of 2003: The Past."
5 **echoing the words:** Raab, "Ravage Continues Far into Day; Gunfire and Bottles Beset Police."
5 **"night of terror":** "The Blackout: Night of Terror."
5 **snipers and flying:** Raab, "Ravage Continues Far into Day; Gunfire and Bottles Beset Police."
5 **during massive riots:** Meier, *Morgenthau*, 683.
6 **413-acre prison island:** Meier, *Morgenthau*, 684.
6 **packed far beyond:** Meier, *Morgenthau*, 685.
6 **immediate medical attention:** Meier, *Morgenthau*, 683.
6 **"[s]he was a very sweet girl":** Jimmy Breslin, "Breslin to .44 Killer: Give Up Now!," *New York Daily News*, June 5, 1977, 3.
6 **"cops can't do":** Meier, *Morgenthau*, 684.
7 **"New York City is a mess":** Vincent Canby, "New York's Woes Are Good Box Office," *New York Times*, November 10, 1974, 141.
7 **"city almost bankrupt":** Pia Beumer, "Bernhard Goetz and the Roots of Kyle Rittenhouse's Celebrity on the Right." *Washington Post*, June 15, 2022.

7 **city workers since:** Andy Soltis, "When the Big Apple Went Bust," *New York Post*, November 16, 2001, https://nypost.com/2001/11/16/when-the-big-apple-went-bust.
7 **city dismissed some:** Soltis, "When the Big Apple Went Bust."
7 **time the city:** Ari L. Goldman, "Teachers Laid Off in '75 Are Rehired," *New York Times*, August 29, 1977, 30.
7 **four thousand hospital staff:** David Bird, "Hospital Staff Protests Layoffs," *New York Times*, August 12, 1975, 35.
7 **municipal workforce between:** Keith Meatto, "City Lit: Union City," *City Limits*, June 1, 2000, https://citylimits.org/2000/06/01/city-lit-union-city.
7 **jobs often threatened:** Áine Cain, "It Might Be New York City's 'Summer of Hell,' but 14 Photos Show How Much Worse the Subway System Was in the 1970s," *Business Insider*, July 18, 2017, https://www.businessinsider.com/history-of-nyc-subway-system-2017-7.
8 **most famous headlines:** "Ford to City: Drop Dead," *New York Daily News*, October 30, 1975, 1.
8 **not before sniping:** Owen Moritz, "State Might Tumble Next, Gov Tells 'Unelected' Ford," *New York Daily News*, October 30, 1975, 3.
8 **transit police force:** Sydney H. Schanberg, "A New Morality Play," *New York Times*, December 29, 1984, 21.
8 **policing the more:** Nicholas Pileggi, "Open City: The Bad Guys Are Winning the War on Crime," *New York*, January 19, 1981, 22.
8 **"I think it's intolerable":** Pileggi, "Open City," 22.
8 **"population had *declined*":** Pileggi, "Open City," 22.
8 **By 1979:** Meier, *Morgenthau*, 708.
8 **By 1984:** Philip Lentz, "After 2 Years of Controversy, Goetz Will Get His Day in Court," *Chicago Tribune*, March 22, 1987, 10.
8 **the worst year:** Leonard Butler, "1980 Called Worst Year of Crime in City History," *New York Times*, February 25, 1981, B3.
8 **insurance and grease:** Pileggi, "Open City," 22.
8 **greet new visitors:** Peter Kihss, "City Unions Join to Fight Layoffs," *New York Times*, July 11, 1975, 10.
8 **"should never ride":** Jen Carlson, "The 1970s Pamphlet Aimed at Keeping Tourists Out of NYC," *Gothamist*, October 19, 2018, https://gothamist.com/arts-entertainment/the-1970s-pamphlet-aimed-at-keeping-tourists-out-of-nyc#photo-1.
9 **to do anything:** Robert D. McFadden, "Robert Morgenthau, Longtime Manhattan District Attorney, Dies at 99," *New York Times*, July 21, 2019, 23.
9 **situation and complained:** Meier, *Morgenthau*, 708.
9 **its white residents:** Richard McGahey, "When Unions Saved New York City from Bankruptcy," *Forbes*, June 28, 2023, https://www.forbes.com/sites/richardmcgahey/2023/06/28/when-unions-saved-new-york-city-from-bankruptcy/?sh=40dd121256e9.
10 **nearly 50 percent:** Megan Roby, "The Push and Pull Dynamics of White Flight: A Study of the Bronx Between 1950 and 1980," *Bronx County Historical Society Journal* 45, no. ½ (Spring/Fall 2008): 34–53.
10 **"out of here":** Barbara Basler, "Black Man Is Killed by Mob in Brooklyn: Attack Called Racial," *New York Times*, June 23, 1982, A1.
10 **tried to run:** M. A. Farber, "The Howard Beach Case: Puzzling Picture of a Racial Attack," *New York Times*, January 5, 1987, B1.
11 **neighborhood with friends:** Ralph Blumenthal, "Black Youth Is Killed by Whites; Brooklyn Attack Is Called Racial," *New York Times*, August 25, 1989, A1.
11 **was seriously injured:** Ari L. Goldman, "The Region; as Blacks Clash with Hasidic Jews in Crown Heights, Who's in Control?," *New York Times*, August 25, 1991, Section 4, 6.
12 **"going to have":** James Stolz, "There's No Help on the Way," *New York Daily News*, July 22, 1980, 31.
12 **notion that people:** Dennis Jay Kenney, "Crime on the Subways: Measuring the Effectiveness of the Guardian Angels," *Justice Quarterly* 3, no. 4 (1986): 481–96.

CHAPTER TWO: CLAREMONT VILLAGE

13 **arcade game that:** Will Freeman, "Space Invaders at 40: 'I Tried Soldiers, but Shooting

People Was Frowned Upon,'" *Guardian*, June 4, 2018, https://www.theguardian.com/games/2018/jun/04/space-invaders-at-40-tomohiro-nishikado-interview.

13 **However simple it:** Richard Stanton, *A Brief History of Video Games: From Atari to Xbox One* (Running Press, 2015), 95–97.

13 **longer they could:** Jeannette DeWyze. "San Diego's Gremlin: How Video Games Work," *San Diego Reader*, July 15, 1982.

14 **machine would track:** Ryan Geddes and Daemon Hatfield, "IGN's Top 10 Most Influential Games," IGN, June 13, 2012, https://www.ign.com/articles/2007/12/11/igns-top-10-most-influential-games.

14 **popular in Japan:** Giles Richards, "A Life Through Video Games," *Guardian*, July 23, 2005, https://www.theguardian.com/technology/2005/jul/24/games.shopping.

14 **period often called:** Stanton, *A Brief History of Video Games: From Atari to Xbox One*, 95.

14 **meant big business:** Mark J. P. Wolf, "Arcade Games in the 1980s," in *The Video Game Explosion: A History from PONG to PlayStation and Beyond*, ed. Mark J. P. Wolf (Greenwood Press, 2008), 94.

15 **teenager to make:** Margot Hornblower, "Subway Vigilante's Victim Says He 'Learned Lesson,'" *Democrat and Chronicle*, January 11, 1985, 3A.

15 **caught might mean:** Trial transcript page 5363, Box 7, Folder 5.

15 **"bad to bust":** Esther B. Fein, "For Goetz Victim's Mother, Worry and Self-Doubt," *New York Times*, January 12, 1985, Section 1, 25.

15 **had probably known:** Trial transcript page 5312, Box 7, Folder 5.

15 **into machines together:** Trial transcript page 5314, Box 7, Folder 5.

15 **"average teenagers with":** Fein, "For Goetz Victim's Mother, Worry and Self-Doubt."

16 **knew his father:** Hornblower, "Subway Vigilante's Victim Says He 'Learned Lesson.'"

16 **out of school:** Margot Hornblower, "Wounded Youth Denies Intent to Rob New York City 'Subway Vigilante,'" *Washington Post*, January 11, 1985, https://www.washingtonpost.com/archive/politics/1985/01/11/wounded-youth-denies-intent-to-rob-new-york-city-subway-vigilante/630d1f27-7295-40cb-bb2c-ed4f880eb1d3/.

16 **and eventually enrolled:** David E. Sanger, "Callers Support Subway Gunman," *New York Times*, December 25, 1981, Section 1, 1.

16 **was likely born:** Hornblower, "Subway Vigilante's Victim Says He 'Learned Lesson.'"

16 **"get a job" . . . "go-getter":** Hornblower, "Subway Vigilante's Victim Says He 'Learned Lesson.'"

16 **facing jail time:** "All 4 Teens Shot by 'Vigilante' Had History of Criminal Arrests," *Orlando Sentinel*, January 10, 1985, https://www.sun-sentinel.com/1985/01/10/all-4-teens-shot-by-vigilantehad-history-of-criminal-arrests/.

16 **"is capable of":** Sanger, "Callers Support Subway Gunman."

16 **described as a "thinker":** *The Company You Keep*, written and directed by Adrian Liang (Stone Age Films, 2018), https://vimeo.com/267236898.

16 **had repeated psychiatric:** Trial transcript page 5647, Box 7, Folder 6.

16 **most severe being:** Trial transcript page 5396, Box 7, Folder 5.

16 **was first arrested:** Mark Lesly with Charles Shuttleworth, *Subway Gunman: A Juror's Account of the Bernhard Goetz Trial* (British American Publishing, 1988), 82.

17 **arrested three months:** Lesly with Shuttleworth, *Subway Gunman*, 76.

17 **poker machine from:** Trial transcript page 5304, Box 7, Folder 5.

17 **video game machine:** Trial transcript page 5305, Box 7, Folder 5.

17 **just three weeks:** Trial transcript page 5307, Box 7, Folder 5.

17 **started snorting cocaine:** Trial transcript pages 5309-10, Box 7, Folder 5.

17 **regular crack smoker:** Trial transcript page 5310, Box 7, Folder 5.

17 **more a day:** Trial transcript page 5311, Box 7, Folder 5.

17 **he was high:** Hornblower, "Wounded Youth Denies Intent to Rob New York City 'Subway Vigilante.'"

17 **at some point:** Bruce Weber, "James Ramseur, Wounded in '84 Subway Shooting, Dies at 45," *New York Times*, December 23, 2011.

17 **four pending warrants:** George P. Fletcher, *A Crime of Self-Defense: Bernhard Goetz and the Law on Trial* (University of Chicago Press, 1990), 3.

17 **born in Queens:** Keith Moore and Don Singleton, "Victim's Mom Not Bitter," *New York Daily News*, January 11, 1985, 3.

17 **food service worker:** Moore and Singleton, "Victim's Mom Not Bitter."

17 **enjoyed dressing up:** Larry McShane, "For One Goetz Victim, Suffering Won't End: Youth Was Immobilized from the Waist Down, Fell into a Coma, Suffered Irreversible Brain Damage. Now 29, He Has the Mental Capacity of a Third Grader," *Los Angeles Times,* January 8, 1995, https://www.latimes.com/archives/la-xpm-1995-01-08-mn-17496-story.html.
17 **make them targets:** Fein, "For Goetz Victim's Mother, Worry and Self-Doubt."
18 **"more to life":** Fine, "For Goetz Victim's Mother, Worry and Self-Doubt."
18 **was awaiting trial:** Marcia Chambers, "Goetz Posts Bail and Is Freed; Youths He Shot Won't Testify," *New York Times,* January 9, 1985, A1.
18 **they would watch zipping:** McShane, "For One Goetz Victim, Suffering Won't End."
18 **Darrell's friends described:** *The Company You Keep,* written and directed by Adrian Liang (Stone Age Films, 2018), https://vimeo.com/267236898.
18 **"was staying outside":** Fein, "For Goetz Victim's Mother, Worry and Self-Doubt."
18 **"situation out there":** Fein, "For Goetz Victim's Mother, Worry and Self-Doubt."
18 **area is given:** David Gonzalez, "What Is New York's Greenest Borough? Probably Not the One You Think," *New York Times,* December 4, 2022, Section MB, 8.
18 **cut a gash:** Robert Caro, *The Power Broker: Robert Moses and the Fall of New York* (Vintage, 1975), 893–94.
19 **refusing services deliberately:** Margot Hornblower, "South Bronx, 10 Years After Fame," *Washington Post,* August 25, 1987, https://www.washingtonpost.com/archive/politics/1987/08/25/south-bronx-10-years-after-fame/e2933cbc-a3c5-4da6-a571-b091822f02f5/.
19 **"most publicized urban":** John J. Goldman, "South Bronx Gears for Rebirth," *Hartford Courant,* September 4, 1981, B14.
19 **buildings had defaulted:** Owen Moritz, "South Bronx Can Be Saved!," *New York Daily News,* October 16, 1977, 5.
19 **simply gave up:** Hornblower, "South Bronx, 10 Years After Fame."
19 **lost to fires:** Hornblower, "South Bronx, 10 Years After Fame."
19 **were an average:** Moritz, "South Bronx Can Be Saved!"
19 **available to make:** Hornblower, "South Bronx, 10 Years After Fame."
19 **merely abandoned buildings:** Hornblower, "South Bronx, 10 Years After Fame."
19 **vacant buildings still:** Goldman, "South Bronx Gears for Rebirth."
20 **"turn it around":** Hornblower, "South Bronx, 10 Years After Fame."
20 **to blast Carter:** Hornblower, "South Bronx, 10 Years After Fame."
20 **to the plight:** Gerald M. Boyd, "Jackson Spends a Night in South Bronx," *New York Times,* March 31, 1984, 28.
20 **Mother Teresa would:** Tony Marcano, "Mother Teresa Has Quiet Day at Her Convent in the Bronx," *New York Times,* May 28, 1997, B2.
21 **multiple smaller housing:** "'Village' Is Rising in Bronx Section," *New York Times,* August 20, 1962, 25.
21 **were originally designed:** Derrick Jackson, "Where Subway Case Hits Home Hard," *Newsday,* January 6, 1985, 4.
21 **half of the:** Jackson, "Where Subway Case Hits Home Hard."
21 **Social Security checks:** Jackson, "Where Subway Case Hits Home Hard."
21 **neighborhoods got rougher:** Fritz Umbach, *The Last Neighborhood Cops: The Rise and Fall of Community Policing in New York Public Housing* (Rutgers University Press, 2011), 138.
21 **New York around:** Umbach, *The Last Neighborhood Cops,* 119.
21 **grew much faster:** Umbach, *The Last Neighborhood Cops,* 142–43.
22 **"get some money":** Trial transcript page 5317, Box 7, Folder 5.
22 **toward Pace University:** Trial transcript page 5318, Box 7, Folder 5.
22 **diversion while others:** Trial transcript page 5314, Box 7, Folder 5.
22 **an extra charge:** Trial transcript page 5322, Box 7, Folder 5.
22 **they snuck through:** Trial transcript page 5323, Box 7, Folder 5.
22 **for the downtown:** Trial transcript page 5323, Box 7, Folder 5.
22 **to the point of her:** Trial transcript page 6250, 6263, Box 7, Folder 5.
23 **described their behavior:** Trial transcript page 6324, Box 7, Folder 5.
23 **little more than:** Trial transcript page 6309, Box 7, Folder 5.
23 **about what they:** Trial transcript page 6981, Box 7, Folder 5.
23 **groups of riders:** Trial transcript page 5906, Box 7, Folder 5.

CHAPTER THREE: BU

24 **"a real man":** "Classic Ads," the official website of Charles Atlas, accessed March 2, 2025, https://www.charlesatlas.com/classicads.html.
25 **"was picked on":** "Wolf or Wimp?," *Chicago Tribune*, December 14, 1986, https://www.chicagotribune.com/1986/12/14/wolf-or-wimp-2/.
25 **"Bernhard is basically":** "Wolf or Wimp?"
25 **"part of human":** "Wolf or Wimp?"
25 **"understand what happened":** Trial transcript page 4769, Box 7, Folder 2.
25 **father, rigidly Lutheran:** George P. Fletcher, *A Crime of Self-Defense: Bernhard Goetz and the Law on Trial* (University of Chicago Press, 1990), 11.
26 **to the farm:** Robert McFadden, "Goetz: A Private Man in a Public Debate," *New York Times*, January 6, 1985, 1.
26 **interest in sports:** McFadden, "Goetz: A Private Man in a Public Debate."
26 **arrested and charged:** McFadden, "Goetz: A Private Man in a Public Debate"; Lillian Rubin, *Quiet Rage: Bernie Goetz in a Time of Madness* (Farrar, Strauss & Giroux, 1986), 86.
26 **by political opponents:** McFadden, "Goetz: A Private Man in a Public Debate."
26 **regarded as troublemakers:** Rubin, *Quiet Rage*, 87.
26 **long been murmurs:** Rubin, *Quiet Rage*.
26 **"father was bisexual":** McFadden, "Goetz: A Private Man in a Public Debate."
26 **Bernhard was bullied:** McFadden, "Goetz: A Private Man in a Public Debate."
27 **from boarding school:** "Wolf or Wimp?"
27 **prep school in:** "Wolf or Wimp?"
27 **seeking psychiatric assistance:** McFadden, "Goetz: A Private Man in a Public Debate."
27 **romantic Elizabeth Boylan:** "Wolf or Wimp?"
28 **speak for the:** "Wolf or Wimp?"
28 **"Elizabeth had hurt":** "Wolf or Wimp?"
28 **incorporated and ran:** McFadden, "Goetz: A Private Man in a Public Debate."
28 **dozing off on the stoop:** Myra Friedman with Michael Daly, "My Neighbor Bernie Goetz," *New York*, February 18, 1985, 35; UPI, "Crime Frustrated Goetz, Neighbors Say," *Los Angeles Times*, January 7, 1985, 16.
28 **it was ordered:** Friedman with Daly, "My Neighbor Bernie Goetz."
28 **neighbors regarded him:** Murray Weiss and Richard Sisk, "Suspect in IRT Shootings Walks in and Surrenders," *New York Daily News*, January 1, 1985, 3.
28 **an "obsessive nature":** Friedman with Daly, "My Neighbor Bernie Goetz."
28 **known for tension:** Friedman with Daly, "My Neighbor Bernie Goetz."
29 **would often brighten:** Friedman with Daly, "My Neighbor Bernie Goetz," 36.
29 **"kind of guy":** Don Gentile and Brian Kates, "'A Little Strange': Neighbors Describe Him as a Zealot," *New York Daily News*, January 1, 1985, 3.
29 **theory of policing:** George L. Kelling and James Q. Wilson, "Broken Windows," *Atlantic*, March 1982, https://www.theatlantic.com/magazine/archive/1982/03/broken-windows/304465/.
29 **"had a feeling":** McFadden, "Goetz: A Private Man in a Public Debate."
29 **particularly riled up:** Suzanne Daley, "Man Tells Police He Shot Youths in Subway Train," *New York Times*, January 1, 1985, 1.
29 **few hours later:** Friedman with Daly, "My Neighbor Bernie Goetz," 35.
29 **Frustrated, he regularly:** United Press International, "Crime Frustrated Goetz, Neighbors Say," *Los Angeles Times*, January 7, 1985, 16.
29 **particularly incensed when:** Daley, "Man Tells Police He Shot Youths in Subway Train."
29 **was seen clearing:** Friedman with Daly, "My Neighbor Bernie Goetz."
30 **enough to rid:** Gentile and Kates, "'A Little Strange': Neighbors Describe Him as a Zealot."
30 **"going to clean":** Clyde Haberman, "NYC; One Question That Matters in Goetz Case," *New York Times*, April 12, 1996, B1; Friedman with Daly, "My Neighbor Bernie Goetz."
30 **they removed him:** Gentile and Kates, "'A Little Strange': Neighbors Describe Him as a Zealot."
30 **given Goetz's number:** Friedman with Daly, "My Neighbor Bernie Goetz," 25.
30 **"get the liberals":** Friedman with Daly, "My Neighbor Bernie Goetz," 35.

31 **January 21, 1981:** "The Crime That Many Cheered and Few Jeered," *New York Post,* January 1, 1985, 1; Suzanne Daley, "Man Tells Police He Shot Youths in Subway Train," *New York Times,* January 1, 1985, 1.

CHAPTER FOUR: THE .38 SMITH & WESSON AIRWEIGHT

32 **the equipment was:** George P. Fletcher, *A Crime of Self-Defense: Bernhard Goetz and the Law on Trial* (University of Chicago Press, 1990), 14.
32 **noise and saw:** Trial transcript page 7421, Box 8, Folder 6; Samuel Maull, "Defense Opens in Goetz Case with Story of 1981 Mugging," Associated Press, May 22, 1987.
33 **saw the three:** Trial transcript page 7421, Box 8, Folder 6.
33 **As Cozza approached:** Trial transcript page 7421, Box 8, Folder 6.
33 **what the boys:** Suzanne Daley, "Man Tells Police He Shot Youths in Subway Train," *New York Times,* January 1, 1985, 1.
33 **Cozza arrested Clarke:** Trial transcript pages 7420–22, Box 8, Folder 6.
33 **would not heal:** Mark Lesly with Charles Shuttleworth, *Subway Gunman: A Juror's Account* (British American Publishing, 1988), 149.
33 **only charged with:** Statement of Bernhard H. Goetz to Concord Police, December 31, 1984, Box 1, Folder 6.
34 **"consider that someone":** Robert McFadden, "Goetz: A Private Man in a Public Debate," *New York Times,* January 6, 1985, 1.
34 **"spent all this":** McFadden, "Goetz: A Private Man in a Public Debate."
34 **"say whatever it":** Trial transcript pages 7431–32, Box 8, Folder 6.
35 **"was equivalent to":** McFadden, "Goetz: A Private Man in a Public Debate."
35 **"never let it":** Marcia Chambers, "Goetz Spoke to One Youth, Then Shot Again, Police Say," *New York Times,* February 28, 1985, A1.
35 **bought at least:** Jan Hoffman, "Fund Linked to N.R.A. Gave $20,000 for Goetz's Defense," *New York Times,* April 16, 1996, A1.
35 **In 1970 Goetz:** Anne Groer, "Orlando Gun Seller Testifies in Goetz Trial," *Orlando Sentinel,* May 13, 1987, A4.
35 **East Village in:** Nancy Grace, "Interview with 'Subway Vigilante' Bernhard Goetz," *Larry King Live,* CNN, December 17, 2004, https://transcripts.cnn.com/show/lkl/date/2004-12-17/segment/01.
35 **had dual residence:** Groer, "Orlando Gun Seller Testifies in Goetz Trial."
35 **supposed to sell:** Stephen McFarland, "In Fla., It's Easy to Take Up Arms," *New York Daily News,* January 3, 1985, 30.
35 **the checks cashed:** McFarland, "In Fla., It's Easy to Take Up Arms."
35 **other people several:** Margot Hornblower, "Intended to Gouge Eye of Teen, Goetz Tape Says," *Washington Post,* May 14, 1987, https://www.washingtonpost.com/archive/politics/1987/05/14/intended-to-gouge-eye-of-teen-goetz-tape-says/4c408078-48d6-4e4d-8ced-eccd3d6e49ee/.
36 **point to have:** United Press International, "Crime Frustrated Goetz, Neighbors Say," *Los Angeles Times,* January 7, 1985, 16, https://www.latimes.com/archives/la-xpm-1985-01-07-mn-11761-story.html.
36 **seen a gun:** Murray Weiss, Randy Diamond, and Don Singleton, "A Quiet, Intense Man," *New York Daily News,* January 2, 1985, 2.
36 **Goetz apparently did:** Gentile and Kates, "'A Little Strange': Neighbors Describe Him as a Zealot."
36 **concealed carry permit:** McFadden, "Goetz: A Private Man in a Public Debate."
36 **Over time, courts:** *In re Klenosky,* 75 App. Div. 2d 793, 428 N.Y.S. 2d 256, 257 (1980).
36 **Merely living in:** *In re Bernstein,* 85 App. Div. 2d 574, 445 N.Y.S. 2d 716, 717 (1981).
36 **"of particular threats":** *In re Martinek,* 294 App. Div. 2d 221, 222, 743 N.Y.S. 2d 80, 81 (2002); *see also In re Kaplan,* 249 App. Div. 2d 199, 201, 673 N. Y. S. 2d 66, 68 (1998) (approving the NYPD's requirement of "extraordinary personal danger, documented by proof of recurrent threats to life or safety" (quoting 38 N. Y. C. R. R. § 5–03(b))).
37 **seen a psychologist:** Weiss et al., "A Quiet, Intense Man."
37 **had not shown:** Frank Faso, Murray Weiss, and Brian Kates, "A Growing Anger," *New York Daily News,* January 3, 1985.
37 **"trying to follow":** Fletcher, *A Crime of Self-Defense,* 13.
37 **"can't give everyone":** Fletcher, *A Crime of Self-Defense,* 72.

38 **"spend time taking":** Grace, "Interview with 'Subway Vigilante' Bernhard Goetz," https://transcripts.cnn.com/show/lkl/date/2004-12-17/segment/01.
38 **"basically consisted of":** Faso et al, "A Growing Anger."
38 **"cowboys and Indians":** Grace, "Interview with 'Subway Vigilante' Bernhard Goetz," https://transcripts.cnn.com/show/lkl/date/2004-12-17/segment/01.
39 **"Easier than typing":** Stone Phillips, "Stone Phillips: 15 Years of *Dateline*," NBC News, July 2, 2007, https://www.nbcnews.com/id/wbna19562622.
39 **Gun safety professionals:** "United States Marine Corps Training Command Safety Rules," USMC, accessed March 5, 2025, https://www.trngcmd.marines.mil/Portals/207/Docs/wtbn/MPMS/DIV%2024%20Pistol%20Weapons%20Handling_Media.pdf?ver=2015-06-15-134604-773; "Firearm Safety—10 Rules of Safe Gun Handling," The Firearm Industry Trade Association, accessed March 5, 2025, https://www.nssf.org/safety/rules-firearms-safety/.
39 **been to walk:** Fletcher, *A Crime of Self-Defense*, 14.
39 **"I was so":** Statement of Bernhard H. Goetz to New York Police Department, December 31, 1984, Box 1, Folder 6.
40 **"hope I catch":** Fletcher, *A Crime of Self-Defense*, 104–5.
40 **"I was pissed":** Fletcher, *A Crime of Self-Defense*, 104–5; Trial transcript page 4793, Box 7, Folder 2.
40 **"gun and showing":** Fletcher, *A Crime of Self-Defense*, 104–5.
40 **"light blue windbreaker":** Trial transcript page 5128, Box 7, Folder 3.
41 **"acquired a year":** McFadden, "Goetz: A Private Man in a Public Debate."
41 **"the stubby revolver":** Michael Wilson, "The Face of Danger Is Changing," *New York Times*, November 14, 2008, https://www.nytimes.com/2008/11/15/nyregion/15thug.html.
41 **"an attractive service weapon":** Matthew Moss, "NYPD Set to Retire Last of Its Revolvers," *The Firearms Blog*, November 30, 2017, https://www.thefirearmblog.com/blog/2017/11/30/nypd-set-retire-last-revolvers/.
41 **stopped wearing gloves:** Lesly with Shuttleworth, *Subway Gunman*, 58.
41 **"I'm not a gun":** Chambers, "Goetz Spoke to One Youth, Then Shot Again, Police Say."

CHAPTER FIVE: CAR 7657

42 **"due to foreclosures":** Margot Hornblower, "Painful 'Renaissance' in Harlem," *Washington Post*, July 31, 1984, https://www.washingtonpost.com/archive/politics/1984/07/31/painful-renaissance-in-harlem/af0fcd9e-24df-4a12-b645-bbb7ddaee3d1/.
43 **"Harlem bled into":** Lee Daniels, "'Gentrification' of 2 Neighborhoods Found Beneficial," *New York Times*, March 23, 1984, B5.
43 **"Governor Mario Cuomo":** Salvatore Arena and Owen Mortiz, "Gov Makes City Plea for Times Sq. Project," *New York Daily News*, October 26, 1984, 27.
43 **rents shot into:** Kirk Johnson, "If You're Thinking of Living in Chelsea," *New York Times*, October 14, 1984, Section 8, 9.
43 **Flores arrived:** Trial transcript page 5877, Box 7, Folder 7.
43 **picking up two baguettes:** Trial transcript page 5876, Box 7, Folder 7.
43 **was an R22 subway:** "The IRT SMEE Fleet (R-12—R-36)," *NYCSubway*, accessed March 2, 2025, https://www.nycsubway.org/wiki/The_IRT_SMEE_Fleet_(R-12_—_R-36).
44 **a fire blazed:** Malcolm Gladwell, "In a Different New York, a Different Goetz Trial," *Washington Post*, April 20, 1996, https://www.washingtonpost.com/archive/politics/1996/04/21/in-a-different-new-york-a-different-goetz-trial/b1369624-e31d-4963-af5f-2953c8d3f565/.
44 **down an average:** Gladwell, "In a Different New York, a Different Goetz Trial."
44 **minefield of hundreds:** Gladwell, "In a Different New York, a Different Goetz Trial."
44 **By the mid-1970s:** Hilary Greenbaum and Dana Rubinstein, "The Origin of Spray Paint," *New York Times Magazine*, November 4, 2011, 22.
44 **What had started:** Gladwell, "In a Different New York, a Different Goetz Trial"; Dimitri Ehrlich and Gregor Ehrlich, "Graffiti in Its Own Words," *New York*, June 26, 2006, https://nymag.com/guides/summer/17406/.
44 **The act of tagging:** Áine Cain, "It Might Be New York City's 'Summer of Hell,' but 14 Photos Show How Much Worse the Subway System Was in the 1970s," *Business Insider*, July 18, 2017, https://www.businessinsider.com/history-of-nyc-subway-system-2017-7.

44 **"going all city":** Ehrlich and Ehrlich, "Graffiti in Its Own Words."
45 **As early as:** Cain, "It Might Be New York City's 'Summer of Hell,' but 14 Photos Show How Much Worse the Subway System Was in the 1970s."
45 **instead of trying:** Suzanne Daley, "Crime Rises and Ridership Drops for New York City Subway System," *New York Times*, May 8, 1984, A1.
45 **like a sneakerhead:** Daley, "Crime Rises and Ridership Drops for New York City Subway System."
45 **felonies a year:** Charles Hanley, "In Subway Crime, N.Y. Still Leads the World," *Los Angeles Times*, March 17, 1985.
45 **some forty a:** Sydney H. Schanberg, "A New Morality Play," *New York Times*, December 29, 1984, 21.
45 **transportation systems across:** Hanley, "In Subway Crime, N.Y. Still Leads the World."
45 **more hospitable environment:** Hanley, "In Subway Crime, N.Y. Still Leads the World."
45 **one police officer:** Michael Kruse, "How Gotham Gave Us Trump," *Politico Magazine*, July/August 2017, https://www.politico.com/magazine/story/2017/06/30/donald-trump-new-york-city-crime-1970s-1980s-215316/.
45 **Signs warned riders:** Dennis Perkins, "In the New York Story, Colin Quinn Looks to Stereotypes for Wisdom—and Finds Some," The A.V. Club, November 18, 2016, https://www.avclub.com/in-the-new-york-story-colin-quinn-looks-to-stereotypes-1798189831.
45 **The system was:** Albert Samaha, "The Rise and Fall of Crime in New York City: A Timeline," *Village Voice*, August 7, 2014, https://www.villagevoice.com/the-rise-and-fall-of-crime-in-new-york-city-a-timeline/.
45 **system still hosted:** Mitchell L. Moss, Sarah M. Kaufman, Sam Levy, Ashley Smith, and Jorge Hernandez, "Subway Ridership 1975–2015," NYU Rudin Center for Transportation, March 2017, 8, https://wagner.nyu.edu/files/faculty/publications/State%20of%20Subway%20Ridership%20-%20Mar717.pdf.
45 **"rider can't ignore":** Schanberg, "A New Morality Play."
46 **his wife, Andrea:** Trial transcript page 6942, Box 8, Folder 4.
46 **half hour from:** Trial transcript page 5949, Box 7, Folder 8.
46 **acting alone, rose:** Trial transcript page 5349, Box 7, Folder 5.

CHAPTER SIX: SHINY EYES

47 **he approached Goetz:** Trial transcript page 5390, Box 7, Folder 5.
47 **"Bernhard Goetz's face":** Trial transcript page 7048, Box 8, Folder 5.
48 **kept the four:** Pete Hamill, "Bernhard Goetz: Notes from the Underground," *Village Voice*, May 12, 1987, https://www.villagevoice.com/bernard-goetz-notes-from-underground/.
48 **with an innocent:** George P. Fletcher, *A Crime of Self-Defense: Bernhard Goetz and the Law on Trial* (University of Chicago Press, 1990), 11–12.
48 **"were just typical":** Nancy Grace, "Interview with 'Subway Vigilante' Bernhard Goetz," *Larry King Live*, CNN, December 17, 2004, https://transcripts.cnn.com/show/lkl/date/2004-12-17/segment/01.
48 **final local stop:** Trial transcript page 5950, Box 7, Folder 8.
48 **Canty was just:** William Kunstler, *My Life as a Radical Lawyer* (Birch Lane Press, 1994), 292–93.
49 **keen interest in:** Trial transcript page 6312, Box 7, Folder 9; Mark Lesly with Charles Shuttleworth, *Subway Gunman: A Juror's Account* (British American Publishing, 1988), 117.
49 **avoid an unpleasant:** David E. Sanger, "The Little-Known World of the Vigilante," *New York Times*, December 30, 1984, Section 4, 6.
49 **would later say:** Grace, "Interview with 'Subway Vigilante' Bernhard Goetz," https://transcripts.cnn.com/show/lkl/date/2004-12-17/segment/01.
50 **turned around and:** Trial transcript page 5340, Box 7, Folder 5.
50 **Goetz swung back:** Trial transcript pages 5343–44, Box 7, Folder 5.
50 **would later say:** Grace, "Interview with 'Subway Vigilante' Bernhard Goetz," https://transcripts.cnn.com/show/lkl/date/2004-12-17/segment/01.
50 **where it hit:** Lesly with Shuttleworth, *Subway Gunman*, 78.
50 **feeling his legs:** Trial transcript page 5347, Box 7, Folder 5.
50 **using his keys:** Trial transcript page 4812, Box 7, Folder 2.
50 **as the loudest:** Trial transcript page 6250, Box 7, Folder 9.

50 **"are you all":** Trial transcript page 5344, Box 7, Folder 5.
51 **shooter might come:** Trial transcript pages 5887–88, 6251, Boxes 7 and 9, Folder 7.
51 **hoping to find:** Trial transcript page 6941, Box 8, Folder 4.
51 **"looked like he":** Samuel Maull, "Goetz Shooting Victim Testifies at Subway Shooter Trial," Associated Press, May 1, 1987.
51 **described his demeanor:** Trial transcript pages 6352–53, Box 8, Folder 1.
51 **Allen was wounded:** Trial transcript page 5346, Box 7, Folder 5.
51 **look of terror:** Trial transcript page 6841, Box 8, Folder 3; Kirk Johnson, "Jury Watches an Angry Goetz on Tape," *New York Times*, May 14, 1987, B1.
52 **Cabey the first:** Marcia Chambers, "Goetz Spoke to One Youth, Then Shot Again, Police Say," *New York Times*, February 28, 1985, A1.
52 **"look so bad":** Chambers, "Goetz Spoke to One Youth, Then Shot Again, Police Say."
52 **"barrel against his":** Trial transcript page 4810, Box 7, Folder 2.
52 **"just kept shooting":** Trial transcript page 5885, Box 7, Folder 7.
52 **"Why did he":** Trial transcript page 5346, Box 7, Folder 5.
52 **up and sat:** Lesly with Shuttleworth, *Subway Gunman*, 62.
52 **knelt down next:** Trial transcript page 5347, Box 7, Folder 5.
53 **"Miss, are you":** Trial transcript pages 6251–52, Box 7, Folder 9.
53 **meaning that someone:** Trial transcript page 5952, Box 7, Folder 8.
53 **saw a calm:** Trial transcript page 5954, Box 7, Folder 8.
53 **Goetz if he:** Trial transcript page 5957, Box 7, Folder 8.
53 **"know why I":** Robert McFadden, "A Gunman Wounds 4 on IRT Train, Then Escapes," *New York Times*, December 23, 1984, 1.
53 **then urged Goetz:** McFadden, "A Gunman Wounds 4 on IRT Train, Then Escapes."
53 **Soler assumed Goetz:** Trial transcript page 5956, Box 7, Folder 8.
53 **how they were:** Fletcher, *A Crime of Self-Defense*, 2, 122–23.
53 **helped at least:** Trial transcript page 5891, Box 7, Folder 7; Lesly with Shuttleworth, *Subway Gunman*, 98–99.
54 **train to prevent:** Grace, "Interview with 'Subway Vigilante' Bernhard Goetz," https://transcripts.cnn.com/show/lkl/date/2004-12-17/segment/01.
54 **panic and brazenness:** Fletcher, *A Crime of Self-Defense*, 2.
54 **Goetz reached the Chambers Street stop:** Suzanne Daley, "Goetz Drove Across New England for Several Days Before Surrender," *New York Times*, January 4, 1985, B3.
54 **Plymouth Gran Fury:** Grace, "Interview with 'Subway Vigilante' Bernhard Goetz," https://transcripts.cnn.com/show/lkl/date/2004-12-17/segment/01.
54 **After walking a block east:** Statement of Bernhard H. Goetz to Concord Police, December 31, 1984, Box 1, Folder 6.

CHAPTER SEVEN: THE MAN IN THE BLUE WINDBREAKER

55 **hysterical individual even:** Trial transcript page 6281, Box 7, Folder 9.
55 **"been shot through":** Trial transcript page 6273, Box 7, Folder 9.
55 **"only asked for":** Trial transcript page 6273, Box 7, Folder 9.
56 **"guy threatened us":** Trial transcript page 4965, Box 7, Folder 3; George P. Fletcher, *A Crime of Self-Defense: Bernhard Goetz and the Law on Trial* (University of Chicago Press, 1990), 140. Cabey would make essentially the same statement to *New York Daily News* columnist Jimmy Breslin in November 1985.
56 **require multiple ambulances:** Trial transcript page 4917, Box 7, Folder 3.
56 **crawling toward the:** Trial transcript page 5020, Box 7, Folder 3.
56 **officer not let:** Trial transcript page 5859, Box 7, Folder 7.
56 **believed he was:** Trial transcript pages 4928–29, Box 7, Folder 8.
56 **blood to his:** Trial transcript page 4928, Box 7, Folder 8.
56 **had been shot:** Trial transcript page 4926, Box 7, Folder 8.
57 **put a tube:** Trial transcript page 6476, Box 8, Folder 1.
57 **of his chest:** Trial transcript pages 4924–25, Box 7, Folder 8.
57 **they would treat:** Trial transcript page 6401, Box 9, Folder 1.
57 **despite having had:** Trial transcript pages 4925–26, Box 7, Folder 8.
57 **wounds burned when:** Trial transcript page 5349, Box 7, Folder 5.
58 **his spinal cord:** Trial transcript pages 4829–30, Box 7, Folder 2.
58 **by this point:** Trial transcript pages 6517–18, Box 8, Folder 1.

58 **he had developed:** Trial transcript pages 6519–20, Box 8, Folder 1.
58 **a deep coma:** Frank Faso and Don Singleton, "IRT Victim in Coma," *New York Daily News*, January 10, 1985, 3; Trial transcript page 6523, Box 8, Folder 1.
58 **did not think:** Trial transcript page 6524, Box 8, Folder 1.
58 **"shouldn't have been":** Paul Tharp, "'I'm Sorry, Mom,'" *New York Post*, January 11, 1985, 3.
58 **speech was slurred:** "Judge Blocks Goetz's Access to Subway Victim," United Press International, May 25, 1990.
58 **incident that got:** Larry McShane, "For One Goetz Victim, Suffering Won't End," *Los Angeles Times*, January 8, 1995, https://www.latimes.com/archives/la-xpm-1995-01-08-mn-17496-story.html.
59 **All they found:** Robert McFadden, "A Gunman Wounds 4 on IRT Train, Then Escapes," *New York Times*, December 23, 1984, 1.
59 **of the assailant:** Robert D. McFadden, "City Strengthens Subway Patrols," *New York Times*, December 24, 1984.

CHAPTER EIGHT: A POLITE NOTE

61 **the gunman outnumbered:** Dorothy Gilliam, "Frontier Judgments," *Washington Post*, January 7, 1985.
61 **"run for mayor":** Sydney H. Schanberg, "A New Morality Play," *New York Times*, December 29, 1984, 21.
61 **mayor was flooded:** Andrew Meier, *Morgenthau: Power, Privilege, and the Rise of an American Dynasty* (Random House, 2022), 709.
61 **kinship with the shooter:** Richard Stengel, "A Troubled and Troubling Life," *Time*, June 24, 2001.
61 **"scary on those":** Bob Kappstatter, "The Story of Bernhard Goetz, the Subway Vigilante," *New York Daily News*, January 12, 2019, https://www.nydailynews.com/2017/08/14/the-story-of-bernhard-goetz-the-subway-vigilante/.
64 **"contact the police":** Myra Friedman with Michael Daly, "My Neighbor Bernie Goetz," *New York*, February 18, 1985, 38.
64 **"frequent and periodic":** Peter McGlaughlin and Don Gentile, "Finest to Flood the Subways," *New York Daily News*, December 24, 1984, 3.
65 **intended to get:** Robert McFadden, "City Strengthens Subway Patrols," *New York Times*, December 24, 1984, 1.
65 **its president calling:** McGlaughlin and Gentile, "Finest to Flood the Subways."
65 **whose radios did:** McFadden, "City Strengthens Subway Patrols."

CHAPTER NINE: THE BUG

68 **"someone a lesson":** Katharine Q. Seelye, "Brian Garfield, Prolific Author of 'Death Wish,' Dies at 79," *New York Times*, January 6, 2019, https://www.nytimes.com/2019/01/06/obituaries/brian-garfield-dies-at-79.html.
68 **immediately began tying:** Joyce Brothers, "Portrait of 'Death Wish' Gunman," *New York Post*, December 27, 1984, 2.
68 **on its cover:** *New York Post*, December 24, 1984, 1.
68 **"the Wild West":** Peter Mathews, "Bronson: Sometimes You Have to Be Vigilante," *New York Post*, January 11, 1985, 3.
68 **"a permanent place":** Brian Kates, "A Fantasy Come True: Death Wish Gunman Captured City's Imagination," *New York Daily News*, January 1, 1985, 2.
68 **"real Charles Bronson":** Ruben Rosario and Don Singleton, "'Death Wish' Gunman Wounds 4," *New York Daily News*, December 23, 1984, 3.
69 **"Something like [a vigilante shooting]":** Jim Levison, interview by the author, March 7, 2024, by Zoom.
70 **appearing in newspapers:** Joseph Berger, "Doctor Recalls His Brother, a Suspect in Rooftop Slaying," *New York Times*, December 9, 1984, 1.
70 **"DEATH OF A DREAM":** *New York Post*, December 4, 1984, 1.
70 **"SLAIN GIRL'S DYING WORDS":** *New York Post*, December 3, 1984, 1.
70 **"Grim Farewell to Slain":** *New York Post*, December 5, 1984, 1.
71 **Alexander Hamilton in:** Wolfgang Saxon, "The New York Post Has a Long History," *New York Times*, November 20, 1976, 23.

71 **previously untouchable figures:** Deirdre Carmody, "Dorothy Schiff Agrees to Sell Post to Murdoch, Australian Publisher," *New York Times*, November 20, 1976, 53.
71 **fear of going:** "Dorothy Schiff, Ex-Post Owner, Dies," *New York Times*, August 31, 1989, B11.
71 **she was thinking:** "The Battle of New York," *Time*, January 17, 1977, 56.
72 **been buried alive:** "The Battle of New York."
72 **Murdoch had figured:** Robert Kolarik, "*San Antonio Express-News* History, Part 3: Wild in the Streets," *San Antonio Express-News*, July 10, 2008; Steve Stecklow, Aaron O. Patrick, Martin Peers, and Andrew Higgins, "In Murdoch's Career, a Hand on the News," *Wall Street Journal*, June 5, 2007.
72 **"provided a daily":** "The Battle of New York."
73 **"carry on vigorously":** Deirdre Carmody, "Dorothy Schiff Agrees to Sell Post to Murdoch, Australian Publisher," *New York Times*, November 20, 1976, 53.
73 **"impression was created":** Thomas Kiernan in "Transcript: Who's Afraid of Rupert Murdoch?," *Frontline*, PBS, accessed May 19, 2024, https://www.pbs.org/wgbh/frontline/wgbh/pages/frontline/programs/transcripts/1404.html.
73 **with sections such:** Susan Mulcahy and Frank DiGiacomo, *Paper of Wreckage* (Simon & Schuster, 2024), 69.
73 **on the loose:** Steve Dunleavy in "Transcript: Who's Afraid of Rupert Murdoch?," *Frontline*, PBS, accessed May 19, 2024, https://www.pbs.org/wgbh/frontline/wgbh/pages/frontline/programs/transcripts/1404.html.
73 **send his missives:** Mulcahy and DiGiacomo, *Paper of Wreckage*, 72.
74 **the same time:** Mulcahy and DiGiacomo, *Paper of Wreckage*, 74.
74 **Elliott sent Murdoch:** Jonathan Mahler, "What Rupert Wrought," *New York*, April 1, 2005, https://nymag.com/nymetro/news/people/features/11673/.
74 **"fine old newspaper":** "Beame Calls The Post a Sensationalist Rag," *New York Times*, August 28, 1977, 42.
75 **didn't just endorse:** Ken Auletta in "Transcript: Who's Afraid of Rupert Murdoch?," *Frontline*, PBS, accessed May 19, 2024, https://www.pbs.org/wgbh/frontline/wgbh/pages/frontline/programs/transcripts/1404.html.
75 **"of the sixty":** Ken Auletta, "Promises, Promises," *New Yorker*, June 25, 2007, https://www.newyorker.com/magazine/2007/07/02/promises-promises-2.
75 **them to quit:** Carey Winfrey, "50 of 60 Reporters on Post Protest 'Slanted' Coverage of Mayor's Race," *New York Times*, October 5, 1977, 30.
75 **"sickening is happening":** Jonathan Mahler, "What Rupert Wrought," *New York*, April 1, 2005, https://nymag.com/nymetro/news/people/features/11673/.
75 **daily war with:** Merrill Brown, "Will Compete with Murdoch's 'Post,'" *Washington Post*, March 15, 1984.
76 **front-page headlines:** Alex S. Jones, "Headlines Blaring, City's Tabloids Step Up Battle," *New York Times*, December 10, 1984, B6.
76 **on the verge:** Brown, "Will Compete with Murdoch's 'Post.'"
76 **"editors and reporters":** "Urgent Appeal to Shooter," *New York Post*, December 24, 1984, 3.
76 **"straphangers to look":** Murray Weiss, Richard Sisk, and Don Gentile, "Riders Cheer Gunman," *New York Daily News*, December 25, 1984, 3.
76 **"wonder if the":** Sydney H. Schanberg, "A New Morality Play," *New York Times*, December 29, 1984, 21.
77 **eighty blocks south:** Alex Michelini, Peter McLaughlin, and Murray Weiss, "Vigilante a W. Side Story," *New York Daily News*, December 25, 1984, 3.
77 **On an express:** Hal Arkowitz and Scott Lilienfeld, "Why Science Tells Us Not to Rely on Eyewitness Accounts," *Scientific American*, January 1, 2010, https://www.scientificamerican.com/article/do-the-eyes-have-it/.
77 **further suggested that:** Marcia Chambers, "Goetz Held at Rikers I. in $50,000 Bail in Wounding of 4 Teen-Agers on IRT," *New York Times*, January 4, 1985, B1; Ruben Rosario and Don Singleton, "'Death Wish' Gunman Wounds 4," *New York Daily News*, December 23, 1984, 3; Chris Oliver and Leslie Gevirtz, "The Victims: We Wanted $5 to Play Video Game," *New York Post*, December 24, 1984, 3.
77 **The falsehood was:** Jimmy Breslin, "Color Us White and Brutal on This Black Day," *New York Daily News*, December 31, 1984, 6.

78 **having previously been:** John Eligon, "Michael Brown Spent Last Weeks Grappling with Problems and Promise," *New York Times*, August 24, 2014, A1.
78 **"not a good":** Margaret Sullivan, "An Ill-Chosen Phrase, 'No Angel,' Brings a Storm of Protest," *New York Times*, August 25, 2014, https://archive.nytimes.com/publiceditor.blogs.nytimes.com/2014/08/25/an-ill-chosen-phrase-no-angel-brings-a-storm-of-protest/.

CHAPTER TEN: JOSEPH ADAMS

80 **"heading north is":** Statement of Bernhard H. Goetz to Concord Police, December 31, 1984, Box 1, Folder 6.
80 **first documented stop:** Suzanne Daley, "Goetz Drove Across New England for Several Days Before Surrender," *New York Times*, January 4, 1985, B3.
81 **the blue windbreaker:** Marcia Chambers, "Goetz Spoke to One Youth, Then Shot Again, Police Say," *New York Times*, February 28, 1985, A1.
81 **his identity hidden:** Daley, "Goetz Drove Across New England for Several Days Before Surrender."
82 **"He was a very nice guy":** Daley, "Goetz Drove Across New England for Several Days Before Surrender."
82 **an antique bookstore:** Daley, "Goetz Drove Across New England for Several Days Before Surrender."
82 **There they could sit:** "End of the Line," *Time*, January 14, 1985, https://time.com/archive/6707530/end-of-the-line/.
82 **he told Stotler:** Tony Burton, "City Out of Control; N.H. Bookseller Recalls Goetz Visit," *New York Daily News*, January 3, 1985, 30.
82 **New York license:** Burton, "City Out of Control; N.H. Bookseller Recalls Goetz Visit."
82 **New Hampshire in:** Burton, "City Out of Control; N.H. Bookseller Recalls Goetz Visit."
82 **from New York:** "End of the Line."
82 **"he had been":** Burton, "City Out of Control; N.H. Bookseller Recalls Goetz Visit."
82 **spoke at length:** "End of the Line."
83 **"not safe in":** Burton, "City Out of Control; N.H. Bookseller Recalls Goetz Visit."
83 **police showed no:** Burton, "City Out of Control; N.H. Bookseller Recalls Goetz Visit."
83 **four young men:** "End of the Line."
83 **had not heard:** Burton, "City Out of Control; N.H. Bookseller Recalls Goetz Visit."
83 **"didn't try to":** "End of the Line."
83 **Stotler and his:** Daley, "Goetz Drove Across New England for Several Days Before Surrender."
83 **"sympathize with him":** Burton, "City Out of Control; N.H. Bookseller Recalls Goetz Visit."
83 **She wore heavy:** Anne Groer, "Orlando Gun Seller Testifies in Goetz Trial," *Orlando Sentinel*, May 13, 1987, A4; Mark Lesly with Charles Shuttleworth, *Subway Gunman: A Juror's Account* (British American Publishing, 1988), 125–26.
84 **previously lived above:** Myra Friedman with Michael Daly, "My Neighbor Bernie Goetz," *New York*, February 18, 1985, 35.
84 **"hardly the closest":** Friedman with Daly, "My Neighbor Bernie Goetz."
85 **predominantly black and brown:** Fox Butterfield, "46th Street 'Restaurant Row' Starts Guardian Angel Patrol," *New York Times*, June 10, 1988, A1.
85 **group has exploded:** "Our Chapters," Guardian Angels, accessed March 4, 2025, https://www.guardianangels.org/divisions.
85 **"The thing about these kids":** Butterfield, "46th Street 'Restaurant Row' Starts Guardian Angel Patrol."
85 **"have a certain":** Butterfield, "46th Street 'Restaurant Row' Starts Guardian Angel Patrol."
85 **"We would prefer":** Butterfield, "46th Street 'Restaurant Row' Starts Guardian Angel Patrol."
85 **"paramilitaries" who ought:** "Trouble with 'Angels' at Gracie Mansion," *New York Daily News*, September 15, 1980, 16.
85 **"People say, 'Oh, the Guardian Angels'":** Curtis Sliwa, interview by the author, December 10, 2024, by Zoom.
86 **Her stomach started:** Friedman with Daly, "My Neighbor Bernie Goetz.

87 **"notes from the police":** Friedman with Daly, "My Neighbor Bernie Goetz," 38.
88 **"until this blows over":** Friedman with Daly, "My Neighbor Bernie Goetz."
88 **"Oh, Myra":** Friedman with Daly, "My Neighbor Bernie Goetz," 39.
88 **"hoodlums" could get away:** Friedman with Daly, "My Neighbor Bernie Goetz."
88 **bag in a shape . . . No response at the door:** Trial transcript pages 6624–27, Box 8, Folder 2.
89 **heavily breathing:** Friedman with Daly, "My Neighbor Bernie Goetz."

CHAPTER ELEVEN: LIVE FREE OR DIE

90 **"I am the person":** Suzanne Daley, "Man Tells Police He Shot Youths in Subway Train," *New York Times,* January 1, 1985, Section 1, 1.
91 **"Although you might say":** Tony Burton, "I'm Your Man," *New York Daily News,* January 1, 1984, 13.
91 **Florida driver's license:** Trial transcript page 5113, Box 7, Folder 3.
92 **he assumed they would let him:** Nancy Grace, "Interview with 'Subway Vigilante' Bernhard Goetz," *Larry King Live,* CNN, December 17, 2004, https://transcripts.cnn.com/show/lkl/date/2004-12-17/segment/01.
92 **on the second floor:** Trial transcript page 5114, Box 7, Folder 3.
92 **"nervous, very nervous":** Trial transcript page 5120, Box 7, Folder 3.
94 **"You have to think":** Statement of Bernhard H. Goetz to Concord Police, December 31, 1984, 11.
94 **"The robbery has":** Statement of Bernhard H. Goetz to New York Police Department, December 31, 1984, 11–12.
94 **"The problem isn't the police" . . . "all the attention":** Statement of Bernhard H. Goetz to New York Police Department, December 31, 1984, 8.
95 **"They say I shot him":** Statement of Bernhard H. Goetz to New York Police Department, December 31, 1984, 30.
95 **"[t]hey know the rules":** Statement of Bernhard H. Goetz to Concord Police, December 31, 1984, 10.
95 **Even being asked . . . "body language":** Statement of Bernhard H. Goetz to Concord Police, December 31, 1984, 8, 44.
96 **"make them suffer":** Statement of Bernhard H. Goetz to Concord Police, December 31, 1984, 12.
96 **"I, in my heart, was a murderer":** Statement of Bernhard H. Goetz to New York Police Department, December 31, 1984, 28.
96 **"[I]f I had more bullets":** Statement of Bernhard H. Goetz to New York Police Department, December 31, 1984, 19.
96 **"You better learn a lesson":** Statement of Bernhard H. Goetz to New York Police Department, December 31, 1984, 31.
97 **"sadistic and savage":** Statement of Bernhard H. Goetz to Concord Police, December 31, 1984, Box 1, Folder 6. Statement of Bernhard H. Goetz to New York Police Department, December 31, 1984, Box 1, Folder 6.
98 **He was charged:** "Fugitive Charges Filed After Arrest in Subway Case," *Washington Post,* January 1, 1985.
98 **one word reply:** "'Vigilante Suspect Agrees to Return to New York City," *Washington Post,* January 2, 1985.
98 **"Oh, do I pity":** Stephen Crane, interview by the author, April 11, 2024, by Zoom.
99 **Lee Harvey Oswald:** Ruben Rosario, Frank Faso, Stuart Marques, and Don Flynn, "Goetz Under Wraps; Beef Up Security in Court," *New York Daily News,* January 4, 1985, 32.
99 **diverted all traffic:** Rosario et al., "Goetz Under Wraps; Beef Up Security in Court."
99 **several of them:** Rosario et al., "Goetz Under Wraps; Beef Up Security in Court."
99 **"Let him go!":** Frank Faso, Ruben Rosario, and Don Singleton, "Goetz' Bail Set at 50G; Intent to Kill Is Cited," *New York Daily News,* January 4, 1985, 3.
99 **"wasn't a great piece" . . . "*Beat him up?*":** Jim Levison, interview by the author, March 7, 2024, by Zoom.

CHAPTER TWELVE: POWER TO THE VIGILANTE

103 **"Ride with Bernie":** Richard Feldman, *Ricochet: Confessions of a Gun Lobbyist* (John Wiley & Sons, 2008), 102.

104 **"You had enough fun":** Susan Mulcahy and Frank DiGiacomo, *Paper of Wreckage* (Simon & Schuster, 2024), 265–66.
104 **"Trigger Happy":** Margot Hornblower, "In City of Strong Opinions, Goetz Trial Pulls a Crowd," *Washington Post,* May 3, 1987, https://www.washingtonpost.com/archive/politics/1987/05/03/in-city-of-strong-opinions-goetz-trial-pulls-a-crowd/3b545df2-dec7-4643-bf73-4036603d8df3/.
104 ***New York Times* polling:** Robert D. McFadden, "Poll Indicates Half of New Yorkers See Crime as City's Chief Problem," *New York Times,* January 14, 1985, A1.
105 **"cheering lustily":** Jimmy Breslin, "The Gunner Grows Smaller as the Facts Mount," *New York Daily News,* January 3, 1985, 6.
105 **He was suspicious . . . "In picking up the guns Goetz":** Les Payne, "A Hero to the Hysterical: A Vigilante Who's Blond," *Newsday,* January 6, 1985, 7.
105 **Mayor Koch complained . . . "In a city like this":** Joyce Purnick, "Koch's Troubles with the Press," *New York Times,* March 3, 1985, Section 4, 6.
106 **a staff editorial:** The Editorial Board, "Vigilance to Justice," *Wall Street Journal,* December 31, 1984.
106 **"What are you supposed":** Mike Royko, "They Deserved It, Sure as Shooting," *New York Daily News,* January 16, 1985, 6.
106 **William F. Buckley analogized:** William F. Buckley Jr., "Before Goetz, There Was Calley," *New York Daily News,* January 22, 1985, 28.
107 **"Take time to think":** John Leo, "Behavior: Low Profile for a Legend Bernhard Goetz," *Time,* Monday January 21, 1985.
107 **Subway Vigilante Game:** Subway Vigilante Game: The Home Version (Paperback Games: Bethesda, Md.), 1985, accessed May 3, 2025, https://boardgamegeek.com/image/5189218/subway-vigilante.
107 **"Subway Vigilante, an ode":** Mike Palumbo, "Race Relations During the Reagan Years," *20th Century History Song Book,* https://20thcenturyhistorysongbook.com/song-book/1980s-the-reagan-years/race-relations-during-the-reagan-years/. Also accessed May 3, 2025, https://www.discogs.com/release/27168639-Ronny-The-Urban-Watchdogs-Subway-Vigilante and https://www.discogs.com/release/27168639-Ronny-The-Urban-Watchdogs-Subway-Vigilante/image/SW1hZ2U6OTU0NDk3MTM=.
107 **"The Executioner":** Palumbo, "Race Relations During the Reagan Years"; *Background Magazine,* "Pallas—The Executioner," posted November 5, 2012, YouTube, 00:05:41, https://www.youtube.com/watch?v=wz3fUH00YSU.
107 **"Shoot His Load":** Genius lyrics, accessed May 3, 2025, https://genius.com/Agnostic-front-shoot-his-load-lyrics. For years after the shooting: "Hold On," track 10 on Lou Reed, *New York,* produced by Lou Reed and Fred Maher, 1989; "B-Boy Bouillabaisse," track 15 on Beastie Boys, *Paul's Boutique,* produced by Beastie Boys, The Dust Brothers, and Mario Caldato Jr., 1989; "Clan in da Front," track 3 on Wu-Tang Clan, *Enter the Wu-Tang (36 Chambers),* produced by RZA, 1993; "We Didn't Start the Fire," track 2 on Billy Joel, *Storm Front,* produced by Billy Joel and Mick Jones, 1989.
108 **Howard Stern:** George Maskian, "Success in the Raw," *New York Daily News,* January 12, 1985.
108 **"Bernhard Hugo Goetz What He Shoots":** "Song of the Vigilante," uploaded by Zsubgirl, YouTube, March 28, 2017, 0:03:08, https://youtu.be/tQoQGULmGr4?si=Ik72jnP2QQ8FX6VB.
109 **"I wish the roles":** "A Lawyer for Bernhard Goetz, Who Was Indicted on Weapons Charges . . . ," Associated Press, January 27, 1985.
109 **"defending New York society":** Associated Press, "Head of State G.O.P. Offered Aid to Goetz," *New York Times,* January 6, 1985, Section 1, 22.
109 **Using language that:** Ashley Jardina and Spencer Piston, "The Politics of Racist Dehumanization in the United States," *Annual Review of Political Science* 26, no. 1 (2023): 369–88.
109 **"because he was scared":** Associated Press, "Head of State G.O.P. Offered Aid to Goetz."
109 **"who tried to harass" . . . "we are living in fear":** Pia Beumer, "Bernhard Goetz and the Roots of Kyle Rittenhouse's Celebrity on the Right," *Washington Post,* June 15, 2022.
109 **"In general":** "Asked About Goetz, Reagan Cites the Law," *New York Times,* January 10, 1985, B3; Ronald Reagan, "The President's News Conference: U.S.-Soviet Relations,"

Ronald Reagan Presidential Library & Museum, January 9, 1985, https://www.reaganlibrary.gov/archives/speech/presidents-news-conference-21.

110 **"I don't blame the police":** Ronald Reagan, "The President's News Conference: U.S.-Soviet Relations," Ronald Reagan Presidential Library & Museum, January 9, 1985, https://www.reaganlibrary.gov/archives/speech/presidents-news-conference-21.

110 **"moral lepers" . . . He focused on improving:** Robert D. McFadden, "Edward I. Koch, a Mayor as Brash, Shrewd and Colorful as the City He Led, Dies at 88," *New York Times*, February 1, 2013.

111 **with antipoverty organizations:** Lee Dembart, "Koch, Criticized by Many Blacks, Seeks to Repair Ties with Them," *New York Times*, February 27, 1979, A1.

111 **His standing with the black:** McFadden, "Edward I. Koch, a Mayor as Brash, Shrewd and Colorful as the City He Led, Dies at 88."

112 **Koch was indeed gay:** Matt Flegenheimer and Rosa Goldensohn, "The Secrets Ed Koch Carried," *New York Times*, May 7, 2022.

112 **"poverty pimps":** Dembart, "Koch, Criticized by Many Blacks, Seeks to Repair Ties with Them."

113 **"I thought we should":** Sam Roberts, "Political Realities and Koch's Decision to Name Black Police Commissioner," *New York Times*, December 24, 1983, Section 1, 27.

113 **A public servant:** Douglas Martin, "Benjamin Ward, New York City's First Black Police Commissioner, Dies at 75," *New York Times*, June 11, 2002, A27.

114 **"He's black":** Murray Weiss and Alex Michelini, "Commish a Man of Many Jobs," *New York Daily News*, November 8, 1983, 60.

114 **"cop's cop" . . . "Many people make the mistake":** Martin, "Benjamin Ward, New York City's First Black Police Commissioner, Dies at 75," A27.

115 **"taking the law into":** Suzanne Daley, "Man Tells Police He Shot Youths in Subway Train," *New York Times*, January 1, 1985, 1.

115 **"I cannot imagine":** Marcia Chambers, "Goetz Rejects Offers on Bail from a Stranger and Family," *New York Times*, January 5, 1985, 25.

CHAPTER THIRTEEN: THREE TO ONE

116 **skyrocketing in value:** Jeffrey Toobin, "The Morgenthau Family's Gilded Path to the Manhattan D.A.'s Office," *New York Times*, October 8, 2022.

117 **a sprawling office:** Robert D. McFadden, "Robert Morgenthau, Longtime Manhattan District Attorney, Dies at 99," *New York Times*, July 21, 2019.

117 **"crime in the streets":** McFadden, "Robert Morgenthau, Longtime Manhattan District Attorney, Dies at 99."

117 **largely leaving the:** Toobin, "The Morgenthau Family's Gilded Path to the Manhattan D.A.'s Office."

117 **Some 250 lawyers:** Frank Faso, Ruben Rosario, and Don Singleton, "Goetz' Bail Set at 50G; Intent to Kill Is Cited," *New York Daily News*, January 4, 1985, 3.

117 **The security inside:** Rosario et al., "Goetz Under Wraps; Beef Up Security in Court."

118 **His face was scruffy:** Marcia Chambers, "Goetz Held at Rikers I. in $50,000 Bail in Wounding of 4 Teen-Agers on IRT," *New York Times*, January 4, 1985, B1.

118 **"Detective Daniel Hattendorf":** Faso, Rosario, and Singleton, "Goetz' Bail Set at 50G; Intent to Kill Is Cited."

119 **Judge Leslie Crocker Snyder:** Marcia Chambers, "Goetz Rejects Offers on Bail from a Stranger and Family," *New York Times*, Section 1, 25.

119 **thought it was too low:** Marcia Chambers, "Goetz Held at Rikers I. in $50,000 Bail in Wounding of 4 Teen-Agers on IRT," *New York Times*, January 4, 1985, B1.

119 **The crush of spectators:** Rosario et al., "Goetz Under Wraps; Beef Up Security in Court."

119 **defendants to lessen:** Chambers, "Goetz Rejects Offers on Bail from a Stranger and Family."

119 **"identified" with Goetz:** Chambers, "Goetz Rejects Offers on Bail from a Stranger and Family."

120 **how they could support Goetz's defense:** Thomas Hanrahan, Murray Weiss, and Don Gentile, "'Where Do I Send Money?' Angry New Yorkers Say They'll Bail Out Suspect," *New York Daily News*, January 4, 1985, 3.

120 **Other offers came in:** Associated Press, "Head of State G.O.P. Offered Aid to Goetz," *New York Times*, January 6, 1985, Section 1, 22.

120 **Despite the easy money . . . "publicly raised bail money":** Chambers, "Goetz Rejects Offers on Bail from a Stranger and Family."

120 **and posted his own . . . kept the release quiet:** Marcia Chambers, "Goetz Posts Bail and Is Freed; Youths He Shot Won't Testify," *New York Times*, January 9, 1985, A1.

123 **made the decision to call the three . . . "excruciating pain":** Chambers, "Goetz Posts Bail and Is Freed; Youths He Shot Won't Testify."

124 **once he got on the stand:** "Goetz Posts Bail and Is Freed; Youths He Shot Won't Testify," *New York Times*, January 9, 1985, https://www.nytimes.com/1985/01/09/nyregion/goetz-posts-bail-and-is-freed-youths-he-shot-won-t-testify.html.

125 **none of whom had overheard:** Jim Dwyer, "Goetz Indicted on Gun Charge, but Not in Shooting of 4 on IRT," *Newsday*, January 26, 1985, 3, 10.

126 **"practically an exoneration" . . . "What kind of hero":** Margot Hornblower, "N.Y. Jury Refuses to Indict Goetz for Attempted Murder," *Washington Post*, January 26, 1985.

126 **Shirley Cabey did not respond . . . "What this says to me":** Dwyer, "Goetz Indicted on Gun Charge, but Not in Shooting of 4 on IRT."

126 **"tantamount to a" . . . "silly" and "unintelligent":** Associated Press, "Some See Goetz Charge as Wise, Others as Racist," *Poughkeepsie Journal*, January 26,1985, 2.

127 **"You don't know":** Marcia Chambers, "Grand Jury Votes to Indict Goetz Only on Gun Possession Charges," *New York Times*, January 26, 1985, 1.

127 **"instant justice":** Joyce Purnick, "Koch's Shifts Reflect Complexity of Goetz and Bumpurs Cases," *New York Times*, February 23, 1985, 27.

127 **violent crimes "Solomonic":** Selwyn Raab, "Mayor Backs Jury on Goetz: Questions Action on Officer," *New York Times*, February 9, 1985, 27.

127 **Days later:** Purnick, "Koch's Shifts Reflect Complexity of Goetz and Bumpurs Cases."

127 **"The rights of society":** Esther B. Fein, "Angry Citizens in Many Cities Supporting Goetz," *New York Times*, January 7, 1985, B1.

127 **"I believe that most":** "Bernhard Goetz Arrested After Allegedly Selling Pot to Undercover Cop," CBS News, November 2, 2013, https://www.cbsnews.com/newyork/news/bernhard-goetz-arrested-after-allegedly-selling-pot-to-undercover-cop/.

128 **asking audiences about:** Purnick, "Koch's Shifts Reflect Complexity of Goetz and Bumpurs Cases."

128 **"We want John Lindsay!":** William H. Conan, "Ed Koch: The Man Behind the Mayor," *New York Times*, February 1, 1981, Section 6, 19.

128 **"Just as I said" . . . "I don't believe if you look at my statements":** Purnick, "Koch's Shifts Reflect Complexity of Goetz and Bumpurs Cases."

129 **"The facts that make":** Associated Press, "Goetz Backers Similar to 'Lynch Mob,'" *Journal News*, February 22, 1985, 4.

130 **"I'm not surprised that":** "Major News in Summary: Ward Weighs In on Goetz Case," *New York Times*, February 4, 1985, Section 4, 1.

130 **directly challenged the police chief's comments:** Marcia Chambers, "Goetz Spoke to One Youth, Then Shot Again, Police Say," *New York Times*, February 28, 1985, A1.

130 **"It was the view":** Chambers, "Grand Jury Votes to Indict Goetz Only on Gun Possession Charges."

130 **"might have made a difference" . . . "We're not interested in tilting":** Sam Roberts, "Morgenthau Says Goetz Case May Go to 2D Grand Jury," *New York Times*, March 1, 1985, A1.

131 **That Robert Morgenthau, who regarded receiving less:** Andrew Meier, *Morgenthau: Power, Privilege, and the Rise of an American Dynasty* (Random House, 2022), 708.

131 **"failing to get a more serious":** Marcia Chambers, "U.S. Attorney Meets with Blacks over Request for Inquiry on Goetz," *New York Times*, January 30, 1985, B6.

131 **"Women—lots of women":** Meier, *Morgenthau: Power, Privilege, and the Rise of an American Dynasty*, 709–10.

131 **"We thought we had":** Richard Stengel, "New Evidence," *Time*, March 25, 1985, https://time.com/archive/6708969/new-evidence.

CHAPTER FOURTEEN: GUNFIGHT IN CINCINNATI

133 **on promoting hunting:** Joel Achenbach, Scott Higham, and Sari Horwitz, "How NRA's True Believers Converted a Marksmanship Group into a Mighty Gun Lobby," *Washington Post*, January 12, 2013.

134 **series of Black Panther protests:** "Mapping the Black Panther Party in Key Cities," *Mapping American Social Movements Project,* accessed May 28, 2025, https://depts.washington.edu/moves/BPP_map-cities.shtml
134 **he got far more vocal:** Adam Winkler, *Gunfight: The Battle over the Right to Bear Arms in America* (W. W. Norton, 2011), 237–45.
135 **No evidence tying Casiano:** John M. Crewdson, "Hard-Line Opponent of Gun Laws Wins New Term at Helm of Rifle Association," *New York Times,* May 4, 1981, B11.
135 **NRA's bylaws gave members:** Joel Achenbach et al., "How NRA's True Believers Converted a Marksmanship Group into a Mighty Gun Lobby."
137 ***Washington Post*/ABC News poll:** Barry Sussman, "Poll Shows Americans Split over Goetz Case," *Washington Post,* January 19, 1985.
137 **"a very bipartisan issue" . . . "things like that":** Richard Feldman, interview by the author, February 27, 2024, by telephone.
138 **Roy Innis wasn't just . . . "morally corrupt":** Robert D. McFadden, "Roy Innis, Black Activist with a Right-Wing Bent, Dies at 82," *New York Times,* January 10, 2017.
139 **"[I]t is because I learned":** "ABC News/*Time* Forum: Guns," *ABC News Special,* January 24, 1990.
139 **He believed that disarming:** James V. O'Connor, "Roy Innis Defines Himself and Politics," *New York Times,* September 22, 1986.
139 **"was not meant":** Emily Langer, "Roy Innis, Embattled Leader of the Congress of Racial Equality, dies at 82," *Washington Post,* January 9, 2017.
139 **"outrageously bad idea":** Owen Fitzgerald, Charles Seaton, and Larry Sutton, "Bernie Triggers Koch Reaction," *New York Daily News,* February 26, 1985, 5.
139 **"avenger for all of us" . . . "I wish it had been me":** John Leo, "Behavior: Low Profile for a Legend Bernard Goetz," *Time,* January 21, 1985.
139 **"nothing to do with race":** David E. Pitt, "Blacks See Goetz Verdict as Blow to Race Relations," *New York Times,* June 18, 1987, A1.
139 **Innis was no stranger . . . "Self-Protection Is Your Right":** Richard Feldman, *Ricochet: Confessions of a Gun Lobbyist* (John Wiley & Sons, 2008), 94.
141 **"Never before have I seen":** Feldman, *Ricochet,* 100.
144 **"We're going to the U.S. Attorney's office":** "Goetz Lawyer: Don't Take Law into Your Own Hands," Associated Press, January 28, 1985.

CHAPTER FIFTEEN: WHEN RUDY MET AL

145 **Young Al Sharpton:** Gabrielle Olya, "How Al Sharpton Dropped an Astounding 176 Pounds," *People,* August 17, 2022.
145 **"The gold medallion":** Reverend Al Sharpton (@TheRevAl), "People always talk about me wearing my medallion, I wore the King medallion just like @RevJJackson & many of King's lieutenants. I continued the tradition of those who mentored me. I was given my King medallion from Hosea Washington for my activism in Howard Beach. #RevAlThrowback," Twitter (now X), May 27, 2019, https://x.com/TheRevAl/status/1133085664214433798.
145 **James Brown, who took Sharpton:** Howard Kurtz, "Al Sharpton, into the Maelstrom," *Washington Post,* July 14, 1988.
145 **He preached his:** Kurtz, "Al Sharpton, into the Maelstrom"; E. R. Shipp, "A Flamboyant Leader of Protests," *New York Times,* July 21, 1988, B6.
145 **While promoting a . . . "For $500,000":** Kurtz, "Al Sharpton, into the Maelstrom."
146 **For years, he had worked:** Shipp, "A Flamboyant Leader of Protests."
146 **he owed his:** Kurtz, "Al Sharpton, into the Maelstrom."
146 **following Sharpton's comments:** Corey Dade, "The Rev. Al Sharpton, in Six True-False Statements," NPR, January 19, 2013.
146 **"done more to heal":** Ron Kampeas, "Al Sharpton Admits to Using 'Cheap' Rhetoric About Jews," *Times of Israel,* May 20, 2019, https://www.timesofisrael.com/al-sharpton-admits-to-using-cheap-rhetoric-about-jews/.
146 **"represents a defiance":** Kurtz, "Al Sharpton, into the Maelstrom."
147 **"We had never gone":** Al Sharpton and Anthony Walton, *Go and Tell Pharaoh: The Autobiography of the Reverend Al Sharpton* (Doubleday, 1996), 89.
147 **"Alfred is the perfect black" . . . "Andy has been aligned":** Kurtz, "Al Sharpton, into the Maelstrom."

147 **he became "attached":** Al Sharpton, interview by the author, March 8, 2024, by Zoom.
148 **"poppycock, nonsense and foolish":** "A Lawyer for Bernhard Goetz, Who Was Indicted on Weapons Charge . . . ," Associated Press, January 27, 1985.
148 **"People feel we're for":** "A Lawyer for Bernhard Goetz, Who Was Indicted on Weapons Charge . . ."
148 **"The precedent to me":** Al Sharpton, interview by the author, March 8, 2024, by Zoom.
149 **local law enforcement officials feared:** Eric Nadler, "Want to Make a Federal Case Out of It?," *New York Daily News*, August 14, 1983, 16–17, 20.
149 **for enforcing laws:** Phil Roura and Tom Poster, "Ron's Top Drug Cop to Get Fed Post Here," *New York Daily News*, March 1, 1983, 9.
149 **He had been born . . . "brilliant" and a master:** Nadler, "Want to Make a Federal Case Out of It?"
150 **a master at cross-examining:** "Man in the News; Nominee for U.S. Attorney," *New York Times*, April 13, 1983, A25.
150 **He was also known as . . . dealing with others on a personal basis:** Nadler, "Want to Make a Federal Case Out of It?"
150 **"The federal civil rights":** Associated Press, "U.S. Prosecution of Goetz Sought," *New York Times*, January 29, 1985, B3; news services and staff reports, "Possible Civil Rights Charges Against Goetz Studied by U.S.," *Washington Post*, January 28, 1985.
150 **"We tried to suggest":** Marcia Chambers, "U.S. Attorney Meets with Blacks over Request for Inquiry on Goetz," *New York Times*, January 30, 1985, B6.
151 **"mildly contentious but not hostile":** Al Sharpton, interview by the author, March 8, 2024, by Zoom.
151 **Goetz acted out . . . the comment was "troubling":** Ellen Cates, "Manhattan U.S. Attorney Rudolph Giuliani Monday Ruled Out . . . ," United Press International, February 25, 1985.

CHAPTER SIXTEEN: REASONABLY REASONABLE REASONABLENESS

154 **thirty-seven-year-old Gregory Waples . . . "on a lark":** E. R. Shipp, "Goetz Prosecutor: Intensity and Talent," *New York Times*, May 30, 1987, Section 1, 33.
155 **"serious," "unpretentious to a fault":** Joseph Borini and Adam Nagourney, "A Trying Day for Goetz," *New York Daily News*, July 9, 1986, 3.
155 **He aggressively avoided . . . was arguably the best:** Shipp, "Goetz Prosecutor: Intensity and Talent."
156 **claimed to be the best . . . "liberty's last champion":** E. R. Shipp, "A Tenacious Slotnick Faces Biggest Test," *New York Times*, May 16, 1987, 33.
156 **watch poking out:** Lesly with Shuttleworth, *Subway Gunman*.
156 **alligator-skin briefcase:** James Patterson and Benjamin Wallace, *The Defense Lawyer* (New York: Little, Brown, 2021), 7.
156 **Slotnick was standing . . . "so-called organized crime figures":** Shipp, "A Tenacious Slotnick Faces Biggest Test."
157 **"Barry was always":** Gillian Coulter, interview by the author, January 29, 2025, by Zoom.
157 **"I don't represent people":** Patterson and Wallace, *The Defense Lawyer*, 32.
157 **hordes of paparazzi:** Patterson and Wallace, *The Defense Lawyer*, 33.
157 **slick courtroom tactics:** Shipp, "A Tenacious Slotnick Faces Biggest Test."
158 **"I want his story":** Sam Roberts, "Morgenthau Says Goetz Case May Go to 2D Grand Jury," *New York Times*, March 1, 1985, A1.
159 **"significant new evidence":** Salvatore Arena and Brian Kates, "Goetz Victim Testifies Before 2d Grand Jury," *New York Daily News*, March 19, 1985, 15.
159 **"That's why we were":** Thomas Hanrahan, "Want to See Goetz Fry: Victim," *New York Daily News*, March 19, 1985, 3.
160 **"Just because we":** Hanrahan, "Want to See Goetz Fry: Victim."
160 **"I want to see Bernie Goetz":** Hanrahan, "Want to See Goetz Fry: Victim."
161 **"a license to kill":** George P. Fletcher, *A Crime of Self-Defense: Bernhard Goetz and the Law on Trial* (University of Chicago Press, 1990), 58–59, note 47.
161 **"whether the evidence creates":** *People v. Goetz*, 502 N.Y.S.2d 577, (N.Y. Sup. Ct. 1986).
162 ***"So there's both":*** *People v. Goetz*, 502 N.Y.S.2d 577, 580 (N.Y. Sup. Ct. 1986).
162 **again hoping to testify:** Marcia Chambers, "Goetz Is Indicted for the Shooting of Four

on the IRT," *New York Times,* March 28, 1985, https://www.nytimes.com/1985/03/28/nyregion/goetz-is-indicted-for-the-shooting-of-four-on-the-irt.html.

164 **"slam dunk" for acquittal:** Stephen Crane, interview by the author, April 11, 2024, by Zoom.

164 **"he reasonably believes":** *People v. Goetz,* 502 N.Y.S.2d 577, 581-84 (N.Y. Sup. Ct. 1986).

164 **"A subjective standard":** Richard Meislin, "Morgenthau to Appeal Ruling on Goetz," *New York Times,* January 18, 1986, Section 1, 31.

165 **a "reasonable belief":** *People v. Goetz,* 68 N.Y.2d 96 (N.Y. 1986).

166 **"Steve, I hope":** Stephen Crane, interview by the author, April 11, 2024, by Zoom.

166 **"GOETZ INDICTMENT REINSTATED":** Gregory Waples, September 11, 2024, interview by the author, by Zoom.

CHAPTER SEVENTEEN: BINGO

167 **the Sixth Amendment:** "Sixth Amendment," Constitution Annotated, accessed March 5, 2025, https://constitution.congress.gov/constitution/amendment-6/.

167 **in initial screens of groups:** George P. Fletcher, *A Crime of Self-Defense: Bernhard Goetz and the Law on Trial* (University of Chicago Press, 1990), 90.

168 **Violent crime rates:** T. J. Deakin, "Crime in the United States 1986," *Law Enforcement Bulletin* 56, Issue 9 (September 1987): 5–12, https://www.ojp.gov/ncjrs/virtual-library/abstracts/crime-united-states-1986-0.

168 **"bio-underclass":** Charles Krauthammer, "Children of Cocaine," *Washington Post,* July 30, 1989.

168 **city was "sick":** Larry Sutton, "Right to Bear Arms?," *New York Daily News,* February 25, 1985, 5, 18.

169 **"MY STORY BY BERNHARD GOETZ":** Thomas Collins, "Goetz Turns on the Spotlight," *Newsday,* March 27, 1985, 138.

169 **Goetz stayed up until 5:30 a.m.:** James Patterson and Benjamin Wallace, *The Defense Lawyer* (New York: Little, Brown, 2021), 137.

169 **"We had those talks repeatedly":** Mark Baker, interview by the author, March 12, 2024, by Zoom.

169 **As media outlets:** Don Terry, "The Teen-Agers Goetz Shot: 4 Years Marked by Struggle," *New York Times,* January 14, 1989.

169 **Barry Allen gave:** Margot Hornblower, "Subway Vigilante's Victim Says He 'Learned Lesson,'" *Democrat & Chronicle,* January 11, 1985, 2.

169 **allowed the paper:** Margot Hornblower, "Wounded Youth Denies Intent to Rob New York City 'Subway Vigilante,'" *Washington Post,* January 11, 1985.

170 **had sold their story to the *National Enquirer*:** Hornblower, "Wounded Youth Denies Intent to Rob New York City 'Subway Vigilante."

170 **ten minutes of:** Mark Lesly with Charles Shuttleworth, *Subway Gunman: A Juror's Account* (British American Publishing, 1988), 77.

170 **broke out into applause:** Lesly with Shuttleworth, *Subway Gunman,* 2.

170 **"You sympathize with me":** Fletcher, *A Crime of Self-Defense,* 86.

171 **brought in a professional psychologist:** Fletcher, *A Crime of Self-Defense,* 88.

171 **George W. Bush claimed:** Steven Munson, "Bush Saw Putin's 'Soul.' Obama Wants to Appeal to His Brain," *Washington Post,* December 1, 2015.

171 **"Greenwich Village types":** Fletcher, *A Crime of Self-Defense,* 88.

172 **"Let's assume":** Fletcher, *A Crime of Self-Defense,* 88.

172 **allowed to "nullify":** Fletcher, *A Crime of Self-Defense,* 98.

173 **forbidden the practice:** *Batson v. Kentucky,* 476 U.S. 79 (1986).

173 **the Court applied the principle:** *Georgia v. McCollum,* 505 U.S. 42, 59 (1992).

173 **"I mean if they have records":** Fletcher, *A Crime of Self-Defense,* 90.

173 **"the last thing we wanted":** Mark Baker, interview by the author, March 12, 2024, by Zoom.

174 **"Sometimes these fears":** Fletcher, *A Crime of Self-Defense,* 85.

174 **Bernie "defended himself":** Philip Lentz, "After 2 Years of Controversy, Goetz Will Get His Day in Court," *Chicago Tribune,* March 22, 1987, 10.

175 **"I think the day of turning":** Esther Pessin, "Selection of Jury Clears Way for Goetz Trial," United Press International, April 8, 1987.

175 **Slotnick's representation of one of John Gotti's:** "Stage Set for Goetz Trial," *New York Times*, March 14, 1987, A32.
175 **a new profile:** Carole Augus, "Wolf or Wimp?": Myths and Realities of Bernhard Goetz, Subway Vigilante," *Chicago Tribune*, December 14, 1986, A1.
175 **an article about:** Gerald McKelvey, "Many Still Undecided on Goetz," *Newsday*, December 22, 1986, 9, 20.
175 **"fool's errand":** Gregory Waples, interview by the author, September 11, 2024, by Zoom.
175 **"Let's just say":** Gregory Waples, interview by the author, September 11, 2024, by Zoom.
175 **an overhead sketch of twelve jurors:** Anthony DeStefano, "The Subway Gunman Trial," *Newsday*, April 27, 1987, 6, 19.
176 **The news organizations apologized:** Lesly with Shuttleworth, *Subway Gunman*, 16–17.
176 **the defense tried to get the trial postponed:** Kirk Johnson, "Goetz Loses Last-Minute Attempt for Trial Delay," *New York Times*, April 25, 1987.
176 **"There comes a point":** Kirk Johnson, "Details Viewed as Key in Goetz Trial," *New York Times*, April 26, 1987, 38.
176 **Prosecutors apparently resisted:** Lentz, "After 2 Years of Controversy, Goetz Will Get His Day in Court," 10.

CHAPTER EIGHTEEN: ROOM 572

178 **"It was insane":** Gillian Coulter, interview by the author, January 29, 2025, by Zoom.
178 **ready to jump in:** Dennis Duggan, "Street Jury Issues Verdict on Goetz," *Newsday*, April 28, 1987, 32.
178 **"Bernhard Goetz: Blame the Criminals":** Margot Hornblower, "In City of Strong Opinions, Goetz Trial Pulls a Crowd," *Washington Post*, May 3, 1987.
179 **Revolutionary Communist Party:** Hornblower, "In City of Strong Opinions, Goetz Trial Pulls a Crowd."
179 **"Mug at Your Own Risk":** "In City of Strong Opinions, Goetz Trial Pulls a Crowd."
179 **"Who, stimulated by":** Hornblower, "In City of Strong Opinions, Goetz Trial Pulls a Crowd."
179 **"Look at that":** Duggan, "Street Jury Issues Verdict on Goetz," 32.
180 **spectators at the:** Mark Lesly with Charles Shuttleworth, *Subway Gunman: A Juror's Account* (British American Publishing, 1988), 30.
180 **Among the daily hundred or so:** Jerry Schwartz, "They Queue Up Every Day for Sensational Trial," Associated Press, May 10, 1987.
180 **several dozen reporters:** Lesly with Shuttleworth, *Subway Gunman*, 20.
180 **Lubavitchers sympathetic to:** Duggan, "Street Jury Issues Verdict on Goetz," 32.
180 **actor Treat Williams:** Schwartz, "They Queue Up Every Day."
180 **Columbia Law School professor George Fletcher:** Margot Hornblower, "Jury Exonerates Goetz in 4 Subway Shootings," *Washington Post*, June 16, 1987, https://www.washingtonpost.com/archive/politics/1987/06/17/jury-exonerates-goetz-in-4-subway-shootings/53973777-a617-4ed5-88ed-e841e0643746/.
180 **Mary Ann Romano:** Hornblower, "In City of Strong Opinions, Goetz Trial Pulls a Crowd."
180 **Barbara Taylor:** Schwartz, "They Queue Up Every Day."
181 **Even Gregory Waples's father:** James Patterson and Benjamin Wallace, *The Defense Lawyer* (New York: Little, Brown, 2021), 285.
182 **his staff seated:** Fletcher, *A Crime of Self-Defense*, 9.
182 **five-hundred-attorney megalith with a:** Robert D. McFadden, "Robert Morgenthau, Longtime Manhattan District Attorney, Dies at 99," *New York Times*, July 21, 2019, A23.
182 **began to address:** Lesly with Shuttleworth, *Subway Gunman*, 23.
182 **"Suddenly, however, that day":** Trial transcript pages 4760–61, Box 7, Folder 2.
183 **"blind, self-righteous, volcanic fury" . . . "hollow-point bullets":** Trial transcript pages 4787–94, Box 7, Folder 2.
184 **"[P]rovidence alone":** Trial transcript page 4761, Box 7, Folder 2.
185 **"For whatever reason":** Trial transcript page 4764, Box 7, Folder 2.
186 **choreographed stage directions:** Lesly with Shuttleworth, *Subway Gunman*, 30.
185 **"[Y]ou're going to see":** Trial transcript page 4891, Box 7, Folder 2.
186 **calling them "vultures" . . . "without pity in their eyes":** Trial transcript pages 4822, 4830, 4834, 4838, 4885, Box 7, Folder 2.

186 **"[Ramseur] will take this witness stand" . . . "And the answer":** Trial transcript pages 4827–29, Box 7, Folder 2.
187 **imaginary witness as:** Lesly with Shuttleworth, *Subway Gunman*, 32–33.
187 **"license to lie":** Trial transcript page 4840, Box 7, Folder 2.
188 **a reasonable doubt is:** "Voir Dire Instructions," New York State Unified Court System, accessed March 5, 2025, https://www.nycourts.gov/judges/cji/5-SampleCharges/CJI2d.Voir_Dire.pdf.
189 **"persons are above":** Fletcher, *A Crime of Self-Defense*, 174n8; Record at 8825.
190 **"meanest-looking photographs":** Mark Baker, interview by the author, March 12, 2024, by Zoom.
191 **He accused Waples:** Trial transcript page 6770, Box 8, Folder 3.
191 **"Mr. Slotnick kept pictures":** Trial transcript pages 6769–70, Box 8, Folder 3.
191 **"life-threatening injuries" . . . "the people have the burden":** Lesly with Shuttleworth, *Subway Gunman*, 196.
192 **"a great place to visit":** Anne Groer, "Orlando Gun Seller Testifies in Goetz Trial," *Orlando Sentinel*, May 13, 1987.

CHAPTER NINETEEN: TWO BIG ITALIAN GUYS

194 **"had not labored":** Trial transcript pages 4779–80, Box 7, Folder 2.
195 **"normal" voice:** Trial transcript page 5786, Box 7, Folder 7.
195 **"Give me five dollars":** Statement of Bernhard H. Goetz to New York Police Department, December 31, 1984, Box 1, Folder 6.
195 **Goetz had paused for:** Kirk Johnson, "Goetz Shooting Victim Says Youths Weren't Threatening," *New York Times*, May 2, 1987, 31.
195 **"Mr. Canty, in December of 1984":** Trial transcript page 5390, Box 7, Folder 5.
196 **Eliciting clipped, enunciated answers:** Kirk Johnson, "Judge Refuses Immunity to Youth Shot by Goetz," *New York Times*, May 12, 1987, B3.
196 **"robbing and stealing":** Trial transcript page 5395, Box 7, Folder 5.
197 **whether there were areas in which Allen could testify:** Johnson, "Judge Refuses Immunity to Youth Shot by Goetz."
197 **"Mr. Allen, do you know" . . . "On advice of":** Trial transcript page 6087, Box 7, Folder 8.
197 **"Mr. Allen, my name is":** Trial transcript page 6104, Box 7, Folder 9.
198 **Slotnick would ask the court:** Trial transcript page 6641, Box 8, Folder 2.
198 **"missing witness":** George Fletcher, *A Crime of Self-Defense: Bernhard Goetz and the Law on Trial* (University of Chicago Press, 1988), 151.
198 **felt about ninety degrees:** Trial transcript page 7882, Box 20, Folder 7.
198 **closed early due to the heat:** Trial transcript page 7129, Box 8, Folder 5.
198 **"It's warm in the courtroom":** Trial transcript page 7877, Box 20, Folder 7.
199 **"I knew he was not going to be a star":** Gregory Waples, interview by the author, September 11, 2024, by Zoom.
199 **"contumacious" on the stand . . . and tried desperately:** Trial transcript page 5829, Box 7, Folder 7.
199 **"there is some persuasiveness":** Trial transcript pages 5911–12, Box 7, Folder 7.
199 **wearing dirty white jeans:** Kirk Johnson, "Youth Shot in Subway Says He Didn't Approach Goetz," *New York Times*, May 20, 1987, B3.
200 **"I'm not taking":** Trial transcript page 5931, Box 7, Folder 8.
200 **"Sorry, your honor, I can't hear":** Trial transcript page 5931, Box 7, Folder 8
200 **a risky step:** Fletcher, *A Crime of Self-Defense*, 131.
200 **With his hands in:** Mark Lesly with Charles Shuttleworth, *Subway Gunman: A Juror's Account* (British American Publishing, 1988), 93.
200 **"draw no inferences and":** Trial transcript page 5934, Box 7, Folder 8.
200 **Now wearing a:** Johnson, "Youth Shot in Subway Says He Didn't Approach Goetz."
201 **"Do you want me to":** Trial transcript page 7247, Box 8, Folder 5.
201 **"Oh shit, Troy":** Trial transcript page 7052, Box 8, Folder 4.
202 **"big Italian guys":** Selwyn Raab, "A Man Goetz Shot Is Charged with Faking Own Abduction," *New York Times*, March 27, 1985, B8.
202 **the cops figured:** Raab, "A Man Goetz Shot Is Charged with Faking Own Abduction."
202 **Goetz's friends would soon:** Fletcher, *A Crime of Self-Defense*, 131.

203 **"If you can't answer yes or no":** Trial transcript page 7232, Box 8, Folder 6.
203 **"If I may":** Trial transcript pages 7245–46, Box 8, Folder 5.
204 **"Weren't you convicted":** Trial transcript pages 7251–52, Box 8, Folder 5.
205 ***flashing a wry*:** Lesly with Shuttleworth, *Subway Gunman*, 171.
205 **Ramseur rocked and:** Johnson, "Youth Shot in Subway Says He Didn't Approach Goetz."
205 **"Do you remember, Mr. Ramseur":** Trial transcript pages 7257–59, Box 8, Folder 5.
207 **"He's playing games with me":** Trial transcript page 7265, Box 8, Folder 5.
207 **"If you are going to get me":** Trial transcript page 7268, Box 8, Folder 5.
207 **"I would respectfully ask" . . . "pleading" or "coaxing":** Fletcher, *A Crime of Self-Defense*, 133.
207 **"I am not a partisan here":** Trial transcript page 7274, Box 8, Folder 6.
208 **"When was the last time prior to":** Trial transcript page 7279, Box 8, Folder 5.
208 **"James, why don't you":** Trial transcript page 7266, Box 8, Folder 5.
208 **cellblock 74:** Mike Pearl and Doug Feiden, "'Toss Out Ramseur Ravings,'" *New York Post*, May 21, 1987, 7, 15.
208 **"pent-up rage":** Otto Friedrich, Roger Franklin, and Raji Samghabadi, "Not Guilty," *Time*, June 29, 1987, 10–11.
208 ***New York Post* ran a large headline:** Pearl and Feiden, "'Toss Out Ramseur Ravings,'" 7, 15.
208 **stand as "sullen":** Gregory Waples, interview by the author, September 11, 2024, by Zoom.
208 **"You're not to speculate as":** Trial transcript pages 7743–44, Box 20, Folder 6.
208 **pity and anger:** Kirk Johnson, "Judge Sentences a Goetz Victim over Outbursts," *New York Times*, May 23, 1987, 31.
208 **"had conveyed viciousness":** Kirk Johnson, "Judge Sentences a Goetz Victim Over Outbursts," *New York Times*, May 23, 1987, 31.
209 **He still refused:** Johnson, "Judge Sentences a Goetz Victim over Outbursts."
209 **As he testified:** Lesly with Shuttleworth, *Subway Gunman*, 176.
209 **Slotnick deliberately cowered:** James Patterson and Benjamin Wallace, *The Defense Lawyer* (New York: Little, Brown, 2021), 337.
209 **three or four guards quickly:** Fletcher, *A Crime of Self-Defense*, 132.
209 **"five o'clock follies":** Kirk Johnson, "Reporter's Notebook: Vagaries of the Goetz Trial," *New York Times*, May 24, 1987, A26.
209 **"If he had a gun":** Fletcher, *A Crime of Self-Defense*, 132.
210 **the man had an itch:** Fletcher, *A Crime of Self-Defense*, 132n42.
210 **least one juror:** Lesly with Shuttleworth, *Subway Gunman*, 176.
210 **"[T]o all of the court officers":** Trial transcript page 7326, Box 8, Folder 6.
210 **Waples, appearing bemused by:** Fletcher, *A Crime of Self-Defense*, 132.

CHAPTER TWENTY: ANTE UP

211 **sleeves down but unbuttoned:** Kirk Johnson, "Reporter's Notebook: Vagaries of the Goetz Trial," *New York Times*, May 24, 1987, A26.
211 **some insight into his mind:** Mark Lesly with Charles Shuttleworth, *Subway Gunman: A Juror's Account* (British American Publishing, 1988), 28.
212 **"there was no way":** Mark Baker, interview by the author, March 12, 2024, by Zoom.
213 **"the brains of the outfit":** Lesly with Shuttleworth, *Subway Gunman*, 14.
214 **adding more microphones:** Lesly with Shuttleworth, *Subway Gunman*, 42.
214 **jurors got a:** Trial transcript page 5162, Box 7, Folder 4.
214 **to keep the antennae:** Trial transcript page 5163, Box 7, Folder 4.
214 **"The mood of the courtroom":** James Patterson and Benjamin Wallace, *The Defense Lawyer* (New York: Little, Brown, 2021), 298.
214 **would snap into:** Trial transcript page 5164, Box 7, Folder 4.
214 **top eight inches:** Johnson, "Reporter's Notebook: Vagaries of the Goetz Trial."
215 **ABC News had aired:** Fred Rothenberg, "ABC's '20-20' Devotes Full Hour to Goetz Case," Associated Press, March 21, 1985.
215 **"was about to be beaten" . . . avoiding looking at:** Frank Faso and Joseph McNamara, "Court Hears Goetz on Tape," *New York Daily News*, May 14, 1987, 5.
215 **"terrible things":** Mark Baker, interview by the author, March 12, 2024, by Zoom.

215 **"We're done" . . . "You're on":** Mark Baker, interview by the author, March 12, 2024, by Zoom.

CHAPTER TWENTY-ONE: EXHIBIT Y

217 **courts to this:** Amanda Hernandez, "Shortage of Prosecutors, Judges Leads to Widespread Court Backlogs," Stateline, January 25, 2024, https://stateline.org/2024/01/25/shortage-of-prosecutors-judges-leads-to-widespread-court-backlogs/.

218 **"the ultimate mensch":** Mark Baker, interview by the author, March 12, 2024, by Zoom.

218 **"lost it more than I probably":** Gregory Waples, interview by the author, September 11, 2024, by Zoom.

218 **asked him to officiate:** Ruth Pollack, interview by the author, April 15, 2025, by telephone.

218 **"worn down" . . . "cut the baby in half":** Gregory Waples, interview by the author, September 11, 2024, by Zoom.

219 **"trapped like a rat":** George Fletcher, *A Crime of Self-Defense: Bernhard Goetz and the Law on Trial* (University of Chicago Press, 1988), 128.

220 **"somewhat involved":** Kirk Johnson, "Goetz Jury Takes Short Trip on Subway," *New York Times,* May 30, 1987, 35.

220 **"class field trip":** Fletcher, *A Crime of Self-Defense,* 128; Johnson, "Goetz Jury Takes Short Trip on Subway," 35.

220 **"he didn't really want":** Esther Pessin, "Jurors in Goetz Trial Ride Subway Train," United Press International, May 30, 1987.

220 **"Bernie! Bernie! Bernie!":** Pessin, "Jurors in Goetz Trial Ride Subway Train."

220 **They rode a few blocks to the Chambers Street:** Johnson, "Goetz Jury Takes Short Trip on Subway."

220 **been stripped down:** Johnson, "Goetz Jury Takes Short Trip on Subway."

220 **used to perform maintenance:** Pessin, "Jurors in Goetz Trial Ride Subway Train."

220 **hop over a six-inch gap:** Frank Faso and Joseph McNamara, "Goetz Jury on Subway," *Daily News,* May 30, 1987, 3.

220 **The car was oriented:** Trial transcript page 7892, Box 20, Folder 7.

220 **totaled about thirty:** Faso and McNamara, "Goetz Jury on Subway."

221 **A transit worker had wiped:** Johnson, "Goetz Jury Takes Short Trip on Subway."

221 **graffiti still covered the car:** Faso and McNamara, "Goetz Jury on Subway."

221 **something big was happening:** Pessin, "Jurors in Goetz Trial Ride Subway Train."

221 **"Is this the Goetz car?":** Faso and McNamara, "Goetz Jury on Subway."

221 **"zoo atmosphere":** Faso and McNamara, "Goetz Jury on Subway."

221 **"circuslike" . . . "fish in an aquarium":** Mark Lesly, with Charles Shuttleworth, *Subway Gunman: A Juror's Account of the Bernhard Goetz Trial* (British American Publishing, 1988), 217–18.

222 **Justice Crane therefore:** Faso and McNamara, "Goetz Jury on Subway."

222 **pause the action:** Trial transcript pages 7922–40, Box 20, Folder 8.

222 **One merely had:** Trial transcript page 7934, Box 20, Folder 8.

222 **and his investigator:** Fletcher, *A Crime of Self-Defense,* 128.

223 **remain in place for:** Mike Pearl and Doug Feiden, "Play It Again, Bernie!," *New York Post,* May 28, 1987, 3.

223 **black teenagers:** Fletcher, *A Crime of Self-Defense,* 128.

223 **reduced to numbers:** Pearl and Feiden, "Play It Again, Bernie!"

223 **Slotnick argued:** Fletcher, *A Crime of Self-Defense,* 128.

223 **"full credit" . . . "Give me the meanest":** Mark Baker, interview by the author, March 12, 2024, by Zoom.

223 **act their most blatantly:** *Trial by Media,* season 1, episode 2, "Subway Vigilante," directed by Brian McGinn, Netflix, May 11, 2020, https://www.netflix.com/title/80198329.

224 **interview for this book:** Curtis Sliwa, interview by the author, December 10, 2024, by Zoom.

224 **"proper heights":** Trial transcript pages 7741–42, Box 20, Folder 6.

224 **courtroom that had now fallen silent:** Anthony DeStefano, "Goetz Defense Replays Shooting on Subway," *Newsday,* May 29, 1987, 2.

224 **Slotnick positioned the four men:** Fletcher, *A Crime of Self-Defense,* 129.

224 **The four muscular:** DeStefano, "Goetz Defense Replays Shooting on Subway."

224 **"They were looming":** Gregory Waples, interview by the author, September 11, 2024, by Zoom.
224 **described as "infuriated":** Mike Pearl and Doug Feiden, "Goetz Jury Taken for a Ride," *New York Post*, May 29, 1987, 5.
225 **"dozens" of objections:** Pearl and Feiden, "Goetz Jury Taken for a Ride."
225 **He sat on:** Trial transcript page 7792, Box 20, Folder 6.
226 **he ordered that court officers:** Fletcher, *A Crime of Self-Defense*, 129–30; trial transcript page 8044, Box 20, Folder 7.
226 **"no legal warrant":** Fletcher, *A Crime of Self-Defense*, 129.
226 **"covert message of racial fear":** Fletcher, *A Crime of Self-Defense*, 208.
226 **of the shooting:** Fletcher, *A Crime of Self-Defense*, 207.
226 **"If one were re-creating":** Fletcher, *A Crime of Self-Defense*, 129.
227 **"the ruddy face":** James Patterson and Benjamin Wallace, *The Defense Lawyer* (New York: Little, Brown, 2021), 341.
227 **"Here's a white guy":** Curtis Sliwa, interview by the author, December 10, 2024, by Zoom.
227 **picked up on the racial dynamics:** Pearl and Feiden, "Goetz Jury Taken for a Ride"; Pearl and Feiden, "Play It Again, Bernie!"
227 **"the threat of light vigilantism":** Al Sharpton, interview by the author, March 8, 2024, by Zoom.
227 **"pervasive and systemic" racism . . . "coon show":** Ronald Smothers, "23 Black Leaders and Koch Attack 'Pervasive' Racism, *New York Times*, January 1, 1987, 1.

CHAPTER TWENTY-TWO: *THE CHAMPION*

230 **"Holy smokes":** Mark Baker, interview by the author, March 12, 2024, by Zoom.
230 **five meandering hours of closing argument:** George Fletcher, *A Crime of Self-Defense: Bernhard Goetz and the Law on Trial* (University of Chicago Press, 1988), 174n5.
230 **case of the laryngitis:** Trial transcript pages 8267–68, Box 21, Folder 1.
230 **"freebasing drugs" . . . "other friends":** Trial Transcript page 8702, Box 21, Folder 6.
231 **"The mind went off":** Trial transcript page 8662, Box 21, Folder 6.
231 **"the most unreliable source":** James Patterson and Benjamin Wallace, *The Defense Lawyer* (New York: Little, Brown and Company, 2021), 359.
231 **confidence jurors felt:** Fletcher, *A Crime of Self-Defense*, 174–75.
232 **"The law protects everyone":** Trial transcript page 8825, Box 14, Folder 6.
232 **Waples reminded the jury:** Fletcher, *A Crime of Self-Defense*, 174–75.
233 **Slotnick had pointed:** Trial transcript pages 8696–97, Box 21, Folder 6.
233 **He pulled up a chair:** Fletcher, *A Crime of Self-Defense*, 176.
234 **"undoubtedly annoyed" and "intimidated" . . . "rambunctious young teens":** Trial transcript page 8971, Box 21, Folder 6.
234 **"If this defendant":** Trial transcript page 8977, Box 14, Folder 7.
235 **"this guy is insulting my intelligence" . . . "alienated everyone":** Fletcher, *A Crime of Self-Defense*, 179–80.
235 **"the kind of comment that reinforced":** Lesly with Shuttleworth, *Subway Gunman*, 317.
235 **"could have filtered the thought" . . . "Maybe it really didn't matter":** Gregory Waples, interview by the author, September 11, 2024, by Zoom.
236 **"The public at large":** Trial transcript page 8828, Box 21, Folder 6.

CHAPTER TWENTY-THREE: SYMPATHY FOR THE VIGILANTE

237 **"I need to start you":** Mark Lesly with Charles Shuttleworth, *Subway Gunman: A Juror's Account of the Bernhard Goetz Trial* (British American Publishing, 1988), 266.
238 **they gradually gave it:** Lesly with Shuttleworth, *Subway Gunman*, 45–46, 298.
239 **they found him guilty:** George Fletcher, *A Crime of Self-Defense: Bernhard Goetz and the Law on Trial* (University of Chicago Press, 1988), 182.
240 **"open and shut":** Fletcher, *A Crime of Self-Defense*, 182.
240 **sold her story:** Trial transcript page 6705, Box 8, Folder 2.
240 **"I have other guns":** Lesly with Shuttleworth, *Subway Gunman*, 277.
241 **"People don't get convicted":** Trial transcript page 8680, Box 21, Folder 6.
241 **They had little:** Kirk Johnson, "Goetz Is Cleared in Subway Attack; Gun Count Upheld; Acquittal Won in Shooting of 4 Youths—Prison Term Possible on Weapon Charge," *New York Times*, June 17, 1987, A1.

241 **"[It was] very tough":** Gillian Coulter, interview by the author, January 29, 2025, by Zoom.
242 **"I don't know why I":** Trial transcript pages 7387–88, Box 8, Folder 6.
242 **"Cabey said he sat down":** Jimmy Breslin, "Shooting Script: In Hospital, the Line from Cabey," *New York Daily News*, November 26, 1985, 5.
243 **"Miss, I've been shot":** Trial transcript page 6273, Box 7, Folder 9.
244 **an "adrenal haze":** Lesly with Shuttleworth, *Subway Gunman*, 295.
244 **One juror suggested that:** Lesly with Shuttleworth, *Subway Gunman*, 294–95.
245 **"near hysteria":** Gail Collins, "'Trapped' by His Fear: Jurors' Pity for Goetz," *New York Daily News*, June 17, 1987, 5.
245 **"[t]he statements of a man":** Lesly with Shuttleworth, *Subway Gunman*, 295.
245 **"get a free trip" . . . have a soft spot:** Fletcher, *A Crime of Self-Defense*, 242n.52.
245 **"disturbed" and "quirky":** Fletcher, *A Crime of Self-Defense*, 188.
246 **"We needed a motive":** Fletcher, *A Crime of Self-Defense*, 186.
246 **"Where have they":** Fletcher, *A Crime of Self-Defense*, 186.
247 **Several burst into:** Lesly with Shuttleworth, *Subway Gunman*, xiv.
247 **Goetz . . . dropped his head:** Lesly with Shuttleworth, *Subway Gunman*, xiv.
248 **Loud gasps shot:** Fletcher, *A Crime of Self-Defense*, 186; Lesly with Shuttleworth, *Subway Gunman*, xv.
248 **Several court officers:** Lesly with Shuttleworth, *Subway Gunman*, xv.
248 **("*Bernie Goetz* in prison?"):** Gillian Coulter, interview by the author, January 29, 2025, by Zoom.
249 **"[d]oesn't it become":** Gillian Coulter, interview by the author, January 29, 2025, by Zoom.
249 **"Can I go home now?":** Kirk Johnson, "Goetz Is Cleared in Subway Attack; Gun Count Upheld; Acquittal Won in Shooting of 4 Youths—Prison Term Possible on Weapon Charge," *New York Times*, June 17, 1987, https://www.nytimes.com/1987/06/17/nyregion/goets-cleared-subway-attack-gun-count-upheld-acquittal-won-shooting-4-youths.html.
249 **Protesters held up:** Otto Friedrich, Roger Franklin, and Raji Samghabadi, "Not Guilty," *Time*, June 29, 1987, 10–11.
249 **"to thank the people of New York" . . . One woman was:** Johnson, "Goetz Is Cleared in Subway Attack," A1.
250 **"GOETZ RACIST MURDERER":** "Ward Rips Changing of Charge by Judge," *New York Daily News*, June 18, 1987, 5.
250 **He had to ask:** Johnson, "Goetz Is Cleared in Subway Attack."
250 **Someone had also:** Johnson, "Goetz Is Cleared in Subway Attack."
250 **like the Beatles:** Collins, "'Trapped' by His Fear: Jurors' Pity for Goetz."
250 **jurors flashed "victory":** Johnson, "Goetz Is Cleared in Subway Attack."
251 **"race or racism":** Collins, "'Trapped' by His Fear: Jurors' Pity for Goetz."
251 **"We were doing":** Friedrich, Franklin, and Samghabadi, "Not Guilty."
251 **Robert Morgenthau gave:** Johnson, "Goetz Is Cleared in Subway Attack."
251 **"I underestimated the":** Andrew Meier, *Morgenthau: Power, Privilege, and the Rise of an American Dynasty* (Random House, 2022), 708–9.
252 **Despite having made:** Fletcher, *A Crime of Self-Defense*, 202.
252 **"This has sent a message":** Fletcher, *A Crime of Self-Defense*, 201.
252 **Mayor Koch broadly:** "Implications of Goetz Verdict Debated," United Press International, June 21, 1987.
252 **write a letter to Justice Crane:** Susan Milligan and Marilyn Thompson, "Black Clerics Bash Koch," *New York Daily News*, June 18, 1987, 5.
252 **"trust the system":** Milligan and Thompson, "Black Clerics Bash Koch."
252 **The event got:** Milligan and Thompson, "Black Clerics Bash Koch."
253 **"I think that if a black":** David Pitt, "Blacks See Goetz Verdict as Blow to Race Relations," *New York Times*, June 18, 1987, A1.
253 **"could well encourage others":** Milligan and Thompson, "Black Clerics Bash Koch."
253 **"Yeah, we were right":** Fletcher, *A Crime of Self-Defense*, 201.
253 **The case proved:** Jaclyn Diaz, "The Central Park 5 Are Exonerated. Trump Doesn't Seem to Think So," NPR, September 11, 2024, https://www.npr.org/2024/09/11/nx-s1-5108632/central-park-five-trump-debate.

254 ***New York Times*/WCBS-TV poll:** Maureen Dowd, "Fear of Crime Seems to Strain Race Relations," *New York Times*, May 16, 1985, B4.
254 **"These kids feel":** Pitt, "Blacks See Goetz Verdict as Blow to Race Relations."
254 **"Robbery is a":** Pitt, "Blacks See Goetz Verdict as Blow to Race Relations."

CHAPTER TWENTY-FOUR: INMATE NO. 78900316

256 **"substantial sentence":** Howard Kurtz, "Goetz Sentenced to 6 Months for Subway Shootings," *Washington Post*, October 20, 1987, https://www.washingtonpost.com/archive/politics/1987/10/20/goetz-sentenced-to-6-months-for-subway-shootings/f4449db4-7aef-4ab5-b571-ed83ecb9c327.
256 **"break the heart":** Goetz-Sentence transcript page 30, Box 21, Folder 2.
256 **Crane decided to sentence:** Kurtz, "Goetz Sentenced to 6 Months for Subway Shootings"; Goetz-Sentence transcript pages 7–8.
257 **"Excuse me your honor":** Goetz-Sentence transcript page 37, Box 21, Folder 2.
257 **"How much more flesh":** Ronald Sullivan, "Goetz Is Given One-Year Term on Gun Charge," *New York Times*, January 14, 1989, Section 1, 1.
257 **"This case is really more about":** "Bernie for the Defense," *New York Daily News*, January 14, 1989, 3.
258 **"My client is":** Sullivan, "Goetz Is Given One-Year Term on Gun Charge."
259 **"He has an expertise":** Vincent Lee and Don Singleton, "Tuned In at Rikers," *New York Daily News*, February 1, 1989, 2.
259 **In all, Goetz took home:** Barbara Goldberg, "Subway Gunman Goetz Gets Out of Jail," United Press International, September 20, 1989, https://www.upi.com/Archives/1989/09/20/Subway-gunman-Goetz-gets-out-of-jail/2344622267200.
259 **He was there:** Goldberg, "Subway Gunman Goetz Gets Out of Jail."
259 **"retribution" . . . "He got screwed":** Paul La Rose, "More Jail for Goetz," *New York Daily News*, August 29, 1989, 7.
260 **Eventually, Goetz served his time:** Stuart Marques, "Goetz Is Free but Not Easy," *New York Daily News*, September 21, 1989, 29.
260 **He dashed from:** Goldberg, "Subway Gunman Goetz Gets Out of Jail."
260 **Even with reporters:** Michael Freitag, "Goetz Released After Spending 8 Months in Jail," *New York Times*, September 21, 1989, B10.

CHAPTER TWENTY-FIVE: PECKERWOOD

261 **"He won't be breakdancing anymore":** Ron Kuby, interview by the author, March 14, 2024, by Zoom.
261 **"deliberately, willfully, and with malice":** Patrick Clark and Robert Carroll, "Lawsuit Accuses Goetz," *New York Daily News*, January 31, 1985, 7.
262 **"fight for the poor":** Website, the Law Office of Ronald L. Kuby, https://www.kubylaw.com/ronaldlkuby.
262 **"There are a lot of things":** Ron Kuby, interview by the author, March 14, 2024, by Zoom.
262 **long, graying ponytail:** Ron Kuby, email message to author, November 7, 2024.
262 **Goetz represented himself:** Larry McShane, "Bernie, Darrell and the American Judicial System," Associated Press, June 14, 1993.
262 **"a series of delaying tactics":** Ron Kuby, email message to author, November 7, 2024.
262 **inability to afford a cab:** McShane, "Bernie, Darrell and the American Judicial System."
263 **"We took a beating financially":** Mark Baker, interview by the author, November 11, 2024, by Zoom.
263 **the city's crime rate:** Clifford Krauss, "New York Crime Rate Plummets to Levels Not Seen in 30 Years," *New York Times*, December 20, 1996, A1.
264 **Much looked different:** Clyde Haberman, "NYC; One Question That Matters in Goetz Case," *New York Times*, April 12, 1996, B1.
264 **"stupid" . . . "I didn't want":** Adam Nossiter, "A Gunman's Tale of Fear, Hatred, and Drugs," *New York Times*, April 13, 1996, 1, https://www.nytimes.com/1996/04/13/nyregion/a-gunman-s-tale-of-fear-hatred-and-drugs.html.
264 **"I walked directly":** Larry McShane, "Goetz Version of Shooting Contradicts Defense," Associated Press, September 26, 1990.
264 **"I was trying to get":** Nossiter, "A Gunman's Tale of Fear, Hatred, and Drugs."
264 **"I've never experienced":** Nossiter, "A Gunman's Tale of Fear, Hatred, and Drugs."

265 **"mental vegetable":** "Judge Blocks Goetz's Access to Subway Victim," United Press International, May 25, 1990.
265 **"I think that would have been":** Stone Phillips, "Stone Phillips: 15 Years of *Dateline*," NBC News, July 2, 2007, https://www.nbcnews.com/id/wbna19562622.
265 **"It would have been better off":** Adam Nossiter, "A Gunman's Tale of Fear, Hatred and Drugs."
265 **"Bernie World" . . . "look at that guy over there":** Jorge Fitz-Gibbon, "Goetz a Jerk, Not a Racist, Jury Told," *New York Daily News,* April 23, 1996, 10.
265 **"Bernie has always been":** Adam Nossiter, "Bronx Jury Orders Goetz to Pay Man He Paralyzed $43 Million," *New York Times,* April 24, 1996, A1.
265 **"a lot of Bernie's words":** Adam Nossiter, "Goetz's Attorney Sums Up, Ruefully," *New York Times,* April 23, 1996, B3.
265 **"clearly Mr. Goetz":** Nossiter, "Bronx Jury Orders Goetz to Pay Man He Paralyzed $43 Million."
266 **"not the first":** Fitz-Gibbon, "Goetz a Jerk, Not a Racist, Jury Told."
266 **They awarded him:** "Judge Rules Bankrupt Goetz Liable for $43 Million Judgement," Associated Press, August 2, 1996; Nossiter, "Bronx Jury Orders Goetz to Pay Man He Paralyzed $43 Million."
266 **He claimed about $17,000:** Garry Pierre-Pierre, "The Black and the Red of Goetz's Balance Sheet," *New York Times,* May 15, 1996, B3.
266 **"To us, this is a case":** Jan Hoffman, "Fund Linked to N.R.A. Gave $20,000 for Goetz's Defense," *New York Times,* April 16, 1996, A1.
267 **Several prospective jurors:** Haberman, "NYC; One Question That Matters in Goetz Case."
267 **"New York's a tough place" . . . "Even David Duke denies":** Haberman, "NYC; One Question That Matters in Goetz Case."
268 **Between 2003 and 2013:** "Stop and Frisk Data," New York Civil Liberties Union, March 14, 2019, https://www.nyclu.org/data/stop-and-frisk-data.

CHAPTER TWENTY-SIX: SAVING THE SQUIRRELS

269 **It became easier:** Norimitsu Onishi, "Court Case Nudges Goetz Out of Cocoon; Subway Gunman Back in Spotlight," *New York Times,* December 31, 1995, 27.
269 **"All he wants right now":** Kirk Johnson, "Goetz Is Cleared in Subway Attack; Gun Count Upheld; Acquittal Won in Shooting of 4 Youths—Prison Term Possible on Weapon Charge," *New York Times,* June 17, 1987, A1.
269 **"just an innocuous":** Marcia Chambers, "Goetz Is Indicted for the Shooting of Four on the IRT," *New York Times,* March 28, 1985, A1.
269 **"He was no longer the story":** Scott Greenfield, interview by the author, November 11, 2024, by Zoom.
270 **He was perplexed:** Jake Halpern, "A Jolly Green Giant," *New Yorker,* November 10, 2002.
270 **"I think eating meat":** Andrea Peyser, "Bernhard Goetz: NYC's Most 'High'-Minded Citizen," *New York Post,* November 7, 2013, https://nypost.com/2013/11/07/bernhard-goetz-nycs-most-high-minded-citizen/.
270 **He has been spotted:** Michael Schwirtz, "Bernard Goetz, Man in '84 Subway Shooting, Faces Marijuana Charges," *New York Times,* November 2, 2013.
270 **"Penelo Pea Pod":** "Veggie Pride Parade," accessed March 5, 2025, https://www.veggiepridepar ade.org.
270 **"I was born":** Halpern, "A Jolly Green Giant."
270 **"I said, oh man":** Curtis Sliwa, interview by the author, December 10, 2024, by Zoom.
271 **"comfort animal":** Rikki Reyna and Stephen Rex Brown, "Squirelly Goetz Picks New Fights," *Daily News,* May 4, 2015.
271 **Goetz claimed that:** Schwirtz, "Bernhard Goetz, Man in '84 Subway Shooting, Faces Marijuana Charges."
271 **"Undercover people are":** Barry Paddock, "Bernie Goetz Has Pot Dealing Case Tossed Because Prosecutors Took Too Long: Judge," *New York Daily News,* September 10, 2014, https://www.nydailynews.com/2014/09/10/bernie-goetz-has-pot-dealing-case-tossed-because-prosecutors-took-too-long-judge.
271 **The case got dismissed:** Paddock, "Bernie Goetz Has Pot Dealing Case Tossed Because Prosecutors Took Too Long: Judge."

272 **"Teen Guess What's in My Pants?":** "DA 02-1336," Federal Communications Commission, June 6, 2002, https://docs.fcc.gov/public/attachments/DA-02-1336A1.pdf.
272 **live broadcast of a blow-by-blow account:** Joel Garreau, "'Opie & Anthony' Off the Air and in Hot Water," *Washington Post,* August 21, 2002.
272 **"GOETZ: It's a group" . . . "No one gives a shit about him":** Time Killing Fuel, "Opie & Anthony - Bernie Goetz Goes After Opie," uploaded November 9, 2017, YouTube video, 01:25:30, https://www.youtube.com/watch?v=mjfCrLv125M.
276 **Four months after:** Pete Hamill, "Bernhard Goetz: Notes from Underground," *Village Voice,* May 12, 1987, https://www.villagevoice.com/bernard-goetz-notes-from-underground; Mark Lesly with Charles Shuttleworth, *Subway Gunman: A Juror's Account of the Bernhard Goetz Trial* (British American Publishing, 1988), 76, referring to "Phoenix House" as "Phoenix Academy."
276 **an automobile mechanic:** Lesly with Shuttleworth, *Subway Gunman,* 77; Associated Press, "3 Other Goetz Victims Move On, Two to Prison," *Los Angeles Times,* January 8, 1995.
276 **got a GED:** Trial transcript page 5366, Box 7, Folder 5.
276 **start cooking school:** Margot Hornblower, "One of the Youths Shot by Goetz Testifies About Words, Glances on Subway," *Washington Post,* May 2, 1987.
276 **bullet "saved" Troy:** Leon Neyfakh, host, Fiasco: Vigilante, episode 6, "Damages," Prologue Projects, July 27, 2023, 37 min, 22 sec., https://www.prologueprojects.com/shows.
276 **watching horror movies:** Larry McShane, "10 Years Later, Goetz Victim Asks: What Happened?," Associated Press, December 19, 1994.
276 **In 1989 he:** "Goetz Victim Held in Mugging," Associated Press, March 7, 1989.
276 **"I didn't do nothing":** *The Company You Keep,* written and directed by Adrian Liang (Stone Age Films, 2018), https://vimeo.com/267236898.
277 **A pill bottle:** Josh Saul, "One of Bernhard Goetz's Victims Kills Self on Anniversary of Subway Shoot," *New York Post,* December 23, 2011; Bruce Weber, "James Ramseur, Wounded in '84 Subway Shooting, Dies at 45," *New York Times,* December 23, 2011, https://www.nytimes.com/2011/12/24/nyregion/james-ramseur-victim-of-bernhard-goetz-subway-shooting-dies-at-45.html.

CHAPTER TWENTY-SEVEN: *PLUS ÇA CHANGE . . .*

281 **March 1, 2024:** Quotes and details in this chapter are taken from my phone interview with Bernhard Goetz, on March 1, 2024, and email exchanges on February 26, 27, and 28; March 1 and 7; and April 1, 2024.
285 **"When Cuomo gave his talk":** Bernhard Goetz, interview by the author, March 1, 2024, by telephone.
289 **"failures of society":** Nancy Grace, "Interview with 'Subway Vigilante' Bernhard Goetz," *Larry King Live,* CNN, December 17, 2004, https://transcripts.cnn.com/show/lkl/date/2004-12-17/segment/01.
290 **"Society is better off without":** Stone Phillips, "15 Years of *Dateline,*" NBC News, July 2, 2007, https://www.nbcnews.com/id/wbna19562622.
293 **multiple witnesses testified:** *See, e.g.,* trial record at 6349, in which Solitaire Macfoy called the car "fairly crowded."
294 ***"Despite the fact":*** Jake Halpern, "A Jolly Green Giant," *New Yorker,* November 10, 2002.

CONCLUSION

297 **widespread power outages:** James Barron, "The Blackout of 2003: The Overview; Power Surge Blacks Out Northeast, Hitting Cities in 8 States and Canada; Midday Shutdowns Disrupt Millions," *New York Times,* August 15, 2003, A1.
298 **"a snow day":** Barron, "The Blackout of 2003: The Overview."
298 **Restaurants rolled their grills:** Eddy Ramírez, "Lighting the Grill Rather Than Cursing the Darkness," *New York Times,* August 12, 2004, B4.
298 **Tourists not allowed:** Richard Lezin Jones and Daisy Hernández, "The Blackout: Visitors; So, Fewer Sights to See? Tourists Take It in Stride," *New York Times,* August 17, 2003, 29.
298 **Moments after the Metropolitan Museum of Art:** Barron, "The Blackout of 2003: The Overview."

298 **There were pockets of looting:** Michael Wilson, "The Blackout: The Neighborhoods; For Owners of Stores Hit by Looters, Low Crime Rate During Crisis Is No Comfort," *New York Times*, August 17, 2003, 30.
298 **"So far, so good":** James Barron, "Power Surge Blacks Out Northeast," *New York Times*, August 15, 2003.
298 **New housing, some of it:** Brent Staples, "Why Once-Violent Neighborhoods Stayed Calm During the Blackout," *New York Times*, August 24, 2003, Section 4, 10.
299 **"He was a bumper sticker":** Gillian Coulter, interview by the author, January 29, 2025, by Zoom.
300 **We're not doing this to support":** Richard Feldman, interview by the author, February 27, 2024, by telephone.
300 **"I don't make judgments about":** Mark Baker, interview by the author, March 12, 2024, by Zoom.
300 **"Sometimes Bernie gives":** "Lawyer Sez He Goetz Nightmares," *New York Daily News*, April 16, 1996.
300 **"Bernie is a nut":** James Patterson and Benjamin Wallace, *The Defense Lawyer* (New York: Little, Brown, 2021), 193.
300 **"All these years later":** Ellis Henican, "Bernie Goetz? We See in Him What We Want to See," *Newsday*, April 12, 1996.
301 **"There are six subway crimes":** Ron Kuby, interview by the author, March 14, 2024, by Zoom.
301 **Al Sharpton's bodyguard:** Julia Marsh, "Eric Adams Was Once Al Sharpton's Bodyguard. Now They Talk Weekly," *Politico*, August 25, 2023.
301 **"never witnessed crime at this level":** Emma G. Fitzsimmons, "Eric Adams Can't Stop Talking About Crime. There Are Risks to That," *New York Times*, July 16, 2022, https://www.nytimes.com/2022/07/15/nyregion/eric-adams-crime-nyc.html.
301 **Even the increase:** Patrick Langan, "The Remarkable Drop in Crime in New York City: Research Summary," Bureau of Justice Statistics, October 21, 2004.
301 **According to FBI:** Federal Bureau of Investigation Crime Data Explorer, https://cde.ucr.cjis.gov/LATEST/webapp/#/pages/explorer/crime/quarterly.
301 **to be religious:** Pew Research Center, "Migrants Living in Each Region," Pew Research Center, August 19, 2024, https://www.pewresearch.org/religion/2024/08/19/migrants-living-in-each-region/.
301 **or be married:** U.S. Census Bureau, "Marital Histories Differ Between Native-Born and Foreign-Born Adults," May 5, 2021, https://www.census.gov/library/stories/2021/05/marital-histories-differ-between-native-born-and-foreign-born-adults.html.
302 **native-born Americans:** National Institute of Justice, "Undocumented Immigrant Offending Rate Lower Than U.S.-Born Citizen Rate," National Institute of Justice, April 15, 2021, https://nij.ojp.gov/topics/articles/undocumented-immigrant-offending-rate-lower-us-born-citizen-rate.
302 **One estimate had:** Ted Gest, "Street Crime: People Fight Back," *U.S. News & World Report*, April 15, 1985.
302 **Boston that year:** Gest, "Street Crime."
302 **"There's no better":** Gest, "Street Crime."
303 **"[Jordan Neely] would have":** Al Sharpton, interview by the author, March 8, 2024, by Zoom.
303 **"Thoughts and deductibles":** Dionne Searcey and Madison Malone Kircher, "Torrent of Hate for Health Insurance Industry Follows C.E.O.'s Killing," *New York Times*, December 5, 2024.
304 **New York's trains:** Ana Ley, "The Voice of the Subway Speaks for Herself, at Last," *New York Times*, January 6, 2024, MB 7.
305 **"[t]hey weren't muggers":** Jim Levison, interview by the author, March 7, 2024, by Zoom.

ILLUSTRATION CREDITS

INTERIOR ILLUSTRATIONS

Page 9: Council for Public Safety

Page 97: *New York Daily News,* January 2, 1985. NY Daily News Archive via Getty Images.

Page 134: Black Panthers on steps of Legislative Building, Olympia, 1969, State Governors' Negative Collection, 1949–1975, Washington State Archives, Digital Archives, http://www.digitalarchives.wa.gov, 2025

Page 225: © Jane Rosenberg

Page 272: Jefferson Siegel/NY Daily News via Getty Images

INSERT ILLUSTRATIONS

Page 1, top: Bettmann Archive via Getty Images; middle: AP Photo/Eddie Adams; bottom: AP Photo/Dave Pickoff

Page 2, top left: AP Photo; top right: Photo by Mike Lipack/NY Daily News Archive via Getty Images; bottom: Photo by Carmine Donofrio/NY Daily News Archive via Getty Images

Page 3, top: AP Photo; bottom: Photo by Rick Maiman/NY Daily News via Getty Images

Page 4: Courtesy Municipal Archives, City of New York

Page 5, top: AP Photo/Mario Suriani; middle: AP Photo/Charles Wenzelberg; bottom: AP Photo/Debbie Hodgson

Page 6, top: AP Photo/Frankie Ziths; middle: AP Photo/Mario Suriani; bottom: AP Photo/G. Paul Burnett

Page 7, top and middle: © Jane Rosenberg; bottom: AP Photo

Page 8, top: AP Photo/David Bookstaver; middle: Photo by John Pedin/NY Daily News Archive via Getty Images; bottom: AP Photo/David Bookstaver

INDEX